A THEORY OF LEGAL ARGUMENTATION

A Theory of Legal Argumentation

The Theory of Rational Discourse as Theory of Legal Justification

ROBERT ALEXY

Translated by

Ruth Adler and Neil MacCormick

OXFORD
UNIVERSITY PRESS

OXFORD
UNIVERSITY PRESS

Great Clarendon Street, Oxford OX2 6DP

Oxford University Press is a department of the University of Oxford.
It furthers the University's objective of excellence in research, scholarship,
and education by publishing worldwide in

Oxford New York

Auckland Cape Town Dar es Salaam Hong Kong Karachi
Kuala Lumpur Madrid Melbourne Mexico City Nairobi
New Delhi Shanghai Taipei Toronto
With offices in
Argentina Austria Brazil Chile Czech Republic France Greece
Guatemala Hungary Italy Japan South Korea Poland Portugal
Singapore Switzerland Thailand Turkey Ukraine Vietnam

Oxford is a registered trade mark of Oxford University Press
in the UK and in certain other countries

Published in the United States
by Oxford University Press Inc., New York

Reprinted 2011

ISBN 978-0-19-958422-2

Printed and bound in Great Britain by CPI Antony Rowe,
Chippenham and Eastbourne

For Edith

Preface

In a leading decision of 14 February 1973 on decisions contrary to statute, the first panel of the German Federal Constitutional Court declared that all judicial rulings must 'be founded on rational argumentation'.[1] This demand for rationality in argument can be extended to any situation in which lawyers engage in debate. So questions about the nature of rational argumentation in general and rational legal argumentation in particular are not only of interest to legal theorists and philosophers of law. They are pressing issues for practising lawyers and a matter of concern for every citizen active in the public arena. Not only the standing of academic law as a scientific discipline, but also the legitimacy of judicial decisions depends on the possibility of rational legal argumentation.

The question of what is to be understood by 'rational legal argumentation', of whether and to what extent it is possible, is the subject-matter of this investigation. The subtitle: 'The Theory of Rational Discourse as Theory of Legal Justification' indicates how these questions are to be tackled. The answer proceeds in two stages. Parts A and B of the book attempt to work out a general theory of practical reasoning, whilst Part C applies this theory to legal argumentation. That the first two parts occupy considerably more space than the third is a reflection of the present objective to lay a foundation for a theory of legal argumentation. A further development of this theory is not only possible but also desirable. If this investigation succeeds in its aim, it will have laid the corner-stone for such future work.

The manuscript of this book was presented as a thesis in the Faculty of Law of the Georg-August University of Göttingen in 1976. The work would not have come to fruition without support from many quarters. I should particularly like to single out Professor Ralf Dreier from all those who helped along the way. It was he who first gave me many of my ideas during the course of countless discussions. My thanks also to Professor Malte Dießelhorst whose criticism saved me from several errors.

1 *BVerfGE* (Decisions of the Federal Constitutional Court) 34,269 (287).

I should also like to record particular thanks at this point to my philosophy teacher Professor Günther Patzig. It would give me particular pleasure if his approach to philosophy were recognizable in the method of this investigation. Finally thanks are due to the *Studienstiftung des deutschen Volkes* which gave both intellectual and financial support throughout many years.

R. A.

Göttingen
January 1978

Preface To The English Edition

This book was first published in German in 1978. It is a great source of pleasure to me that it is now appearing in English. I should like to express special thanks to the translators, Ruth Adler and Neil MacCormick. They gave me their manuscript to read before it went to the printers, and I was very gratified to find that they had captured my meaning entirely, even in those places where differences in the two languages precluded a literal translation. I believe that the book has been improved by their work. I also owe many thanks to William Twining who initially supported the idea of a revival of translations of contemporary scholarly work in legal theory. Finally, I must express my gratitude to the editorial staff of Oxford University Press for the care they took in seeing the manuscript through the Press, and in particular for their detailed help with the bibliography.

R. A.

Kiel
September 1988

Contents

List of Logical Symbols used in the Text

$\neg$ = not (negation)

$\wedge$ = and (conjunction)

$\vee$ = or (disjunction)

$\rightarrow$ = if . . . then . . . (conditional)

$\leftrightarrow$ = if and only if . . . then . . . (biconditional)

(x) = for all x (universal quantifier)

O = it is obligatory that . . . (deontic operator)

Introduction

1. THE PROBLEM OF THE JUSTIFICATION OF LEGAL DECISIONS

'It can . . . no longer be seriously maintained that the application of laws involves *no more* than a logical subsumption under abstractly formulated major premises'.[1] This observation by Karl Larenz marks one of the few points of agreement in contemporary discussions of legal methodology. In many cases the singular normative statement which expresses a judgment resolving a legal dispute is not a logical conclusion[2] derived from formulations of legal norms presupposed valid[3] taken together with statements of fact which are assumed or proven to be true. There are at least four reasons for this: (1) the vagueness of legal language,[4] (2) the possibility of conflict between norms,[5] (3) the fact that there are cases requiring a legal statement which do not fall under any existing valid norm,[6] and finally (4) the possibility, in special cases, of a decision which is contrary to the wording of a statute.[7]

[1] K. Larenz, *Methodenlehre der Rechtswissenschaft*, 3rd edn. (Berlin, Heidelberg and New York, 1975), 154.

[2] On the concept of logical conclusion cf. A. Tarski, 'On the Concept of Logical Consequence', in his *Logic, Semantics, Metamathematics* (Oxford, 1956), 409 ff. On the possibility of relations of inference between normative propositions cf. below, pp. 188–9.

[3] What is to count as 'a legal norm presupposed valid' may remain an open question here. The claim made in the text also holds good where further sources of law such as precedent are recognized in addition to legislation and custom.

[4] Cf. H. L. A. Hart, *The Concept of Law* (Oxford, 1961), 121 ff. and id., 'Positivism and the Separation of Law and Morals', *Harvard Law Review*, 71 (1958), 606 ff.

[5] H. Kelsen, *Pure Theory of Law*, trans. M. Knight (Berkeley, Calif. 1967), 205–8.

[6] Cf. Larenz, *Methodenlehre*, pp. 354 ff.

[7] It is not only possible that this enumeration may be incomplete; one might also be of the view that it contains too many reasons. Thus on the one hand (3) and (4) are missing from the reasons cited by Kelsen for the 'indefiniteness of

A legal judgment J, which follows logically from formulations of legal norms N_1, N_2 . . . N_n whose validity has to be presupposed together with empirical statements A_1, A_2 . . . A_n, can be described as *justifiable* in terms of N_1, N_2 . . . N_n together with A_1, A_2 . . . A_n. However, if there are judgments which do not follow logically from N_1, N_2 . . . N_n together with A_1, A_2 . . . A_n, the question arises of how such judgments can be justified. This problem is the fundamental problem for legal methodology.

The theory of legal methodology could solve the problem of how fully to justify a legal judgment if it were able to provide rules or procedures according to which it could be shown either that the transition from N_1, N_2 . . . N_n and A_1, A_2 . . . A_n to J is permissible (even where J does not follow logically from N_1, N_2 . . . N_n and A_1, A_2 . . . A_n) or that in addition to the presupposedly valid norms and the proven empirical statements, further propositions with a normative content N'_1, N'_2 . . . N'_n can be adduced such that J follows logically from N_1, N_2 . . . N_n together with N'_1, N'_2 . . . N'_n and A_1, A_2 . . . A_n.

The most widely discussed candidates for the role of rules or

the law-applying act', while on the other, he cites the discrepancy between the will and the expression of the norm-stipulating authority as a reason (5) in addition to (1) and (2) (Kelsen, *Pure Theory of Law*, p. 350 and 'Zur Theorie der Interpretation', in *Die Wiener rechtstheoretische Schule* . . ., ed. H. Klecatsky, R. Marcic, and H. Schambeck (Vienna, Frankfurt, Zurich, Salzburg, and Munich, 1968), ii. 1365). (5) may be regarded as a reason for (4) or (1). What is problematic is whether and to what extent decisions classified under (3) and (4) are constitutionally admissible. In both instances the judge assumes a role in an area which, according to the principle of the separation of powers, would seem to be the province of the legislature. However, this problem cannot be discussed here. It will only be pointed out that there are cases of (3) (indirect breach of contract) and (4) (compensation for non-physical injury (*BGB*, para. 253)) in which the creation of new legal norms through legal judgments and the non-application of legal norms, has been generally recognized or held to be in accordance with the constitution by virtue of a declaration of the Federal Constitutional Court (*BVerfGE* 34, 269 (286–7)). The subject-matter of this book is not the question of the constitutionality of decisions falling under (3) and (4), but rather that of whether such decisions in their turn can also be rationally justified within the framework of legal methodology. However, an answer to this question should also be of significance in addressing the problem of their constitutional admissibility.

procedures to take on this task are the so-called 'canons of interpretation'.

Even the number of these canons remains in dispute. Savigny, for instance, distinguished the grammatical, the logical, the historical, and the systematic elements of interpretation.[8] According to Larenz there are five criteria of sound interpretation: the literal meaning of the statute; its contextual meaning; the regulatory purposes, aims, and normative intentions of the historical legislator; objective-teleological criteria; and finally conformity of interpretation to the constitution.[9] To cite a further example, Wolff recognizes philological, logical, systematic, historical, comparative, genetic, and teleological interpretations.[10]

More significant than the problem of the *number* of canons is the question of their rank order. Different canons may lead to quite different results. In the light of this fact, they would only be capable of yielding a single correct answer by way of a well-grounded result if it were possible to articulate strict criteria for ranking them. No one has as yet succeeded in doing this.[11] A further difficulty is the indeterminacy[12] of the canons of

[8] F. C. von Savigny, *System des heutigen Römischen Rechts*, vol. i (Berlin, 1840), 212 ff.

[9] Larenz, *Methodenlehre*, pp. 307 ff.

[10] H. J. Wolff and O. Bachof, *Verwaltungsrecht*, 9th edn. (Munich, 1974), vol. i, para. 28. III. c. (The paragraph number refers to Wolff's section of the textbook.)

[11] Cf. M. Kriele, *Theorie der Rechtsgewinnung*, 2nd edn. (Berlin, 1976), 85 ff.; J. Esser, *Vorverständnis und Methodenwahl in der Rechtsfindung*, 2nd edn. (Frankfurt-on-Main, 1972), 124 ff. Larenz, who makes an attempt at a rank ordering, also observes that 'there exists no definite ranking between them' (*Methodenlehre*, p. 334). The difficulty of justifying a rank order is closely related to the difficulties of determining the goal of interpretation. A decision about the goal of interpretation presupposes a theory regarding the function of adjudication, and this in its turn presupposes an answer to the question whether and to what extent rational legal argumentation is possible. In this regard Engisch is to be supported in his view that it requires 'a more penetrating perspective to assign to each method of interpretation its relative validity and its particular logical setting' (K. Engisch, *Einführung in das juristische Denken*, 5th edn. (Stuttgart, Berlin, Cologne, and Mainz, 1971), 84. The theory of legal reasoning proposed here constitutes an attempt to discover such 'more penetrating perspectives'.

[12] Cf. Kriele, *Theorie der Rechtsgewinnung*, p. 86.

interpretation. A rule such as: 'Interpret every norm so that it achieves its purpose' leads to divergent outcomes when each of two interpreters has a different view as to the purpose of the norm in question.[13]

The weakness of the canons of interpretation indicated above does not mean that they should be dismissed out of hand. But it does exclude the possibility of considering them as sufficient in themselves as rules for constructing justifications of legal judgments.

One might give up the search for a *system of justificatory rules* and try instead to establish a *system of propositions* from which the missing normative premises necessary for the purposes of justification could be deduced. Justification in terms of such a system would be conclusive whenever the system consisted solely of propositions derivable from the set of presupposedly valid norms. In such a case, however, the system would not contain any regulations which went beyond the presupposedly valid set of norms.[14]

On the other hand, if, like Canaris for example, one understands by such a system, a system of the general principles of legal order (an 'axiological-teleological' system)[15] the question immediately arises as to how such principles are to be established. They do not follow logically from the presupposed norms. The application of such principles for the justification of legal judgments is also problematic.

The principles allow of exceptions and may be mutually inconsistent and even contradictory; they do not claim to have all-or-nothing applicability; their real meaning only unfolds through a two-way process of adjustment and limitation; and for their actual implementation, they require concretization via subordinate prin-

[13] In light of the uncertainty of the canons, it is open to doubt whether they are to count as rules at all. Thus Müller sees them as 'short-hand descriptions for certain ways of proceeding in an investigation' and Rottleuthner as instructions 'to ask for standards of relevance' (F. Müller, *Juristische Methodik*, 2nd edn. (Berlin, 1976), 167; H. Rottleuthner, *Richterliches Handeln* . . . (Frankfurt-on-Main, 1973), 30). The question of the logical status of the canons is discussed in more detail below. See pp. 244–5.

[14] Cf. Kriele, *Theorie der Rechtsgewinnung*, p. 98.

[15] C.-W. Canaris, *Systemdenken und Systembegriff in der Jurisprudenz* (Berlin, 1969), 46 ff.

ciples and *particular value-judgments* with an independent material content.[16]

The axiological-teleological system is not such as to yield any unique decision about the proper weighing and balancing of legal principles in a given case or about which particular values should be given priority in any particular situation.[17]

This does not mean to say that it is impossible to base arguments on a system of values and goals, that is to argue from an axiological-teleological system, or on some other system. Arguments from systems, however these systems are characterized, play a significant part both in the practice of the courts and in the field of legal science.[18] However, it does make it quite clear that this type of argumentation is never entirely conclusive.

1.1 Suppose that there are situations in which the decision of an individual case does not follow logically from either empirical statements taken together with presupposed norms or strictly grounded propositions of some system however conceived, and also that such decisions cannot be completely justified by reference to rules of legal method. In such cases it must follow that the decision-maker has discretion inasmuch as the case is not fully governed by legal norms, rules of legal method, and doctrines of legal dogmatics. Accordingly there is a choice to be made between competing solutions.

It is this choice on the part of the decision-maker which

[16] Ibid., 52–3 (my italics). Cf. Larenz, who notes that 'at each stage of concretization, additional value judgments [are] needed, which must be taken on first by the legislature and only subsequently, within the framework of any remaining scope for judicial discretion, by the judge' (Larenz, *Methodenlehre*, p. 462).

[17] In view of this state of affairs, Wieacker considers whether it might not 'perhaps after all be better to abandon any postulated system of (relatively) closed deductive relations' (F. Wieacker's review of Canaris, *Systemdenken und Systembegriff*, *Rechtstheorie*, 1 (1970), 112). Cf. further Esser, *Vorverständnis und Methodenwahl*, p. 100, where he writes of the 'multiple valency of the evaluative content of a principle' and observes: 'It is not the principles which act but rather the person who has to determine the law. The correct relation cannot be "extracted from" the system without examining the problems of conflict.'

[18] For a number of examples which stress precisely this point cf. U. Diederichsen, 'Topisches und systematisches Denken in der Jurisprudenz', *NJW* 19 (1966), 698 ff.

determines which singular normative proposition is to be asserted (as the conclusion of a piece of legal research, for example) or to be pronounced by way of a judgment in a case. The content of such a singular normative statement is an assertion or determination of that which is required of, forbidden to, or permitted for certain individuals.[19] Hence the decision, regardless of the question at which level of justification it is reached, is a decision about what ought to or may be done or not done. In this decision a state of affairs or an action or type of behaviour on the part of one or more persons is given preference over other states or actions or kinds of behaviour on the part of these persons. Giving preference in this way involves a judgment that the chosen option is in some sense the better one, and to this extent there is a 'value-judgment'[20] as the basis of[21] the decision. Almost all contemporary methodological discussions emphasize the fact that law cannot dispense with such value-judgments.

[19] It is not being asserted here that all legal judgments directly express commands, prohibitions, or permissions. This is not the case in respect of judgments altering legal relations, for example. The weaker thesis that all judgments are reducible to basic forms which contain only those normative expressions which are basic deontic operators such as 'commanded' 'forbidden', and 'permitted', will not be put forward here, although there are arguments in favour of it. Here it will suffice to say that legal judgments at least imply commands, prohibitions, or permissions. Regarding this problem area, cf. W. N. Hohfeld, 'Some Fundamental Legal Conceptions as Applied in Judicial Reasoning', in his *Fundamental Legal Conceptions as Applied in Judicial Reasoning and Other Legal Essays*, ed. W. W. Cook (New Haven, Conn., 1923), 23 ff. and, in particular, A. Ross, *Directives and Norms* (London, 1968), 106 ff.

[20] On the concepts of 'giving preference', 'choice', and 'better' cf. G. H. von Wright, *The Logic of Preference* (Edinburgh, 1963), 13 ff. The expression 'value-judgment' can be used to designate either the actual giving of preference or the judgment that a particular alternative is the better one, or the rule of preference underlying this judgment (and thereby the preference). Concerning this last cf. A. Podlech, 'Wertungen und Werte im Recht', *AöR* 95 (1970), 195–6. Many use the expression to mean all these and more at the same time. Since there is no need for greater precision for present purposes, it will be omitted.

[21] Cf. Wieacker, 'Zur Topikdiskussion in der zeitgenössischen deutschen Rechtswissenschaft' in *Xenion*, Festschrift for P. J. Zepos, ed. E. von Caemmerer, J. H. Kaiser, G. Kegel, W. Müller-Freienfels, and H. J. Wolff (Athens, 1973), 407: 'Outwith the core of the law which is amenable to subsumption and particularly in the realm of making new law . . . all problems concerning the application of law . . . can be formulated as decisions between alternative value-judgements.'

Thus Larenz speaks of the 'insight that the application of law is not exhausted by a process of subsumption, but rather requires a wide range of value-judgments on the part of those applying the law.'[22] Müller is of the opinion that 'law devoid of decisions and value-judgments ... [would be] neither practical nor realistic'.[23] Esser observes that 'in all but the least problematic decisions ... value-judgments [are of] central significance'.[24] Kriele comes to the conclusion that one 'cannot by any means escape from evaluative, normative-teleological, and political elements inherent in every interpretation',[25] and Engisch is forced to recognize that

> even today, statutes, in all branches of the law, [are] constructed in such a way that both judges and administrators do not make and justify their decisions purely by subsumption under fixed legal concepts whose content will be revealed unambiguously through interpretation, but are rather called upon to judge independently and from time to time to decide and decree in the manner of legislators.[26]

The problem has been identified rather than resolved by the above observations. The question is where and to what extent value-judgments are required, how the relationship between these value-judgments and the methods of legal interpretation as well as the propositions and concepts of legal dogmatics are to be determined, and how these value-judgments can be rationally grounded or justified.

Finding answers to these questions is of great theoretical and practical significance. At the very least, the scientific status of jurisprudence is dependent on the answers we give. In addition, our answers will have considerable bearing on the problem of the legitimacy of regulating social conflicts by judicial decisions. For if it is the case that judicial rulings are based on value-judgments, and if these value-judgments cannot be rationally grounded, then at least in a large number of cases it is the *de facto*, extant, normative convictions or decisions of a professional body[27] which form the basis for such

[22] Larenz, *Methodenlehre*, p. 150.
[23] Müller, *Juristische Methodik*, p. 134.
[24] Esser, *Vorverständnis und Methodenwahl*, p. 9.
[25] Kriele, *Theorie der Rechtsgewinnung*, p. 96.
[26] Engisch, *Einführung in das juristische Denken*, p. 107.
[27] This holds true at least for courts presided over by professional judges.

conflict-resolution, a basis which neither has nor can have any further justification.

The questions: (1) where and to what extent value-judgments are necessary; (2) how these value-judgments relate to arguments designated as 'specifically legal' and to legal dogmatics; and (3) whether such value-judgments are rationally justifiable, cannot be answered in advance in the Introduction. They are rather the subject-matter of this investigation. Nevertheless, in order to avoid the risk of certain quite probable misunderstandings, I shall assume a position in respect of some of these issues.

The thesis that law cannot proceed without value-judgments does not mean that the outcome of every case is uncertain. Legal norms or dogmatic doctrines or precedents will often dictate a unique answer. It can even be assumed that there are considerably more such cases than there are debatable or 'hard' cases.[28] Yet it must be said that the clarity of a so-called 'clear case' is not such a simple matter either.[29] Whoever claims that a decision is uncontroversial is to be understood as asserting that there are no arguments which might give rise to serious doubts. Such arguments are, however, always conceivable. The assertion that every such counter-argument is bad or legally irrelevant does not follow conclusively from the set of presupposed norms. In view of this one might wish to assert that the categorization of a case as 'clear' constitutes a 'negative value-judgment'[30] with respect to all potential counter-arguments. But this touches a problem which need not be pursued any further here.

It is sometimes suggested in the literature that the value-judgments required for legal decision-making should be understood as moral evaluations. Thus Kriele writes: 'With this, the last veil has fallen: every exercise of jurisdiction is guided by

[28] Cf. Canaris, *Systemdenken und Systembegriff*, p. 147.

[29] Cf. Kriele, *Theorie der Rechtsgewinnung*, pp. 212 ff.

[30] The idea of such a negative value-judgment is alluded to by T. Heller: 'Every legal act of subsumption already involves a value-judgment to the extent that, in order to be applied at all, the law must have been deemed to be of value in the form in which it is handed down' (*Logik und Axiologie der analogen Rechtsanwendung* (Berlin, 1961), 59). Cf. Esser, *Vorverständnis und Methodenwahl*, p. 175: 'Basically, the wording of a legal norm only becomes "clear" if the outcome with which one is faced does not offend.'

considerations of social morality'.[31] On the other side, Hart is of the opinion that the decision-maker may be guided by almost any social objectives whatever their moral value might be; he is not confined to moral reasons.[32]

In order to solve these problems, one would have to elucidate concepts such as 'considerations of social morality', 'moral reason', etc. Such elucidation can, however, be avoided for the present since the discussion does not depend on the strong thesis that the prerequisite value-judgements are always to be conceived as moral judgments, but rather on the much weaker claim that they are always *morally relevant*.

This at least cannot be denied if it is admitted that (1) every legal judgment touches on the interests of at least one person and that (2) the question whether or not some action encroaching on the interests of an individual is justified can always be treated also as a moral question.

The observation that the inevitable value-judgments present in many legal decisions are morally relevant does not in itself say very much. It is, however, the presupposition of the thesis to be justified below: the thesis that legal decision-making *ought* (*ought* from a legal point of view) to be guided by morally sound value-judgments of a legally relevant kind.

1.2 It would be wrong to conclude from the fact alone that law cannot proceed without value-judgments, that those applying the law can give free reign to their own subjective moral convictions whenever such value-judgments are required. Such

[31] Kriele, 'Offene und verdeckte Urteilsgründe. Zum Verhältnis von Philosophie und Jurisprudenz heute', in *Collegium Philosophicum*, Festschrift for J. Ritter, ed. E.-W. Böckenförde *et al.* (Basle and Stuttgart, 1965), 112.

[32] Hart, 'Positivism and the Separation of Law and Morals', pp. 608 ff. Cf. N. Hoerster, 'Grundthesen analytischer Rechtstheorie', *Jahrbuch für Rechtssoziologie und Rechtstheorie*, 2 (1972), 123. The question of whether or not the value-judgments which are necessary in the context of legal decision-making, but which cannot be directly extracted from the law itself, are to be regarded as moral judgments, is quite separate from the question of whether or not legal decisions can be distinguished from moral decisions at all. The latter would have to be emphatically answered in the affirmative by referring to the special character of legal justification to be expounded in the theory of legal discourse. Cf. W. K. Frankena, 'Decisionism and Separatism in Social Philosophy', in *Rational Decision*, ed. C. J. Friedrich, NOMOS, 7 (1964), 18 ff.

a conclusion would only follow if there were no possibility at all of objective evaluation. Many suggestions and attempts have been made to further this end. Three are of particular interest in relation to this investigation.

First there is the seemingly plausible suggestion that the decision-maker should be guided by the 'value-judgments of the community at large or of a specific group'.[33] There are several objections to this proposal. In many cases it is simply not possible to establish exactly what are the value-judgments of the community. Even with the help of social survey methodology, it is often not possible to capture popular value-judgments in a form that is sufficiently concrete to serve as the basis for a decision. In order to overcome this problem, the community would have to become thoroughly acquainted with each individual case to be decided. Furthermore such a procedure would frequently yield divergent value-judgments. Which should the decision-maker pursue? This question arises even where the relevant value-judgments are those of a 'specific group', of which two of the most obvious are lawyers or, from within this class, judges. Even among these, it is not rare to meet quite divergent views. Moreover, if one settles for the convictions of a specific group, it is necessary to give reasons for making the opinions of the members of this group the decisive ones. Finally it is necessary to question whether a normative conviction can count as a justifying basis for legal decisions simply on the ground that it is commonly held. It could perhaps be argued that certain normative convictions are pervasive only because they have as yet not been subjected to critical

[33] Engisch, *Einführung in das juristische Denken*, p. 124. Cf. C. Perelman, *Justice* (New York, 1967), 67, where he says of judges that they 'ought to exercise their mandates in conformity with the aspirations of the community they represent'. Indeed, he says this of 'the legislators, the executives, and judges who are elected or appointed by those who possess the confidence of the people'. He wishes to leave the search for rational value-judgments to the philosophers. Cf. further R. Zippelius, *Einführung in die juristische Methodenlehre*, 2nd edn. (Munich, 1974), who recommends first ascertaining 'which interpretation or supplementation of the law would best correspond to the ethico-legal ideas prevailing in the community' (p. 76). Should it prove impossible to arrive at an unambiguous outcome in this way, the judge should be allowed 'to pursue his or her own sense of rightness, his or her personal notions of expediency' (p. 85).

examination. This point, however, has more limited application to the convictions held by lawyers. These are, at their best, the outcome of continuous and institutionalized critical discussion.

On the other hand it must be stated that since the decision-maker in the role of judge pronounces judgment 'in the name of the people', he or she should not be indifferent to the beliefs of those in whose name judgment is handed down.[34] Moreover the results of the deliberations of numerous generations of lawyers can only be neglected by decision-makers at their peril. It can be seen from these observations that it cannot be a matter of straight alternatives; of being guided by one's own convictions or by those of the people in whose name justice is administered or those individuals who have long made it their practice to discuss legal questions. What is required is rather a model which on the one hand can take into account both commonly held convictions and the results of prior legal discussions, and on the other hand leaves room for criteria of correctness. The theory to be presented here claims, amongst other things, to provide just such a model.

Almost more attractive than the reference to widely held beliefs is recourse to the 'inner evaluative coherence of the legal order'[35] or to the 'legal order's meaning taken in its entirety'.[36] This model is correct to a degree but it is also inadequate. It is inadequate because a concept such as the evaluative coherence of the legal order has no fixed meaning which would restrict any decision-maker to a specific value-judgment. The different norms are crystallizations of wholly different, often diverging evaluative perspectives. Perhaps no principle is unrestricted in practical application. In addition it is often quite unclear what values in particular a given norm is supposed to embody. This

[34] Cf. Zippelius, *Einführung in die juristische Methodenlehre*, p. 21: 'The idea of democracy already advocates that as many people as possible should participate in determining the form of the social order, and that as a representative of this community, the judge should follow the ideas prevailing in it.'

[35] Wieacker, 'Zur Topikdiskussion', p. 408, and similarly in his 'Über strengere und unstrenge Verfahren der Rechtsfindung' in *Im Dienst an Recht und Staat*, Festschrift for W. Weber, ed. H. Schneider and V. Götz (Berlin, 1974), 439.

[36] Larenz, *Methodenlehre*, p. 420.

means that a further decision has to be made as to the weight to be assigned to the various evaluative perspectives bearing on the case.

If it is indeed the case that for the reasons given above, legal decisions cannot be fully justified in terms of the evaluative coherence of the legal order, it is nevertheless beyond dispute that the evaluative perspectives expressed in the constitution as well as in other laws or embodied in a variety of norms and decisions are relevant for any potential decision. Just as on the model which takes into account the convictions of the general public, here too it is less important to postulate compliance with these evaluative perspectives than it is to determine more precisely the forms in which, and the rules according to which, they can and should enter into the justification of a particular decision.

A third possibility would be to appeal to some objective order of values, whether independent of the law or as expressed in the constitution or in the totality of the legal order, or to a set of objectively recognizable doctrines of natural law. This is what the *Bundesverfassungsgericht* (Federal Constitutional Court)[37] and the *Bundesgerichtshof* (Federal Supreme Court)[38] have done in Germany.[39] Such a proposal involves what have repeatedly been shown to be highly questionable philosophical premisses.[40] More will be said about this later, in the discussion of meta-ethical intuitionism. Equally strong is the objection that the relatively specific propositions necessary for justifying a given decision can hardly be deduced from an order of values whatever its ontological status.[41]

On the other hand it must be admitted that some of the propositions established in this way, although vague in the

[37] Cf. *BVerfGE* 2, 1 (12); 6, 32 (40–1); 7, 198 (205) 27, 1 (6); 30, 173 (193).

[38] Cf. *BGHZ* (Decisions of the Federal Supreme Court in civil matters) 8, 243 (248); *BGHSt* (Decisions of the Federal Supreme Court in criminal matters) 6, 47 (53).

[39] On the subject of the combination of mainly theologically shaded natural law motives together with elements of the Scheler and Hartmann ethics of value underlying this approach to legal decision-making cf. H. Welzel, *Naturrecht und materiale Gerechtigkeit*, 4th edn. (Göttingen, 1962), 225.

[40] Cf. W. Weischedel, *Recht und Ethik* (Karlsruhe, 1956); Welzel, *Naturrecht*, pp. 226 ff.: Podlech, *Wertungen und Werte im Recht*, pp. 201 ff.

[41] On this cf. Wieacker, *Gesetz und Richterkunst* (Karlsruhe, 1958), 10.

extreme, are nevertheless entirely acceptable. Consider for example 'Liberty and equality are constant fundamental values of state unity.'[42] What is lacking is some more satisfactory foundation for such principles and some procedure defining them more precisely.

The proposals discussed so far for the objectivization of value-judgments can be divided into three groups:

(1) Proposals using as a starting-point actual extant convictions and points of consensus as well as actually valid or accepted non-legal norms.
(2) Proposals making a reference to values which can in some way by extracted from the existing fabric of the law (including past decisions).
(3) Proposals involving principles which go beyond the positive law.

A further possibility has not been discussed, namely:

(4) An appeal to empirical findings (over and above those involved under (1)).

Such empirical findings are of considerable significance in the process of legal justification of legal decisions, but normative premises cannot be deduced from them *alone*.[43]

There is much to be said in favour of the view that none of the procedures listed above, nor indeed any combination of like procedures, could solve the problem of the justification of legal judgments. Certainly, in modern society there are divergent views on almost every practical problem. Actual consensus, at least consensus sufficient to deal with concrete practical questions, is rare. Divergent values are always apparent within the overall framework of a legal order and these can lead to divergent outcomes in their application to particular concrete cases. An appeal to self-evident truths or to pre-ordained laws of

[42] *BVerfGE* 2, 1 (12).

[43] On the problem touched on here of the derivation of an 'ought' from an 'is' cf. the review of the literature by E. Morscher, 'Das Sein-Sollen-Problem logisch betrachtet. Eine Übersicht über den gegenwärtigen Stand der Diskussion', *conceptus*, 8 (1974), 5 ff.; Hoerster, 'Zum Problem der Ableitung eines Sollens aus einem Sein in der analytischen Moralphilosophie', *ARSP* 55 (1969), 11 ff.; F. von Kutschera, *Einführung in die Logik der Normen, Werte und Entscheidungen* (Freiburg and Munich, 1973), 66 ff. and below, pp. 34ff., 59.

nature is—at least from the methodological point of view—a very doubtful way of proceeding. Moreover, any principles discovered in this way can be applied quite differently. Finally it is possible to draw sets of mutually opposed normative consequences from any given judgments of fact.

Should we conclude from this that in the last analysis it is after all the non-intersubjectively-testable value-judgments of the decision-maker that are the decisive factor, value-judgments which can perhaps be explained in sociological or psychological terms but cannot be justified any further? This is certainly not a desirable conclusion as far as concerns the legitimacy of judicial decision-making and the scientific character of legal dogmatics in its concern with normative questions. This is not in itself an argument against drawing the conclusion, but it is a good reason for searching for an alternative solution.

2. THE FUNDAMENTAL IDEAS OF THIS ENQUIRY

Such a search would appear promising in the light of the results of modern discussions on ethics, of contemporary linguistic philosophy, and also of current developments in the theory of argumentation, all of which meet at various points. It is the aim of this investigation to discuss critically some theories developed in these different areas and to apply them to the field of fundamental juristic inquiry.[44]

Legal reasoning will be understood here as a linguistic activity which occurs in many different situations from courtroom to classroom. This linguistic activity is concerned, in a sense yet to be more precisely defined, with the correctness of normative statements. It will be expedient to designate such activity 'discourse' and, further, since it concerns the correctness

[44] In connection with the Swedish legal theorist Ivar Agge, Dreier characterizes contemporary legal theory as a 'frontier post discipline' with the task of testing 'the findings, whether empirical or theoretical, of neighbouring sciences for their relevance to legal science in the narrower sense' (*Was ist und wozu Allgemeine Rechtstheorie?* (Tübingen, 1975), 21). This investigation may be regarded as an attempt to contribute to the completion of this task.

of normative statements, as 'practical discourse'. Legal discourse is a special case of general practical discourse.[45]

Legal discourse can be conceived of in a variety of ways. It can be looked at from an empirical, an analytical, or a normative standpoint. It is *empirical*, for example, where it describes or seeks to explain the relative frequency of given types of arguments;[46] the correlation between groups of speakers, the speech situations and the use of certain types of argument or their application; the force of arguments; the motivation to use certain arguments or the views prevalent among given groups of people concerning the validity of arguments. Theoretical work in such subjects belongs to the behavioural study of legal practices in general and of judicial activity in particular[47] and has to be pursued by social scientific methods.

It is *analytical* where the focus is on the logical structure of actual or possible arguments. Finally, it is *normative* where it proposes and justifies criteria for the rationality of legal discourse.

These three approaches are not sharply distinguished in traditional German legal methodology. This, however, is not necessarily a shortcoming, for a whole series of relationships exists between them. Thus the empirical approach presupposes at least a rough classification of the different types of argument. The normative perspective requires insights into the logical structure of possible arguments. The relationship between the normative and the empirical approaches is more problematic. Can it be said, for example, that the majority view in a given group as to the validity of an argument is a test for its rationality? Questions such as this can only be raised at this stage; they are to be discussed more fully during the course of the present investigation.

Criteria for the rationality of legal discourse will be at the forefront of the enquiry. Since the elucidation of such criteria includes an analysis of the logical structure of justifications, the

[45] On the justification of this thesis cf. below, pp. 212 ff.

[46] On this cf. E. Eichenhofer, 'Frequenzanalytische Untersuchungen juristischer Argumentation', *Rechtstheorie*, 5 (1974), 216 ff.

[47] Cf. Rottleuthner, *Richterliches Handeln*, pp. 61 ff.

approach pursued in this book can be termed 'normative-analytical'. An attempt will be made to develop a theory of legal discourse that is both normative and analytical.

The conception of legal discourse as a special case of general practical discourse will be of central significance. Both legal discourse and general practical discourse are concerned with the correctness of normative statements. This is what they have in common. It will be argued that both in the assertion of a general practical statement and in the assertion or pronouncement of legal statements a claim is made to correctness.[48] Legal discourse is a *special* case because legal argumentation occurs in the context of a number of limiting conditions. In particular one must include here its statute-bound character; its necessary regard to precedents; its involvement with doctrinal studies as developed through an institutionally organized profession of academic lawyers, as well as—and this of course is not true for academic legal discourse—its subjection to the requirements of procedural ordinances and regulations.

The claim to correctness involved in the assertion of any legal statement is the claim that, subject to the constraints set by these limiting conditions, the assertion is rationally justifiable. This claim matches the precept in Article 20, paragraph 3 of the Constitution (*Grundgesetz*) under which every act of adjudication is subjected to 'legislation and the rule of law'. The question is how we are to understand the formula 'rationally justifiable, subject to the constraints set by these limiting conditions'.

In order to answer this question it would seem appropriate to begin by investigating what might be meant by saying that a normative statement is 'rationally justifiable'. To this end a number of relevant theories will be discussed in considerable detail. The theories in question belong partly to the field of analytical moral philosophy, in particular those of Stevenson, Hare, Toulmin, and Baier, together with Habermas's consensus theory of truth, the Erlangen School's theory of practical deliberation, and finally Perelman's theory of argumentation. The results of these discussions will be integrated into a general theory of rational, practical discourse. The core of this theory

[48] Cf. below, pp. 214 ff.

will consist of five groups containing a total of twenty-two explicitly formulated rules and a table of six forms of argument.[49] The explicit formulation of these rules and forms of argument may seem pedantic, redundant, or even presumptuous. Perhaps its most important function is to reveal their shortcomings the more plainly. These deficiences may relate to the content of the rules, their incomplete enumeration, the redundancy of particular rules and forms of argument, as well as the lack of precision in their formulation. Insofar as shortcomings of this kind do not render the rules and forms of argument entirely pointless, they present something akin to a code of practical reason.

The efficacy of these rules and forms of argument should be neither overestimated nor undervalued. They are not axioms from which certain normative propositions can be deduced, but rather a group of rules and forms of various logical rankings which an argument must satisfy if the conclusion it establishes is to have the correctness it purports to have. At the same time, the rules do not by any means completely determine the conclusion of such an argument in each and every case. But they do exclude some (as 'discursively impossible' ones) from the class of possible normative propositions, and thereby establish the validity (as 'discursively necessary' ones) of the contradictories of those excluded. In the case of a large number of normative propositions, however, they, together with their contradictions, are entirely consistent with the rules of discourse ('discursively possible'). This can be explained by the fact that the rules of rational practical discourse do not prescribe the premises from which the parties to any discourse have to set out. The starting-point of any discourse consists in the first instance of the initially given (i.e. actual extant) normative convictions, desires, and perceived needs of, and empirical information possessed by, the speakers. The rules of discourse lay down how one may arrive at well-founded normative statements from this starting-point but without fully prescribing every step. Since it is possible to start

[49] Cf. below, pp. 188 ff. On the concept of an argument form cf. below, p. 92. On the difference between rules and forms cf. below, p. 188 n. 29.

from quite different normative convictions, desires, and perceived needs, and since it is not certain how perceptions of need change or how normative convictions are to be modified or desires subjected to limits, there remains a possibility to quite diverse outcomes.

It could be said that the rules of discourse define a decision-making process in which it is uncertain what is to form the basis of decision and in which not every step is prescribed. This can be viewed as a shortcoming on the one hand and an advantage on the other. The shortcoming is obvious. The advantage consists of the fact that the overall basis of the decision and a series of individual steps in the decision-making process are not fixed by any expert in decision theory who in turn would have to begin from his or her own preconceptions, but are rather left to the individuals immediately involved. The task of discourse theory can be seen precisely as that of putting forward rules which on the one hand are sufficiently weak—that is, of such limited normative content that individuals of quite different normative outlook can agree to them—and on the other hand so strong that any discussion which abides by them can be acknowledged as 'rational'.

The weakness of the rules of discourse outlined above is made more pronounced by the fact that some of the rules are formulated in such a way that they can only be adhered to approximately. However, this does not make the rules pointless. They certainly cannot reduce the field of what is discursively possible to any sort of final certainty. Nevertheless they are of considerable importance in explaining the claim to correctness, as a criterion for judging the correctness of normative statements, as a critical device for weeding out whatever is not rational in a purported justification, and/or for sharpening an ideal worth striving for.

This vindicates discourse theory as a promising enterprise for legal theory. A norm or individual directive which satisfies the criteria determined by the rules of discourse can be deemed '*just*'. Hence the theory of discourse is one of what are probably several possible ways of analysing a central concept of jurisprudence.

The discussion has already alluded to the fact that legal discourse can be distinguished from general practical discourse in that the former is, in short, restricted in its scope by statute, precedent, legal dogmatics, and—in the case of actual judicial proceedings—by procedural legislation and regulations.

The wide range of what is merely discursively possible, the tentative nature of any conclusions, and the need to resolve many practical questions in a limited time-span, constitute three of the reasons for regarding these constraints as not merely acceptable but rather both rational and necessary. It can be assumed that any participants in a process of rational deliberation which has as its object the limits of general practical discourse, would decide in favour of the introduction of procedures for creating rules of positive law as well as procedures for the scientific analysis and for the application of these rules. That is, they would decide in favour of the institutionalization of scientific legal studies and of some form (not necessarily the currently practised form) of judicial discourse. The introduction of positive legal rules, their courtroom application, and their compulsory enforcement have not least among their functions that of securing the possibility of general practical discourse.

In saying that legal discourse takes place within a framework of limiting conditions, nothing has been said as to how this delimitation is to occur in practice. To this end it will be necessary to determine in more detail both the rules according to which the limiting conditions are to be taken into account and the actual forms of argument in which reference may be made to them.

It is possible to make a distinction between those rules and forms which are valid for all kinds of legal discourse and those which play a role only in certain forms of discourse. Only some of the general rules and forms can be discussed in this enquiry.

A particularly important problem to be examined in this connection is the question of the relationship of legal argumentation to general practical argumentation. The 'special case' thesis is open to at least three interpretations.

The first possible meaning is the claim that the actual process of justification or deliberation should proceed (and in ideal cases does indeed proceed) according to the criteria of general practical discourse, and that legal justification only serves as a secondary legitimation of any conclusions arrived at in this way.

This thesis can be called the 'Subordination Thesis'. According to this thesis, whenever cases arise whose solution cannot be derived conclusively from statute law, legal discourse is nothing more than general practical discourse behind a legal façade.[50]

If the Subordination Thesis is rejected, two possibilities remain. It might be claimed that legal argumentation can take one part of the way, to a point at which specifically legal arguments are no longer available. It is here that general practical argumentation must intervene. This thesis can be designated the 'Supplementation Thesis'. Finally there is the view that specifically legal arguments and general practical arguments should be combined at all levels and applied jointly. This interpretation, which can be labelled the 'Integration Thesis', is the one adopted here.

Of course, little has been achieved by the mere assertion of the Integration Thesis. The question remains how the integration which it demands should be fostered. To put it another way, in Esser's words, the question is that of how to determine the relationship of 'tests for correctness' with 'tests for coherence' in respect of the reconcilability of the solution offered with the positive law, due account being taken of other legislative solutions and of 'dogmatic elements'.[51] Ascertaining this is one of the aims of the theory of legal reasoning put forward in this book.

3. TOPIC THEORY AND ITS LIMITS

Anyone putting forward a theory of legal reasoning, may well be understood to be proposing some version of the Theory of Legal Topics, which has played such a significant part in discussions of methodology during the last twenty years. But this would be a

[50] Müller has claimed that Kriele advocates this thesis (*Juristische Methodik*, pp. 93 ff., 196–7). Some of Kriele's remarks can be understood in this way (cf. perhaps his *Theorie der Rechtsgewinnung*, p. 218). However, Kriele also speaks of the 'characteristic value' of legal justifications which have the capacity of 'influencing the outcome, or at least its range of variations' (ibid., 220). Most recently Kriele has come out expressly against Müller's interpretation (cf. ibid., epilogue, pp. 319–20).

[51] Esser, *Vorverständnis und Methodenwahl*, p. 19.

case of mistaken identity, and as such would have the unfortunate consequence that any objections put forward against topic theory would be automatically transferred, without further inquiry, to the theory of legal reasoning in question. In order to avoid this it would seem appropriate to ask briefly how the theory developed here relates to Viehweg's thesis[52] that legal thinking is best understood as a 'topic-orientated' form of thought.

In order to answer this question it is necessary to know what is to be understood by 'topic theory'[53] in this context. Adapting from Otte, with minor modifications,[54] it can signify three different things: (1) a technique of searching for premisses for an argument; (2) a theory as to the nature of premisses; and (3) a theory about the application of premisses in justificatory arguments at law. As a technique of searching for premisses, the theory of topics advocates the consideration of every possible point of view with a bearing on the question at issue. It is here that catalogues of 'topoi' are meant to come in useful.[55] Struck, presumably with criticism in mind, undertook the work of putting together such a catalogue of sixty-four topoi. Amongst these are to be found such disparate items as: 'Lex posterior derogat legi priori',[56] 'Nothing unconscionable may be demanded',[57] and 'Purpose'.[58] Even the heuristic value of such compilations must be subject to doubt.[59] In any event, nothing comparable will be attempted in this investigation.

The theory of topics considered as a theory of the nature of premisses is of greater interest. According to this theory, whenever argumentation proceeds with a topos as the starting-point, the propositions from which one starts are neither proven

[52] T. Viehweg, *Topik und Jurisprudenz*, 5th edn. (Munich, 1974).

[53] From the extensive literature on topic theory cf. in particular Kriele, *Theorie der Rechtsgewinnung*, pp. 114–53; G. Otte, 'Zwanzig Jahre Topik-Diskussion: Ertrag und Aufgaben', *Rechtstheorie*, 1 (1970), 183 ff.; Wieacker, 'Zur Topikdiskussion', pp. 391 ff.; A. Bokeloh, 'Der Beitrag der Topik zur Rechtsgewinnung', thesis (Göttingen, 1972).

[54] Otte, 'Zwanzig Jahre Topik-Diskussion', p. 184.

[55] Viehweg, *Topik und Jurisprudenz*, p. 35.

[56] G. Struck, *Topische Jurisprudenz* (Frankfurt-on-Main, 1971), 20.

[57] Ibid., 33.

[58] Ibid., 34.

[59] Cf. Otte, 'Zwanzig Jahre Topik-Diskussion', p. 187.

truths nor mere assertions of arbitrary will but are rather ἔνδοξα[60]—that is, plausible, reasonable, generally accepted, or probable propositions.[61] There is a measure of truth in this, but it is open to misinterpretation and is too general and partly false. It is too general because it does not differentiate sufficiently between the various premisses necessary to the process of legal justification of decisions. Struck's assertion: 'A statute is one "topos" among others, but an extremely important one',[62] does not do justice to the role played by valid enacted legal norms in legal discourse.[63] In addition to this weakness there is also the inability of topic theory to do justice to the authoritative character of legal reasoning both in the context of institutionally pursued legal dogmatics[64] and in that of case-law.[65] An adequate theory of legal reasoning, however, must include a theory both of the status of legal dogmatics and of the proper evaluation of precedents.

Apart from its failure to grasp the significance of statute,

[60] Cf. Aristotle, *Topica*, 100^{b}.

[61] Translations of ἔνδοξα vary. Rolfes's translation uses the expression *wahrscheinlich* 'likely' (Leipzig, 1922), p. 1. Viehweg favours instead *meinungsmässig*, 'reasonable' (*Topik und Jurisprudenz*, p. 21). Referring to English translations, Kriele considers 'generally accepted opinions' as most appropriate (*Theorie der Rechtsgewinnung*, p. 135) and Wieacker views *probabel* 'probable', as a free but nevertheless suitable suggestion ('Zur praktischen Leistung der Rechtsdogmatik', in *Hermeneutik und Dialektik*, Festschrift for H.-G. Gadamer, vol. ii, ed. R. Bubner, K. Cramer, and R. Wiehl (Tübingen, 1970), 328 n. 46).

[62] Struck, *Topische Jurisprudenz*, p. 7.

[63] On this point of criticism cf. Canaris, *Systemdenken und Systembegriff*, pp. 142 ff.; Diederichsen, 'Topisches und systematisches Denken', p. 702.

[64] Cf. in particular Diederichsen, 'Topisches und systematisches Denken', pp. 698 ff.

[65] Nor is this weakness remedied by the idea of a system of topics considered by Viehweg. Such a system as understood by Viehweg can be defined by means of four characteristics: (1) orientation to the problem (2) ordering of the 'topics' corresponding to the problems (3) continual movement by means of (4) rational argumentation ('Some Considerations Concerning Legal Reasoning', *Law, Reason, and Justice: Essays in Legal Philosophy*, ed. G. Hughes (New York and London, 1969), 268; similarly in his 'Systemprobleme in Rechtsdogmatik und Rechtsforschung', *System und Klassifikation in Wissenschaft und Dokumentation*, ed. A. Diemer (Meisenheim am Glan, 1968), 104). The introduction of a system of topics defined in this way is little more than the introduction of a new name for what was previously simply called 'Topics'.

dogmatics, and precedent, the fundamental problem with the theory of topics is its exclusive orientation to considering the surface structure of standard arguments. Struck's catalogue of topoi is illustrative of this. Little can be achieved with formulas like: 'Purpose' and 'Nothing unconscionable may be demanded'. What really matters is the logical analysis of such arguments. It is only in this way that their character as structures comprising various sentences, some of which have the all-important feature of being normative, can be grasped. In any rational discourse, these are the true objects of discussion.[66]

However, if one analyses the deep structure of such topoi as: 'Whatever is intolerable is not lawful',[67] which in a general formulation can plausibly be counted among ἔνδοξα 'which appear true to all or to the majority or to the wise and from among the wise, once again either to all or to the majority or to the most famous and respected',[68] one finds more specific normative sentences to which these criteria do not necessarily apply. But these are precisely the sentences which matter, for a phrase like 'Whatever is intolerable is not lawful' becomes quite useless the moment there is disagreement as to what is intolerable. To respond to this problem by producing additional formulations at the same level of generality, is to evade the issue.

Finally, topic theory as a theory about the application of premisses in the justification of individual decisions, is also problematic. The relevant rule supported by the theory here is the requirement of considering all aspects.[69] But this says nothing at all on the question of which aspect is decisive, nor does it even lay down what is to count as a point of view in the first place. In this respect Viehweg's observation that 'discussion apparently remains the only forum of control'[70] is vacuously true. But what does a 'forum of control' mean? Should every actually achieved consensus be regarded as a guarantee of the correctness of what is agreed on? This cannot be the case, if only because subsequent discussion may reveal defects inherent in a

[66] On the requirement 'to give preference to open evaluations over "topical" justifications' cf. Wieacker, 'Zur Topikdiskussion', p. 409.

[67] Struck, *Topische Jurisprudenz*, p. 33.

[68] Aristotle, *Topica*, 100^{b}.

[69] Cf. Struck, *Topische Jurisprudenz*, p. 7.

[70] Viehweg, *Topik und Jurisprudenz*, p. 43.

prior consensus. It would at least be necessary to demand that in any such discussion certain rules are to be followed which mark out the discussion as a rational one. Struck alludes to several such rules.[71] However, these rules are inadequate from the outset in that they contain nothing about the role of statute, dogmatics, and precedent.

Perhaps the picture drawn here of topic theory is too negative. It can at least be said that there is a sense in which the present investigation incorporates the intentions of topic theory as it has been applied to law.[72] However, it is precisely this which makes it imperative to expose its shortcomings as clearly as possible. A theory of legal reasoning will be judged by reference to the extent and degree to which it succeeds in avoiding these shortcomings. To recapitulate once again, these shortcomings consist of underestimating the significance of statute, dogmatics, and precedent, of insufficient analysis of the deep structure of arguments, and of an insufficiently precise concept of discussion.

It is, however, important to hold on to some aspects of topic theory—in particular the view that in areas where there are no conclusive justifying grounds it is not necessary to leave the field wide open to irrational decision-making, and also the belief that there is a close conceptual connection between the idea of rational justification and that of rational discussion.

4. TOWARDS ASSESSING WHETHER CONTEMPORARY METHODOLOGICAL DISCUSSIONS REVEAL A NEED FOR A THEORY OF RATIONAL LEGAL ARGUMENTATION

The theory of legal argumentation put forward here can be understood as extending and developing many of the points alluded to in the literature on legal method. It is not only

[71] Struck, *Topische Jurisprudenz*, pp. 99 ff.

[72] This applies in particular to the proposal for a formal 'topic' as presented by Viehweg. The subject-matter of such a formal topic should be the rules of the pragmatics of the language. By 'pragmatics' Viehweg understands, following Morris's famous distinction, the theory of the relationship between signs, speaker, and situation. (Cf. C. W. Morris, 'Foundations of the Theory of Signs', *International Encyclopedia of Unified Science* (Chicago, 1938), vol. i, no. 2, pp. 1 ff.) On this, Viehweg refers to findings in modern logic, linguistic philosophy, and moral philosophy (*Topik und Jurisprudenz*, pp. 111 ff.). This usage is adopted in the present study.

Viehweg who considers it necessary to work out a 'fully developed and up-to-date theory of argumentation as rhetoric'.[73] Hassemer speaks of the need for a theory of legal reasoning as 'one of the most urgent desiderata of legal science'.[74] Rottleuthner is of the opinion that 'as a normative discipline, legal science [is to be understood as] . . . a theory of argumentation'.[75] Rödig points out that 'judges [are not able] to pass judgment . . . solely on the basis of expertise in drawing logically valid conclusions'. 'They must therefore also understand how to argue rationally in areas in which the preconditions for logical proofs do not exist. It is quite clear that such areas exist; much less clear as yet is the method of arguing "rationally" within them.'[76]

The desirability of clarifying what is to be understood by 'rational argumentation' is also evident from several remarks in a recent decision of the Federal Constitutional Court. The court first observes that in the light of Article 20, paragraph 3 of the Constitution (*Grundgesetz*) '[the] law . . . is not identical with the totality of statutes'. Hence 'according to the Basic Law (*Grundgesetz*) [judges are not] required merely to implement instructions of a legislative kind within the limits of possible literal meanings in individual cases.' The task of administering justice according to law can sometimes

> demand in particular that those value-judgments immanent in the constitutional order but not receiving any expression or receiving only imperfect expression in the actual texts of statutes, should be brought into the open and realized in actual decisions by an act of evaluative cognition inevitably involving a discretionary element. Judges must guard against arbitrariness in this process; their decisions must be founded in *rational argumentation.* It must be shown that the written law does not fulfil its task of providing a just resolution to a legal problem. In such cases the judicial decision closes that gap in accordance with the standards of *practical reason* and the community's well-founded general conceptions of justice.[77]

[73] Viehweg, *Topik und Jurisprudenz*, p. 111.

[74] Hassemer, 'Juristische Argumentationstheorie und juristische Didaktik', *Jahrbuch für Rechtssoziologie und Rechtstheorie*, 2 (1972), 467.

[75] Rottleuthner, *Rechtswissenschaft als Sozialwissenschaft* (Frankfurt-on-Main, 1973), 188.

[76] J. Rödig, *Die Theorie des gerichtlichen Erkenntnisverfahrens* (Berlin, Heidelberg and New York, 1973), 116.

[77] *BVerfGE* 34, 269 (287) (my italics).

These statements of the Federal Constitutional Court might be viewed as questionable on constitutional grounds. From the point of view of legal theory, they raise the question of what is to be understood by 'rational argumentation' and 'practical reason'. This is the question to be pursued here. The answer also has a bearing on the constitutional problem. If it were to transpire that there is no such thing as rational argumentation or that its role is quite minimal, then there is more likely to be an attempt to limit the extent of judicial competence.

Esser and Kriele in particular argue for the possibility of legally relevant rational argumentation. In his book *Vorverständnis und Methodenwahl in der Rechtsfindung,* Esser tries to show

> that there is in fact such *rationality in argument* outside the dogmatic system and its 'methods'—inasmuch as *the marshalling of a consensus on the reasonableness of a solution* within the framework of legally given alternatives constitutes the actual process of persuasion in law.[78]

However, neither the concept of rational argumentation nor that of a consensus is clarified in Esser's work. Hence several uncertainties remain. In particular, the nature of the relationship between general practical argumentation, which corresponds to what Esser calls 'ways of checking the correctness [of an argument]' with what is specifically legal in arguments, 'ways of checking coherence',[79] as he puts it, remains unclear. Questions also remain concerning the concept of a consensus. Several remarks by Esser give rise to the suspicion that he uses the term to mean actual consensus. Thus he speaks of the 'social correctness for which consensus is the only verifiable indicator'.[80] On the other hand he speaks of an 'anticipation of a common conception to be established or achieved'[81] and of 'partners amenable to rationally conceivable arguments'.[82] There is a need for further clarification here.

For Kriele, the concept of reason is one of the central concepts of legal science: 'considerations of right reason govern the law through and through'.[83] Deliberating on the consequences of the

[78] Esser, *Vorverständnis und Methodenwahl*, p. 9.
[79] Cf. ibid., 19.
[80] Ibid., 28; cf. further pp. 132, 165.
[81] Ibid., 23.
[82] Ibid., 25.
[83] Kriele, *Theorie der Rechtsgewinnung*, p. 227.

maxims underlying a judgment plays a decisive role in the types of rational argument which Kriele considers to be possible and necessary. These consequences should be assessed from the standpoint of the *general interest*, or, in cases of a conflict of interests, from that of the *more fundamental interest*.[84] This formula is not a readily applicable criterion. Its application presupposes an answer to the question of what is to be regarded as the general interest or what is to be considered as the more fundamental interest.[85] To this end it is necessary to articulate more precise criteria or rules. Kriele himself points the way to their discovery in that he calls for a more extensive reciprocal exchange of ideas between contemporary ethics and legal theory.[86] In this regard he refers in particular to the theories of the Erlangen School, and of Habermas and Perelman, and to the results of modern linguistic philosophy, as well as to more recent work on the principle of universalizability. The importation of these approaches into discussions of the foundations of legal theory has shaped the present investigation.

There are of course authors who take the view that the path mapped out in this book is foredoomed not to reach its destination. Luhmann in particular must be cited here:

> However justified the concern of Viehweg, Perelman, Kriele, Habermas, and others to refute the thesis that there is an apparently unbridgeable gap between rational logic and irrational evaluation as an epistemological misconception, yet discursive, reasonable forms of elucidation of both acceptable and unacceptable evaluative stances must remain stuck in the domain of experience. The central claim of practical philosophy, namely that in the course of argument over what are today termed 'values' one might come nearer to *action*, can no longer be sustained in today's world, which offers many more options than ever before. Our way of choosing from our experiences is too different from our way of choosing actions.[87]

The incantation of the 'Myth of Reasonableness'[88] is inadequate

[84] Ibid., 198, 314.

[85] Cf. on this Larenz, *Methodenlehre*, p. 146.

[86] Kriele, *Theorie der Rechtsgewinnung*, epilogue, pp. 343 ff.

[87] N. Luhmann, 'Gerechtigkeit in den Rechtssystemen der modernen Gesellschaft', *Rechtstheorie*, 4 (1973), 144 n. 33.

[88] id., 'Die Systemreferenz von Gerechtigkeit. In Erwiderung auf die Ausführungen von Ralf Dreier', ibid. 5 (1974), 203.

in the light of the complex nature of modern societies. With respect to the legitimacy of decisions what matters is 'not so much motivated convictions but much more . . . acceptance . . . which is free of motives and independent of individual (personal) idiosyncrasies.'[89]

It is not possible to discuss Luhmann's theory here. It will be examined to some extent in the discussion of Habermas's views. It will there become evident that an approach based on Luhmann's System Theory is, in a certain sense, compatible with the one advocated here. This investigation is therefore not to be understood as a direct attack on Luhmann's position. However, should the theory expounded here prove to be tenable, it would indeed provide a weighty argument against the purportedly omnicompetent character of System Theory.

The following discussion is divided into three parts. The first part contains a detailed discussion of the theories of Stevenson, Hare, Toulmin, Baier, Habermas, Lorenzen and Schwemmer, and Perelman. In the second part the results of these discussions are integrated to yield a general theory of practical discourse. Building on this, the third part will work out the rudiments of a theory of rational legal discourse. It will thereby become clear what remains to be done. In particular, there is a need for analytical studies of the argument structure in particular decisions[90] and in scientific discussions, of the rules which are followed and the argument forms which are deployed in different areas of the law,[91] of the structure of argumentation in series of decisions,[92] and of the structure of argumentation in court cases.[93] These analytical investigations would have to be supplemented by empirical studies of legal decision-making behaviour.

[89] id., *Legitimation durch Verfahren*, 2nd edn. (Darmstadt and Neuwied, 1975), 32.

[90] On such an analysis cf. K. Lüderssen, *Erfahrung als Rechtsquelle. Abduktion und Falsifikation von Hypothesen im juristischen Entscheidungsprozeß. Eine Fallstudie aus dem Kartellstrafrecht* (Frankfurt-on-Main, 1972), 109 ff.

[91] Cf. E. von Savigny, J. Rahlf, and U. Neumann, *Juristische Dogmatik und Wissenschaftstheorie* (Munich, 1976).

[92] On this cf. M. Dießelhorst, *Die Natur der Sache als außergesetzliche Rechtsquelle, verfolgt an der Rechtsprechung zur Saldotheorie* (Tübingen, 1968), 50 ff.

[93] On the concepts 'argument structure', 'argument form', and 'structure of argumentation' cf. below, pp. 92–3.

It might be seen as a defect in the current work that these things are not attempted here. It is, however, not possible for everything to happen at once. It would be enough if the investigations presented here could make a contribution to the foundation of a theory of rational legal argumentation—a theory which, it is to be hoped, will one day be so firmly grounded and so widely developed that it will not only clarify the character of legal science as a normative discipline but will also provide practical guidelines for the practising lawyer.

A. REFLECTIONS ON SOME THEORIES OF PRACTICAL DISCOURSE

I. Practical Discourse in Analytic Moral Philosophy

In order to know whether and indeed how normative sentences, utterances, or propositions[1] can be justified, one must know what counts as a normative sentence, utterance, or proposition. A theory of their justification presupposes a theory of normative language.[2]

In recent decades, the analysis of normative language in general, and of moral language in particular, has been the subject of numerous investigations within the broader framework of analytic philosophy. The result has been the development of 'meta-ethics' as a special field of study. Since a theory of normative language forms the basis of any theory of the justification of normative sentences, propositions, etc. it will be necessary to begin by discussing the various meta-ethical theories. Such a preliminary discussion becomes all the more necessary on realizing that there are several meta-ethical theories which are inconsistent with the theory of rational discourse to be put forward in this study.

The simplest model of practical discourse is that of a discussion between two people who are arguing about whether A ought to be done or about whether A is good. There are two possible ways of reaching agreement. The first involves one of the parties proving the truth of his or her claim to the other,

[1] For the time being, these three concepts can be defined in the following way: A sentence is a particular sequence of spoken or written signs, an utterance is the use of a sentence in a specific situation, and a proposition is that which is expressed by a sentence, its meaning. These concepts will need to be clarified further. It will, in particular, be shown why it makes sense to speak of 'normative propositions'. Where nothing hangs on the distinction the following text will refer to both 'propositions' and 'sentences'.

[2] Cf. J. O. Urmson, *The Emotive Theory of Ethics* (London, 1968), 9: 'But as soon as we raise the question how a certain type of assertion, the moral, the mathematical or the aesthetic, for example, can be reasonably arrived at or defended, it is clearly necessary to determine the general character of such assertions, to make explicit what sort of claims in what sort of field they make.'

justifying it, providing grounds for it, etc. The second involves inducing the other party to agree by some other means. There is a large number of such means. They include every method of persuasion, of psychological pressure, and of propaganda. The first way involves the *justification* of a moral conviction.[3] The second involves a process which can at best be *explained* psychologically. The question to be considered in the following pages is as follows: Is justification of moral convictions possible, and, if so, how?

1. NATURALISM AND INTUITIONISM

There are two meta-ethical theories which answer this question unequivocally in the affirmative: naturalism and intuitionism. If either of these theories was tenable, there would be no need for a theory of rational practical discourse like the one proposed here.

1.1. Naturalism

Following Moore, the term 'naturalistic' will be applied to any theory which proceeds on the assumption that normative expressions such as 'good' and 'ought' can be defined in terms of descriptive expressions.[4] If this were possible, then the norma-

[3] There are several differences but also important points of similarity between the concepts of justification (*Rechtfertigung*) and substantiation (*Begründung*) of a conviction, claim, proposition, etc. On the one hand the concept of justification is wider than that of substantiation. Thus it is possible to speak of justifying an utterance both when a speaker admits that it is unsubstantiated but was necessary to avoid disaster and when it is in fact substantiated. On the other hand the concept of justification is more restricted. Justification is the term used, in particular, where reasons are brought forward to meet objections or doubts. However, in many contexts the two are interchangeable. The following text will, in the main use them interchangeably. [*Translator's Note:* It is not at all clear that the distinction holds in English at all, particularly as there exists a further German word for 'substantiation'. Both words are translated 'justification' throughout.]

[4] Cf. G. E. Moore, *Principia Ethica* (Cambridge, 1903), 40: 'I have thus appropriated the name Naturalism to a particular method of approaching Ethics . . . This method consists in substituting for "good" some one property

tive expressions occurring in normative sentences could be replaced by descriptive expressions. In this way every normative proposition would become a descriptive one. As such, it would be amenable to testing according to the procedures of the natural sciences and of the social sciences. The task for ethics or moral philosophy would then be restricted to translating normative expressions into descriptive ones. In such a case, normative sentences would be equivalent to descriptive ones, and the old dispute concerning the possibility of deriving an 'ought' from an 'is' would be settled in the affirmative.

1.1.1. Moore's attack on this thesis (rarely put forward explicitly) resulted in the development of meta-ethics around the turn of the century. He accuses naturalism of a fallacy, the so-called 'naturalistic fallacy'.[5] This accusation is grounded first and foremost in his now famous 'open-question argument'.[6]

If 'good' is defined in terms of some such empirical predicate as 'sought after by the majority', then wherever 'good' appears it can be replaced by 'sought after by the majority'. But it can still be asked: 'A is sought after by the majority, but is A also good?' If the descriptivist theory were correct, this question should make just as little sense as the question 'A is sought after by the majority, but is A also sought after by the majority?' This is, however, not the case. The first question makes sense, while the

of a natural object or of a collection of natural objects; and in thus replacing Ethics by some one of the natural sciences.' Naturalism, which had long been considered exploded, has found adherents again in recent times. Cf. G. J. Warnock, *Contemporary Moral Philosophy* (London and Basingstoke, 1967), 62–77; P. Foot, 'Moral Arguments', *Mind*, 67 (1958), 502–13; and ead., 'Moral Beliefs' in *Theories of Ethics*, ed. ead. (Oxford, 1967), 83–100. The ideas of these writers, designated 'neo-naturalists', are considerably more finely textured than the thesis cited above. It will be necessary to come back to them in discussing more recent ethical theories.

[5] This is rather an unfortunate choice of terminology. As W. K. Frankena has shown, the core of Moore's objection is directed to the attempt at defining 'good' at all. Moore does not only attack definitions stated in terms of descriptive expressions. He employs the term 'naturalistic fallacy' with respect to definitions by means of metaphysical expressions too. (Cf. Moore, *Principia Ethica*, pp. 39, 114). Frankena therefore speaks of a 'definist fallacy'; cf. Frankena, 'The Naturalistic Fallacy', in *Theories of Ethics*, ed. Foot, 57.

[6] Cf. Moore, *Principia Ethica*, pp. 15 ff.

second does not. Thus the meaning of 'good' is *at least not completely* co-extensive with that of 'sought after by the majority'. Any other predicate or combination of predicates can be substituted for 'sought after by the majority': 'Whatever definition be offered, it may always be asked, with significance, of the complex so defined, whether it is itself good.'[7] From this it follows that the naturalistic thesis of the descriptivity of value terms cannot be correct.

1.1.2. The 'open-question argument' has been severely criticized for several reasons. Three particularly important points of criticism will be mentioned here.[8]

It has been objected that, although it may be that the argument remains true for all the definitions put forward to date, this does not exclude the possibility of finding a definition of which this is not true at some time in the future.[9] In the light of the many cases for which Moore's point holds true, this objection will gain weight only if and when the purely abstract possibility of finding a satisfactory definition emerges in some more concrete form.

A further objection rests on the possibility of 'covert synonymity'. The meaning of two expressions can be identical without being immediately apparent. If this were the case, 'good' would indeed be definable, despite the contrary claim of the 'open-question argument'.[10] This objection, like the first, cannot be strictly refuted but its weight may be limited. It would nevertheless seem justifiable not to attribute too much significance to the possibility of 'covert synonymity', so long as no grounds can be adduced for its existence.[11] The strength of the

[7] Ibid., 15.

[8] For further objections cf. K. Nielsen, 'Problems of Ethics', in *Encyclopedia of Philosophy*, ed. P. Edwards (New York and London, 1967), iii. 127–8.

[9] Cf. G. C. Kerner, *The Revolution in Ethical Theory* (Oxford, 1966), 19–20; Hoerster, 'Zum Problem der Ableitung eines Sollens aus einem Sein in der analytischen Moralphilosophie', *ARSP* 55 (1969), 20–1.

[10] R. B. Brandt, *Ethical Theory* (Englewood Cliffs, NJ 1959), 165; Hoerster, 'Zum Problem der Ableitung eines Sollens aus einem Sein', pp 19–20.

[11] Cf. K. Nielsen, 'Covert and Overt Synonymity: Brandt and Moore and the "Naturalistic Fallacy"', *Philosophical Studies*, 25 (1974), 53–4.

'open-question argument' thus rests on the fact that as yet no such grounds have been convincingly expounded.[12]

It has been further pointed out that, although 'good' as the most general moral expression cannot be defined independently of various contexts, in specific contexts it does indeed assume a fixed descriptive meaning such that it is possible to define it. To this there is a counter-objection: true as it is that there are *limits*[13]—indeed narrow limits—to possible uses of the term 'good' in particular contexts and of relatively concrete moral expressions like 'badly behaved' in all contexts, nevertheless within these limits, doubts or conflicts of opinion are always possible. This is sufficient for the viability of the 'open-question argument'.

1.1.3. The objections discussed above make it quite plain that naturalism has not been conclusively refuted by the 'open-question argument'. Nevertheless, the discussion shows that this argument does indeed provide good grounds for the view that the meaning of normative expressions, at the very least, does not correspond entirely to that of descriptive expressions.[14] Inasmuch as naturalism asserts such a correspondence, it cannot be accepted. Moral discourse cannot therefore be reduced to purely empirical discourse.

1.2. Intuitionism

If expressions such as 'good' and 'ought' cannot be defined by empirical expressions, it seems natural to assume that they stand for some kind of non-empirical properties or relations. Such is the thesis of intuitionism. It is called 'intuitionistic' because

[12] Cf. ibid., 55.

[13] The thesis of neo-naturalism to be discussed below, to the effect that there exist such limits (cf. Warnock, *Contemporary Moral Philosophy*, pp. 66 ff.), belongs to the most plausible assumptions of this theory. Nevertheless it is not to be confused with the 'definition thesis' under discussion here.

[14] These grounds gain considerably in strength from the theses of those meta-ethical theories which have elaborated the special function of normative expressions. Cf. R. M. Hare, *The Language of Morals* (London, Oxford and New York, 1952), 91: 'Value-terms have a special function in language, that of commending; and so they plainly cannot be defined in terms of other words which themselves do not perform this function.' This will be discussed further below.

those non-empirical entities are not cognizable through the five senses but rather by a further faculty. Several authors regard this additional faculty as something akin to a sixth sense, others see it more as a capacity for a priori insight,[15] while yet others combine the two.[16] Furthermore, it remains a matter of controversy precisely which entities are open to cognition in the ways indicated. Moore is of the opinion that there exists only one immediately recognizable moral property, which is the property of being 'good'. This property, like the property 'yellow', for example, is simple and unanalysable.[17] Ross holds that there are two such indefinable terms, namely 'good' and 'right'.[18] According to Scheler, on the other hand, there are four kinds of values: values concerning the pleasant and unpleasant, 'vital' values, intellectual values, and values concerning the divine. There is an a priori rank ordering amongst these values such that those of the pleasant and unpleasant are in the lowest position and the values concerning the divine in the highest.[19] These are only a few of the intuitionist approaches.

According to all intuitionist theories, the business of practical discourse would be conducted by appeal to evident truths of some kind or another. Within the range covered by these evident truths, there is no room for argument. A quotation from Moore illustrates this very clearly: 'It is untrue, because it is untrue, and there is no other reason: but I *declare* it untrue because its untruth is evident to me, and I hold that that is a sufficient reason for my assertion.'[20]

Many arguments have been put forward against intuitionism.[21] Probably the strongest of these is this: given that

[15] Cf. W. D. Ross, *The Foundations of Ethics* (Oxford, 1939), 320.

[16] Cf. M. Scheler, *Der Formalismus in der Ethik und die materiale Wertethik*, 5th edn. (Berlin and Munich, 1966), 87: 'The actual seat of all a priori value (and also of a priori ethical value) is 'value cognition' and 'value perception' respectively which are built up through feeling, preferring, and ultimately loving and hating.'

[17] Moore, *Principia Ethica*, p. 7.

[18] Ross, *The Right and the Good* (Oxford, 1930).

[19] Scheler, *Der Formalismus in der Ethik*, pp. 122 ff.

[20] Moore, *Principia Ethica*, p. 144.

[21] Cf. P. H. Nowell-Smith, *Ethics* (Harmondsworth, 1954), 36–47; P. Edwards, *The Logic of Moral Discourse* (New York and London, 1955), 94–103; S. E. Toulmin, *The Place of Reason in Ethics* (Cambridge, 1950), 10–28; E. von Savigny, *Die Philosophie der normalen Sprache*, 1st edn. (Frankfurt-on-Main, 1969), 196–9.

different people in fact respond in different ways to the same evidence, the theory fails to provide any criteria for distinguishing correct and incorrect, genuine and false intuitions.[22] But the theory must provide such criteria if it wishes to substantiate its claim of having established the possibility of objective knowledge and moral truth in the field of ethics. In the absence of such criteria for choosing between alternatives, intuitionism amounts to no more than ethical subjectivism.[23] However well-founded the objections of intuitionism against naturalism may be, it is an equally untenable theory.

2. EMOTIVISM

Normative statements are thus neither the same as statements about empirical objects nor the same as statements about non-empirical objects. In view of this, it would seem appropriate to conclude that the function of the expressions used in normative statements is at least not exhausted in referring to something. They either have a quite different role from that of referring or—a less extreme thesis—serve an additional purpose over and above that of referring. According to the various emotivist theories, this added function is that of expressing and/or evoking feelings and/or attitudes. In contrast to naturalism and intuitionism, emotivism thus advocates a new conception of moral language.[24] The most impressive version of emotivism, strengthened by subjectivist[25] and descriptive elements, is that defended by Stevenson.[26]

[22] P. F. Strawson, 'Ethical Intuitionism', *Philosophy*, 24 (1949), 27. Cf. also A. Podlech, 'Recht und Moral', *Rechtstheorie*, 3 (1972), 135.

[23] Cf. Kerner, *The Revolution in Ethical Theory*, p. 33.

[24] This is clearly stressed by C. L. Stevenson in *Ethics and Language* (New Haven, Conn. and London, 1944), 117: 'The error of treating language as though its function were always cognitive is almost incredibly naïve; and yet it is an error which is largely responsible for the impracticalities of traditional ethical theory.'

[25] Subjectivism must be distinguished from emotivism. According to subjectivism, normative propositions do not serve to express or evoke but rather to describe the feelings or attitudes of the speaker. Subjectivism is thus a special case of naturalism. On this cf. G. Grewendorf and G. Meggle, 'Zur Struktur des metaethischen Diskurses', *Seminar: Sprache und Ethik. Zur Entwicklung der Metaethik, (Frankfurt-on-Main, 1974), 13–14; Urmson, The Emotive Theory of Ethics*, p. 15.

[26] In addition to Stevenson's main work already cited (*Ethics and Language*)

According to Stevenson, the essential function of moral judgments is not that of referring to facts but rather that of *influencing* people. 'Instead of merely describing people's interests they *change* or *intensify* them.'[27] Moral expressions are instruments for exerting psychological influence.[28] They have an emotive function in addition to their cognitive one. It was with this thesis, published in 1937, that, as Urmson points out, Stevenson became the first to propose a programme for ethics which on the one hand is non-cognitive, yet on the other hand takes ethics seriously as an independent discipline.[29]

2.1. In order to analyse moral expressions in their emotive role, Stevenson makes use of two patterns of analysis. In embarking on analysis on the first pattern he uses the following definitions, which he designates as 'working models':

(1) 'This is wrong' means 'I disapprove of this; do so as well'.

(2) 'He ought to do this' means 'I disapprove of his leaving this undone; do so as well'.

(3) 'This is good' means 'I approve of this; do so as well'.[30]

In all three definitions, the *definiens* consists of two parts. The first part, a statement about the speaker's attitude, expresses the *descriptive* meaning of the analysed terms; the second part, an imperative, expresses the *emotive* meaning. By the 'emotive' meaning of a word, Stevenson understands 'the power that the word acquires, on account of its history in emotional situations, to evoke or directly express attitudes, as distinct from describing or designating them.'[31] The imperatives contained in the

cf. the collection of essays by him in *Facts and Values* (New Haven Conn. and London, 1963). Further advocates of this theory, widely held, particularly in the field of logical empiricism, are: A. J. Ayer (*Language, Truth and Logic* (Harmondsworth, 1971), 26–9, 136–51); R. Carnap (*Philosophy and Logical Syntax* (London, 1935), 22–6); and C. K. Ogden and I. A. Richards (*The Meaning of Meaning* (London, 1923)). On the history of emotivism cf. Urmson, *The Emotive Theory of Ethics*, pp. 12–23.

[27] Stevenson, 'The Emotive Meaning of Ethical Terms', in *Facts and Values*, p. 16.

[28] Ibid., 17.

[29] Urmson, *The Emotive Theory of Ethics*, p. 22.

[30] Stevenson, *Ethics and Language*, p. 21.

[31] Ibid., 33; cf. also pp. 41, 59, 61.

definiens, however, only incompletely represent this emotive meaning:

> Ethical judgements alter attitudes, not by an appeal to self-conscious efforts (as is the case with imperatives), but by the more flexible mechanism of *suggestion*. Emotive terms present the subject of which they are predicated in a bright or dim light, so to speak, and thereby *lead* people, rather than command them, to alter their attitudes.[32]

The listener (at least as a general rule) is not conscious of the psychological pressure exercised by moral expressions.[33]

The analysis according to the second pattern also makes use of the distinction between descriptive and evaluative meaning. It is based on the following schema of definition:

> 'This is good' has the meaning of 'This has qualities or relations X, Y, Z . . .', except that 'good' has as well a laudatory emotive meaning which permits it to express the speaker's approval, and tends to evoke the approval of the hearer.[34]

While on the first model the descriptive meaning remains constant, on the second it can change almost at will.[35] This opens the possibility of persuasive definition. Persuasive definitions serve the process of influencing attitudes by determining or changing the descriptive meaning whilst preserving the emotive meaning.[36] The word 'democracy' has, for example, a positive

[32] Ibid., 33.

[33] Stevenson himself subsequently questioned the adequacy of his first analytic model. According to his later view 'I approve of X' is no longer part of the meaning of 'X is good'. 'X is good' merely tends to express the positive attitude of the speaker (see 'Retrospective Comments' in *Facts and Values*, pp 210 ff). The formulation: 'Let us approve of X' has to be acknowledged as conveying a far more appropriate analysis of 'X is good' than 'I approve of X; do so as well' (ibid., 214). This modification will not be introduced here. The substantial and historical significance of Stevenson's original views justifies concentrating on them. 'These views are interesting, and it is they that I discuss, not their authors at a later period of their thought' Urmson, *The Emotive Theory of Ethics*, p. 8. Added to this, Stevenson's modification of his theory hardly touches on his theory of moral reasoning, which is the part of his theory of most interest here.

[34] Cf. Stevenson, *Ethics and Language*, p. 207.

[35] According to Stevenson there are 'certain boundaries' to what can be substituted for X, Y, and Z. Stevenson, however, only observes that such boundaries exist; he does not say what they are (cf. ibid., 207–8).

[36] id., 'Persuasive Definitions', *Mind*, 47 (1938), 336–7 and *Ethics and Language*, pp. 210 ff.

emotive meaning. This meaning may be linked to the most diverse political ideas and in this way may be used to influence people.

The two analytic models are not mutually exclusive. They complement each other.[37] A choice between them has, in particular, no bearing on the question of the *possibility of providing a justification* for moral utterances (as analysed according to the two models).[38]

2.2. A considerable part of Stevenson's investigation is devoted to this question. In addressing it Stevenson develops a theory of moral reasoning. This is perhaps the most interesting part of his work.

The basic thesis of Stevenson's theory of moral reasoning is that, except in a small number of cases in which the point at issue is that of non-contradiction in the logical sense,[39] the relations between the reasons (G), adduced for or against a normative statement, and the normative statement (N) itself,[40] are not *logical relations* (either deductive or inductive) but rather only *psychological*.[41]

> *Any* statement about *any* matter of fact which *any* speaker considers likely to alter attitudes may be adduced as a reason for or against an ethical judgement. Whether this reason will in fact support or oppose the judgement will depend on whether the hearer believes it, and upon whether, if he does, it will actually make a difference to his attitudes.[42]

Although Stevenson thereby excludes moral reasoning from the realm of logic, yet he makes a distinction between rational and non-rational methods of justification. A justification is *rational* where facts are adduced as grounds; it is *non-rational* or

[37] id., *Ethics and Language*, pp. 89, 209, 227.

[38] Ibid., 229.

[39] On these cases cf. ibid., 115 ff.

[40] Stevenson does not use the letters 'G' and 'N' but rather 'R' (for 'reasons') and 'E' (for 'ethical conclusion'). The shorthand versions chosen above are necessary because the letter 'R' is to be used for different purposes in this book. There is no danger of confusion through this change in notation, since there is no question of generally applied symbols but rather of a shorthand occasionally used by Stevenson (and Toulmin).

[41] Stevenson, *Ethics and Language*, pp. 30–1, 36, 113.

[42] Ibid., 114–15.

persuasive when one resorts to other ways of influencing people.[43] Within these two methods Stevenson distinguishes many argument forms and structures of argumentation[44] without laying any claim to having produced an exhaustive list.[45] He uses fictitious dialogues to illustrate them. Following the terminology of the Erlangen School (to be discussed below), the two participants in such a dialogue will be called the 'proponent' (P) and the 'opponent' (O). The rational modes of justification will be examined first.

As already indicated, there are special cases in which the statements adduced stand in logical relations to one another. This would be the case if, for example, P first claimed N and then $\neg$N (not N). O can put this forward as an overwhelming argument against P.[46] The rules of logic hold good for practical discourse too.

More numerous and of greater significance are those cases in which the statements adduced as reasons are not self-contradictory on the one hand but neither do they imply N on the other hand. Here one can talk of the non-logical relations between G and N. This kind of non-logical relation exists whenever O draws P's attention to *properties*[47] of whatever is to be evaluated, to the *consequences*[48] of some action or rule, to the *motive*[49] of an agent, to the consequences of *generalizing*[50] an action, to *authorities*,[51] and to the fact that P does not practise what he or she preaches.[52]

Of particular interest is the possibility opened up by Stevenson of changing an attitude by explaining its *genesis*.

[43] Ibid., 139–40.

[44] The expression 'argument form' refers to the structure of statements expressed by a *single* speaker, the expression 'structure of argumentation' refers to the structure of the statements of *several* speakers. A more precise definition of these concepts will be given below.

[45] Stevenson, *Ethics and Language*, pp. 129–30.

[46] Ibid., 115–16.

[47] Stevenson speaks of 'factual contingent statements about the object itself' as well as of the 'nature' of the adjudged object. Cf. ibid., 118–19.

[48] Stevenson quite correctly points out that there exists a string of borderline cases in which it is not possible to distinguish between properties and consequences. Cf. ibid., 119–20.

[49] Ibid., 121.

[50] Ibid., 94–5, 112.

[51] Ibid., 125–6.

[52] Ibid., 127–8.

According to Stevenson, it is very difficult to give a psychological explanation of the process whereby one changes one's attitude by coming to understand its genesis. He cites as one reason the discovery that the circumstances justifying a moral rule have ceased to exist.[53] Scrutinizing moral opinions in terms of their origin has been developed into a particular method of practical reasoning by the Erlangen School, presumably independently of Stevenson.[54] It will be discussed in more detail below.

Whenever parties to a discussion adduce facts as arguments, as in the cases described above, Stevenson calls the argumentation 'rational'. In all other cases it is non-rational or persuasive. Stevenson cites the following as examples of persuasive argumentation: the use of persuasive definitions,[55] reiteration of ethical terms,[56] metaphorical modes of speech,[57] and didactic narration.[58] It is important to note here that, according to Stevenson, the persuasive and rational elements are combined in most practical reasoning.[59]

2.3. Stevenson himself puts the question whether the relations between G and N in the cases designated 'rational' by him are really no more than purely psychological in nature:

> Perhaps the usual rules for demonstrative and inductive inference need to be *supplemented* by special rules for inferences from R to E—rules which are enough like the others to be said, generically, to mark off *valid* inferences, but which are enough unlike the others to mark off a distinct *kind* of validity.[60]

This question is a variant on one of the basic questions of this investigation: *Are there rules for distinguishing between valid and invalid justifying grounds of normative statements?*

[53] Ibid., 123–4.

[54] Cf. P. Lorenzen, *Normative Logic and Ethics* (Mannheim and Zurich, 1969), 84 ff., id. and O. Schwemmer, *Konstruktive Logik, Ethik und Wissenschaftstheorie* (Mannheim, Vienna, and Zurich, 1973), 190 ff.

[55] Stevenson, *Ethics and Language*, pp. 235, 240–1.

[56] Ibid., 141.

[57] Ibid., 142–3.

[58] Ibid., 144.

[59] Ibid., 142.

[60] Ibid., 153. The letters 'R' and 'E' have been replaced by 'G' and 'N' for the reasons explained in n. 40 above.

Stevenson answers this question in the negative. In *Ethics and Language* he justifies this conclusion by arguing that the use of 'valid' would only be appropriate if the results of the justificatory process could be called 'true'. According to the first analytic model, moral judgments can only be adjudged true inasmuch as they purport to declare the attitudes of the speaker.[61] But the truth or falsity of the report of the speaker's attitude is not what is in dispute. The subject-matter of the dispute is the changing of attitudes.[62] But attitudes do not have truth-value. Therefore, according to Stevenson, it is not possible to speak of the validity of any transition from G to N.[63] Even giving priority to the rational over the persuasive methods is inappropriate. For quite apart from the fact that each can be individually justified,[64] the choice of method would once again depend on a value-judgment and hence on an attitude of mind.[65]

2.4. The most significant objection directed against Stevenson's theory focuses on his psychological approach to moral discourse.[66] According to this, the emotive meaning of moral expressions consists in their causal potency for bringing about a change of or a strengthening in emotional attitudes. Arguments are then no more than instruments for exerting psychological pressure. To be sure, words and sentences do have psychological effects. But understanding such effects is not the same as understanding the meaning of the words and the nature of

[61] Ibid., 26, 155.

[62] Ibid., 155 and id., 'Retrospective Comments', p. 212.

[63] Already in *Ethics and Language* Stevenson observes that in everyday parlance, normative statements are said to be 'true' even when there is no question of a report about the attitude of a speaker. But in such cases, 'true' is only an expression of emotive agreement. This atypical use of 'true' is said not to justify calling moral judgments 'valid' (pp. 169 ff.). In 'Retrospective Comments' Stevenson aligns himself with those theories of truth according to which 'is true', even in respect of empirical propositions, serves only as expressing one's state of being convinced or one's assent. ('Retrospective Comments', p. 219). This exposes the argument cited in the text to doubt. Stevenson's thesis could, however, also be justified directly by arguing that moral disputes are concerned only with attitudes.

[64] *Ethics and Language*, p. 156.

[65] Ibid., 158, 'Retrospective Comments', p. 197.

[66] Cf. G. C. Kerner, *The Revolution in Ethical Theory* (Oxford, 1966), 52.

sentences as arguments. It is only possible to speak of 'meaning' where there are correct and incorrect ways of understanding.[67] But correct and incorrect ways of understanding require rules for distinguishing the one from the other. 'Meaning is a conventional matter.'[68] Furthermore, it could be said that it only makes sense to speak of an 'argument' where what is adduced as an argument is either adjudged valid or invalid.[69] Whoever says: 'I put forward G as an argument against your claim; however, this argument is neither valid nor invalid' is not making a meaningful statement. Either G is not an argument at all, or G is valid or invalid. But if arguments are either valid or invalid there must be rules or conventions for distinguishing valid from invalid arguments. The decisive error in Stevenson's theory is thus his failure to grasp the character of moral discourse as *rule-governed activity*.

In addition, the thesis presented by Stevenson in *Ethics and Language* to the effect that it is not possible to speak of valid and invalid moral arguments because moral judgments cannot be adjudged true or false, is also debatable. It should be pointed out at this juncture that the question of whether or not normative statements can be true or false remains to be decided. On the one hand the validity of an argument may well depend on the possibility that the conclusion it justifies can be true or false. But on the other hand it is conceivable that the possibility of ascribing truth or falsity to a statement may depend on the possibility of validating the supporting arguments for it. Although this makes it impossible to follow Stevenson's theory in its key points, his theory is nevertheless of considerable significance for the present undertaking.

(1) It makes it clear that the function of moral language is far more than that of mere description, as assumed by both naturalism and intuitionism. At the very least it also serves to direct and co-ordinate behaviour.

(2) Stevenson's investigations highlight the central problem

[67] Grewendorf and Meggle, 'Zur Struktur des metaethischen Diskurses', p. 18.

[68] Urmson, *The Emotive Theory of Ethics*, p. 34. Cf. Kerner, *The Revolution in Ethical Theory*, p. 47: 'Meaning must always be governed by linguistic rules.'

[69] Urmson, *The Emotive Theory of Ethics*, p. 86: 'It might well be thought to be analytic that every argument is either valid or invalid.'

of the present investigation, the question of the existence of rules for distinguishing valid from invalid justifying grounds for normative statements.

(3) Stevenson's distinction between rational and persuasive methods is of considerable importance for any theory of rational discourse.

(4) Furthermore, Stevenson's classification of different forms of argument and of argumentation deserves to be kept in mind, despite its lack of completeness and of precision. The analysis and classification of possible forms of argument in practical discourse is one of the central tasks for any theory of practical discourse. Stevenson's theory thus belongs to the class of philosophical theories whose significance is diminished but not negated by its shortcomings.[70]

3. PRACTICAL DISCOURSE AS A RULE-GOVERNED ACTIVITY

The strongest objection to Stevenson's theory was that it failed to recognize the nature of moral discourse as a rule-governed activity. The meta-ethical theories investigated next differ on many points. However, they are united in their view of moral discourse as a rule-governed activity. The discussion of these theories will therefore focus on the *quest for the rules which govern moral discourse*.

3.1. The Foundations in Linguistic Philosophy: Wittgenstein and Austin

The above-mentioned approach to moral discourse draws on the work of the later[71] Wittgenstein and J L. Austin in linguistic

[70] For similar positive judgments cf. ibid., 148, Kerner, *The Revolution in Ethical Theory*, p. 41.

[71] It has now become usual to make a distinction between the earlier and the later philosophy of Wittgenstein. The most important single work of the first period is the *Tractatus Logico-philosophicus*, that of the second the *Philosophical Investigations*. The view has frequently been expressed that there is a break between the early and the late philosophy (cf. e.g. W. Stegmüller, *Hauptströmungen der Gegenwartsphilosophie*, 4th edn. (Stuttgart, 1969), 524, 562;

philosophy. This does not mean that the theories to be discussed are simple applications of these ideas in linguistic philosophy. However, even apart from a number of direct references,[72] the influence of these two writers is discernible at many points.[73] Even where their influence is felt to be negligible or is completely denied in the case of some authors, it has to be admitted that the meta-ethical theories put forward by these writers can be better understood in the light of Wittgenstein's and Austin's theories in linguistic philosophy.

It is not possible, and indeed in view of many prior studies[74] it is quite unnecessary, to present and discuss the views of these two writers in detail. The discussion will be limited to a few remarks on Wittgenstein's concept of a language game and on Austin's concept of a speech act.

Savigny, *Die Philosophie der normalen Sprache*, p. 15). More recently, however, strong reasons have been put forward for the unity of Wittgenstein's philosophy (cf. A. Kenny, *Wittgenstein* (London, 1973), 219 ff). In what follows, only the later philosophy will be discussed.

[72] Cf. S. E. Toulmin, *The Place of Reason in Ethics* (Cambridge, 1950), 83; Hare, 'Austin's Distinction between Locutionary and Illocutionary Acts', in his *Practical Inferences* (London and Basingstoke, 1971), 100–14; J. Habermas, 'Sprachspiel, Intention und Bedeutung. Zu Motiven bei Sellars und Wittgenstein', in *Sprachanalyse und Soziologie*, ed. R. Wiggershaus (Frankfurt-on-Main, 1975), 324 ff. For references to Wittgenstein in the field of legal methodology cf. Larenz, *Methodenlehre der Rechtswissenschaft*, 3rd edn. (Berlin, Heidelberg, and New York, 1975), 178–9; G. Roellecke, 'Grundfragen der juristischen Methodenlehre und die Spätphilosophie Ludwig Wittgensteins', in Festschrift for G. Müller, ed. T. Ritterspach and W. Geiger (Tübingen, 1970), 323–39.

[73] Cf. Hare, *Freedom and Reason* (Oxford, 1963), 89.

[74] On Wittgenstein cf. A. Ambrose and M. Lazerowitz (edd.), *Ludwig Wittgenstein: Philosophy and Language* (London and New York, 1972); Kenny, *Wittgenstein*; G. Pitcher, *The Philosophy of Wittgenstein* (Englewood Cliffs, NJ, 1964); R. Rhees (ed.), *Discussions of Wittgenstein* (London, 1970); Savigny, *Die Philosophie der normalen Sprache*, pp. 15–90; E. K. Specht, 'Die sprachphilosophischen und ontologischen Grundlagen im Spätwerk Ludwig Wittgensteins', *Kant-Studien*, 84 (1963); Stegmüller, *Hauptströmungen der Gegenwartsphilosophie*, pp. 524–696; *Understanding Wittgenstein* (Royal Institute of Philosophy Lectures, London and Basingstoke, 1974); P. Winch (ed.), *Studies in the Philosophy of Wittgenstein* (London and New York, 1969). On Austin cf. I. Berlin *et al.*(edd.), *Essays on J. L. Austin* (Oxford, 1973); M. Furberg, *Saying and Meaning: A Main Theme in J. L. Austin's Philosophy* (Oxford, 1971); Savigny, *Die Philosophie der normalen Sprache*, pp. 127–66; K. T. Fann (ed.), *Symposium on J. L. Austin* (London and New York, 1969).

3.1.1. *Wittgenstein's concept of a language game.*

According to the theory of language put forward in the *Tractatus Logico-philosophicus*, the function of language is to present a picture of the world. Wittgenstein himself characterizes his former theory in *Philosophical Investigations* in the following way: 'The individual words in language name objects—sentences are combinations of such names.'

Wittgenstein contrasts this 'picture of the essence of human language'[75] with his concept of a language game.[76] However, the concept of a language game is neither discussed in a systematic way nor defined in precise terms.[77] Instead one is presented with an almost confusing plethora of allusions and examples. Several features of language games which are of interest for this study will be culled from these. No attempt will be made to grasp the concept in all its aspects.[78]

According to Wittgenstein there is a 'prodigious diversity'[79] of language games. In paragraph 23 of *Philosophical Investigations* he gives the following examples:

> Giving orders, and obeying them—Describing the appearance of an object, or giving its measurements—Constructing an object from a description (a drawing)—Reporting an event—Speculating about an event—Forming and testing a hypothesis—Presenting the results of an experiment in tables and diagrams—Making up a story; and reading it—Play-acting—Singing catches—Guessing riddles—Making a joke; telling it—Solving a problem in practical arithmetic—Translating from one language into another—Asking, thanking, cursing, greeting, praying.[80]

[75] Wittgenstein, *Philosophical Investigations*, trans. G. E. M. Anscombe (Oxford, 1953), p. 2, para. 1.

[76] On the origin of this term in Wittgenstein cf. Specht, 'Die sprachphilosophischen . . . Grundlagen', pp. 40–1; Kenny, *Wittgenstein*, pp. 159 ff.

[77] Cf. Kenny, *Wittgenstein*, pp. 164–5; H. Lenk, 'Zu Wittgensteins Theorie der Sprachspiele', *Kant-Studien*, 58 (1967), 464.

[78] A whole series of writers have attempted to pin down this concept more precisely. Cf. e.g. the definitions and distinctions in Specht, 'Die sprachphilosophischen . . . Grundlagen', pp. 41 ff.; Stegmüller, *Hauptströmungen der Gegenwartsphilosophie*, p. 589; G. Pitcher, *The Philosophy of Wittgenstein*, pp. 247–8; Lenk, 'Zu Wittgensteins Theorie der Sprachspiele', pp. 466 ff.; P. F. Strawson, 'Philosophical Investigations by Ludwig Wittgenstein', *Mind*, 63 (1954), 71 n. 1.

[79] Wittgenstein, *Philosophical Investigations* p. 224.

[80] Ibid., 11–12, para. 23; for further examples cf. Kenny, *Wittgenstein*, pp. 165–6.

It is clear from this enumeration that the concept of a language game cannot be made precise by indicating a number of fixed features. There is rather what Wittgenstein terms a 'family resemblance' between the various language games: 'A complicated network of similarities overlapping and criss-crossing; sometimes overall similarities, sometimes similarities of detail.'[81]

Furthermore these examples show that the descriptive function of language is only one among several. The implication of this for ethics is that there is no need at all to be guided (either in a naturalistic or in an intuitionistic direction) by a paradigm of the descriptive or explanatory sciences. Both moral and legal discourse are language games *sui generis*.

A further characteristic of the examples is that they display a strong link between speaking and acting. This is precisely what the term 'language game' is meant to express: 'I shall also call the whole, consisting of language and the actions into which it is woven, the "language-game".'[82]

Language games, like any other games, are rule-governed activities.[83] This does not mean that they are determined in every aspect. There is after all no rule 'for how high one throws the ball in tennis, or how hard; yet tennis is a game for all that and has rules too.'[84] Furthermore, there are quite different kinds of rules. Just as with language games, they too are linked only by family resemblances.[85] The rules constituting language games range from technical rules (rules of cookery, for example) to syntactical rules (rules of declension, for example).[86]

The concept of a language game thus entails reference to the concept of a *rule*. This concept in its turn is likewise elucidated only by examples and individual allusions. Wittgenstein gives the following, among others, as examples: a table which matches words and pictures,[87] a signpost,[88] and also the rules of

[81] Wittgenstein, *Philosophical Investigations*, p. 32, paras. 66, 67.

[82] Ibid., 5, para. 7, similarly para. 23; cf. Kenny, *Wittgenstein*, pp. 208 ff.

[83] Stegmüller, *Hauptströmungen der Gegenwartsphilosophie*, p. 590; Kutschera, *Sprachphilosophie* (Munich, 1971), 223; Kenny, *Wittgenstein*, p. 170.

[84] Wittgenstein, *Philosophical Investigations*, p. 33, para. 68.

[85] Lenk, 'Zu Wittgensteins Theorie der Sprachspiele' p. 477.

[86] On the great variety of kinds of rules cf. Kenny, *Wittgenstein*, pp. 171–2.

[87] Wittgenstein, *Philosophical Investigations*, p. 40, para. 86, and also his *Blue and Brown Books* (Oxford, 1975), 90.

[88] *Philosophical Investigations*, p. 39, para. 85, p. 80, para. 198.

chess.[89] For a rule to exist it is necessary for *several* people to follow it on *several* occasions. 'It is not possible that there should have been only one occasion on which someone obeyed a rule. . . . To obey a rule, to make a report, to give an order, to play a game of chess, are *customs* (uses, institutions)'.[90] Moreover, there is a strong relationship between the concept of a rule and that of a *mistake*.[91] On the one hand mistakes can only occur where there is a rule for distinguishing between correct and incorrect behaviour; on the other hand the way in which a participant in a language game reacts to mistakes is an important distinguishing mark for the existence of a rule.[92]

Closely bound up with the concept of a language game is another concept, that of a '*form of life*'. By this Wittgenstein understands the shared practices of everyday life[93] which underlie given language games and which have been moulded by certain fundamental convictions and rules. The rules and fundamental convictions which define a form of life constitute a system, however it may be determined,[94] of the sort which Wittgenstein calls a 'world picture'.[95] This world picture constitutes 'the substratum of all my enquiring and asserting'.[96] As such, it is to be conceived 'as something that lies beyond being justified or unjustified; as it were, as something animal'.[97] Thus world pictures and forms of life are neither right nor

[89] Ibid., 80, para. 197.

[90] Ibid., p. 81, para. 199.

[91] Cf. P. Winch, *The Idea of a Social Science*, 4th edn. (London, 1965), 32.

[92] Wittgenstein, *Philosophical Investigations*, pp. 26–7, para. 54. On the concept of a rule in Wittgenstein cf. A. Kemmerling, 'Regel und Geltung im Lichte der Analyse Wittgensteins', *Rechtstheorie*, 6 (1975), 104 ff.

[93] This definition of the concept of a form of life relies in particular on his last work, *On Certainty*, ed. G. E. M. Anscombe and G. H. von Wright (Oxford, 1969); cf. p. 2, para. 7, p. 46, para. 358. In *Philosophical Investigations* this concept is used on p. 8, para. 19, p. 11, para. 23, and p. 88, para. 241, and pp. 174, 226. For an attempt at a definition of the concept based on this cf. J. F. M. Hunter, '"Forms of Life" in Wittgenstein's *Philosophical Investigations*', *American Philosophical Quarterly*, 5 (1968), 233–43.

[94] Cf. Wittgenstein, *On Certainty*, pp. 15–16, para. 102, p. 21, para. 141–2, p. 21, para. 144, p. 52, para. 410–11, pp. 79–80, para. 603.

[95] On the relation between the concept of a world picture with that of a form of life cf. G. H. von Wright, 'Wittgenstein on Certainty', in id. (ed.), *Problems in the Theory of Knowledge* (The Hague, 1972), 58.

[96] Wittgenstein, *On Certainty*, p. 23, para. 162.

[97] Ibid., 47, para. 359.

wrong. Whosoever wishes to induce somebody else to adopt one can only do so by persuasion, not by giving a justifying reason for so doing[98] for such reasons exist only within a form of life or a world picture.[99]

This sketch of the concept of a language game and the related concepts of a rule and a form of life is sufficient for present purposes. It highlights four points of interest for a theory of rational practical discourse:

(1) The descriptive or explanatory use of language is only one among many. As such, it is not to be viewed as the essential or fundamental use. There is therefore no ground at all for reducing normative language to descriptive language or for regarding the former as less important or of less value than the latter.

(2) The logic (in Wittgenstein's broad sense of the word) of language games can only be grasped by taking into account non-verbal behaviour and other extant conditions.

(3) Language games, including moral and legal discourse, are rule-governed activities.

(4) The world pictures and forms of life underlying language games are not amenable to justification and are therefore unamenable to criticism.

It is worth holding on to the first three points. The fourth, on the other hand, is very problematic. If one is of the opinion that there are different human 'forms of life' and is in agreement with the thesis that they can be neither justified nor criticized, one is forced to abandon the idea of the universality of moral discourse. Moral discourse would be relative to forms of life. In opposition to this view it can be pointed out that discussions about forms of life and world pictures do in fact take place.[100] Thus it is possible to have a dialogue between Christians and Communists. Perhaps even more important is the following: it is necessary to distinguish between the observation that neither

98 Ibid., 81, para. 612, p. 34, para. 262.

99 Ibid, 16, para. 105.

100 In this connection B. F. McGuinness points out the argumentation of Descartes for a change in the philosophical world picture of his time ('Comments on Professor von Wright's "Wittgenstein on Certainty"', in *Problems in the Theory of Knowledge*, ed. Wright (The Hague, 1972), 65).

the process of justification nor that of criticism can proceed without presuppositions or assumptions[101] and the thesis that what is presupposed or assumed is in the last analysis not open to discussion (that is, is open neither to justification nor to criticism). The latter does not follow from the former. The view that *all* presuppositions or assumptions may be questioned is of course open to the objection that in discussing one lot of assumptions further assumptions have to be made, so that it is impossible to conceive of a situation which is well-founded in all its aspects.[102] However, the thesis that every assumption is open to discussion does not maintain that everything can be justified *simultaneously*. It says only that there is no assertion such that the possibility of some argument being advanced for or against it is excluded a priori.[103]

3.1.2. *Austin's Theory of Speech Acts*

Austin, like Wittgenstein, is opposed to the view that the only, or even the most fundamental, task of language is to describe the world. He terms this view the 'descriptive fallacy'.[104] However, Austin does not agree with Wittgenstein's thesis concerning the 'prodigious diversity'[105] of the uses of language. He is, furthermore, of the opinion that in order to analyse the limited number of the uses to which language can be put, a more precise

[101] Cf. Wittgenstein, *Philosophical Investigations*, p. 85, para. 217, and his *On Certainty*, p. 28, para. 204.

[102] Such a state of affairs would only be conceivable if one were to admit circular justifications.

[103] On this cf. Popper's criticism of what he calls 'The Myth of the Framework': 'I do admit that at any moment we are prisoners caught in the framework of our theories; our expectations; our past experiences; our language. But we are prisoners in a Pickwickian sense: if we try, we can break out of our framework at any time. Admittedly, we shall find ourselves again in a framework, but it will be a better and roomier one; and we can at any moment break out of it again. The central point is that a critical discussion and a comparison of the various frameworks is always possible' ('Normal Science and its Dangers', in *Criticism and the Growth of Knowledge*, ed. I. Lakatos and A. Musgrave (Cambridge, 1970), 56).

[104] J. L. Austin, *How to Do Things with Words* (London, Oxford and New York, 1962), 3 and 'Performative Utterances', in his *Philosophical Papers* (London, Oxford, and New York, 1970), 234, as well as 'Truth' in the same volume, p. 131.

[105] Cf. Wittgenstein, *Philosophical Investigations*, p. 224.

conceptual framework is needed than, for example, that adopted by Wittgenstein.[106] It is through the elaboration of just such a framework that his theory gains considerably in certainty and concreteness over the theory of language games.[107]

The fundamental concept of Austin's theory is the concept of a speech act. Speech acts are actions which are performed whenever something is said.[108] For example, whosoever says: 'I promise that I shall come tomorrow' or 'I assure you that I saw Peter' is not only saying something but is also doing something: in the first example making a promise, in the second uttering an assertion. According to Austin it is possible to distinguish two, often three acts within a single speech act:[109] the locutionary, the illocutionary, and the perlocutionary act.

The *locutionary act* consists of the utterance of a sentence with a specific meaning. It can in its turn be subdivided into three acts: phonetic, phatic, and rhetic.[110] The phonetic act is the utterance of certain noises, the phatic act the utterance of words according to a particular grammar, the rhetic act the use of the words to say something determinate (sense) about some determinate subject (reference).[111] The rhetic act thus determines what is

[106] Austin, 'Performative Utterances', p. 234.

[107] Austin's theory of speech acts has been pursued further, particularly by J. R. Searle (*Speech Acts* (Cambridge, 1969).) Searle's theory differs from Austin's on a number of points. Of particular significance is his analysis of the rules underlying speech acts.

[108] Cf. Austin, *How to Do Things with Words*, p. 6, and his 'Performative Utterances', p. 235. At an earlier stage of his theory, Austin still distinguished utterances which observe something ('constative utterances') from those by means of which something is done ('performative utterances'). Later he simply understands the constative utterances as one of several kinds of speech act (*How to Do Things with Words*, pp. 132 ff., 146). In what follows only the later, more generalized version of Austin's theory will be discussed. On the development of Austin's theory cf. Hare, 'Austin's Distinction between Locutionary and Illocutionary Acts', in his *Practical Inferences*, pp. 100–5.

[109] These acts are not to be regarded as successive elements of some activity, as is the case with something like cooking; they are rather distinct aspects of one action. Austin therefore speaks of 'different senses or dimensions of the "use of a sentence" or of the "use of language"' (*How to Do Things with Words*, pp. 108–9.).

[110] Ibid., 92–3.

[111] Ibid., 93. On the concepts of 'sense' and 'reference' cf. id., 'How to Talk', in his *Philosophical Papers*, pp. 134–5.

traditionally called 'meaning'. Austin therefore also speaks of the locutionary meaning of a speech act.[112]

The truly original part of Austin's theory is the concept of the illocutionary act. The *illocutionary act* is that which is performed in saying something.[113] What is done *in* saying something must be distinguished from what is being done *by* saying something. The former depends on *conventions*, the latter on what is *actually brought about* in a particular situation. In saying to someone: 'I promise to help you with your move', I am making a promise and by so doing may also surprise, please, or shock the promisee. Bringing about such effects by making utterances is what Austin calls the *perlocutionary act.*[114] Stevenson's error was to consider the perlocutionary act alone.[115]

At the heart of Austin's theory stands the speech act in its character as illocutionary act, that is, as conventional mode of action. The fact that speech acts are conventional actions means that they are not possible in the absence of the rules on which they are based.[116] The concept of the speech act, like that of the language game, thus points to the concept of a rule. Unlike Searle,[117] Austin does not attempt to formulate such rules explicitly. Instead he works out a classification of the possible ways in which speech acts can go wrong. This 'doctrine of the

[112] Austin's theory of locutionary meaning is not without problems. According to Austin, the command 'The door will be shut!' has the same locutionary meaning as the assertion 'The door will be shut.' In both cases, the same thing is being said about the same object. On the other hand Strawson has pointed out that it makes sense to distinguish, for example, between imperatives and assertions, even at the level of locutionary meaning (cf. P. F. Strawson, 'Austin and "Locutionary Meaning"', in *Essays on J. L. Austin*, ed. I. Berlin *et al.* (Oxford, 1973), 56 ff.; similarly Hare, 'Austin's Distinction between Locutionary and Illocutionary Acts', pp. 105 ff.). This criticism will be looked at in more detail in the context of the discussion of Hare's thesis.

[113] Cf. Austin, *How to Do Things with Words*, pp. 99 ff.

[114] Ibid., 101 ff. The separation of the illocutionary from the perlocutionary act gives rise to a whole number of difficulties. On this cf. Savigny, *Die Philosophie der normalen Sprache*, pp. 131 ff.

[115] Cf. Urmson, *The Emotive Theory of Ethics*, p. 27, 130 ff.

[116] Cf. Austin, *How to Do Things with Words*, p. 118; Searle, *Speech Acts*, p. 37. On the conventionality of speech acts (or transactions) cf. D. Wunderlich, 'Zur Konventionalität von Sprechhandlungen', in *Linguistische Pragmatik*, ed. id. (Frankfurt-on-Main, 1972), 11 ff.

[117] Cf. Searle, *Speech Acts*, 62 ff.

infelicities' describes the ways in which speech acts as actions may succeed or fail.[118]

An infelicitous speech act occurs where, for example, someone asserts something without believing it. Whosoever asserts something, evinces their belief in it. One cannot say: 'The cat is on the mat but I do not believe it is', although this sentence is neither logically nor grammatically flawed.[119] It becomes clear that underlying speech as actions there are further rules besides those of logic and grammar. It is one of the merits of the theory of speech acts that it has made clear the significance of these rules, now usually called 'pragmatic rules'.

It follows that a speech act may be flawed not only in the sense that what is being said is false or incorrect, but also in the sense of being, as Austin expresses it 'unhappy'. Austin therefore distinguishes two dimensions of assessment: the dimension bearing on the illocutionary act (the 'happiness/unhappiness dimension'), and the dimension bearing on the locutionary meaning (the 'truth/falsehood dimension').[120]

Of particular interest in Austin's doctrine of the two dimensions of assessment is the opinion he holds that normative statements can also be judged in the dimension of truth or falsity in basically the same way as descriptive statements.[121]

According to Austin in *How to Do Things with Words*, 'true' and 'false' do not stand for a simple relation nor for a simple quality nor for anything simple at all, but rather 'for a general dimension of being a right or proper thing to say as opposed to a wrong thing, in these circumstances, to this audience, for these purposes and with these intentions.'[122] Such an evaluation should occur in assessing whether a piece of advice was good, or a verdict was just, as well as in debating the truth of an assertion.

[118] Austin, *How to Do Things with Words*, pp. 14 ff.

[119] Ibid., 15, 39 ff.

[120] Ibid., 147.

[121] Ibid., 147 ff.

[122] Ibid., 144; similarly in his 'Performative Utterances' (*Philosophical Papers*, pp. 250–1) and 'Performative und konstatierende Äußerung', in *Sprache und Analysis*, ed. and trans. R. Bubner (Göttingen, 1968), 152–3. Austin did not always hold this view. In 'Truth' (*Philosophical Papers*, p. 122), he advocates a correspondence theory of truth. Yet here too he already speaks of 'various degrees and dimensions of success in making statements' (p. 130).

In all these cases the question which arises, in basically the same way, is whether in view of the facts and the purposes of the speaker, and in light of the whole situation, the speech act was the *proper* thing to say.[123]

In order to substantiate his thesis Austin shows that on the one hand even speech acts like convictions, warnings, and advice can be tested in regard to facts, while on the other hand judging descriptive statements requires a multiplicity of further considerations besides drawing on facts.

One might say that this may indeed turn out to be true, but checking a descriptive statement like 'This pond is deep' against the facts nevertheless presents a special case. Austin gives a series of examples against this objection. Thus the statement 'France is hexagonal', cannot be designated as true simply on a basis of confronting the facts. It may be true for the man in the street but not for a geographer. It is, above all, crude. 'It is a rough description; it is not a true or a false one.'[124] In any case, assessing it requires a multiplicity of considerations which are analogous to those employed in judging advice, warnings, and convictions.

It is to be doubted whether this is sufficient to substantiate the thesis that normative statements are to be assessed in basically the same way as descriptive statements, even at the level of truth and falsity.[125] It does, however, at least show that it is not the case that there are no common features here. This is not unimportant. During the course of the investigation it will become apparent that there exist several further common features, apart from those stressed by Austin. Together they could furnish sufficient reasons for putting normative and descriptive statements on a par, at least in principle, with respect to their truth-value.

Austin's theory of speech acts is therefore of importance for the present investigation for three reasons: (1) it contains a refinement of what it means to say that speaking a language is a rule-governed activity; (2) it makes it plain that in several

[123] Austin, *How to Do Things with Words*, p. 144.

[124] Ibid., 142, similarly his 'Performative und konstatierende Äußerung', p. 152.

[125] Cf. Strawson, 'Austin and "Locutionary Meaning"', pp. 62 ff.

important respects the use of normative language is not to be distinguished from that of descriptive language; (3) it offers a system of basic concepts whose fruitfulness will become evident during the course of the investigation.

Several meta-ethical theories will be discussed in the following pages, some of them directly influenced by Wittgenstein's and Austin's theories, all of them more comprehensible against the background of their views. In this regard it will be useful to keep in mind the simple mode of moral discourse already used above. A proponent (P) and an opponent (O) argue about a normative statement (N) in that they cite grounds or reasons (G) for or against N. The questions governing the discussion are as follows: which rules are to count in such discourse and, in particular, are there rules which mark out certain reasons G as good reasons for or against N?

3.2. Hare's Theory

Probably the most influential meta-ethical theory developed within the framework of analytic linguistic philosophy is that of the Oxford philosopher R. M. Hare. According to Hare's views in *The Language of Morals*: 'Ethics . . . is the logical study of the language of morals.'[126] However, as he stressed in his book *Freedom and Reason* eleven years later, ethics should not stop here:

> [I]t is necessary not merely to achieve an *understanding of* the *moral concepts*, but to use this understanding in order to give an *account of moral reasoning*—showing that moral arguments proceed as they do because the logical character of the concepts is what it is.[127]

There are therefore two tasks for ethics: that of logical analysis of moral expressions, and that of investigating moral reasoning. These two areas are not unconnected. Analysis of moral expressions reveals the rules of moral reasoning. Accordingly Hare's investigation of moral expressions will be examined first.

3.2.1. *Hare's Theory of the Language of Morals*

Hare's theory of the language of morals was developed without

[126] Hare, *The Language of Morals*, Preface, p. iii.
[127] id., *Freedom and Reason*, p. 4 (my italics).

direct reference to Austin's theory of speech acts.[128] But he later gave critical consideration to Austin's theory and its conclusions, and in this process modified his own approach and stated it in more concrete terms. This did not, however, affect his basic tenets. For the present, the theory can therefore be discussed in its original form.

Hare's theory consists of two closely connected parts: an analysis of imperatives, and an analysis of value-words. The two parts are connected by the thesis that moral judgments imply imperatives.[129] This is one of Hare's key theses, the thesis of prescriptivism.

In his investigation of imperatives Hare introduces the now famous distinction between the phrastic and the neustic. The two sentences 'Shut the door' and 'You are going to shut the door' correspond to the sentences: 'Your shutting the door in the immediate future, *please*' and 'Your shutting the door in the immediate future, *yes*'. The first part of these sentences is what Hare calls the 'phrastic', the second part ('please' and 'yes') the 'neustic'.[130] According to this analysis, commands and statements have the same phrastic; they are to be distinguished only by their neustics. This distinction forms the kernel of Hare's argument against the derivability of imperatives from purely descriptive statements. Only what is already contained in them can follow from any set of premisses. Purely descriptive statements, by definition, do not contain any imperative neustic.[131] Hence, no imperative can follow from purely descriptive statements.[132] Value-judgments are not deducible from them either. According to Hare, value-judgments imply imperatives. If value-judgments could be deduced from descriptive statements, then imperatives would be likewise deducible. The thesis of prescriptivism thus leads to the thesis: 'that there can be no logical deduction of moral judgements from statements of fact'.[133]

In his analysis of value-words Hare concentrates mainly on

[128] Probably the first reference to the theory of speech acts is to be found in id., 'Geach: Good and Evil', *Analysis*, 17 (1956/7), 105 n. 1.

[129] id., *The Language of Morals*, pp. 171–2.

[130] Ibid., 18. [131] Ibid., 164, 168–9. [132] Ibid., 28, 32.

[133] id., *Freedom and Reason*, p. 2.

the words 'good' and 'ought'.[134] Corresponding to the distinction between phrastic and neustic in the field of imperatives is the distinction between evaluative or prescriptive[135] and descriptive meaning. The *evaluative meaning* of the word 'good' consists in the fact that it is used to commend something.[136] This evaluative meaning must be strictly distinguished from Stevenson's emotive meaning. The latter denotes the effect of an utterance, the perlocutionary act; the former denotes what the utterance counts as, the illocutionary act. The *descriptive meaning* consists in those properties and relations on the basis of which something is designated 'good'. A brief reflection will show that 'good' always has descriptive as well as evaluative meaning. One cannot say: 'This object is exactly like that one in all respects save one, it is not good'.[137] This makes it clear that the application of 'good' is tied to the presence of certain

[134] Hare applies the term 'value judgments' both to assertions such as 'X is good' and to assertions such as 'A ought to do X' (*The Language of Morals*, pp. 168–9). But he does allow that it can make sense for certain purposes to make a terminological distinction between them (*Freedom and Reason*, p. 27 n. 1). The distinction will be regarded as helpful here. Value-judgments and judgments of obligation will be distinguished. The prototype of the value-judgment is the proposition 'X is good', the prototype of the judgment of obligation is the proposition 'A ought to do X'. Classifying a judgment into one of these two sub-classes is not always straightforward. How, for example, should one classify the proposition 'His decision is unjust'? It envisages, among other things, the application of several rules which can be expressed in terms of judgments of obligation. In order to overcome these difficulties, it makes sense to make a simple stipulation. All those normative propositions which can be formulated with the help of the basic deontic terms 'commanded', 'prohibited' or 'permitted' will be called 'judgments of obligation'; all others 'value-judgments'. This terminology might lead to difficulties because, according to it, even a judgment like 'X is permitted', which expresses a permission rather than an obligation, is to be classified as a 'judgment of obligation'. However, 'X is permitted' can be reformulated as 'X is not forbidden' or 'X is not forbidden and not commanded'. On the concepts of 'value-judgment' and 'judgment of obligation' cf. P. Edwards, *The Logic of Moral Discourse* (New York and London, 1955), 141; W. K. Frankena, *Ethics* (Englewood Cliffs, NJ, 1963), 21–8.

[135] In *The Language of Morals*, Hare uses only the expression 'evaluative meaning'; 'prescriptive meaning' is introduced in *Freedom and Reason* to clarify the prescriptive character of moral words (p. 27).

[136] id., *The Language of Morals*, 91–2, 117, 148.

[137] Ibid., 80–1.

characteristics. To call something 'good' is to say that it meets a certain standard, satisfies certain criteria. These criteria are the descriptive meaning of 'good'. Unlike the evaluative meaning, the descriptive meaning may change according to the speaker, the subject-matter of the conversation, and the situation. A racing-driver recommending a car applies a different standard from that applied by a philosopher who calls a certain form of government 'good'.

The 'ought' can be similarly analysed. It too has more than prescriptive meaning. To say that a certain course of conduct A ought to be followed is to imply the acceptance of a principle demanding A.[138] This is what distinguishes those sentences in which the word 'ought' occurs (judgments of obligation) from imperatives. It is of course possible to give reasons for imperatives, but one is not committing any logical error in denying that there are any.[139]

Hare's analysis of moral expressions has encountered sharp criticism. Searle argues, against Hare, that even though moral words like 'good' are frequently used to perform the speech act of commendation this is still insufficient for an analysis of the meaning of such expressions. There are many uses of 'good' in which 'good' is not employed to perform the speech act of commendation and which are to be regarded neither as derivative nor as secondary uses.[140] Searle gives the following utterances as examples: 'If this is good, then we ought to buy it', 'This used to be good', and 'I wonder whether this is good'.[141] Hare does not do justice to these expressions. He over-hastily equates one use of 'good' with its whole meaning. He thereby over-extends the Wittgensteinian thesis of the equivalence of

[138] Ibid., 156–7. As for what Hare understands by 'implies', his following statement makes this clear: 'Type C (You ought to pay him back the money) implies type B (One ought always to pay back money which one has promised to pay back) in the stronger sense that it would be logically illegitimate to give a type C prescription while denying that there was any principle on which it depended. By "logically illegitimate", I mean that my usage of the word "ought" would be so eccentric as to make people wonder what I meant by it' (ibid., 157; the brackets contain Hare's example from p. 156).

[139] Ibid., 157 and *Freedom and Reason*, p. 36.

[140] On this cf. *The Language of Morals*, pp. 124 ff.

[141] Searle, *Speech Acts*, p. 139.

meaning and use.[142] Searle calls this error the 'speech act fallacy'.[143]

Hare modified his theory in response to this criticism. In the original version the occurrence either of an evaluative word like 'good' or of an imperative is an indicator of the illocutionary role of the utterance, that is, of what is *done* with the utterance. According to this, Hare's descriptive meaning would be equivalent to Austin's locutionary meaning, that is, to be understood as what is *said* by uttering the expression. The modification of his theory consists in acknowledging that the evaluative meaning is not exhausted by the illocutionary meaning but is also part of the locutionary meaning. Locutionary meaning includes a general characterization of what is being said, for example as an assertion, imperative, or question.[144] Hare calls this characterization 'tropic'.[145] Figure A.1 shows the structure of Hare's analysis in its modified form.[146]

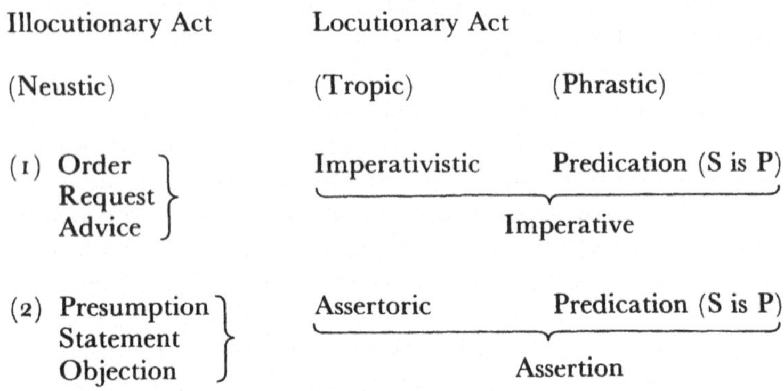

Fig. A.1

[142] Cf. Wittgenstein, *Philosophical Investigations*, p. 20, para. 43: 'For a *large* class of cases—though not for all—in which we employ the word "meaning" it can be defined thus: the meaning of a word is its use in the language.'

[143] Searle, *Speech Acts*, p. 147.

[144] Hare, 'Austin's Distinction between Locutionary and Illocutionary Acts', p. 107.

[145] id., 'Meaning and Speech Acts', in his *Practical Inferences*, p. 90.

[146] For a similar analysis, as well as a critique of Hare's older distinction between neustic and phrastic cf. Ross, *Directives and Norms*, pp. 12 ff.

In the case of judgments of value and of obligation it is more appropriate to talk of a prescriptive or evaluative tropic rather than an imperativistic one. In the case of a judgment of obligation this tropic may be expressed through a deontic operator, for example the operator: 'It ought to be that . . .' (O). It is more difficult to say how the tropic is to be expressed in the case of a value-judgment. Hare gives some guidance here. He calls expressions containing a word like 'good', 'potentially commendatory'.[147] It is then natural to choose the word 'commendable' as the expression of the tropic.[148] In this way it becomes possible to avoid the difficulties pointed out by Searle.

Hare's later analysis is not only a modification of his former views but includes a criticism of Austin's distinction between locutionary and illocutionary acts. This criticism is the same as the one by Strawson mentioned earlier.[149] According to Austin, only what Hare calls the 'phrastic' belongs to locutionary acts; according to Hare, part of what Austin calls' illocution' belongs as tropic to the locutionary act. The moral judgment of an action is accordingly to be distinguished from its description not only at the level of what is done but also at the level of what is said. In the first case a value-judgment is expressed, in the second a descriptive statement.

The views of Hare and Strawson are a decided advance upon those of Austin. According to Austin's doctrine of the two dimensions of assessment, the locutionary meaning is the subject-matter of the judgment in the truth/falsity dimension. However, as indicated above, there are common features when judging this dimension—for example, with respect to statements

[147] Hare, 'Meaning and Speech Acts', p. 93.

[148] It would be possible to introduce an evaluative operator 'e' as an analogue to the deontic operator 'O'. If in addition '!' is used as an imperative operator, the following three basic forms of the locutionary acts intrinsic to normative utterances can be distinguished: '! (S is P)' (imperative) 'O (S is P)' (judgment of obligation), and 'e (S is P)' (value-judgment). Nevertheless, it remains uncertain whether the introduction of such an evaluative operator 'e' is significant. It might be objected that what is being said in a value-judgment is not that it is to be recommended that S have the characteristic of P, but rather that S is to be recommended because it has this characteristic, and that this makes a considerable difference. Because of this difficulty, the following will dispense with the application of an operator like 'e'.

[149] Cf. Strawson, 'Austin and "Locutionary Meaning"', pp. 60–1.

of fact and commendations—but there are also important differences. It therefore makes sense to make distinctions in respect of the locutionary meaning of such markedly different speech acts. In what follows, Hare's and Strawson's analyses will be taken as the starting-point.

A further criticism is levelled against Hare's prescriptivism. Warnock points out that moral expressions are not only used to commend or prescribe. They can be used to perform a multiplicity of speech acts.[150] This is indeed the case. It is, in particular, possible to express judgments of value and of obligation in the speech act of making a statement. But this need not amount to a refutation of prescriptivism. The thesis of prescriptivism declares 'that moral judgments, in their central use, have it as their function to guide conduct'.[151] This function can be fulfilled by quite different forms of speech acts. The only important factor is that there is always a relationship to actions.[152] Such a relationship is also possible in stating judgments of value or obligation. Thus it is not self-consistent to state that X is better than Y and then, without further explanation, to choose Y. The thesis of prescriptivism therefore seems to be entirely consistent with the observation that moral judgments may also be expressed in the speech act of making a statement.[153] Such a speech act has the structure shown in

[150] Warnock, *Contemporary Moral Philosophy*, pp. 34 ff. On the great variety of the use of moral expressions cf. Nowell-Smith, *Ethics*, p. 98.

[151] Hare, *Freedom and Reason*, p. 70.

[152] Cf. ibid., 51–85, for the claim that the existence of particular cases in which one's actions diverge from one's moral professions does not refute prescriptivism.

[153] In such a case, the prescriptive character of an utterance only finds expression in its tropic. This seems to be entirely consistent with Hare's thesis to the effect that prescriptivity is a part of the meaning of evaluative terms (*Freedom and Reason*, p. 67). Assertions of value-judgments and judgments of obligation frequently only relate indirectly to actions. They find their most typical application in deliberations about actions. Expressions in deliberations about practical questions are characterized by the fact that individual expressions do not as yet stand in direct relation to an action. It is precisely the purpose of deliberations to revise individual expressions before taking action. This holds even though it is not possible simply to say in the course of deliberation that X is better than Y and then abandon the deliberation and choose Y. Beyond such a direct relation to actions, assertions of normative propositions have an indirect relation to actions inasmuch as the result of any practical deliberation constitutes a decision as to how to act. All in all, it can

Figure A.2. There is much to support the view that Hare's theory of the language of morals, in the modified form presented here, can stand firm against the attacks of the theory of speech acts as well as the objections of the opponents of prescriptivism.

Illocutionary Act	Locutionary Act	
(Neustic)	(Tropic)	(Phrastic)
Statement	Prescriptive	Predication (S is P)
	Judgment of value or obligation	

Fig. A.2

3.2.2. *Hare's Theory of Moral Reasoning*

Hare's theory of moral reasoning is based on his analysis of moral language. The most important conclusion of this analysis is the distinction drawn between descriptive and evaluative (prescriptive) meaning. Corresponding to this distinction are two ground rules of moral reasoning: the principle of universalizability and the principle of prescriptivity.

The existence of these 'rules of practical reasoning'[154] justifies talk of the rationality of moral discourse.[155] The rules of moral discourse are indeed different from those of reasoning in the natural sciences but, according to Hare, it would be a mistake to assume that there is only one kind of rational discourse.[156]

3.2.2.1. In his justification of the principle of universalizability (PU) Hare takes the universalizability of descriptive expressions as his starting-point. Subsequently he shows that evaluative expressions share this characteristic because of the

therefore be said that assertions of normative propositions in practical deliberations have a prescriptive character for the same reason as evaluative expressions in general: 'it is because we have to make decisions that we have a use for this sort of language' (ibid., 61).

[154] Hare, 'Wissenschaft und praktische Philosophie', in *Philosophie und Wissenschaft*, ed. L. Landgrebe, Ninth German Philosophy Congress (Meisenheim am Glan, 1972), p. 82.

[155] Cf. id., *The Language of Morals*, p. 45, and *Freedom and Reason*, p. 2.

[156] id., 'Wissenschaft und praktische Philosophie', p. 81.

descriptive elements in their meaning.[157] By the universalizability of descriptive expressions Hare refers to the fact that a statement of the kind '*a* is red' constitutes a commitment to say of every other object, like *a* in all the relevant respects, that it too is red. The statement: 'This is red' entails the statement: 'Everything like this in the relevant respects is red'. Whoever agrees with the first but not with the second statement is not using the word 'red' properly.[158]

When we call *a* 'good' we do so *because a* has certain non-moral properties. These properties are the descriptive meaning which we apply in our use of 'good' in this particular case. The PU commits the speaker likewise to designate as 'good' any object at all which possesses these properties.

The fact that *a* has the stated properties is the *reason* for asserting that *a* is good.[159] The PU requires that this reason should count in every case. In this way it creates a link between the assertion '*a* is good' and the reason for saying it.

This link consists of a moral *rule* according to which the fact that something has certain properties is a reason for calling it 'good'. The connection between the concept of a reason and that of a rule is clearly expressed in the following words of Hare's:

> When we make a moral judgement about something, we make it *because* of the possession by it of certain non-moral properties. Thus both views hold that moral judgements about particular things are made for reasons; and the notion of a reason, as always, brings with it the notion of a rule which lays down that something is a reason for something else.[160]

The rules presupposed by moral judgments may be of quite different orders of generality. The rule never to lie is of a high

[157] id., *Freedom and Reason*, pp. 10, 30.

[158] Ibid., 11. [159] Ibid., 21.

[160] Ibid., 21. In *Generalization in Ethics* M. G. Singer puts forward a view very similar to Hare's thesis: 'The generalization principle [which corresponds to Hare's principle of universalizability], I shall argue, is involved in or presupposed by every genuine moral judgment, for it is an essential part of the meaning of such distinctively moral terms as "right", "wrong", and "ought", in their distinctively moral senses. It is also an essential feature of moral reasoning, for it is presupposed in every attempt to give a reason for a moral judgment. It thus determines what can count as a moral reason . . . It follows from this that there can be no genuine moral judgment apart from reasons, and no moral reasons apart from the generalization principle' ((New York, 1961),

order of generality; the rule to tell one's wife the truth in money matters is of a low order of generality.[161]

Hare calls all these rules moral principles.[162] What is crucial is not the level of their generality but that they are universal, that is, that no singular expressions such as proper names occur in them.[163] It is often not possible to formulate such a rule at the first attempt. However, it is always at least possible to say that all cases like *a* should be treated like *a*.[164] This already constitutes a rule. Such a rule could be designated a 'minimal rule'.

The application of some common logical symbols may make Hare's thesis clearer. The form of rules underlying the use of 'good' can be expressed as follows:

$$(x)\ (F_1x \wedge F_2 \wedge \ldots F_nx \rightarrow \text{good } x)$$ [165]

The requirement of the PU can be formulated by stating that in order to be correct value-judgments must follow logically from such rules together with descriptive statements. Underlying correct value-judgments, therefore, there is an inference type of the form:[166]

York, 1961), 34). According to Singer, the PU fulfils yet another important function. The *burden of proof* that there exists a relevant difference between A and B falls on the individual who wishes to treat a person A differently from a person B (ibid., 31). This point will be returned to below.

[161] Cf. Hare, *Freedom and Reason*, pp. 39–40. On the concept of generality cf. also his 'Principles', PAS 73 (1972/3), 2–3.

[162] id., *Freedom and Reason*, pp. 30 ff.

[163] id., 'Principles', p. 4.

[164] id., 'Universalisability', PAS 55 (1954/5), 306–7. An expression such as 'like *a*' can always be transformed into an expression without individual constants. If there are no readily available expressions for this, it is possible to coin one (cf. id., *Freedom and Reason*, p. 11).

[165] 'F_1'–'F_n' stand for any descriptive predicates. '(x)' is the universal quantifier (for all *x* it is the case that . . .), '*x*' an individual variable, '$\wedge$' the sign for conjunction (and), '$\rightarrow$' the sign for a conditional (if . . . then . . .). On the reasons for using the expression 'conditional' rather than the frequently used expression 'implication', cf. W. V. O. Quine, *Methods of Logic*, (London, 1952), 33 ff. and G. Patzig, 'Sprache und Logik', in his *Sprache und Logik* (Göttingen, 1970), 20 ff. An example of a rule of the cited form would be 'For all *x*, if *x* is a strawberry and is large and juicy and red, then *x* is good.'

[166] Cf. Hare, *The Language of Morals*, pp.145–6: 'A statement of the characteristics of the man (the minor or factual premiss) *together with* a specification of a standard for judging men morally (the major premiss) entails a moral judgement upon him.'

.(1) $(x)(F_1x \wedge F_2x \wedge \ldots F_nx \rightarrow \text{good } x)$
.(2) $F_1a \wedge F_2a \wedge \ldots F_na$
(3) good a (1), (2)[167]

a here stands for the name or the definite description of an arbitrary object.

The analysis of judgments of obligation is similar to that of value-judgments.

When I tell someone that he ought to do something, I am committed to the same view with respect to anyone in exactly the same situation. If I say 'You ought to do *x* although there might be someone in exactly the same situation as you who should not do *x*', I am contradicting myself.[168]

If 'ought' is symbolized by the deontic operator 'O',[169] as is common in deontic logic, then the deontic syllogism underlying the judgment of obligation is as follows:

.(1) $(x)(F_1x \wedge F_2x \wedge \ldots F_nx \rightarrow OHx)$
.(2) $F_1a \wedge F_2a \wedge \ldots F_na$
(3) OHa (1), (2)[170]

[167] The dots to the left of the numbers mean that the expression lying to their right has not been derived from other expressions. The numbers to the right of an expression indicate those expressions from which it logically follows. The inference type presented does not exhibit all the steps. For this purpose it can be supplemented through the premisses: '$F_1a \wedge F_2a \wedge \ldots F_na \rightarrow \text{good } a$' (1'). (1') follows from (1) by the substitution rule through insertion of '*a*' for '*x*', (3) from (1'), and (2) through the detachment rule. The following will dispense with the citation of (1') for simplicity's sake. On the substitution and the detachment rule cf. A. Tarski, *Introduction to Logic and to the Methodology of Deductive Sciences*, 3rd edn. (Oxford and New York, 1965), pp. 54 ff.

[168] Hare, 'Wissenschaft und praktische Philosophie', p. 86.

[169] It is debatable whether something like a deontic logic is needed at all in order to grasp the logical structure of judgments of obligation. Thus Rödig holds the view that modern predicate logic is sufficient for this purpose ('Über die Notwendigkeit einer besonderen Logik der Normen', *Jahrbuch für Rechtssoziologie und Rechtstheorie*, 2 (1972), 163 ff.). It would not seem impossible for both ways to be practicable. On arguments for deontic logic cf. E. Morscher and G. Zecha, 'Wozu deontische Logik?', *ARSP* 58 (1972), 363 ff.

[170] It might be objected to the formalization of conditional obligation undertaken here, that it gives rise to a number of paradoxes (paradox of derived obligation, paradox of commitment, paradox of contrary-to-duty imperatives). (Cf. R. M. Chisholm, 'Contrary-to-Duty Imperatives and Deontic Logic', *Analysis*, 24 (1963), 33 ff.; Wright, *An Essay in Deontic Logic and the General Theory of Action* (Amsterdam, 1968), 77; id., 'A New System of Deontic Logic', in *Deontic Logic: Introductory and Systematic Readings*, ed. R.

'*a*' stands for the name or the definite description of a person, 'F_1'–'F_n' and 'H' for arbitrary complex properties of persons, 'H' perhaps for 'pays damages'.

The two formalizations give information as to how Hare imagines the transition from a reason or ground G to a normative statement N; it is mediated by a moral rule R, which together with G implies N.

This immediately gives rise to the next question: How can this rule be justified? The PU alone has nothing to contribute here. It only requires that one act according to *some* rule; it says nothing about what *content* such a rule must have. Every rule is consistent with it. It merely demands consistency on the part of the speaker. The PU thus sets out a necessary but not a sufficient condition for the rationality of moral discourse. More stringent conditions are needed.

3.2.2.2. According to Hare such a stronger condition is to be found by combining the PU with the principle of prescriptivity (PP).

Hare attempts to elucidate[171] this by means of a simple example taken from a biblical parable.[172] A owes money to B and B owes money to C. It is the law that creditors may exact their debts by putting their debtors into prison. B asks himself whether he should have A put in prison. He is inclined to do this but wants to know whether he is morally justified in doing this or even obliged to do it.[173] He is concerned with the moral

Hilpinen (Dordrecht, 1971), 108–9; B. Hansson, 'An Analysis of Some Deontic Logics', ibid., 133.) These paradoxes are instances of the so-called 'paradox of material implication' (cf. Kutschera, *Einführung in die Logik der Normen, Werte und Entscheidung* (Freiburg and Munich, 1973), 28). Many diverse ways have been proposed to avoid these actual or supposed paradoxes. The most suitable is the application of modern semantic methods (model theory) (cf. D. Føllesdal and R. Hilpinen, 'Deontic Logic: An Introduction', *Deontic Logic*, p. 26). With the help of these methods it would seem possible to provide an interpretation of the formulas used in the text, which would avoid the aforementioned difficulties.

[171] Hare, *Freedom and Reason*, p. 90 f.

[172] Matt. 18: 23.

[173] In Hare's example B asks whether he *ought* to put A into prison. It has been remarked that it would be more appropriate to let B ask whether he *may* do this. It is not possible here to enter into the problems resulting from such a reformulation. On this cf. D. P. Gauthier, 'Hare's Debtors', *Mind*, 77 (1968), 400 ff.; M. T. Thornton, 'Hare's View of Morality', *Mind*, 80 (1971), 617–18; N. Hoerster, 'R. M. Hare's Fassung der Goldenen Regel', *Philosophisches Jahrbuch*, 81 (1974), 188 ff.

judgment: 'I ought to put A into prison because he will not pay his debts' (N_1). B then observes that if he accepts N_1, then by virtue of the PU he is obliged to accept the rule: 'Anyone who is in my position ought to put his debtor into prison if he does not pay' (R). Applied to B, R yields the following: 'C ought to put me (B) into prison' (N_2). If B accepts N_1, then according to the PU he must also accept N_2. The PP says that B only accepts N_2 if he is prepared to accept the singular prescription: 'Let C put me into prison', that is if he is prepared to be put into prison. He will, however, not be prepared to do this, since this contravenes his inclinations and interests. But, if he is not prepared to do this, he must reject N_1. Hence he is not morally justified in putting A into prison.

In the example quoted, A stands to B in exactly the same relation as B to C. The person judging and the person judged are in the very same situation. Cases of this kind are rare. According to Hare it is not, however, necessary to have such an actual correspondence. It is sufficient for the individual making the judgment to put himself hypothetically into the position of the person being judged[174] and to ask himself whether, even in this position, he could accept the consequences of the disputed moral rule.[175]

[174] On the difficulties to which this gives rise cf. C. C. W. Taylor, review of R. M. Hare, *Freedom and Reason*, *Mind*, 74 (1965), 286 ff.; H. S. Silverstein, 'A Note on Hare on Imagining Oneself in the Place of Others', *Mind*, 81 (1972), 448 ff.

[175] Hare, *Freedom and Reason*, p. 93. In *Freedom and Reason* Hare starts out from the view that the requirement to place oneself in the position of the person being judged is yielded by the PU. Thus the postulate 'everyone is entitled to equal consideration' is said by Hare to be a 'corollary of the requirement of universalizability' (p. 118). Nevertheless, there is something to be said for the view that this is in fact an independent requirement going beyond the PU and the PP. The PU and the PP are satisfied where the person judging is prepared to accept the consequences of his or her moral judgment for him or herself too. It would hardly contradict the PU and the PP if one were to limit their use to those cases in which the consequences do in fact apply to the person judging. That one should also transpose oneself into the situation of others when one knows or can start from the position that one will never oneself be in this situation, goes considerably further. In a later publication, Hare himself is no longer certain whether or not the requirement of a hypothetical exchange of roles is an independent condition (cf. his 'Rawls' Theory of Justice', *Philosophical Quarterly* 23 (1973), 154). Underlying the requirement of a

The special feature of the Hare's argument is that it claims to make it possible for one to arrive at a conclusion as to the correctness or incorrectness of a moral judgment solely on the basis of the *logic* of normative language expressed through the PP and the PU, the recognition of the *facts*, and the *inclinations* and *interests* of those affected and the *imagination* of the predicament of others.[176] Hence moral judgments can be arrived at without the application of normative premisses. Hare expressly emphasizes that this does not mean that normative statements are derivable from statements of fact. In terms of the Popperian model, he characterizes his procedure as a 'kind of exploration'.[177] The *modus tollendo tollens* $([p \rightarrow q] \wedge \neg q \rightarrow \neg p)$ forms the core of his argument. In the example N_2 follows from N_1. B cannot accept N_2, so he must also reject N_1. Thus, according to Hare, what is essential in moral reasoning is not the deduction of particular judgments from this or that principle but the testing of the acceptability of their logical consequences.[178]

hypothetical exchange of roles is the requirement of the acknowledgement of the other as having equal rights. This requirement will be justified below as a basic principle of moral argument. Hare's argument will therefore be treated as though the requirement of hypothetical exchange of roles, which, it would seem, is not justified in Hare's theory, has been justified.

[176] Cf. id., *Freedom and Reason*, p. 94.

[177] Cf. ibid., 88.

[178] Making essential that discussants must be ready to accept the consequences of the rules presupposed by their moral expressions, is what distinguishes Hare's theory from that of neo-naturalists like Foot and Warnock. According to their view, there exist, particularly in relation to concrete moral expressions such as 'rude' and 'courageous', rules which lay down that where one agrees to certain assertions about facts one must also accept certain value-judgments. In this sense, moral judgments are said to be derivable from factual assertions (cf. Foot, 'Moral Arguments', p. 509). 'Anyone who uses moral terms at all, whether to assert or deny a moral proposition, must abide by the *rules for their use*, including the rules about what shall count as evidence for or against the moral judgement concerned. For anything that has yet been shown to the contrary these rules could be *entailment rules*, forbidding the assertion of factual propositions in conjunction with the denial of the moral proposition' (ibid., 510, my italics). These 'rules about the grounds' (ibid., 511) correspond to Hare's rules or principles presupposed in moral judgments. Whether or not a discourse is to be viewed as a moral discourse at all is said to depend on their application (ibid., 510; similarly

Serious objections can be raised against Hare's procedure. The most important objection concerns the fact that Hare relies on the inclinations and interests of the person making the judgments, with regard to the question of the acceptability of a particular moral judgment in a real or imaginary case. This objection corresponds to one often raised against the Golden Rule which has a broad though not complete similarity with Hare's argument.[179]

In his criticism, Alf Ross translates Hare's biblical example into contemporary terms. He observes that according to the criteria proposed by Hare, it would be morally inadmissible to take proceedings involving measures of compulsion against a debt defaulter, for nobody, including the creditor, *likes* to have legal proceedings instituted against him or herself.[180] This objection can be pushed to its limits by saying that according to Hare's criteria nobody can ever be required to place restrictions on his or her inclinations and interests, for if, as Hare suggests, you take inclinations and interests alone as your starting-point, everyone wishes and desires that these should remain unrestricted.

However, there is another variant on the argument to be

Warnock, *Contemporary Moral Philosophy*, p.68). Hare emphatically comes out against such ideas. It may well be the case that in a given society, many firmly established moral convictions are reflected in rules for the descriptive meaning of moral expressions, but those who argue about morals are not strictly bound by these rules. Thus it is always possible for the individual who does not share these convictions either not to use certain evaluative expressions at all, or to use them differently or in a non-evaluative sense (*Freedom and Reason*, pp. 187 ff.). For a critique of Foot's theory cf. also R. W. Beardsmore, *Moral Reasoning* (London, 1969), 14 ff.

[179] On the differences between Hare's argument and the Golden Rule cf. Hoerster, 'R. M. Hares Fassung der Goldenen Regel', p. 193. On the Golden Rule cf. H. Reiner, 'Die "Goldene Regel"', *Zeitschrift für philosophische Forschung*, 3 (1948), 74 ff.; G. Spendel, 'Die Goldene Regel als Rechtsprinzip', in Festschrift for F. von Hippel, ed. J. Esser and H. Thieme (Tübingen, 1967), 491 ff.; Kelsen, 'Das Problem der Gerechtigkeit', *Reine Rechtslehre*, 2nd edn. (Vienna, 1960) 367–8 (not included in *Pure Theory of Law*, trans. M. Knight (Berkeley, Calif., 1967), but cf. Kelsen, *What is Justice?* (Berkeley, Calif., 1959), chap. 1).

[180] A. Ross, 'On Moral Reasoning', *Philosophical Yearbook*, 1 (1964), 127 ff.

found in Hare.[181] It is of particular significance where the interests of many people have to be taken into consideration. Hare makes this clear in the much debated case of a judge about to pass judgment on an offender.[182] In such a case, it is not sufficient for the judge to put him or herself into the position of the offender and to ask him or herself what he or she would wish in such a situation, he or she must rather take into account the inclinations and interests of all those who may be somehow affected by the decision.[183] The decision must be acceptable to the judge not only from the standpoint of the offender but rather from that of anyone in any way affected by it. One is then faced with the problem 'how, when we have considered all these interests, we combine the consideration of them all into a single answer to our moral problem'.[184]

Hare's argument cannot resolve this problem of the combination of the interests of many individuals. Nor does Hare claim that it can do so. His argument only stipulates 'that everyone is entitled to equal consideration'.[185] Hare believes that a combination of his procedure with utilitarianism may be of further assistance here. However, he declines to show how this might be possible. He only points to several problems concerning utilitarianism. Worth mentioning are the problems of the commensurability of different interests, desires, and inclinations of the same person as well as those of different people, the question of whether an equal but incomplete satisfaction on the part of everyone is to be preferred to the complete satisfaction of

[181] Ross admits, in his critique, that he is somewhat reluctant to reduce Hare's argument to the version discussed to date, in which the only relevant factors are the wishes or interests of the person judging (ibid., 127 n. 25). He justifies the fact that he does so, nevertheless, through numerous expressions of Hare's which in fact speak in favour of understanding it in this way. Hare can be criticized for not elaborating the differences of the two versions sufficiently clearly. He simply presents the second version as an extension of the first.

[182] Hare, *Freedom and Reason*, pp. 115 ff.

[183] It should be stressed that this means that in order to test a normative assertion, not only its logical consequences but, above all, the factual consequences of the validity of the rule underlying it are of significance.

[184] Ibid., 117.

[185] Ibid., 118.

the majority at the expense of the minority, and the difficulty of distinguishing higher and lower desires.[186]

In this light it becomes clear that the application of Hare's argument presupposes normative standards for reconciling different interests. The person passing judgment, who puts him or herself in the shoes of all the people affected by the decision, must ask with respect to each of them what infringement of interests he or she could accept as reasonable or morally justified. A decisive advantage of Hare's procedure is lost in such a process. It is, after all, not possible to do without normative premisses, whose justification is external to the procedure.

This last point bears on all cases involving the interests of more than two persons (multilateral cases). Multilateral cases occur more frequently than Hare would seem to believe. In the debt case, for example, B must not only ask whether in A's place, he or she would wish to accept the consequences of the rule that it is permissible to proceed against default debtors by means of compulsory measures, but B must also take into consideration the interests of everyone in the existence of such a rule. A further example discussed by Hare of two people in adjacent rooms, one of whom likes playing the trumpet while the other enjoys listening to classical music,[187] shows that it is not possible to resolve the issue in bilateral cases either, without recourse to additional normative premisses. All that can be said on the basis of Hare's procedure alone is that the interests of both are to be given consideration. It remains an open question how they are to stand in relation to each other. After all, it should hold true even for the debt case that the interests of both are to be taken into consideration. There is no reason to suppose that B should automatically waive his or her rights. He or she must judge the situation both from his or her point of view and from A's.[188] Hare does not offer any criteria for making such a judgment.

That the application of Hare's criterion presupposes norma-

[186] Ibid., 119 ff. On this, and on the arguments for and against utilitarianism generally, cf. J. J. C. Smart and B. Williams, *Utilitarianism For and Against* (Cambridge, 1973). On utilitarianism cf. also the bibliography in D. W. Brock, 'Recent Work in Utilitarianism', *American Philosophical Quarterly*, 10 (1973), 241–76.

[187] Cf. Hare, *Freedom and Reason*, pp. 112 ff.

[188] On this cf. Hoerster, 'Hares Fassung der Goldenen Regel', p. 195.

tive premisses does not imply that it has no value. It is entirely sensible to demand that I should only expect of others what I would regard as acceptable behaviour according to my *moral convictions* if I were in their situation.

However, this immediately gives rise to a new difficulty. According to this weaker version, any moral judgments at all may be justified, provided the speaker is prepared to regard the limitations or restrictions in question as morally acceptable even when they affect him or her. In this connection Hare quite often cites the example of a Nazi who would regard his being killed as quite right should he turn out to be a Jew.

Hare attempts to meet these difficulties by making a distinction between two kinds of moral argument. The first kind is characterized by the fact that the speakers are pursuing their own interests[189] and are accordingly bound by the PU and the PP to take into account the interests of their fellow human beings in the same way as their own. The distinguishing feature of the second kind is that the speaker is not concerned with interests but rather with ideals.[190] To have an ideal is to regard something as pre-eminently good.[191] Hare's argument is said to be suited to striking a balance as between interests, but not as between interests and ideals, nor as between ideals. This presents no problems until somebody attempts to impose his or her ideals against the interests of others and even against his or her own interests. A serious problem only arises where an individual is prepared to sacrifice both personal interests and those of fellow human beings to his or her ideals. Hare calls such a person a 'fanatic'. Moral arguments cannot but be powerless against him or her.

Hare's main example to illustrate this point is that of the Nazi

[189] Hare defines the concept of interest by recourse to the concept of wanting: 'To have an interest is for there to be something which one wants (or may want), or which is (or may be) a means, necessary or sufficient, for the attainment of something which one wants (or may want)' (*Freedom and Reason*, p. 157; cf. also p. 122). The concept of wanting, in its turn, is determined by means of the concept of assenting to a prescription: 'To want something, is to assent to a prescription of some sort' (Hare, 'Wrongness and Harm', in his *Essays on the Moral Concepts* (London and Basingstoke, 1972), 98).

[190] In this connection Hare speaks of 'two kinds of grounds' (*Freedom and Reason*, p. 149).

[191] Ibid., 159.

who, should it transpire that he was a Jew, would genuinely and in full awareness of the facts be prepared to go to the gas chamber.[192] It is argued that nothing can be achieved against him by means of moral reasoning.[193]

Hare's strict separation of arguments relating to interests and arguments based on ideals, is in itself not unproblematic.[194] It has already been shown that a mere swapping of roles is not sufficient for a judgment as to the correctness of a moral rule. There is a need for additional criteria as to the moral correctness or justice of the balancing of interests. Of course such criteria could be called 'ideals'. It should be noted, furthermore, that both what a person considers to be his or her own interests and what he or she takes to be the interests of others, depend on his or her views on what is good or bad, obligatory or forbidden. This becomes clear in Hare's example of the drug addict.[195] Hare is of the opinion that taking such a person to an institution and compulsorily detaining him or her there would be in the individual's interest. It could be objected here that only someone convinced of the correctness of a certain way of life can argue in this way.

The weaknesses of the distinction between interests and ideals do not render it useless. It does make a difference whether someone rigidly implements a principle or takes into account the interests of fellow human beings, interests which do of course owe their form and meaning to normative considerations. But it becomes clear that for Hare's argument it is not only the question of how different desires and interests, etc. of varying intensity on the part of different people are to be brought to bear on each other, which presupposes normative premisses, but also the question of what are to be counted as desires and interests, etc. Bearing this in mind, an argument of the following kind, as envisaged by Hare, is entirely reasonable:

Everyone who makes a normative statement that presupposes a rule with certain consequences for the satisfaction of the interests of other persons must be able to accept these consequences, even

[192] Ibid., 170 ff.

[193] Ibid., 151.

[194] For a critique of this distinction cf. R. N. Berki, 'Interests and Moral Ideals', *Philosophy*, 49 (1974), 265 ff.

[195] Hare, *Freedom and Reason*, p. 174.

in the hypothetical situation where he or she is in the position of those persons.

To be sure, as it stands, this form is as yet not sufficient for the justification of normative statements, for 'to be able to accept' means 'to be able to accept as morally justified'. This, however, presupposes normative premisses which would in their turn need to be justified. Nevertheless it does distinguish those normative statements which the person judging could not accept according to his or her normative convictions, were he or she to be placed in the situation of any other person.

3.2.2.3. The question, of the sense in which Hare can be said to have established the PU and the PP, has been passed over until now. According to Hare, these principles are theses about the meaning of moral expressions.[196] It is not impossible to use words such as 'good' and 'ought' in a non-prescriptive and non-universalizable way. However, in such cases one is no longer engaged in moral discourse.[197] One has ceased to speak the language of morals and has thereby left the 'moral "game"'.[198] Most people do in fact play this game,[199] but it is not possible to give a moral justification for so doing.[200] In order to do this, it would be necessary to proceed in accordance with the very rules which have yet to be accepted.

The PU and the PP can therefore only be said to be established in the sense that Hare has shown them as definitive of a language game, a language game which, as a rule, is played whenever people discuss practical questions.

This thought is reminiscent of the theory of the complete justification of a decision presented by Hare in *The Language of Morals*, and to which he sometimes refers in *Freedom and Reason*.[201]

A complete justification of a decision would consist of a complete account of its effects, together with a complete account of the principles which it observed, and the effects of observing those principles—for, of course, it is the effects (what obeying them in fact consists in) which give content to the principles too. Thus, if pressed to justify a decision completely, we have to give a complete specification of the *way of life* of which it is a part.[202]

[196] Ibid., 30–1, 97.
[197] Ibid., 98–9, 164.
[198] Ibid., 89.
[199] Ibid., 98.
[200] Ibid., 101.
[201] Ibid., 37.
[202] *The Language of Morals*, p. 69 (my italics).

A way of life, however, cannot (according to Hare) itself be justified. One can only opt for it and attempt to live one's life in accordance with it. The relationship of this idea to Wittgenstein's theory of forms of life is quite apparent. It also lies at the heart of the thesis which states that in the last analysis it is impossible to decide between different ideals such as Nazism and Liberalism.[203]

3.2.3. *Towards a Critique of Hare's Theory of Moral Reasoning*

Probably the two most important objections to Hare's theory of moral reasoning have already been rehearsed. In order to provide a justification of Hare's procedure, there would seem to be a need for a normative principle, such as the principle that everyone is entitled to equal consideration, in addition to the PU and the PP, which are principles based on the logic of moral language. This gap would not seem to be too serious since, as shown below, sufficient grounds can be established for a principle of the aforementioned kind. More problematic are the objections to the efficiency of the procedure. In relying on what those concerned would like to have, one arrives at unacceptable results. Alternatively, in taking considerations of what is right as the starting-point one presupposes additional normative premisses. The latter does not render the procedure useless, but it does show that it cannot stand on its own. If possible it needs to be supplemented.

In addition, there are problems surrounding the strict separation of interest-based and ideal-based arguments. This separation cannot be rigidly maintained. However, the distinction between arguments which take no account at all of interests and those which do, remains both possible and useful.

Furthermore, the thesis concerning the impossibility of justifying—and hence of criticizing—ideals and ways of life must not go unquestioned. There is no doubt that in practice every piece of justificatory reasoning must end somewhere. But still it has to be asked whether it might not always be conceivable that some further reasons could be put forward.[204] In any event Hare fails to consider one possible line of criticism

[203] Cf. Hare, *Freedom and Reason*, p. 163.
[204] Cf. above, pp. 52–1.

already mentioned by Stevenson, namely an investigation of how ideals and ways of life come into being. This procedure will be examined further in connection with the discussion of the Erlangen School's theory of rational deliberation.

Despite these points of criticism Hare's theory contains very significant findings for a theory of rational practical discourse.

(1) First, Hare's modification of Austin's conception of evaluative or prescriptive speech acts ought to be retained.

(2) Hare's account of the universalizability of moral judgments is also of fundamental importance. To utter a moral judgment is *eo ipso* to presuppose some rule. This rule establishes what is to count as a reason or ground G for a moral judgment N. The concept of a reason or ground is thus intimately bound up with that of a rule. With regard to Stevenson's question concerning the relationship between G and N, this means that N follows logically from G together with a rule R which provides that G is a reason for N. This rule may be very specific provided that it is universal.

(3) Equally important is Hare's account of the testing of moral judgments. Whoever utters a moral judgment must be prepared to accept whatever restrictions on interests are required by the rule presupposed in the judgment even if these restrictions apply to the person making the judgment him or herself. 'Accepting' here means 'accepting as morally justified'.

(4) Finally it is worth drawing attention to Hare's account of moral discourse as a rational activity of equal status with the empirical sciences.

3.3. Toulmin's Theory

Toulmin, like Hare, comes out against the conception of moral reasoning as a phenomenon which can at best be explained in psychological terms. He takes as his starting-point Stevenson's problem about the relationship between a reason or ground G and a normative statement N.[205] His central question is as follows: 'What is it that makes a particular set of facts, R, a good

[205] Cf. above, pp. 44–5.

reason for a particular ethical conclusion, E?'[206] In reply to this, Toulmin advances the thesis that in addition to logical and scientific inferences (which Toulmin understands as inductive ones) there are forms of inference 'peculiar to ethical arguments'. These inferences make it possible to pass from factual reasons (G) to normative conclusions (N). Toulmin calls this kind of inference 'evaluative inference'.[207]

3.3.1. *The Function of Ethics*

In order to locate such inferences or, to put it another way, to find criteria of what are good reasons, Toulmin takes up Wittgenstein's notion of language as a tool which is used for a multiplicity of purposes.[208] Its uses range from description to word games. The criteria for its proper use depend on the particular function it is to fulfil within the framework of a particular social context.[209] In the case of descriptions, Toulmin claims that the relevant criterion is the correspondence theory of truth;[210] with word games it may, for example, be a certain starting letter for the words.[211] The criterion for the correct use of moral language can be discovered by examining the function of moral language within the particular social context in which it operates.[212]

In order to find such criteria, Toulmin compares the function of scientific explanations with that of ethical statements. A stick held in water looks as though it is bent. This is surprising. According to Toulmin, the task[213] for scientific explanation

[206] Toulmin, *The Place of Reason in Ethics* (Cambridge, 1950), 4. For the reasons given on p. 42, the letters 'G' and 'N' are used in this study instead of 'R' and 'E'.

[207] Ibid., 38; cf. also pp. 3, 56.

[208] Wittgenstein, *Philosophical Investigations*, p. 6, para. 11: 'Think of the tools in a tool-box: there is a hammer, pliers, a saw, a screw-driver, a rule, a glue-pot, glue, nails and screws.—The functions of words are as diverse as the functions of these objects.'

[209] Toulmin, *The Place of Reason in Ethics*, p. 84.

[210] Ibid., 72 ff.

[211] Ibid., 81–2.

[212] Ibid., 84, 223.

[213] The expressions 'task', 'function', and 'purpose' are here, as in Toulmin's text, used in their everyday colloquial meaning. Sentences containing one of these expressions are transformable into sentences containing the others.

consists in transforming this surprise into something which is to be expected.[214] This is achieved by ordering the totality of available experience according to the criteria of predictive reliability, of coherence with theories established in adjacent fields of study, and of convenience.[215] In this way the statement 'This stick looks bent', which is a direct report or expression of experience, is transformed into the 'fully-fledged scientific judgment': 'The stick is not really bent; its appearance is an optical illusion.'[216]

What is important is that in ethics too one finds this difference between immediate, unconsidered reports and expressions of experiences, and fully-fledged moral judgments. Such fully-fledged moral judgments result from a process of mulling over all available experience.[217] Nevertheless, there is one important difference: scientific explanations do not change the experiences which they explain. By contrast, the essence of moral reasoning consists in modifying unconsidered moral experiences.[218]

Science and ethics thus share the process of mulling over initially unreflective physical or emotional experiences. Nevertheless, the functions they fulfil are distinct. The logic of the process of mulling over is therefore not the same in the two cases. The function of ethics is: '. . . to correlate our feelings and behaviour in such a way as to make the fulfilment of everyone's aims and desires as far as possible compatible.'[219] 'Ethics is concerned with the harmonious satisfaction of desires and interests.'[220] By completing this task, ethics serves its prime goal of preventing unnecessary suffering.[221]

3.3.2. *Toulmin's Analysis of Moral Reasoning*

Toulmin believes that this function is the source from which emerge the criteria for what constitutes a good reason for a

[214] Ibid., 88.

[215] Ibid., 95.

[216] Ibid., 122–3.

[217] Ibid., 124–5. For a very similar distinction between direct reports of experience and feeling on the one hand and judgments on the other Cf. K. Baier, *The Moral Point of View* (Ithaca and London, 1958), 48 ff.

[218] Toulmin, *The Place of Reason in Ethics*, p. 127.

[219] Ibid., 137; cf. also pp. 145, 168.

[220] Ibid., 223.

[221] Ibid., 142.

normative statement. To this end he distinguishes two forms and two levels in moral reasoning.

The first form is present when some action is justified in terms of being required by a valid moral rule of the speaker's community. The second form is applied where justification of some action (or rule) consists in pointing out that it gives rise to less suffering than the alternative under discussion.[222] The first form involves justification by appeal to some rule, the second by reference to consequences. The first form is deontological, the second teleological.[223] The second form directly serves the goal of ethics cited above, namely to avoid unnecessary suffering. The first form achieves this only to the extent that the valid moral norms of a particular society harmonize the actions and desires of its members in such a way that unnecessary suffering is in fact avoided. Toulmin is of the opinion that this, in general, is the case.[224]

The first form of argument ties moral reasoning to existing moral norms. The second form serves the development of its critical function. This critical function is fulfilled in that moral systems are adapted to new circumstances and brought closer to their goal of preventing unnecessary suffering. Moral reasoning thus on the one hand ties in with existing conditions and on the other hand serves the ideal of a society 'in which no misery or frustration is tolerated within the existing resources and state of knowledge'.[225]

The two *levels* of a moral reasoning are to be distinguished from the two *forms*. The first level is concerned with the justification of individual actions, the second with the justification of moral rules. Justification of individual actions proceeds in the first form.[226] The second form only comes into play where

[222] Ibid., 132. The second argument form is concerned with a variant of negative utilitarianism. On this concept cf. K. R. Popper, *The Open Society and its Enemies*, vol. i, *The Spell of Plato*, 5th edn. (London, 1966), chap. 5, n. 6; chap. 9, n. 2; critical of this is R. N. Smart, 'Negative Utilitarianism', *Mind*, 67 (1958), 542–3. However, Toulmin also holds a positive view, consistent with his theory (cf., *The Place of Reason in Ethics*, pp. 159–60).

[223] On these concepts cf. Frankena, *Ethics*, pp. 14–15, and C. D. Broad, *Five Types of Ethical Theory* (London, 1930), 206–7.

[224] Toulmin, *The Place of Reason in Ethics*, pp. 136, 223.

[225] Ibid., 223.

[226] Ibid., 145–6.

two rules are in conflict or where none of the rules valid in the speaker's community is applicable.[227] By contrast, only the second form is concerned with the justification of moral rules *per se.*[228]

3.3.3. *Toulmin's General Theory of Reasoning*

As indicated above, Toulmin puts forward the thesis that there exist specific rules of inference in moral argument which allow the transition from statements of fact (G) to normative statements (N). The existence of such rules would make it possible to distinguish between valid and invalid moral arguments. Toulmin goes even further than this. According to him, a moral statement is *true* whenever good reasons can be adduced for it.[229] Hence, it is not only the possibility of distinguishing valid from invalid moral arguments but also the possibility of normative statements being true or false which depends on the existence of such rules.[230] Toulmin thereby stands Stevenson's argument (discussed above) on its head: the possibility of distinguishing valid from invalid arguments does not presuppose the possibility of normative statements being true or false; rather the possibility of these statements being true or false presupposes the possibility of making such a distinction.

The Place of Reason in Ethics contains no explicit formulations of evaluative inference rules.[231] It offers only descriptions of the two forms of arguments as well as individual arguments based

[227] Ibid., 146 ff.

[228] Ibid., 148 ff. Toulmin's view of moral reasoning can thus be seen as a variant of rule utilitarianism. Characteristic of this variety of utilitarianism is that individual actions are not judged directly by their consequences (act utilitarianism); rather individual acts are judged according to rules and only these rules are judged according to their consequences. On rule utilitarianism cf. in particular, J. Rawls, 'Two Concepts of Rules', *Philosophical Review*, 64 (1955), 3 ff. Critical of this view is J. J. C. Smart, 'Extreme and Restricted Utilitarianism', *Philosophical Quarterly*, 6 (1956), 344 ff.; Hare, *Freedom and Reason*, pp. 130 ff.

[229] Toulmin, *The Place of Reason in Ethics*, pp. 53, 72 ff.

[230] For Toulmin's combination of the theory of moral reasoning with a theory of the possibility of normative statements being true or false cf. Kerner, *The Revolution in Ethical Theory*, pp. 107 ff.

[231] On this cf. Nielsen, 'Good Reasons in Ethics: An Examination of the Toulmin-Hare Controversy', *Theoria*, 24 (1958), 18, n. 20.

on such rules.[232] In order to arrive at an explicit formulation, as well as a clearer determination of the logical character of such rules, it will be helpful to refer to Toulmin's *The Uses of Argument*.[233]

The subject-matter of this investigation is the logic of actual reasoning ('working logic'[234] or 'applied logic'[235]). By 'logic' Toulmin does not mean what is nowadays termed mathematical or formal logic, but rather the theory of the justification of assertions and the assessment of arguments.[236] Logic, understood in this way, has more in common with jurisprudence than with mathematics.[237] Just as jurisprudence describes rules for putting forward 'claims-at-law', for example, so logic determines the rules according to which 'claims-in-general' are justified and refuted. According to Toulmin, logic and jurisprudence are so alike that he advances the thesis that 'logic . . . is generalised jurisprudence'.[238] Toulmin thus abandons the tradition of logic since the time of Aristotle—the tradition which makes mathematics its ideal. He criticizes this tradition for being geared solely to the syllogism as its paradigm,[239] according to him a rather insignificant form of argument in judging practical reasoning. In this way the relationship of logic to practical reasoning is said to have been lost.[240] In order to re-establish this relationship, there is a need for 'a radical re-ordering of logical theory'.[241] The demand for such a radical reordering does not mean that traditional logic is no longer of any value. No valid argument may ever contradict it. Rather, the reordering is needed because traditional logic is insufficient to ground a judgment of the strengths and weaknesses of non-analytic ('substantial') arguments.[242]

For purposes of achieving such a reordering, Toulmin

[232] See Toulmin, *The Place of Reason in Ethics*, pp. 132, 150, p. 224.
[233] id., *The Uses of Argument* (Cambridge, 1958).
[234] Ibid., 9.
[235] Ibid., 255, 95.
[236] Ibid., 6–7.
[237] Ibid., 7–8, 15, 96, 143, 147, 171, 255.
[238] Ibid., 7.
[239] Ibid., 149.
[240] Ibid., 147.
[241] Ibid., 253.
[242] Ibid., 173.

examines the arguments employed in such different fields as physics, jurisprudence, and ethics. He comes to the conclusion that they have basically the same structure. In all fields, to make an assertion raises the implied claim that its underlying assumptions are such as to be accepted.[243] Where this claim is doubted there is a need for justification. This takes place by putting forward facts as grounds or reasons. Thus the assertion that Harry is a British subject (C = claim or conclusion) can be substantiated through the fact that Harry was born in Bermuda (D = data). This argument is open to attack in two ways. The truth of D may be questioned or it may be doubted whether D settles the question of C. In the latter case it is necessary to justify the step from D to C. Such justification cannot result from producing further facts. There is a need for a proposition of a new logical form, an 'inference-licence'.[244] Such 'inference-licences' or rules of inference are as follows: 'Data such as D entitle one to draw conclusions, or make claims, such as C'.[245] Toulmin calls such rules 'warrants' (W). In the example cited above, W is as follows: 'A man born in Bermuda will be a British subject'. Even these rules of inference are open to question. In the case alluded to, one might, for example, refer to the fact that a specific statute was enacted by parliament to vindicate the warrant W.[246] Toulmin calls this kind of allusion 'backing' (B).[247] This yields the argument structure shown in Figure A.3.[248] C thereby follows logically from D and W.[249] In the above

[243] Ibid., 11, 97.

[244] The idea that there are rules underlying arguments, which allow the transition from one proposition to another, was taken over by Toulmin from Ryle (cf. *The Uses of Argument*, p. 260; O. Bird, 'The Re-Discovery of the Topics', *Mind*, 70 (1961), 534). On the concept of inference-licence cf. G. Ryle, *The Concept of Mind* (New York, Melbourne, Sydney, and Cape Town, 1949), 121 ff., 306.

[245] Toulmin *The Uses of Argument*, p. 98.

[246] For a non-trivial example of the application of Toulmin's schema cf. D. Wunderlich, *Grundlagen der Linguistik* (Reinbek, 1974), 71 ff.

[247] Toulmin, *The Uses of Argument*, p. 103.

[248] Ibid., 104. Toulmin introduces further basic concepts by way of the qualifier (Q) and the condition of rebuttal (R). The qualifier determines the modality (necessary, possible, probable, etc.) in which C can be asserted given D and W; the condition of rebuttal indicates when W fails to warrant the transition from D to C (ibid., 100 ff.).

[249] Ibid., 119, 123.

example, this inference has the following form:

.(1) $(x)\ (Fx \rightarrow Gx)$ (W)
.(2) Fa (D)
(3) Ga (C) (1), (2)[250]

In the example given, however, C does not follow from D and B. Nevertheless, there are arguments in which this would be so. Toulmin gives as an example the argument shown in Figure A.4.[251] Toulmin calls arguments of this kind *analytic*. He contrasts them with *substantial* arguments in which C does not follow from D and B.[252]

With the help of the distinctions made so far it is possible to elucidate what Toulmin understands by evaluative rules of inference.

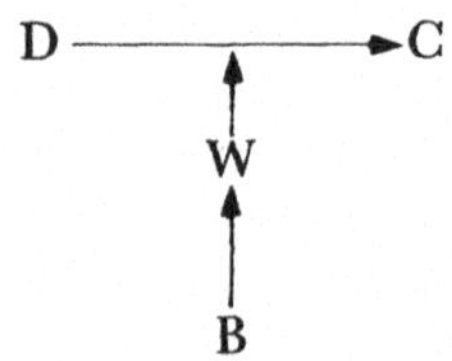

Fig. A.3

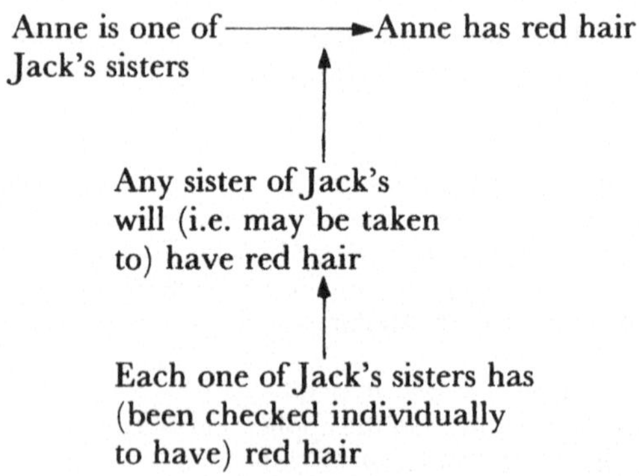

Fig. A.4

[250] Toulmin's justification of C through D and W thereby corresponds to Hare's of N through G and R cf. above, pp. 67 ff.

[251] Ibid., p. 124.

[252] Ibid., 123 ff.

Suppose the normative statement to be justified (C) runs: 'A's behaviour was morally bad'. The ground or reason cited for this might be: 'A told a lie' (D). The relevant rule of inference would be a proposition as follows: 'Lying is morally wrong' (W). This rule of inference can in its own turn be justified by, for example, pointing to the bad consequences of lying (B). W itself thereby becomes a subject for justification at the second level (C′). It is of decisive significance that rules of inference also come into play at this second level.[253] According to Toulmin's theory of morals, such a rule of inference at the second level is a rule of the following kind: 'A rule, adherence to which avoids unnecessary suffering, is good' (W′). W′ facilitates the transition from B (= D′) (Lying as a practice gives rise to unnecessary suffering) to C′, which is the same as W at the first level. The argument in question thus has the structure shown in Figure A.5.[254]

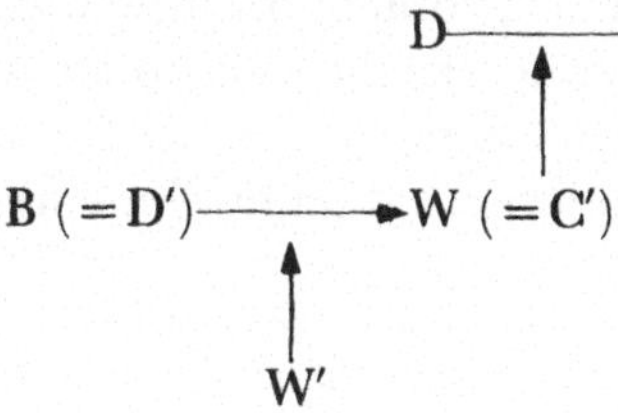

Fig. A.5

The question at once arises as to the possibility of justifying W′. But according to Toulmin this question is to be thrown back at the questioner. If rational argumentation is not to be confined to analytic arguments, then it is not possible to question and justify all the rules of inference. Unless at least some rules of inference are accepted by the speakers from the start, it is impossible for the reasoning process to begin.[255] It is indeed possible to argue about the rules of inference, but such a dispute only makes sense where there is agreement about the rules of inference of the next level.[256]

253 On the use of rules of inference to justify rules of inference cf. ibid., p. 106.
254 Cf. id., *The Place of Reason in Ethics*, 132, 150.
255 id., *The Uses of Argument*, pp. 100, 106.
256 Ibid., 175–6.

3.3.4. *Problems with Toulmin's Theory*

3.3.4.1. Toulmin's theory raises a succession of problems. One widely discussed problem is Toulmin's account of the existence of evaluative rules of inference. Hare in particular criticized this vigorously. According to Hare only the rules of logic should be counted as rules of inference. But Toulmin's evaluative rules of inference are not rules of logic. They do not depend on the meaning of the expressions between which they are supposed to establish a relationship. Moreover, it is possible to deny such rules without self-contradiction. They really have the character of substantive moral rules[257] which are understandable without further arguments as the premisses of practical syllogisms.[258] It is of no significance that the majority of speakers refrain from citing such rules as premisses when giving reasons for what they do or believe. Their arguments are enthymematic.[259]

There is an analogous problem in the theory of science (*Wissenschaftstheorie*). It concerns the question of whether laws of nature featuring in explanations are to be understood as premisses or as rules of inference. Stegmüller correctly observed

[257] Cf. Kerner, *The Revolution in Ethical Theory*, p. 103.

[258] Hare's review of Toulmin, *The Place of Reason in Ethics*, *Philosophical Quarterly*, 1 (1950/1), 374; Hare, *The Language of Morals*, pp. 45, 48 ff.; id., *Freedom and Reason*, p. 87. For an account of the controversy cf. N. Pike, 'Rules of Inference in Moral Reasoning', *Mind*, 70 (1961), 391 ff. The concept 'practical syllogism' will be used here as it is by Hare, to indicate those inferences in which a normative conclusion is derived from a normative premiss together with at least one non-normative premiss (cf. Hare, review of Toulmin, p. 374; id., *The Language of Morals*, p. 26 n. 1). On the concept of practical syllogism in Aristotle (e.g. *The Nichomachean Ethics*, 1147[a]), see Wright, 'On So-called Practical Inference', *Acta Sociologica*, 15 (1972/3), 39–40; G. Kalinowski, *Einführung in die Normenlogik*, trans. W. Klein (Frankfurt-on-Main, 1973), 15 ff. For a different application of the expression 'practical syllogism', which is concerned with the connection between intentions and actions, cf. Wright, 'On So-called Practical Inference', pp. 40 ff.; id., *The Varieties of Goodness* (London and New York, 1963), 162 ff.; id., *Explanation and Understanding* (Ithaca and London, 1971), 96 ff.

[259] On the concept of enthymeme cf. R. George, 'Enthymematic Consequence', *American Philosophical Quarterly*, 9 (1972), 113–16; A. R. Anderson and N. D. Belnap, 'Enthymemes', *Journal of Philosophy*, 58 (1961), 713–22; Quine, *Methods of Logic*, pp. 185 ff. On the concept of enthymeme in Aristotle cf. J. Sprute, 'Topos und Enthymem in der aristotelischen Rhetorik', *Hermes*, 103 (1975), 68 ff.

that this discussion ends in a pseudo-discussion. Either alternative remains a possibility.[260]

This is true for ethics too. To be sure, it must be pointed out, following Hare, that the moral principles to be grasped as evaluative rules of inference are different from rules of logic. They have normative content and are by no means self-evident.

The classification of the controversy between Hare and Toulmin as a 'pseudo-discussion' should not be taken to imply that such discussion is of no relevance. It is to be supposed not only that all moral principles may be conceived as rules of moral argument but also that numerous rules of moral discourse may be conceived as moral principles. This could be of considerable significance. It is quite possible that there are rules which, when conceived as moral principles, can only be the subject of a decision for or against, but when conceived as rules of rational discourse on practical questions can still be supported by reasons.[261]

3.3.4.2. A further problem with Toulmin's theory of evaluative rules of inference is the problem of their justification. Toulmin states that he arrived at both his rules and the distinction between the different levels and forms of moral argumentation through a *description* of moral discourse: 'This description has led us to see how, in *particular types* of ethical question and argument, good reasoning is distinguished from bad, and valid argument from invalid'.[262]

It is, of course, possible to argue according to other rules and forms. However, according to Toulmin, what one is then doing is beyond the realm of moral argument.[263] The rules and forms worked out by Toulmin hence define[264] the language game of

[260] W. Stegmüller, *Probleme und Resultate der Wissenschaftstheorie und Analytischen Philosophie*, vol. i, *Wissenschaftliche Erklärung und Begründung* (Berlin, Heidelberg, and New York, 1974), 98.

[261] Hare's principle of universalizability would seem to be an example of this. Hare himself mentions the possibility of understanding this principle both as a thesis about the logical characteristics of moral judgments, and to this extent as a rule of moral reasoning, and also as an (analytic) moral judgment (cf. *Freedom and Reason* p. 33).

[262] Ibid., 160.

[263] Ibid., 161.

[264] On the use of the expression 'to define' in connection with language games and rules cf. Wittgenstein, *Philosophical Investigations*, p. 82, para. 205.

morals. But the question of whether or not one should enter into this game cannot be put in a meaningful way as a moral question.[265] Toulmin and Hare are in agreement on this. If it could be answered at all it could only be answered from *within* ethics. But anyone wishing to answer it from within ethics would necessarily be presupposing the answer from the outset.

The procedure chosen by Toulmin for substantiating the rules of moral argument may be called '*empirical-definitional*'. It is empirical (or descriptive), because Toulmin arrives at his rules through a description of the practice of moral argumentation. This description is undertaken, to borrow an expression of Hart's, from the 'external point of view'.[266]

It is definitional because he chooses to distinguish one of the multiplicity of actually occurring language games as the game of morality, and denies that any other language game has this characteristic.[267] This combination of description and definition is problematic. Why should only the one language game described by Toulmin be designated 'moral' or 'ethical'?[268] According to their colloquial usage, the expressions 'moral' and 'ethical' can certainly also be used to designate other rules of reasoning or argumentation. This is particularly the case with regard to the rule which prescribes the avoidance of unnecessary suffering. This means that Toulmin has in fact proposed only one of several possible definitions of moral argument. Add to this that a simple reference to actual adherence to a rule is at best to be designated as its justification in a very weak sense, and one must conclude that Toulmin has given only a very incomplete

[265] Toulmin, *The Place of Reason in Ethics*, p. 162.

[266] On this concept cf. H. L. A. Hart, *The Concept of Law* (Oxford, 1961), 86–7.

[267] One might ask whether Toulmin does not employ yet another mode of justification. He formulates his rules in such a way that they are suited to serve specific purposes, namely that of avoiding avoidable suffering and that of the harmonious satisfaction of needs and interests. Such a justification, in which the rules of moral reasoning are put forward as a means to specific purposes, can be termed '*technical*'. The first aim, however, is identical with the content of one of the rules to be justified, the second is so general that Toulmin does not use it in justification. Toulmin's theory thus clearly demonstrates the weakness of the technical mode of justification. On this weakness as well as on the other modes of justification cf. below, pp. 181 ff.

[268] In this connection Toulmin uses both expressions with almost the same meaning (*The Place of Reason in Ethics*, pp. 160–1).

solution to the problem of justifying the rules of moral reasoning.

A further weakness of Toulmin's theory is the vagueness of its fundamental rule. A formula such as 'Avoid unnecessary suffering' merely introduces the general idea of a utilitarian theory. What is to count as suffering? How is one person's suffering to be compared with another's? And, above all, how does the suffering of an individual or of a lesser number stand in comparison to avoidance of the suffering of a majority? May the former be tolerated in order to secure the latter? Toulmin's theory raises more questions than it answers in this area.

Despite these weaknesses, the theory nevertheless contains several findings which are useful for a theory of rational practical discourse.

(1) His thesis that there are rules of moral discourse which mark out certain assertions of fact (G) as good grounds or reasons for certain value-judgments (N) is of considerable interest. Since the normative content of these rules of argumentation corresponds to the normative content of moral principles, it is certainly not permissible to equate these rules with the rules of logic.

(2) The parallel drawn by Toulmin between direct reports of perceptual experiences and direct reports concerning moral experiences on the one hand and fully-fledged scientific and moral judgments on the other hand, is worth maintaining as the discussion proceeds. The fully-fledged judgment (in both cases) is the outcome of working through all the relevant material in accordance with specific rules.

(3) Also important is Toulmin's observation that in justifying judgments of value and obligation we first take account of existing moral norms and only proceed to criticism at a second stage. Moral reasoning cannot begin from nothing. It is tied to the historically evolved material of normative discourse.

(4) Toulmin's general theory of reasoning is not an appropriate substitute for formal logic. However, it does furnish interesting insights into the structure of the premisses used in the process of justification, and it makes plain the nature of the various levels of the process. The realization that some kind of premisses or rules must be presupposed in order for any argumentation to take place at all, is of particular importance.

(5) In addition, Toulmin's way of distinguishing the different forms and levels of argument, especially the distinction between the justification of a singular normative statement and that of a rule, is worth holding on to.

(6) Finally, the idea that the rules of a language game can be discovered by analysing its function or purpose is also of interest.

All in all, Toulmin's theory cannot be regarded as an adequate theory of practical discourse, but it yields significant pointers for the development of such a theory.

3.3.5. *Refining Terminology*

Using Toulmin's distinctions as a basis, it is possible to refine the terminology used so far. In this connection it is possible to make use of the fact that Toulmin's rules of inference (warrants) can be understood as premisses at any level.

The expression 'argument form' denotes the structure which comprises a proposition (C) asserted by a speaker together with the propositions (D and W) advanced or presupposed as directly supporting this proposition. The term 'structure' includes not only the logical form of these propositions but also their character, as, for example, empirical, normative (moral, proclaimed by the legislator), already accepted, open to question, etc. The advanced or presupposed propositions (D and W) 'directly' support the proposition to be justified (C), if the effect of omitting any of them is that the proposition in question (C) no longer follows logically from the rest of them.

An *argument* consists of the propositions belonging to a single argument form which are adduced in support of a further proposition. Accordingly, a *plurality* of arguments is in play in a case in which the proposition to be justified follows from *each* of several sub-sets of the advanced or presupposed propositions. An argument against a proposition is an argument in favour of a proposition which contradicts it.

The expression 'argument structure' refers to the logical relations between several arguments of a given speaker. The most important relation is that of connectedness. There are two kinds of connectedness. In the one kind the proposition to be justified through one argument is itself a proposition used as a justifying one in the other argument. In such a case one can speak of arguments of different levels. In the other kind different arguments of the same form or of different forms serve to justify the same proposition. Here the concern is with arguments on the same level.

The expression 'structure of argumentation', finally, refers to the logical relations of the assertions uttered by several speakers.

The definitions given above could be refined to a considerably greater degree, but they are nevertheless sufficient for present purposes.

3.4. Baier's Theory

Baier's theory of moral reasoning is significant for the present investigation in two main ways: it contains (1) an analysis of the structure of moral argument which is developed beyond Toulmin's theory and (2) a version of the concept of generalizability which stands in marked contrast to Hare's.

3.4.1. *Baier's Analysis of Moral Reasoning*

According to Baier, the question 'What shall I do?' means the same as 'What is *the best* thing I can do?'[269] The best course of action is that 'which is supported by the best reasons'.[270]

In order to establish which are the best reasons it is necessary to embark on a certain activity. Baier calls this activity 'deliberation'.[271] This expression covers the reflections of an individual as well as the discussions of several speakers. What count as good reasons are thus discovered in the course of reflection or discussion.

Baier distinguishes two levels of reflection and discussion. The first level involves looking at the facts and questioning their relevance, that is, 'the surveying of the facts'. The second level involves weighing up the reasons discovered at the first level, that is, 'the weighing of the reasons'.

The first level of deliberation asks what might be considered as a reason for a singular normative statement. Baier's answer is similar to that of Toulmin and Hare in that he too is of the

[269] Baier, *The Moral Point of View*, p. 85.
[270] Ibid., 88.
[271] Ibid., 93.

opinion that it is rules which make something count as a reason. Baier calls these rules 'consideration-making beliefs' or 'rules of reason'. However, he leaves open the question of whether they are to be deemed 'inference-licences', as Toulmin claims, or as major premisses of practical syllogisms, as Hare assumes.[272]

According to Toulmin, the rules to be applied at the first level of reasoning generally make possible a decision on what is to be done. In contrast to this, Baier starts from the position that in normal cases not only reasons for but also reasons against certain courses of action can be brought forward. The course of action which one ought to follow is the one supported by the *best* reasons. Thus the fact that there is a reason G in favour of an action A only implies that A ought to be done if there are no better reasons for refraining from A. These facts which are distinguished as reasons by the 'rules of reason' therefore only provide a presumption in favour of what is to be done.[273]

There is a further important respect in which Baier's rules differ from those of Toulmin. They not only have the function of facilitating the transition from reasons (G) to a normative statement (N), they also serve above all to identify the relevant facts in the first place.[274] This, together with the presumptive character of the reasons arrived at through the rules, justifies calling these rules 'rules of relevance' in the manner of E. von Savigny.[275]

Where there are both grounds for doing A and grounds for not doing A, a state of affairs which Baier accurately describes as 'extremely frequent',[276] it becomes necessary to weigh up which of the reasons is the better.

Underlying this weighing of reasons which occurs at the second level are rules which lay down which reasons belonging to a certain type of reasons, and which types of reasons, are to be given the highest ranking. Baier calls these rules 'rules of superiority'[277] or 'rules of priority'.[278]

[272] Ibid., 94.
[273] Ibid., 102.
[274] Ibid., 94.
[275] Savigny, *Die Philosophie der normalen Sprache*, p. 174.
[276] Baier, *The Moral Point of View*, p. 171.
[277] Ibid., 99.
[278] Ibid., 106.

3.4.2. *The Moral Point of View*

This sketch of practical reasoning highlights one of the most typical features of practical argument: the advancing of reasons 'for' and 'against'. Precisely in the discussion of complex questions such as legal ones there are nearly always reasons both for and against any particular solution. The decision is made at the level of rules of superiority or priority. The question therefore arises of how these are to be justified. One solution would be that of Toulmin: they might be justified in terms of the rule: 'Avoid unnecessary suffering' by pointing out their consequences. Baier's theory would then be no more than a refinement of Toulmin's. But Baier chooses a path which is perhaps more like that of Hare: the theory of the moral point of view.

According to Baier, the moral point of view is defined in terms of a set of rules, criteria, or conditions to which moral judgments must conform if they are to be accepted as such. In Baier's view a moral judgment which meets these conditions is to be counted 'true'.[279] It must therefore be asked which conditions (criteria, rules) characterize this point of view.

3.4.2.1. Baier makes a distinction between formal and material conditions. The first of the *formal conditions* is the demand that action must be guided by *rules* and not by purposes determined by self-interest.[280] According to the second formal condition, these rules must be valid for everyone: 'they are principles *meant for everybody*.'[281] From this follows Baier's next important step, that these rules must be open and universally teachable.[282] From this *demand for 'universal teachability'*,[283] which may be viewed as a special variant of the idea of universalizability, emerge three criteria for the judgment of moral rules:

(1) Moral rules may not be '*self-frustrating*'. They can be said

[279] Ibid., 173 ff., 184. On Baier's thesis concerning the truth-value of normative assertions cf. Nielsen, 'On Moral Truth', *Studies in Moral Philosophy*, American Philosophical Quarterly, Monograph Series, i (Oxford, 1968), 9 ff.

[280] Baier, *The Moral Point of View*, pp. 191 ff.

[281] Ibid., 195.

[282] Ibid., 195–6.

[283] Baier's requirement of universal teachability corresponds to Kant's requirement of publicity: 'All actions relating to the right of other men are unjust if their maxim is not consistent with publicity' ('Perpetual Peace', in *On History*, trans. L. W. Beck (Indianapolis, 1963), 129).

to be such whenever their purpose is thwarted in the event of any actual universal instruction to act on them, which would result in nobody acting as they prescribe. One such self-frustrating rule is the maxim: 'When you are in need, ask for help, but never help another man when he is in need.'[284]

(2) Furthermore, moral rules must not be '*self-defeating*'. They are such whenever the purpose of an agent is thwarted as soon as it is known that he or she is following them. One such rule would be: 'Give a promise even when you don't intend to keep it.'[285]

(3) It would be pointless to teach the aforementioned rules universally, but it would be possible. However, there are rules which could not conceivably be universally taught. An example of such a '*morally impossible*' rule is the rule: 'Always assert what you think is not the case.' Open teaching of this rule would result in the listener simply adding a negation to every assertion. In such a case it would not be the art of deception but some new rule of language which was being taught.[286]

3.4.2.2. Baier similarly discusses three criteria in regard to the *material conditions* of the moral point of view. They are intended as explanations of the demand that moral rules must be 'for the good of everyone alike'.[287]

(1) The first criterion is met when adherence to a rule contributes *immediately* to '*the common good of everyone*'. Such immediate good for all is present when production rises and everybody's standard of living is raised as a result. It becomes clear from this that the area of the applicability of this criterion is limited to those cases in which the interests of all coincide at least

[284] Baier, *The Moral Point of View*, pp. 196–7.

[285] Ibid., 197.

[286] To be sure, such a ruling would not be desirable. To the question whether it is raining outside, I would have to answer in the affirmative, if I knew that it was not raining outside. Since the person asking the question would know the new rule, he or she would thereby have the desired information. Should he or she, however, ask how late it is, I would be able, provided I know that it is 12 o'clock, to say not only that it is not 12 o'clock but also that it is, for example, 6.15, 18.07, or 22.44 hours. Should I choose the latter possibility, my information would be fairly useless to the inquirer. He or she would have to go to some trouble to obtain the correct information. To say that such a rule is undesirable for this reason does not, however, deny that it is possible.

[287] Baier, *The Moral Point of View*, p. 200.

in part. It is therefore not applicable in any case involving a conflict of interests.[288]

(2) In such cases, which are much more common, the criterion of '*reversibility*', regarded as a key criterion by Baier, comes into play: the behaviour in question must be acceptable to those affected by it irrespective of whether they are on the 'giving' or 'receiving' end of it.[289] This criterion corresponds to Hare's procedure, which has already been fully discussed. It shares its weaknesses too, for it fails to say when a rule is morally acceptable from the point of view of those affected by it. However, it has been shown that despite its weaknesses such a criterion is not entirely useless.[290]

(3) Finally, Baier's third condition coincides with Singer's generalization argument. An action is forbidden if its *general adoption would have undesirable consequences*.[291] In everyday discussions this criterion turns up in the shape of the following question: 'What if everyone did that?' It plays an important part in such discussions. Yet both its justifying grounds and its range of application remain controversial. If everyone were to produce clothing humanity would starve. Does this mean that nobody should produce clothes? What happens if a certain number is assigned to the activity in question such that the undesirable consequences are bound to follow? Does this argument in its turn oblige every individual to abstain from the activity? How is the opposite case, when it is established that there will definitely not be any undesirable consequences, to be judged? These and a whole series of further problems have been discussed in depth in connection with M. G. Singer's book *Generalization in Ethics*.[292] The argument alluded to above appears in the middle of this book. It is not possible to go into

[288] Ibid., 201. [289] Ibid., 202, 208. [290] See above, pp. 76–7.

[291] Baier, *The Moral Point of View*, pp. 209 ff. For a more precise version of this argument form cf. Singer, *Generalization in Ethics*, p. 61: 'If everyone were to do *x*, the consequences would be disastrous (or undesirable); therefore no one ought to do *x*.'

[292] Cf. e.g. N. Hoerster, *Utilitaristische Ethik und Verallgemeinerung*, 2nd edn. (Freiburg and Munich, 1977); J. H. Sobel, 'Generalization Arguments', *Theoria*, 31 (1965), 32–60; W. C. Lycan and A. Oldenquist, 'Can the Generalization Argument be Reinstated?' *Analysis*, 32 (1971/2), 76–9; D. Lyons, *Forms and Limits of Utilitarianism* (Oxford, 1965), 198 ff.

this discussion here. However, one might hazard a guess that once subjected to some limitations and qualifications, this argument can be acknowledged as a thoroughly useful one.

The question arises of how the rules, conditions, or criteria defining the moral point of view are to be justified. Why should one accept this point of view? Reference to self-interest is not enough. Whoever adopts the moral point of view is often required to limit considerations of self-interest. Baier's justification of it therefore proceeds in the following way. If one wishes to provide justifying grounds for the moral point of view, one should not ask why a particular individual in a particular situation should adopt it. The question should rather be put as follows: whether a world in which people adopt this point of view is not better from the point of view of *anyone* than one in which everyone behaves immorally.[293]

3.4.3. *Towards a Critique of Baier's Theory*

It must remain a matter of some doubt whether such a justification will stand up. In order to justify the moral point of view, one must presuppose the standpoint of anyone at all. But in taking personal factors out of the account and assuming the viewpoint of anyone at all, one has already accepted something very like the moral point of view. The justification thus becomes circular.

Furthermore, it is questionable whether the defining conditions of the moral point of view are sufficient to serve as criteria for testing moral judgments. A whole set of dubious moral rules is compatible with the requirement of 'universal teachability' and the three criteria derived from it. One only has to think of publicly promulgated racial laws. The formula of immediate service to the common good of everyone leaves many questions unanswered. One can speak of a common advantage both when A and B each receive four rather than two of some unit and when A obtains three rather than two and B five rather than two. This last, however, would hardly be adjudged just without further explanation.[294] The condition of reversibility is exposed to the

[293] Baier, *The Moral Point of View*, p. 310.

[294] On such distributive problems cf. J. Rawls, *A Theory of Justice* (Cambridge, Mass., 1971), 60 ff.

arguments already adduced against Hare's theory of moral reasoning. The rule which forbids those actions which lead to bad consequences if generally carried out, does not, in the last analysis, state what are to count as bad consequences. But knowing this is a necessary condition for applying the rule. Baier's conditions for the moral point of view thus leave many problems unresolved.

Despite these weaknesses Baier's theory is of some significance for the present investigation.

(1) Baier's distinction between those rules which determine grounds or reasons and those which establish a ranking among such rules, is an important addition to Toulmin's analysis of moral argument.

(2) Baier's analysis of the moral point of view reveals many aspects of the concept of generalizability. This concept is central to a theory of rational practical discourse.

4. SOME INTERIM RESULTS

There are many more theories both in the field of meta-ethics and, more generally, in the field of analytical ethics, but we shall not draw on them here. In particular one should mention numerous recent investigations in utilitarian ethics[295] as well as Rawls's *A Theory of Justice*.[296] Discussion of these theories,

[295] On this cf. Brock's bibliography, 'Recent Work in Utilitarianism', *American Philosophical Quarterly*, 10 (1973), 241–76 and also Smart and Williams, *Utilitarianism For and Against*.

[296] As a variant of a contractarian theory, Rawls's theory of justice, despite several significant differences, has many points of contact with the discourse theory advocated here. It must be viewed as an open question whether it would be sufficient as a foundation of a theory of legal reasoning—not something it claims for itself. The subject-matter of Rawls's theory is the basic structure of society (*A Theory of Justice*, p. 7). By contrast, the subject-matter of a theory of legal reasoning is the treatment of individual practical questions. Rawls's theory contains only a few observations on this theme (cf. ibid., 199–200, and p. 339), where Rawls himself asks in relation to the natural duties justifiable in his system: 'How are these duties to be balanced when they come into conflict, either with each other or with obligations, and with the good that can be achieved by supererogatory actions?' He also observes: 'There are no obvious rules for settling these questions.'). On the other hand, discussion of individual practical problems is always dependent on the

though surely useful, would extend beyond the framework set for this investigation.

Before moving on to a discussion of Habermas's theory, we ought to draw together a certain number of particularly important results of the discussion so far:

(1) Contrary to the claims of naturalism and intuitionism, the function of moral language is not exhausted by the description of empirical or non-empirical objects, properties, or relations.

(2) Moral discourse is rather a *rule-governed* activity *sui generis* concerned with balancing interests in a reasonable way. The most important task for a theory of practical discourse is the articulation of the rules governing this activity. In doing this, it is important to distinguish between describing and analysing the rules of actually existing language games and justifying or grounding such rules. The former belong to the empirical and analytical part of a theory of practical discourse, the latter to the normative part.

(3) The *rules* of practical reasoning are to be distinguished from the various *argument forms*.

(4) Normative statements are *universalizable*. As Hare has shown, this means that the person who cites a reason G for a normative statement N, presupposes a rule to the effect that G is a reason or ground for N. The idea of generalizability takes several different forms over and above the concept of universalizability.

(5) Practical reasoning is governed by different rules from, for instance, reasoning in the natural sciences. This, however, is no reason to deny it the character and title of *rational activity*.

All in all it can be said that the theories discussed so far do indeed leave many problems unresolved, but they also contain a considerable number of valuable pointers for the construction of a theory of rational practical discourse to be attempted here and which is strong enough to serve as the basis of a theory of legal reasoning.

practical questions relating to the basic structure of the society. To this extent Rawls's theory is of significance for a theory of legal reasoning too. A discussion of Rawls's theory, its relationship to the theory of discourse advocated here, as well as its relevance for a theory of legal reasoning would be the subject-matter for a separate investigation.

II. Habermas's Consensus Theory of Truth

For the present investigation, the most significant of the theories of the justification of normative statements developed in the German language are Habermas's consensus theory of truth and the theory of practical deliberation of the Erlangen School. Each of these theories has as its focal point the discussion of practical questions. Habermas's theory will be dealt with first.

In his consensus theory, Habermas claims that normative utterances such as commands and value-judgments can be justified in basically the same way as empirical statements.[297] The *truth* of empirical statements thereby corresponds to the *correctness* of normative utterances.[298]

1. HABERMAS'S CRITIQUE OF THE CORRESPONDENCE THEORY OF TRUTH

In order to substantiate his thesis, Habermas first contrasts the consensus theory which he has developed with classical theories

[297] Habermas, 'Wahrheitstheorien', in *Wirklichkeit und Reflexion*, Festschrift for W. Schulz, ed. H. Fahrenbach (Pfullingen, 1973), 220, 242 ff., 252 ff.; id., *Legitimation Crisis*, trans. T. A. McCarthy (London, 1976), 102 ff. There are of course a number of differences in actual details id., 'A Postscript to Knowledge and Human Interests', *Philosophy of the Social Sciences*, 3 (1973), 171 ff. There will be a need to refer to these differences in the course of the discussion.

[298] id., 'Wahrheitstheorien', pp. 220, 226 ff. As a rule Habermas uses the expression 'correctness' with regard to normative utterances and the expression 'truth' in regard to non-normative statements. However, he also speaks of the 'truth-value of practical questions': 'If we understand "truth" extensively as the rationality of an understanding attainable in a free and unlimited communication, then practical questions can in this sense lack truth-value only in the eyes of those who in a positivistic way adhere to a pictorially conceived theory of truth or who in a pragmatic way like Luhmann, theorize truth as a function of the generation of certainty' ('Theorie der Gesellschaft oder Sozialtechnologie? Eine Auseinandersetzung mit Niklas

of truth, in particular the correspondence theory. He tries to show that the classical theories cannot solve the problems associated with the concept of truth, and does this with a view to exhibiting the solutions to these problems which his own theory can offer.

According to the consensus theory's criterion of truth,

I may predicate something of an object, if and only if every individual who *could* enter into conversation with me *would* predicate the same thing of the named object. In order to distinguish true from false statements, I refer to the judgment of others—indeed to the judgment of all others with whom I might ever engage in conversation (here I include, counterfactually, all speech-partners whom I might encounter if my life history were co-extensive with that of humankind). The condition for the truth of statements is the potential agreement of *everyone* else.[299]

In contrast to this, the correspondence theory of truth[300] holds that a sentence (or an assertion or a proposition or a statement)[301] is to be called true if and only if the state of affairs to which the sentence gives expression does actually exist. A state of affairs which exists is a fact.[302] Truth can thus be defined as a correspondence between sentence and fact.

Luhmann', in Habermas and N. Luhmann (eds.), *Theorie der Gesellschaft oder Sozialtechnologie—Was leistet die Systemforschung?* (Frankfurt-on-Main, 1971), 241. Cf. also id., *Legitimation Crisis*, pp. 102 ff.) Habermas often makes a further distinction between the correctness of commands and the suitableness of value-judgments (cf. id., 'Wahrheitstheorien', p. 242).

[299] id., 'Vorbereitende Bemerkungen zu einer Theorie der kommunikativen Kompetenz', in Habermas and Luhmann, *Theorie der Gesellschaft*, p. 124; id., 'Wahrheitstheorien', p. 219. The formulation cited is the same verbatim in both texts. On this see also what is of course the more weakly formulated thesis of Frankena, who says that with the use of expressions such as 'good', 'right', 'justified', 'valid', 'true', 'real', and 'rational' one raises 'implicit claims to a hypothetical consensus' ('Decisionism and Separatism in Social Philosophy', *Nomos*, 7 (1964), 23).

[300] On correspondence theory cf. G. E. Moore, 'Facts and Propositions', *Proceedings of the Aristotelian Society*, suppl. vol. 7 (1927), 171–206; Austin, 'Truth', *Philosophical Papers*, pp. 117–33; A. Tarski, 'The Semantic Conception of Truth and the Foundations of Semantics', *Philosophy and Phenomenological Research*, 4 (1943/4), 341–75.

[301] On that of which it may be said that it is true or false cf. A. R. White, *Truth* (London and Basingstoke, 1970), 7 ff.

[302] On this terminology cf. Wittgenstein, *Tractatus Logico-philosophicus*, no. 2: 'What is the case—a fact—is the existence of states of affairs.'

At a first glance the correspondence theory of truth appears unproblematic and even trivially true. Scarcely anyone would gainsay Aristotle's dictum that 'to say of what is that it is, or of what is not that it is not is true.'[303] Problems only arise on closer investigation. One of the most difficult problems which comes to the fore arises in connection with answering the question of what it is to which the sentence (or proposition, etc.) must correspond if it is to be true, in short: of what is to count as a fact.

This is precisely the point which Habermas takes up. Together with Strawson he makes a distinction between facts and objects of experience. 'Facts are what statements (when true) state; they are not what statements are about. They are not, like things or happenings on the face of the globe, witnessed or heard or seen . . .'.[304] Objects of experience are in the world. By contrast, as Patzig says, 'Facts . . . are not first what they are and secondly, in addition, what is represented by true sentences.'[305] 'Without sentences, there could be no facts; facts are essentially language-dependent.'[306]

Facts are thus not something in the world in the same way as objects are. But, according to Habermas, this is what they would have to be if the correspondence theory were to make sense. Otherwise the correspondence theory would be limited to the realm of language. But this is not consistent with the requirement that statements should be governed by facts and not facts by statements. For a theory of truth to be adequate, it must do justice to what Patzig calls the 'internal duality'[307] in the concept of fact, meaning thereby that facts are on the one hand dependent on language while on the other hand the truth-value of sentences is dependent on the facts. According to Habermas, only a consensus theory of truth can meet these requirements.[308]

[303] Aristotle, *Metaphysics*, 1011^{b}.

[304] P. F. Strawson, 'Truth' in *Truth*, ed. G. Pitcher (Englewood Cliffs, NJ, 1964), 38.

[305] G. Patzig, 'Satz und Tatsache', in id., *Sprache und Logik* (Göttingen, 1970), p. 43; trans. 'Facts and Sentences', *Contemporary German Philosophy*, vol. ii, ed. D. E. Christensen *et al.* (Pennsylvania, 1983), 179.

[306] id., 'Facts and Sentences', p. 179.

[307] Ibid., 182.

[308] Habermas, 'Wahrheitstheorien', p. 217.

2. COMBINING SPEECH ACT THEORY AND A THEORY OF TRUTH

Habermas's consensus theory builds on the theory of speech acts[309] discussed above.[310]

According to Habermas, truth is an '[implicit] claim to validity which we annex to constative speech acts. A statement is true when the claim to validity implicated in the speech act whereby we assert the statement by means of sentences is justified.'[311] The soundness of an assertion should therefore no longer be dependent on the truth of what is asserted, as has been traditionally supposed, but on the contrary, the truth of what is asserted is made to depend on the soundness of the assertion. The concept of truth is shifted, so to speak, from the level of the semantic to that of the pragmatic.

Should such a solution be possible, two goals would have been achieved. First, it could be shown that truth does not consist of some problematic relation between sentences and the world. Second, an important step would have been made towards setting normative and non-normative statements on an equal footing with respect to their truth-value. However, it remains to be shown that there can be such a thing as a sound assertion of a normative statement. If there exist such sound assertions of normative statements, then, going beyond Habermas, one could even speak of normative facts. Just as the sentence 'Snow is white' can correspond to the fact that snow is white,[312] so too can

[309] id., 'Vorbereitende Bemerkungen zu einer Theorie der kommunikativen Kompetenz', pp. 102 ff. For a full discussion of Habermas's theory in contrast to speech act theory cf. his 'What is Universal Pragmatics?' in *Communication and the Evolution of Society*, trans. T. A. MacCarthy (Boston, 1979), 1–68. At the same time Habermas understands his theory as a continuation of Wittgenstein's analysis of language games: 'Had Wittgenstein developed *a theory of language games*, it would have had to adopt the form of universal pragmatics' ('Sprachspiel, Intention und Bedeutung. Zu Motiven bei Sellars and Wittgenstein', *Sprachanalyse und Soziologie*, ed. R. Wiggershaus (Frankfurt-on-Main, 1975), p. 327).

[310] Cf. above, pp. 53 ff.

[311] Habermas, 'Wahrheitstheorien', p. 218.

[312] On this cf. Tarski, 'The Semantic Conception of Truth and the Foundations of Semantics', *Philosophy and Phenomenological Research*, 4 (1943/4), 343.

the sentence 'X ought to be done' correspond to the fact that X ought to be done.[313]

3. DISTINGUISHING BETWEEN ACTION AND DISCOURSE

A decisive step in Habermas's theory is the fact that the theory of speech acts is embedded in a general theory of communication which distinguishes two fundamentally different forms of communication: 'action' [*Handlung*] and 'discourse' [*Diskurs*].

'Actions' are language games[314] in which the claims to validity implicated in speech acts are tacitly recognized. By contrast, in 'discourses' claims to validity which have become problematic are made the subject-matter and are scrutinized as to their soundness.[315] In 'actions' the questions of whether the assertion made in a speech act is true, of whether the state of affairs expressed in it exists—that is, is a fact—are not raised. The theme of such communication is rather experience of objects in the world. Items of information are exchanged concerning these experiences. These items are reliable or unreliable[316] according to whether the information is founded on subjective or objective experiences. It is founded on objective experience where actions supported by it are successful.[317] As soon as doubts are raised about the items of information—that is, as soon as the truth of the statement used to convey the information is questioned—the realm of 'action' is abandoned and one finds oneself in the other realm of communication, that of 'discourse'.

In discourses there is said to be no 'room for procedures aimed at *obtaining* information; discourses are unencumbered by action and free of experience. Items of information are fed into discourses and the output of discourses consists of the recogni-

[313] On this cf. White, 'Truth', pp. 59 ff.

[314] On the concept of a language game cf. above, pp. 49 ff.

[315] Habermas, 'Wahrheitstheorien', p. 214, and his *Theory and Practice*, trans. J. Viertel (London, 1974), 18.

[316] id., 'Wahrheitstheorien', p. 218.

[317] Ibid., 388–9. This makes it clear that Habermas's theory of objectivity is a pragmatic one. In connection with K.-O. Apel, Habermas speaks of a 'transcendentally inclined pragmatism' ('Wahrheitstheorien', p. 233. Cf. also Apel, *Towards a Transformation of Philosophy*, trans. G. Adey and D. Frisby (London, Boston, and Henley, 1980), pp. 77 ff.).

tion or rejection of problematic claims to validity. Nothing apart from arguments is produced in the process of discourse.'[318] To say that discourses are free of experience does not therefore mean that experiences do not enter into them, but only that no experiences can be acquired in the course of them. Discourses presuppose the totality of experiences gained in actions, apart from those which are made problematic. It is possible for ever increasing parts of the matter given in experience to be processed through progressive problematizations.

The relationship between 'action' and 'discourse' presents a number of problems. One problem is that of simple statements of observation. It might be thought that, in order to ground the statement: 'This ball is red', a corresponding experience can be immediately invoked.[319] This would show that, at least in some cases, truth does after all consist of a relation between statements and the world which is not mediated by argumentation. The distinction between 'action' and 'discourse' would then be superfluous, at least as far as concerns simple statements of observation.[320]

This objection, however, is untenable. Popper has shown that simple statements of observation, which he calls 'basic statements', are not something fixed and firmly founded on experience. Even these sentences have the character of hypotheses because of the 'universal names' (predicates) which they employ.[321] As such, they are theory-dependent. Thus 'the word "red" [implies] a theory of colours'.[322] This means that not even basic sentences are uncontestable. They too can be falsified. Underlying their acceptance is an agreement.[323] Drawing attention to simple statements of observation is thus no objection to the possibility of discursively testing them.

What is true of simple statements of observation is all the more

[318] Habermas, *Erkenntnis und Interesse*, 2nd edn. (Frankfurt-on-Main, 1973), 386; trans.: 'A Postscript to Knowledge and Human Interests', p. 168.

[319] id., *Erkenntnis und Interesse*, p. 389; 'A Postscript to Knowledge and Human Interests', p. 170.

[320] It is characteristic of writers who hold to the correspondence theory that they discuss mainly statements of this type. Cf. e.g. Austin, 'Truth', pp. 118 ff.

[321] Popper, *The Logic of Scientific Discovery* (New York, Hagerstown, San Francisco, and London, 1968), 94–5.

[322] Ibid., 111.

[323] Ibid., 104 ff.

so for complex forms of statement. The truth of negative, general, and modal statements cannot be determined by an immediate confrontation with something in the world.

As a result of the distinction between 'action' and 'discourse', one arrives at the following definition of fact: a fact is what a discursively justifiable statement states. The dependency on language remains. On the other hand 'discourse' (in part because experiences enter into it whereby the fact-world connection is guaranteed) secures the dependency of statements on facts without these facts thereby having to become objects in the world. In this way, the conditions for the adequacy of a definition of a fact would be satisfied.

4. THE JUSTIFICATION OF NORMATIVE STATEMENTS

The fact that truth does not consist of a simple statement-world relation, provides an important argument against the thesis that normative statements have no truth-value. Nevertheless, in order to show that they positively do have such truth-value something more is needed by way of substantiation. It must be shown that within the framework of a consensus theory it is possible to distinguish sound or justified assertions from unsound or unjustified ones, valid arguments from invalid, and sound transitions from statements of fact (G) to normative statements (N) from unsound ones. It is a presupposition that it is possible to formulate rules which allow these distinctions to be made. Hence one is putting the same question in connection with Habermas's theory as that which stood at the centre of the discussion of meta-ethics in the field of analytical philosophy.

Habermas's answer builds on the doctrine of claims to validity implicated in speech acts. According to Habermas, a successful language game presupposes the mutual recognition of four claims to validity: 'Claims as to the *intelligibility* of the utterance, of the *truth* of its propositional element, the *correctness* or suitability of its performative element, and the *veracity* of the speaker.'[324] The claim to intelligibility is made with respect to every speech act, the claim to truth in respect of constative

[324] Habermas, *Theory and Practice*, p. 18 (my italics); cf. also 'Wahrheits-theorien', pp. 220 ff.

speech acts such as assertions. The claim to correctness or suitability is associated with regulative speech acts. According to Habermas, the following, among others, are to be reckoned regulative speech acts: orders or commands, suggestions, and promises. Finally, the claim to veracity arises in speech acts which express the intentions, attitudes, etc. of the speaker. Habermas calls these speech acts 'representative speech acts'.[325]

According to Habermas, the claim to intelligibility is a precondition and not an object of communication.[326] The claim to veracity is not settled through discourse. I can only recognize by his or her actions whether a speaker is veracious.[327] By contrast, the claim to correctness or suitability implicated in regulative speech acts can, in common with claims to truth implicated in constative speech acts, only be discursively settled. Judgments of value and judgments of obligation are thereby basically put on an equal footing with empirical judgments in respect of their truth-value.

However, Habermas's conception of claims implicated in regulative speech acts contains several obscurities. These relate to his not entirely unproblematic adoption of the theory of speech acts.[328]

Speech acts can be performed through explicit performative utterances[329] such as: 'I promise that I shall come tomorrow' or

[325] For Habermas's classification of speech acts cf. his 'Vorbereitende Bemerkungen zu einer Theorie der kommunikativen Kompetenz', pp. 111–12; and his 'Wahrheitstheorien', p. 228. There will be no discussion here of the many problems to which this classification gives rise. It will only be pointed out that Habermas's divisions are quite different from those of Austin (*How to Do Things with Words*, pp. 150 ff.)

[326] Habermas, 'Wahrheitstheorien', p. 222. This assumption is not unproblematic. It is also possible to have discussions concerning intelligibility, something which Habermas moreover recognizes throughout. More will be said about the 'discussability' of problems of intelligibility in the discussion of the theses of the Erlangen school.

[327] Ibid., 221 and *Theory and Practice*, p. 18.

[328] For a criticism of Habermas's adoption of speech act theory cf. Y. Bar-Hillel, 'On Habermas' Hermeneutic Philosophy of Language', *Synthèse*, 26 (1973), 1 ff. Bar-Hillel's criticism must be accepted at many points. But his thesis that Habermas's lack of clarity and misunderstandings give rise to falsification of his whole theory is unacceptable.

[329] On this concept cf. Austin, *How to Do Things with Words*, pp. 68–9 and Wunderlich, 'Zur Konventionalität von Sprechhandlungen', pp. 16 ff.

'I affirm that I saw Mr. Lauben'. Relying on Searle's terminology,[330] Habermas calls the first part of such a sentence (I promise that . . .) the 'performative sentence' and the second part (I shall come tomorrow) the 'dependent sentence with propositional content'.[331] The first part expresses what is done by the utterance, the second what is said. Austin designates the former 'illocutionary force', the latter 'locutionary meaning'.[332]

With the constative speech acts it was the propositional content, the statement, which was subject to testing. By contrast, the claim to correctness is supposed to relate to the performative element of the regulative speech act. This performative element is supposed to be tested for whether it can be regarded as the 'fulfilment' of a justified norm. The object of discursive testing is therefore not the regulative speech act itself, but rather the norm which it is to be considered as satisfying.[333] Thus, for example, it should be possible for an order 'to be justified by reference to a valid norm which confers appropriate order-giving competence'.[334]

It must be objected to this that, even with respect to quite a number of the speech acts which Habermas calls 'regulative', a distinction can and must be made between judging what was done and judging what was said.[335] Thus one can judge in respect of an order whether it was issued in the scope of someone's order-giving competence, but one can also judge whether what was ordered was correct or appropriate. The necessity for distinguishing between judging what is done and what is said becomes particularly clear with utterances such as: 'I maintain that this decision is unjust'. Whoever wishes to judge such an utterance must (at the very least) test the soundness of the value-judgment (this decision is unjust) stated in the utterance. The fact already shown in the discussion of Hare's theses,[336] that in this case it is necessary to test the rule (or

[330] Searle, Speech Acts, p. 24.

[331] Habermas, 'Vorbereitende Bemerkungen zu einer Theorie der kommunikativen Kompetenz' p. 104.

[332] Austin, *How to Do Things with Words*, pp. 99, 147; cf. above, pp. 54 f.

[333] Habermas, 'Wahrheitstheorien', pp. 220, 228–9, and his *Theory and Practice*, p. 18.

[334] id., 'Wahrheitstheorien', p. 228.

[335] 'Do' here relates to the illocutionary and 'say' to the locutionary act.

[336] Cf. above, pp. 66 f.

standard) presupposed in such a value-judgment, does not prevent us from speaking of the judgment as being 'justified'. This is so because the judgment may be mistaken because of a wrong assessment of the facts as well as the unjustified nature of the rule presupposed by it. The rule presupposed in such a value-judgment is not to be confused with the rules which can be said to be 'acted upon' when one performs a regulative speech-act. A rule presupposed in such a value-judgment is not to be confused with the rules which can be said to be 'acted upon' when one performs a regulative speech act. A rule which empowers a non-commissioned officer to issue orders is something different from a rule which lays down what is a good order to issue in a particular situation.

Habermas's divergent conception seems to result from two factors. On the one hand he does not see what Hare and Strawson have made clear,[337] namely that in regard to a number of the speech acts, which Habermas calls 'regulative', the categorization of what is said as a value-judgment or a judgment of obligation is a categorization of its locutionary meaning. This is true, for example, of admonitions (You ought to return the stolen money to him) and of recommendations (This helpful action is good), as well as of the simple assertion of such judgments. Habermas here makes the same mistake as Austin, for whom the locutionary meaning was exhausted by assigning a particular 'sense' to a particular 'reference'.[338] On the other hand Habermas combines into a single class of speech acts both those speech acts which have normative statements (judgments of value and obligation) as their locutionary meaning and speech acts such as promises which do not have a normative statement as their locutionary meaning, but rather a statement about future behaviour. These quite diverse speech acts are then treated in the same way.[339]

In order to avoid these difficulties, it would be possible to subdivide the concept of regulative speech acts. The term

337 Cf. Hare, 'Austin's Distinction between Locutionary and Illocutionary Acts', p. 107, and his 'Meaning and Speech Acts', p. 90; Strawson, 'Austin and "Locutionary Meaning"', p. 60; and above, pp. 62 ff.

338 Austin, *How to Do Things with Words*, pp. 92–3.

339 On those speech acts which Habermas calls 'regulative' cf. his 'Wahrheitstheorien', p. 228.

'normative speech act' could be applied to all those speech acts which had as their locutionary meaning a normative statement (a judgment of value or obligation). Normative speech acts can be constative inasmuch as the assertion of a normative statement is a normative speech act.[340] Testing of those regulative speech acts which do not fall into this subdivision, such as the act of making an apology or an excuse, for example, would proceed by adjudging a singular normative statement concerning the regulative speech act in question—for example, 'A's apology was appropriate/inappropriate'—which can be asserted in a normative speech act. Regulative speech acts which are not normative speech acts are thus judged in the same way as any other kind of 'action'.

5. THE LOGIC OF DISCOURSE

According to the consensus theory, the potential agreement of all is the condition both of the truth of a non-normative statement and of the correctness of a normative statement. This criterion of truth suffers from two weaknesses: on the one hand it cannot be satisfied and on the other hand, even if it could be, it would not be sufficient. The agreement of all is unattainable, if only because those who have died can no longer participate in a conversation and it cannot be established what their opinions would have been. And even if everyone were in a position to express an opinion, a contingently occurring agreement could not serve as a criterion of truth.[341] It might, for example, rest on an error or on coercion.

In his essay on theories of truth, Habermas tries to counter these difficulties by stipulating that only a *well-grounded consensus* can serve as a criterion of truth:[342]

> The meaning of truth lies not in the circumstance that some consensus is actually achieved, but rather in this: that at any time and in any place if we but enter into discourse, a consensus can be achieved under certain conditions which prove this to be a well-grounded consensus.[343]

[340] Cf. above, p. 65.
[341] Habermas, 'Wahrheitstheorien', p. 239.
[342] Ibid., 239.
[343] Ibid., 239–40.

A well-grounded consensus is said to be a consensus which rests on 'the strength of the better argument'. But what is it that makes one argument better than another, and in what does the strength of the better argument consist?

Habermas attempts to settle these matters within the framework of a logic of discourse.[344] The subject-matter of a logic of discourse is the formal characteristics of the links between steps in an argument. What is decisive is that such linked steps in an argument do not consist of sentences but of speech acts. The logic of discourse must therefore be a pragmatic logic.[345]

At the centre of the logic of discourse stands argument: 'An "argument" is that justificatory ground which is deemed to give us reason to acknowledge the claim to validity implicit in an assertion or a command, or, as the case may be, an evaluation.'[346] In order to describe the formal structure of an argument, Habermas uses Toulmin's schema, already discussed above[347] (see Figure A.6).[348]

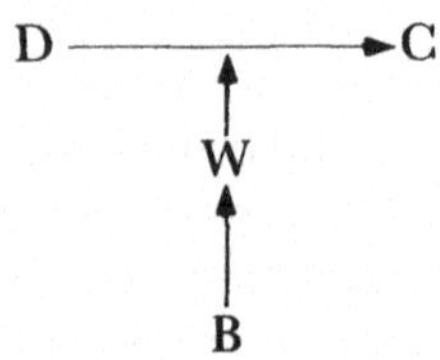

Fig. A.6

This argument structure is used to deliver explanations in theoretical discourse. It forms the basis of justification in practical discourse. Thus the order (C) 'A shall return 50 DM to B by the end of the week' can be justified through the fact (D) that B made A a loan of 50 DM for this period via the rule (W) 'Loans are to be repaid within the prescribed period of time'.

[344] Ibid., 240.
[345] Ibid., 241.
[346] Ibid., 241–2.
[347] Cf. above, pp. 84 ff.
[348] Toulmin, *The Uses of Argument*, pp. 95 ff.

This rule itself (W) can be justified in its turn by, for example, pointing to the direct and indirect consequences of following the norm (B).[349] What is crucial here is that the relation between B and W is non-deductive. W does not follow from B. The strength of the argument therefore depends on the acceptability of the transition from B to W.

It was shown above that the transition from B to W is definitely to be accepted where it is possible to presuppose a rule W′ from which, together with B, W follows.[350] This immediately gives rise to the question of whether, and if so how, W′ can be justified. This question corresponds to the problem discussed by Habermas, that of the origin of the consensus-achieving strength in respect of the transition from B to W. This question involves a variant of the problem already discussed by Stevenson, namely the relation of a ground or reason G to a normative statement N: are there such things as valid and invalid transitions from G to N, or does the readiness to accept such a move depend solely on the psychological make-up, the social standing, and cultural affiliation of the person concerned? If the latter should be the case, the readiness to move from G to N could at best be explained; it could not be justified. A theory of rational discourse would then be impossible, or at any rate would be only a theory concerning effective discursive means. This characterizes the weight of one answer eventually given by Habermas.

According to Habermas, the consensus-achieving strength of the transition from B to W is dependent on the adequacy of the language-system applied in the reasoning process. The language-system used in argumentation has to determine which classes of experiences may be brought into the reasoning process as 'backing'. These experiences are observational and survey data in theoretical discourses, and interpretations of need in practical discourses. It is supposedly possible for the language-system to determine which classes of experiences are admissible as 'backing', because underlying the 'fundamental predicates of reliable languages of justification' there are cognitive

[349] Cf. Habermas, 'Wahrheitstheorien', p. 244.
[350] Cf. above, p. 87.

schemata.[351] Habermas's concept of cognitive schemata is linked to Piaget's genetic epistemology. According to Piaget the fundamental structures of cognitive capacity are cognitive schemata which are neither pure reflections of some given order of the external world, as assumed by empiricism, nor something innate or genetically determined, as maintained by rationalism. They are rather to be understood as constructs produced by subjects with a specific genetic inheritance, through their actions in a determinately structured world and within the framework of a determinate society in the course of their development. These constructs are a precondition and determinant of every cognition.[352]

The transition from B to W is thus mediated through cognitive schemata. According to Habermas, induction, the transition from a number of singular statements to a general statement, is thereby rendered trivial, 'namely the repetition by way of example of exactly that kind of experience from which the cognitive schemata which always enter into the basic predicates of the language of justification have been previously developed.'[353]

The consensus-achieving strength of an argument thus rests 'on a cognitive development which guarantees the adequacy of the descriptive system and which precedes every individual argumentation'.[354] It might be thought fitting at this point to define truth in terms of the adequacy of the language-system. However, Habermas explicitly rejects such a move. Language-systems and systems of concepts cannot have truth-value; truth can only be established in respect of statements and the reasoning put forward to substantiate them. The decisive step for Habermas consists in his claim that the 'naturally evolved and internally regulated' language-system on which every argumentation rests in the first instance must, in turn, itself be the subject of argumentation. It is in this way that Habermas arrives at his criterion for a well-founded consensus: 'A

351 Ibid., 246.

352 J. Piaget, 'Piaget's Theory', in *Carmichal's Manual of Child Psychology*, ed. P. H. Mussen, 3rd edn. (New York, London, Sydney, and Toronto, 1970), i. 703 ff.

353 Habermas, 'Wahrheitstheorien', p. 246.

354 Ibid., 249.

consensus arrived at through argument may be viewed as a criterion of truth if and only if it is structurally possible to call into question, modify, and replace the prevailing language of justification in which experiences are interpreted.'[355]

This criterion of truth is certainly not unproblematic. Nevertheless, it cannot be discussed here in all its aspects. The discussion will be limited to the question of its suitability as a criterion of the rationality of practical discourse. The following paragraphs will speak of the 'logic of practical discourse' rather than the 'logic of discourse' in general.

The part played by induction in theoretical discourses is said to be played by generalizability in practical discourses. Habermas describes the 'principle of universalization'[356] as 'the only principle in which practical reason expresses itself'.[357] Unfortunately he declines to give a systematic investigation of this concept, regardless of the multiple ambiguities revealed by a cursory glance at the conceptions of Hare, Baier, and Singer.[358]

Habermas's version of the idea of generalizability rests on his theory of the 'ideal speech-situation', which will be discussed more fully below. All speakers have equal rights in the ideal speech situation; there is no element of coercion. It is obvious that in such a situation a consensus is possible only about those orders, norms, etc. which '*all* can want'.[359] According to Habermas, norms regulate the possibility of satisfying needs and the pursuit of interests respectively.[360] A norm which '*all* can

[355] Ibid., 250. It is worth mentioning that a similar idea is expressed in the jurisprudential writings of Josef Esser. He begins by observing that language too is 'a part of one's preconceptions'. 'The modalities of social outlook characteristic of a language are "re-actualized" with every use of the language without this fact being at all recognized. The interpretative process is already guided by this, yet the interpreter does not recognize it. What may be called a "traditional nexus" is constituted by these *thought-schemata inherent in language* and it often remains operative for generations. . . . Jurisprudence has hitherto failed to give any clear account of the unconscious power of traditions. However, all these frames of reference ought to be taken into account if the conditions of our process of finding legal solutions is to be rational' Esser, *Vorverständnis und Methodenwahl*, pp. 10–11 (my italics).

[356] Habermas, 'Wahrheitstheorien', p. 251.

[357] id., *Legitimation Crisis*, p. 108.

[358] Cf. above, pp. 65 ff., 95 ff.

[359] Habermas, *Ligitimation Crisis*, p. 108.

[360] id., 'Wahrheitstheorien', p. 251.

want' is thus such that *everyone* can accept its direct and indirect consequences in respect of the satisfaction of the needs of *each and every individual*.[361]

This formula differs both from that of Hare and from Singer's generalization argument. According to Hare it is sufficient that the *judging individual* accepts the consequences *for all*,[362] while Singer demands that the consequences of *everybody* following the norm be acceptable.[363] It is neither necessary nor meaningful to make some kind of decision in favour of one of these three versions of the idea of generalizability, to which further ones may be added—for instance, the demand for *consistency*[364] expressed through the principle of universalizability and the demand for *universal teachability* (Baier).[365] It would seem highly probable that they can be combined with each other. No question of incompatibility arises, except possibly as between Hare's argument and Habermas's formula. This possibility can be removed by adopting a priority rule in favour of Habermas's formula. Such a priority rule would in no way render Hare's argument superfluous. As will become clear, Habermas's formula is, as a rule, only approximately attainable. It rather defines an ideal than a fixed criterion. In these circumstances it makes sense to stipulate the satisfaction of Hare's criterion as a minimal requirement.

It is another question whether and to what degree the different cited variants of the principle of generalizability are reducible to one another. There would have to be extensive logical analysis to discover this. In what follows, this matter will

[361] id., *Legitimation Crisis*, p. 108: 'The discursively formed will may be called "rational" because the formal properties of discourse and of the deliberative situation sufficiently guarantee that a consensus can arise only through appropriately interpreted, *generalizable* interests, by which I mean needs *that can be communicatively shared*.' A similar criterion is suggested by Frankena: 'Our judgment or principle is really justified if it holds up under sustained scrutiny of this sort from the moral point of view on the part of *everyone*' (Frankena, *Ethics*, p. 95 (my italics)).

[362] See above, pp. 72 ff. This is a requirement which is said to be yielded by combining the principle of universalizability with the principle of prescriptivity.

[363] See above, pp. 97–8.

[364] See above, pp. 65 ff.

[365] See above, pp. 95–6.

only be alluded to in passing. A systematic analysis would require a separate investigation.[366]

According to Habermas's version of the principle of generalizability, for there to be a consensus about a norm there has to be something which must be accepted as a need by anyone and everyone. In order to settle this point Habermas falls back on his theory of cognitive schemata. People's needs are not something predetermined in nature. It is perhaps possible to put forward a number of conditions for survival. If one were also to include the premiss that people ought to survive, then in this way one might resolve several practical problems—that is, in the sense of a theory of the minimal content of natural law.[367] However, quite apart from the fact that what are to count as conditions for human survival remains open to dispute, only a very small number of questions could be decided in this way. The reason for the inadequacy of such a starting-point lies in the fact that, as Kamlah[368] stressed, human needs are culturally shaped. They

[366] The results of such an analysis would at the same time deliver the basis for an interpretation of the various versions of Kant's categorical imperative, particularly the formulation: 'Act only on that maxim through which you can at the same time will that it should become a universal law' (*Groundwork of the Metaphysic of Morals*, trans. H. Paton, in *The Moral Law*, 3rd edn. (London, 1964), 88) and also the principles, such as that of freedom, contained in Kant's legal philosophy, and resting on the idea of generalizability, which required that: '. . . only the united and consenting will of all—that is, a general united will of the people by which each decides the same for all and all decide the same for each—can legislate' (*The Metaphysical Elements of Justice* (i.e. *Metaphysik der Sitten*) trans. J. Ladd (Indianapolis, 1965), 78) and that of equality, which demands that 'no one can lawfully bind another without at the same time subjecting himself to the law by which he also can be bound' ('Perpetual Peace', p. 93 n. 2) and that of publicity which lays down that: 'All actions relating to the right of other men are unjust if their maxim is not consistent with publicity' (ibid., 129). Even these few quotations suggest the supposition that all the variants of the idea of generalizability cited above are contained in Kant's theory. Should this prove to be the case, and to the extent that these variants on the principle of generalizability enter into the theory of rational practical discourse, this theory can be called 'Kantian'. In order to confirm the supposition it would be necessary to examine Kant's theory in the light of the five (and possibly more) formulae; refining this assertion would require an analysis of the relationship of the theory of rational practical discourse to Kant's theory.

[367] Hart, *The Concept of Law*, pp. 189 ff.

[368] W. Kamlah, *Philosophische Anthropologie* (Mannheim, Vienna, and Zurich, 1973), 52 ff.

are individually experienced only in the context of certain interpretations. These interpretations occur within the framework of cognitive schemata or, as Habermas occasionally writes, within the framework of 'world-pictures'.[369]

Rather than talking of 'cognitive schemata' or 'world-pictures', it can also be said that the labelling of a need as one which is to be generally accepted, is rule-governed. These rules in their turn underlie historically evolved moral convictions and thereby also the language of morals. Habermas's demand for discursive testing of the adequacy of the language-system which determines the interpretation of needs can therefore be understood as a demand for discursive testing of the moral rules which underlie moral language. An example of such rules would be those governing the use of the expression 'courageous'.[370]

In order to facilitate such discursive testing of the rules underlying moral expressions, discourse must be constructed in such a way as to allow for the revision of the originally chosen language-system. According to Habermas, this presupposes the possibility of free interchange between the different levels of discourse. Four levels and four corresponding steps are distinguished.

The first step in theoretical discourse ('entry into discourse') consists of the transition from 'action' to 'discourse' by problematization of an assertion. The second step ('theoretical discourse') consists of the submission of at least one argument. The third step ('meta-theoretical discourse') is the transition to a modification of the originally chosen language-system. The last step consists of the transition to 'reflection on the systematic changes of the language of justification',[371] in which 'with the help of the peculiarly circular movement of rational *post factum* construction, we determine what *ought* to count as cognition'.[372]

369 Habermas, 'Theorie der Gesellschaft oder Sozialtechnologie?' p. 286.

370 For a view of such rules as rules determinative of moral argumentation cf. the neo-naturalist Philippa Foot, 'Moral Arguments', pp. 509–10. Hare stresses in regard to neo-naturalism that those arguing morally are not strictly bound to these rules. They can use and justify other rules (on this cf. above pp. 71–2). There is a certain correspondence between this view of Hare's and Habermas's demand for discursive testing of the moral language-system.

371 Habermas, 'Wahrheitstheorien', p. 253.

372 Ibid., 253.

At this last stage we come upon the practical foundation of the basic norms of theoretical discourse.

In an analogous way, entrance into practical discourse occurs through problematization of, for example, orders and prohibitions. The second step consists of the submission of at least one argument. In the third step the adequacy of the language-system becomes the subject-matter of the discourse. The last step consists of 'reflecting on how our structures of needs depend on the level of our knowledge and know-how. We come to an agreement on the interpretations of our needs in the light of available information concerning the scope of what is possible and what is attainable.'[373] The fourth step is the meeting-place of practical and theoretical discourse.

In both forms of discourse, the consensus-achieving strength of an argument rests on the ability to move in an uninhibited way from one level to another and back again until a consensus is reached. The formal characteristics of discourse must therefore be such as to secure freedom of movement between the levels of discourse.

6. THE IDEAL SPEECH SITUATION

The formal characteristics which satisfy these conditions are the characteristics of the ideal speech situation.[374] Habermas calls a speech situation ideal when 'communication in it is hampered neither by external contingent factors, nor by constraints which are internal to the structure of communication itself'.[375] Communication remains free from constraints 'where there is a symmetrical distribution of opportunities among all the participants in the discourse to choose and execute speech acts.'[376] From this general requirement of symmetry, Habermas derives four demands corresponding to the four different classes of speech-acts distinguished by him.

(1) All potential participants in a discourse must have an equal

[373] Ibid., 254.
[374] Ibid., 255 ff.
[375] Ibid., 255.
[376] Ibid., 255.

opportunity of contributing communicative speech-acts,[377] so that they may at any time initiate discourses and carry them on through dialogue and a process of question and answer.

(2) All participants in discourses must have an equal opportunity to put forward interpretations, assertions, recommendations, explanations, and justifications and to problematize, justify, or refute their respective claims to validity in such a way that no opinion can remain permanently free from thematization and criticism.[378]

These two requirements relate entirely to discourse. The next two requirements are concerned rather with the way in which discourse is always embedded in a context of actions.

(3) Only those speakers are admitted to discourse who, as acting subjects have equal opportunities to use representative speech-acts, that is to express their attitudes, feelings, and intentions . . .

(4) Only those speakers are admitted to discourse who, as acting subjects, have equal opportunities to use regulative speech acts, that is to issue orders, objections, permissions, and prohibitions or promises and acceptances of promises, or to call people to account or to accept account rendered and so on.[379]

The last two requirements are said to make explicit the fact that the realization of the ideal speech situation presupposes both the realization of openness in everyday life as well as the achievement of freedom of action.

It is questionable whether it makes sense to formulate these conditions so stringently. It is undoubtedly correct that the hypocrisies and constraints of everyday life can have an adverse effect on discourse. But why should it not be possible to be further advanced in the realm of discourse than in that of everyday dealing? It is, for example, entirely conceivable for certain norms to be justified as sound norms in discourse even though they contradict those which are binding in the context of action. Furthermore, it is entirely possible that discourse could

[377] The communicative speech acts cited in the first demand have not been mentioned until now. They are not bound up with a special claim to validity, but rather serve to express 'the pragmatic sense of speech generally'. Verbs such as 'to say', 'to contradict', and 'to quote' belong to them. (id., 'Vorbereitende Bemerkungen zu einer Theorie der kommunikativen Kompetenz', p. 111).

[378] Ibid., 255.

[379] Ibid., 256.

bring into being new modes of conduct, for example a certain degree of openness, which as yet remain unusual outwith the realm of discourse. Moreover, if realization of the conditions for the ideal speech situation were indeed wholly dependent on realization of what Habermas calls 'pure communicative action', this would make it impossible to change the actually obtaining conditions through discourse. It therefore makes sense not to tie conditions for the ideal speech situation strictly to ideal conditions for conduct in general.[380] This, moreover, corresponds to what Habermas says in speaking of a 'sufficient realization of the requirements which we impose upon discourse.'[381] Such sufficient realization is said to exist 'when both external constraints and those immanent in speech are neutralized to such a degree that there exists no danger of a pseudo-consensus (resting on deception and self-deception)'.[382] Even a weaker formulation of the concept of the ideal speech situation, along the lines indicated, gives rise to a whole range of objections.

Probably the most frequent objection relates to the fact that the ideal speech situation is unrealizable.[383] Thus Habermas himself observes that it is excluded by the 'spatio-temporal limitations of the communication process as well as the limited psychic capacity of the participants in any discourse'.[384] Noticeably related to this is the objection that it is never possible to establish with certainty whether or not the ideal speech situation has in fact been realized. It is always possible, for example, to be deceived about the existence of constraints.[385] Habermas meets this objection with his theory of the counterfactual character of the ideal speech situation. According to this

[380] Similarly F. W. Stallberg, 'Legitimation und Diskurs—Zur Habermas-Analyse Wolfgang Fachs', *Zeitschrift für Soziologie*, 4 (1975), 98.

[381] Habermas, 'Wahrheitstheorien', p. 257.

[382] A letter from Habermas to the author written 17 Dec. 1974 and quoted with his permission.

[383] Cf. Luhmann, 'Systemtheoretische Argumentationen. Eine Entgegnung auf Jürgen Habermas', in Habermas and Luhmann (edd.), *Theorie der Gesellschaft oder Sozialtechnologie—Was leistet die Systemforschung?* (Frankfurt-on-Main, 1972), p. 336; H. Schnelle, *Sprachphilosophie und Linguistik* (Reinbek, 1973), 41.

[384] Habermas, 'Wahrheitstheorien', p. 257.

[385] Ibid., 257.

theory, to quote Habermas's own formulation, the ideal speech-situation is 'neither an empirical phenomenon nor a pure construct, but rather an inescapable underpinning for discourse reciprocally assumed by the parties'.[386] The anticipation of the achievement of an ideal speech situation

> is a guarantee of its being proper to couple with an actually attained consensus, the claim that it is a reasonable one; at the same time it provides a critical standard for questioning it and testing whether any actual consensus is a sufficient indicator for a well-founded consensus.[387]

> The structure of possible speech is such that in performing a speech act we counter-factually behave as though the ideal speech situation were not a mere fiction but rather a present reality; this is just what is meant by an 'underpinning'. The normative foundation of linguistic communication is therefore two-sided: it exists in anticipation but as an anticipated foundation it is already operative.[388]

> No matter how the intersubjectivity of mutual understanding may be deformed, the design of an ideal speech situation is necessarily implied with the structure of potential speech; for every speech, even that of intentional deception, is oriented towards the idea of truth.[389]

This version of the theory of the ideal speech situation has the advantage of avoiding the reproach of being unrealizable in practice. It is definitely possible to pursue an ideal that can never be realized. However, it has the disadvantage of failing to provide a criterion of decision-making which yields clear, unambiguous results in each case. Yet this weakness is tempered in two ways. First, the rules defining the ideal speech situation provide criteria for the criticism of norms. Second, it should be

[386] Ibid., 258.

[387] Ibid.

[388] id., 'Vorbereitende Bemerkungen zu einer Theorie der kommunikativen Kompetenz', p. 140. Cf. also 'Historischer Materialismus und die Entwicklung normativer Strukturen', in his *Zur Rekonstruktion des Historischen Materialismus* (Frankfurt-on-Main, 1976), 11. [*Translator's note:* This essay also appears in *Communication and the Evolution of Society*, trans. T. A. MacCarthy (Boston, 1979.] Here Habermas remarks concerning communication theory that it is able to locate in the four mentioned claims to validity 'a gentle but obstinate, a never silent although seldom redeemed claim to reason.' id., *Communication and the Evolution of Society*, p. 97.

[389] id., 'Towards a Theory of Communicative Competence' in *Recent Sociology*, ed. H. P. Dreitzel, vol. ii (London, 1970), 144.

remembered that an approximate realization of the ideal speech situation is possible. In this sense Habermas draws attention to the fact that unequal distributions of opportunities to use speech acts can be neutralized by institutional measures.[390]

According to Habermas, the basic norms of rational speech defined in terms of the ideal speech situation are not only presupposed in discourses they also underlie the claims to validity made in the ordinary transactions of everyday life. Habermas therefore maintains that anyone and everyone involved in any form of communication whatsoever already presupposes the ideal speech situation, however much he or she may in fact deviate from its postulates.[391] This can only be avoided by withdrawing from all forms of communication. But, according to Habermas, an individual who did so would lose his or her identity.[392]

If these observations are correct, something might have been gained towards solving the problem of how to substantiate the basic norms of rational speech. K.-O. Apel calls a justification of the type presented by Habermas 'transcendental-pragmatic'.[393] It is said to be transcendental inasmuch as the rules are justified by showing that their validity is a condition of the possibility of linguistic communication. It is pragmatic because these rules are rules of speech which do not deal exclusively with syntax or semantics, but go beyond this to regulate the relationship of the speaker to his or her own utterances.[394] Habermas, who still

[390] Habermas, 'Wahrheitstheorien', p. 257.

[391] id., *Legitimation Crisis*, p. 159 n. 16: 'The socio-cultural form of life of communicatively socialized individuals produces the "transcendental illusion" of pure communicative action in *every* interaction context and, at the same time, it structurally refers *every* interaction context to the possibility of an ideal speech situation in which the validity claims accepted in action can be tested discursively.' Cf. also id., 'Zwei Bemerkungen zum praktischen Diskurs' in his *Zur Rekonstruktion des Historischen Materialismus* (Frankfurt-on-Main), p. 339: 'The idea of rational speech, if I may express myself in this way, is not first set out in the general structures of discourse and justification, but rather in the basic structures of linguistic activity.' For a very similar view cf. Apel, *Towards a Transformation of Philosophy*, p. 259.

[392] id., *Legitimation Crisis*, p. 159 n. 16; similarly Apel, *Towards a Transformation of Philosophy*, p. 269.

[393] Apel, *Towards a Transformation of Philosophy*, pp. 256 ff.

[394] On the distinction between syntax, semantics, and pragmatics cf. C. W. Morris, 'Foundations of the Theory of Signs', pp. 1 ff.

spoke of the 'transcendental character of ordinary language'[395] in 1973, has since expressed doubts about using Kantian terminology. He suggests instead the expression 'universal-pragmatic'.[396] The problem of the distinguishing characteristic of the justification chosen by Habermas will be examined later in the discussion of possible ways of justifying rules of discourse. Here it will first be asked whether, and to what extent, the arguments put forward by Habermas can be viewed as tenable, irrespective of how they are to be classified.

7. CRITICAL DISCUSSION OF HABERMAS'S THEORY

This question leads to a general critical discussion of Habermas's theory. The present discussion will focus primarily on its tenability and usefulness as a theory of practical discourse.[397]

7.1 One of the most prominent opponents of discourse theory is Niklas Luhmann. Luhmann advocates the thesis that attempts such as those of Habermas are doomed to failure 'under the prevailing conditions of a world which grows ever richer in possibilities'.[398] The present-day problem is no longer that of the substantive correctness of decisions or norms but is rather said to be that of coping with complexity. Hence the problem of justice is to be severed from its old connection with truth and justifiability and reformulated as a question concerning the 'adequate complexity of the legal system'.[399]

To this very general objection to the relevance of traditional questions concerning truth, justifiability, and justice in modern societies, is added the claim that discussions can be more adequately understood through the approach of system theory

[395] Habermas, *Legitimation Crisis*, p. 110.

[396] id., 'What is Universal Pragmatics?', pp. 21 ff.

[397] As such it is most likely to be acceptable. Thus Habermas himself observes that 'a consensus theory of correctness does not (encounter) the same objections as a consensus theory of truth' ('Wahrheitstheorien', p. 250).

[398] Luhmann, 'Gerechtigkeit in den Rechtssystemen der modernen Gesellschaft', p. 144 n. 33.

[399] Ibid., 142. For a critique of Luhmann's theory of justice cf. R. Dreier, 'Zu Luhmanns systemtheoretischer Neuformulierung des Gerechtigkeitsproblems', *Rechtstheorie*, 5 (1974), 189 ff.

than through that of a theory of speech. A system-theoretical approach does not, it is said, stop with the postulation of ideal conditions. It can work out the limitations of the performance of any discursive system whatever, and can demonstrate the possibilities of improved performance through alternative organizations of discourses.[400]

A general discussion of Luhmann's system theory would go beyond the subject-matter of this investigation. Hence only some arguments will be brought to bear here which offer a plausible alternative to Luhmann's objections to the possibility and relevance of discourse theory, at least to the extent of not condemning outright from the start the project of a theory of rational practical discourse. A more thoroughgoing debate with Luhmann would have had to be conducted at the level of a comprehensive comparison of theories rather than that of an exchange of individual arguments. This would immediately require the development of the theory of rational discourse beyond the stage of first conceptions. The present aim is to contribute to such a development, not least through the expansion of the theory of rational practical discourse into the realm of legal reasoning. Debate with Luhmann therefore really occurs only indirectly in this work. It occurs indirectly inasmuch as the arguments brought forward here in favour of discourse theory can be seen as arguments against system theory, to the extent that discourse theory is incompatible with system theory.

The question of the degree to which discourse theory is incompatible with system theory leads back to Luhmann's two objections cited above.

Suppose that the system-theoretical approach is well adapted to working out the performances and limitations of any discourse system whatever, and to demonstrating the possibilities for improving performances through alternative organizations of discourses. This would only count as a point against discourse theory if it were the case that discourse theory was in fact obliged to remain stuck at the postulation of ideal conditions. But this is not the case. It is one of the tasks of discourse theory to investigate how, even under limiting conditions, rational argument can and does proceed, and how

[400] Luhmann, 'Systemtheoretische Argumentationen', pp.328 ff.

the possibility of rational argument can be improved in the presence of limiting conditions. To this end there is a need to know the working capacity of different discursive systems and whether it is possible to expand their capacity. To the extent that system theory can assist in finding this out, it is not only useful but indispensable for discourse theory.

The decisive question is therefore whether the approach of discourse theory as such makes sense—that is, whether the traditional questions concerning truth, justifiability, and justice have today lost their relevance, and whether the problem of justice should accordingly be removed from its old connection with truth and justifiability and rather regarded as the question of whether or not the legal system has adequate complexity. It can be pointed out immediately that it is quite conceivable that the formula of 'adequate complexity' contains a pointer to a necessary condition of justice in decision-making.[401] It is, however, to be doubted whether it is indeed the case 'today' that norms no longer carry any implicit claim to correctness or justifiability. Thus Dreier,[402] referring to Habermas, points out that the abandonment of this implicit claim would presuppose the development of a 'another mode of socialization' which had been disconnected from norms in need of justification.[403] It is already open to doubt whether such a 'mode of socialization' is really possible.[404] In any case a glance at the practice of debates about legal policy or courtroom deliberations or jurists' controversies or indeed reasons in everyday life shows that there is something to be said for the view that this 'mode' has not taken

[401] Cf. Dreier, 'Zu Luhmanns systemtheoretischer Neuformulierung', p. 200.

[402] Ibid., 199.

[403] Habermas, *Legitimation Crisis*, p. 94.

[404] It might be said against this possibility that as long as people can question, doubt, set up claims, and argue, they are in a position to criticize and likewise to justify the norms according to which they live. If one accepts the premiss—of course not unproblematic—that when people have a capacity, they also have an interest in making use of this capacity, the result is that a mode of socialization, uncoupled from norms in need of justification, may spread widely but cannot ultimately and generally assert itself. This argument is only brought in as an aside because of the weakness of the thesis concerning an interest in rational justification. It will suffice to observe here that there in fact exists something like a practice of rational deliberation.

effect, at least not yet. The system-theoretical objection does then perhaps reveal the limits to discourse theory. But it cannot be accepted as an argument against the possibility of and need for such a theory.

7.2 The core of the 'universal-pragmatic' justification of the basic norms of rational speech is formed by the thesis that every speaker attaches to his or her utterances implicit claims to intelligibility, veracity, correctness, and truth. Whoever utters a judgment of value or obligation[405] implicitly makes a claim to correctness, that is, that the judgment uttered is rationally justifiable.

This thesis goes beyond merely maintaining that practical discourse presupposes the possibility that practical decisions are justifiable, for this would not entail that a claim to justifiability is implicitly raised with *every* utterance of a judgment of value or obligation. One might be of the opinion that although any discussion concerning the correctness of particular utterances does indeed raise this very claim, nevertheless moral positions can be expressed without making any such claim. On this view the basic norms of rational speech would only be significant for those who had *decided* to participate in the language game of practical reasoning. Habermas's 'universal-pragmatic' justification would collapse. To back up this view, it could be pointed out that many people make assertions without being ready to justify them with reasons. In many cases they are not even in a position so to do.

This cannot, however, be reckoned a very telling objection. The fact that someone is unable or unwilling to substantiate a claim says nothing as to the existence of the claim. The claims implicated in speech acts are not dependent on the wishes of the speaker but rather on the rules underlying the speech acts. Suppose that someone makes a normative assertion and in response to the question 'Why?' either refuses to give any answer and gives no reasons for this refusal or responds by saying that there are no reasons for the assertion in question. In such a situation one might react with responses such as 'But you should give reasons for this' or 'If there is no reason for saying that A has

[405] On these concepts cf. above, p. 60.

a duty to help B, you ought not to say it'. The deontological expressions 'should' and 'ought' occurring in these sentences are a sign that the speaker is referring to a rule which requires supporting grounds.[406] Normally the addressee of such remonstrances will accept them as such and respond by giving reasons or otherwise letting it be known why he or she is not offering any. These reasons, like the reasons for the original assertion, are open to discussion. Such reasons are frequently accepted.

The above discussion makes it clear that although speakers do indeed presuppose a rule which requires justification, yet this rule does not demand that everyone must give reasons for every statement made, at any time, to anyone. It is enough that he or she gives reasons for being unable to unwilling to give reasons in the given situation, or refers one to the competency of others to give reasons. This rule does not require an individual justification on the part of the speaker for every assertion, but it does ordain that all utterances are open to discussion. The reasons for not giving any reasons are also open to discussion. The legitimacy of a reference to the competence of others to provide justificatory reasons can be tested. Thus it may be asked whether the authority invoked by the speaker really does guarantee the correctness of his or her thesis. It may, though, be possible and often necessary to go into the substantive correctness of the claim here. In order to ensure discussability of the authority-invoking argument, the speaker has to be restricted to appealing only to certain specific authorities. It is not permissible for him or her, without giving any reasons, simply to be of the opinion that someone at some time will be in a position to give reasons for his or her statement.

It is of course possible to express sentences related to practical questions, without in this sense having to give reasons. In such cases, however, one is not presented with a judgment of value or obligation but rather, for example, an announcement concern-

[406] Cf. Hart, *The Concept of Law*, p. 56: 'What is necessary [for the existence of a rule] is that there should be a critical reflective attitude to certain patterns of behaviour as a common standard, and that this should display itself in criticism (including self-criticism), demands for conformity, and in acknowledgements that such criticism and demands are justified, all of which find their characteristic expression in the normative terminology of "ought", "must", and "should", "right" and wrong".'

ing a feeling, an attitude, or a desire. But in regarding something as a judgment of value or obligation one must always conceive it as being subject to an implicit claim to justifiability.

This corresponds to what Patzig writes:

It is only by reference to this essential claim to justifiability, which is always implicit in moral value judgments by virtue of their meaning, that one can grasp such statements in their sense as judgments. If one does not wish to miss the meaning of such judgments one must not regard them as merely spontaneous utterances of an emotional reaction, but must rather take them as genuine assertions, which, because they are genuine assertions, can be false (and can of course also be true).[407]

The following requirement can now be formulated as a rule underlying the speech act of assertion:

Every speaker must give reasons for what he or she asserts when asked to do so, unless he or she can cite reasons which justify a refusal to provide a justification.[408]

This rule will be called the '*general justification rule*'.

It is possible to have a succession of utterances containing no assertions. Nevertheless, a long continuous communication without any assertions at all is only possible in artificial conditions, for example by arrangement. Such an arrangement could hardly be sustained for life. In any case even such an agreement would presuppose the justification rule. It is not

[407] Patzig, 'Relativismus und Objektivität moralischer Normen', in his *Ethik ohne Metaphysik* (Göttingen, 1971), 75.

[408] On a rule of this kind cf. Wunderlich, 'Zur Konventionalität von Sprechhandlungen', p. 21; Searle, *Speech Acts*, pp.65–6; Schnelle, *Sprachphilosophie und Linguistik*, pp. 42–3. The status of such a rule is a matter of dispute. One might be of the view that it is constitutive of the speech act of assertion. (On the concept of constitutive rules cf. Searle, *Speech Acts*, pp. 33 ff.) In contrast to this, Schnelle is of the view that the concept of asserting, unlike that of promising, is not bound up with such a duty. A rule like the justification rule cited should therefore only be regarded as a general postulate of conversation (*Sprachphilosophie und Linguistik*, pp. 42–3). On the concept of a postulate of conversation cf. H. P. Grice, *Logic and Conversation* (typescript, 1968), 32 ff. There is quite a lot to be said in favour of the view that if one links the claim to truth or correctness with the concept of asserting, one must also view the justification rule as constitutive of the assertion. Of interest here, not as an argument (nor as some kind of authority), is the definition of assertion which Kant gave: to '*assert* anything, that is, declare it to be a judgment necessarily valid for everyone . . .' (*Critique of Pure Reason*, trans. N. K. Smith (London, 1933), p. 646).

possible to agree not to keep to a rule unless some such rule exists. Thus anyone who participates in any communication becomes subject to the justification rule.

7.3 The general justification rule stands in close relation to the conditions of the ideal speech situation. Whoever gives justifying grounds for something at least pretends to accept the other as a speaking partner with equal rights, at least with respect to what concerns the justificatory process, and neither to practise coercion him or herself nor to rely on coercive means practised by others. Furthermore, he or she claims to be able to vindicate his or her assertion to anyone at all. Language games which are not at least alleged to satisfy these requirements cannot be viewed as justificatory arguments. Thus utterances such as 'If you don't believe it, you will lose your job' or 'Mr. F. would easily be able to disprove it, but you should accept it for reason G', are hardly to be designated justificatory arguments.

The demands for equal rights, universality, and lack of coercion can be formulated as three rules. These rules correspond to the conditions drawn up by Habermas for the ideal speech situation in the attenuated version accepted above.[409] The first rule concerns entry into discourse. It goes as follows:

(1) Everyone who can speak may take part in discourse.[410]

The second rule governs freedom of discussion. It can be subdivided into three requirements:

(2) (a) Everyone may problematize any assertion.
(b) Everyone may introduce any assertion into the discourse.
(c) Everyone may express his or her attitudes, wishes, and needs.

[409] Cf. above, pp. 120–1.

[410] Popper presents a further justification of such a rule which is different from the above and interesting: 'The fact that the rationalist attitude considers the argument rather than the person arguing is of far-reaching importance. It leads to the view that we must recognize everybody with whom we communicate as a potential source of argument and of reasonable information; it thus establishes what may be described as the "rational unity of mankind"' (*The Open Society and its Enemies*, ii. 225).

(c) is of significance particularly in practical discourse. It articulates the requirement of openness. Finally, the third rule has the task of shielding discourses from every kind of coercion. It goes as follows:

(3) No speaker may be prevented from exercising the rights laid down in (1) and (2) by any kind of coercion internal or external to the discourse.

It may be questioned whether (3) is a rule of discourse at all. It could also be regarded as a condition for the realization of (1) and (2). For the moment, however, it is sufficient simply to note that (3) has a special status.

(1)–(3) define the most important conditions for the rationality of discourses. They are therefore to be called '*rationality rules*'.

It might be thought that little has been gained by drawing up these rules. It has already been mentioned above that they cannot be fully realized. Nevertheless this objection was not seen as proving them to be pointless.[411] They (1) define an ideal which can be approximately achieved, (2) provide an instrument for criticizing unjustifiable limitations on the rights and opportunities of discourse partners, (3) provide thereby at least a hypothetical and negative criterion of correctness or truth, and (4) offer an interpretation of the claim to correctness or truth.[412]

7.4 Both the ideal character of the rationality rules and the possibility of making mistakes about the degree to which it is being observed do indeed show that no actually achieved consensus gives any guarantee of the validity of the outcomes of

[411] On the objection that rules like those given above cannot actually be met, and on the function of such rules, cf. the apposite remarks of Kant: 'Nothing, indeed, can be more injurious, or more unworthy of a philosopher, than the vulgar appeal to so-called adverse experience. Such experience would never have existed at all, if at the proper time those institutions had been established in accordance with ideas . . .'. 'This perfect state may never, indeed, come into being; none the less this does not affect the rightfulness of the idea, which, in order to bring the legal organisation of mankind ever nearer to its greatest possible perfection, advances this maximum as an archetype' (*Critique of Pure Reason*, pp. 311–12).

[412] For a fuller discussion on the use of these rules cf. below, pp. 193–4.

the discourse.[413] The rules proposed do not provide a procedure whereby a lawyer, for example, can resolve a certain case in a certain situation. It might be concluded from this that, although Habermas's theory describes a fine ideal, it offers little for the conduct either of everyday moral argument or of the normative sciences such as jurisprudence.[414]

This must, however, be disputed. On the one hand further rules of practical argument can be derived from Habermas's theory and on the other hand this theory is not only in need of development but is also capable of it.

It must first be observed that the rationality rules already exclude certain outcomes. It is not compatible with them for an individual, even one who consents, to accept a lasting status without rights—that is, the status of a slave. Everyone must have the right to demand the discursive testing of every norm at any time. A norm which excludes this is inadmissible. It is *discursively impossible*. It is a not insignificant accomplishment of discourse theory that it can provide justifying reasons for the inadmissibility of such norms.

The number of discursively impossible norms is certainly small. Yet Habermas's theory also gives several pointers for the realm of the discursively possible.

First one must mention Habermas's reference (in reliance on Toulmin) to forms of argument. Habermas, however, refers to two argument forms only, the justification of a judgment of value or obligation by means of a rule and the justification of a rule by reference to its direct and indirect consequences for the satisfaction of needs.

As the discussions of Stevenson's and Baier's theories showed, there are considerably more forms to be considered. These will be enumerated and systematized in due course. It must certainly be admitted that an analysis of argument forms still cannot offer any guidance on how to argue substantively. But this analysis is necessary for the establishment of rules which do influence the substance of reasoning.

[413] Cf. Posner, 'Diskurs als Mittel der Aufklärung. Zur Theorie der rationalen Kommunikation bei Habermas und Albert', in *Linguistik und Sprachphilosophie*, ed. M. Gerhard (Munich, 1974), 295.

[414] Thus H. Rüssmann, 'Die Begründung von Werturteilen', *Juristische Schulung*, 15 (1975), 355.

Habermas's principle of generalizability constitutes such a rule. According to this a norm is capable of being generalized if its direct and indirect consequences for the satisfaction of *everyone's* needs are acceptable to *everyone*.[415] For the time being, this rule can be formulated as follows:

The consequences of a norm for the satisfaction of everyone's needs must be acceptable to everyone.

Discourse is thereby bound to the currently prevailing interpretations of the legitimacy of needs. Which needs are actually regarded as generalizable is a point which depends on the individually and socially formed moral convictions of the speaker. Habermas's doctrine of the criticism of justificatory language comes in here. The basic moral convictions evolved in the course of the development of an individual, of a society, and also in the course of the development of humankind as a species have entered into the language of morals. They can be formulated as rules which underlie the use of evaluative expressions such as 'good' or 'ought', 'immoral' or 'greed'. These rules govern the interpretation of one's own and others' needs as being generalizable or not. The central question for discourses is therefore: which interpretation is correct?

This must first be answered by saying that the question cannot be elucidated in a theory of practical discourse but only from within discourse itself. Formulas such as: 'Objectively more valuable needs are to take preference over objectively less valuable needs' or 'Satisfying more fundamental needs should take precedence over satisfying less fundamental needs' either presuppose an untenable intuitionist or naturalist meta-ethical theory—as shown above[416]—or turn out to be empty formulas. Of course, mere allusion to clarification in discourse is not enough either. A theory of practical discourse must provide rules and forms according to which the correctness of interpretations of needs and hence the correctness of the moral rules underlying them, can be tested.

Habermas only hints at such a way of proceeding in the framework of his theory of discourse. Here he makes a connection with the 'critical genesis' procedure as worked out

415 Cf. above, pp. 111 ff. 416 Cf. above, pp. 34 ff.

by himself in carrying forward[417] the thoughts of Hegel, Marx, and Freud from epistemological points of view and which has been elaborated in its technicalities by Lorenzen and Schwemmer.[418] 'Critical genesis' is the process whereby the emergence of moral rules in the life history of individuals and of the species is brought to final fruition by the participants in discourse.[419] This makes it possible to determine to what extent, at different developmental stages, the conditions of the ideal speech situation were realized. It likewise makes possible criticism of moral rules generated by this developmental process and exerting influence on our thinking and reasoning. Habermas formulates this as follows:

How would the members of a social system, at a given stage in the development of productive forces, have collectively and bindingly interpreted their needs (and which norms would they have accepted as justified) if they could and would have decided on organization of social intercourse through discoursive will-formation, with adequate knowledge of the limiting conditions and functional imperatives of their society?[420]

The idea of 'critical genesis' will not be examined in more detail until the discussion of Lorenzen's and Schwemmer's views. Here let it simply be taken as established that if such a procedure should prove meaningful a further rule of discourse would have been discovered, which for the time being can be formulated as follows:

The interpretation of needs as ones which have to be generally accepted must be able to stand up to examination in terms of 'critical genesis'.

[417] Habermas, *Erkenntnis und Interesse*, pp. 14 ff., 36 ff., 262 ff.

[418] P. Lorenzen and O. Schwemmer, *Konstruktive Logik, Ethik und Wissenschaftstheorie* (Mannheim, Vienna, and Zurich, 1973), 209 ff. For explicit references by the Erlangen School to Hegel and Marx cf. Lorenzen, *Normative Logic and Ethic* (Mannheim and Zurich, 1969), 84 ff., and Schwemmer, *Philosophie der Praxis* (Frankfurt-on-Main, 1971), 14.

[419] It might therefore make more sense to speak of a 'critical testing of genesis' rather than of 'critical genesis'.

[420] Habermas, *Legitimation Crisis*, p. 113; cf. also his 'Einige Bemerkungen zum Problem der Begründung von Werturteilen', in *Philosophie und Wissenschaft*, ed. L. Landgrebe, Ninth German Philosophy Congress (Meisenheim am Glan, 1972), p. 99 and 'Theorie der Gesellschaft oder Sozialtechnologie?', p. 164.

This rule, and also Habermas's principle of generalizability, differ from the previously mentioned argument forms in that they include criteria for the substantive testing and justifying of norms. They are therefore to be called: '*justification rules*'.

7.5 Even a discourse accomplished according to the rules worked out so far, and in the forms analysed to date, brings no guarantee for the correctness of the result. This is only not the case with respect to certain discursively necessary norms. However, the majority of norms are merely *discursively possible.* This means that both they and their negations are compatible with the rules of discourse. This is a consequence of the fact that the rules of discourse do not prescribe which normative conceptions are to form the starting-point for participants in a discourse and how these conceptions are to be modified. That this is left up to the participants in a discourse is not, however, a shortcoming but rather one of the decisive advantages of a theory of discourse. It is through this that the weakness of decision-theory approaches is avoided. These approaches must presuppose certain needs, orders of preferences, or conceptions of value in order to arrive at a specific result.[421] This is not to say that approaches in terms of decision theory are incompatible with those of discourse theory. There are several indications that they can be made viable within the framework of a theory of discourse.

If a norm is merely discursively possible, then even with a consensus there can be no talk of its final justification. There can be many reasons for rejecting a norm which has been generally accepted to date. The interpretation of needs may change. Empirical knowledge acted upon hitherto may be shown to be inadequate. Certain direct or indirect consequences may not have been considered. Attention is only drawn later to conflicts

[421] On this cf. O. Höffe, 'Rationalität, Dezision oder praktische Vernunft. Zur Diskussion des Entscheidungsbegriffs in der Bundesrepublik', *Philosophisches Jahrbuch*, 80 (1973), 348; B. Schlink, 'Inwieweit sind juristische Entscheidungen mit entscheidungstheoretischen Modellen theoretisch zu erfassen und praktisch zu bewältigen?' *Jahrbuch für Rechtssoziologie und Rechtstheorie*, 2 (1972), 332: 'A critique of the informational and evaluative base drops out of the efforts of decision theory to arrive at a normative principle of decision making'. On the applicability of decision theories to legal decision making processes cf. also W. Kilian, *Juristische Entscheidung und elektronische Datenverarbeitung* (Frankfurt-on-Main, 1974), 149 ff.

of norms. The conditions of the ideal speech situation may subsequently prove to have been inadequately realized. Discursively possible norms are therefore to be regarded as justified only for the present.[422] They are permanently falsifiable.[423]

Consideration might be given to supplementing discourse theory through the introduction of a principle of falsification. This, however, is not necessary. The rationality rules already open up the possibility of problematizing any norm again, at any time, and if need be showing it to be unsubstantiated. To be sure, they do not stipulate for the duty[424] but only for the right to seek refutation.

7.6 This makes it possible to counter a further objection to the practicality of Habermas's theory. It is sometimes pointed out that in many actually occurring practical deliberations, it is not possible to establish a consensus, even though all the participants are striving to reach a correct outcome. This is particularly so when decisions have to be made under pressure of time, as with a bench of judges for example.

Yet, even with respect to situations such as this, consensus theory makes a considerable contribution. It makes explicit the implicit claim under which even such deliberations take place. Here too there is a search for the right or just outcome. Moreover, it makes it clear that such discussions are also determined by the basic norms of rational speech. The rules of rational argument thus constitute an instrument for the critique of such deliberations, and the forms of argument sketched out

[422] Cf. Posner, 'Diskurs als Mittel der Aufklärung', pp. 295 ff.

[423] On the concepts 'falsification' and 'falsifiability' in the empirical sciences cf. Popper, *The Logic of Scientific Discovery*, pp. 78 ff. For an application of Popper's basic ideas to practical philosophy cf. H. Albert, *Traktat über kritische Vernunft*, 2nd edn. (Tübingen, 1968), 73 ff. The possibility that a false consensus can disguise a mistake (about the fulfilment of the conditions for the ideal speech situation) leads Habermas himself to treat the idea of fallibility as necessary. 'From discourse theory follows . . . the fallibility maxim, which says that we can at any time attempt to establish retrospectively whether an alleged discourse actually took place under distorting restrictions' Habermas, letter to the author (17 Dec. 1974)).

[424] On this cf. Albert (*Traktat über kritische Vernunft*, p. 43) who sets up the requirement: 'Always look for relevant inconsistencies in order to expose current convictions to the risk of destruction, so that they have the opportunity of proving themselves.'

merely in a preliminary way by Habermas provide a means of analysing the justificatory reasons expounded there. Furthermore, it is possible to provide discursive justification for rules which apply where no agreement is reached—for example, rules of voting and principles of tolerance. Finally, it is not unthinkable that there should be further discussion of a decision made under pressure of time. This occurs for example in the discussion of judicial decisions amongst academic lawyers.

7.7 In the light of these findings one is prompted to ask whether the consensus theory can still be held as a theory of truth. It contains no certain criteria of truth and falsity. Even an actually existing consensus is no criterion of truth. It may have been realized under deficient conditions. However, an explanation of the concept of truth does not require the elaboration of a method of establishing the truth which leads to definite outcomes. 'Discourse theory's conception of truth simply takes those rules of rational talk (intuitively mastered but still capable of reconstruction) as conditions of adequacy which every possible test for truth must satisfy.'[425] By elaborating the basic rules of procedures for testing the truth or correctness of statements, Habermas's consensus theory has at least brought to light several aspects of the concept of truth. Whether this is a sufficient analysis of this concept and how the approach of the consensus theory relates to other approaches are matters to be settled in a separate investigation.

To sum up, it can be said that despite a number of critical points Habermas's theory contains many important findings for a theory of rational argumentation. The points to be retained have already been elaborated and partially reformulated and furnished with new justifying grounds in the course of discussing the theory. What has to be stressed once again here are the three rationality rules built on to the general justification rule and the two justification rules. They form the basic rules for a general theory of rational practical discourse.

[425] Habermas, letter to the author (17 Dec. 1974).

III. The Theory of Practical Deliberation of the Erlangen School

The theory of practical deliberation of the Erlangen School makes a further significant contribution to a theory of practical discourse. This theory as expounded by Lorenzen, and particularly in Schwemmer's more developed version of it, is an attempt to apply the constructive method to the realm of ethics.[426]

1. THE PROGRAMME OF THE CONSTRUCTIVE METHOD

The constructive method in its original character was a position in the debate on the foundations of mathematics. It was known by the name of 'intuitionism'. In 1907 Brouwer had questioned the *tertium non datur*, the assumption that every mathematical statement must be either true or false.[427] Brouwer's starting-point was the difficulties encountered with respect to statements concerning infinite realms. Take a mathematical statement like Goldbach's suggestion that every even number is the sum of two prime numbers. This statement can be tested with any number of numbers but will still not have been proven, for there will always be more numbers which have not been the subject of testing. Traditional logic claims here that, although one may not know whether this statement is true or false, one does know that it is *either* true or false. According to constructivism it is precisely this which is an unfounded assumption, a jump in

[426] The present investigation will discuss in particular the works of Lorenzen and Schwemmer. On the theories of other authors to be included among the members of the Erlangen School cf. F. Kambartel (ed.) *Praktische Philosophie und konstruktive Wissenschaftstheorie* (Frankfurt-on-Main, 1974), and J. Mittelstraß (ed.), *Methodologische Probleme einer normativ-kritischen Gesellschaftstheorie* (Frankfurt-on-Main, 1975).

[427] L. E. J. Brouwer, *Over de Groundslagen der Wiskunde* (Amsterdam and Leipzig, 1907) (trans.: A. Heyting (ed.), *Collected Works*, vol. i (Amsterdam and New York, 1975), pp. 11–101).

thought.[428] Such jumps, however, are to be avoided at all costs in the realm of science. Every step should follow on from another according to fixed rules. This presupposes that 'there are rules for making decisions as to the right to assert (or to dispute) a statement'.[429]

An example of such rules are the rules of dialogue proposed by Lorenzen for the purposes of constructing logic. These rules of dialogue lay down how a compound statement can be attacked and defended. The use in dialogue of a sentence governed by a universal quantifier, for example, is regulated by a rule such that anyone that is any proponent asserting $(x)\ Fx$ (for example, in a conversation about ravens: 'All are black') must defend against any opponent the proposition Fa ('This raven is black') for every a (for each individual raven) indicated by the opponent.[430] In the diagrams used by Lorenzen this can be represented as shown in Figure A.7:

O Opponent	P Proponent
a?	$(x)\ Fx$ Fa

Fig. A.7

The ban on admitting anything which has not been methodically introduced extends not merely to the procedure of justification but also to the language of justification. This in its turn is to be built up constructively without resort to any assumptions. In particular, it is deemed inadmissible to use ordinary language as a meta-language to speak about the artificial language of logic, as occurs in traditional logic. In order to clarify the constructivist position Lorenzen employs a metaphor in which he compares language with a ship which finds itself on the high seas without ever being able to put into port. Both hermeneutics and analytic philosophy are said to take as their starting-point work on and about this ship, which

[428] W. Kamlah and P. Lorenzen, *Logische Propädeutik oder Vorschule des vernünftigen Redens*, rev. edn. (Mannheim, Vienna, and Zurich, 1967), 195.

[429] Ibid., 196.

[430] Cf. Lorenzen and Schwemmer, *Konstruktive Logik, Ethik und Wissenschaftstheorie*, p. 46.

was built in the past. According to the constructivist conception we should rather 'have the courage to jump into the water and start afresh'.[431] We must 'transpose ourselves into a setting without a ship, that is without language, and must try to comprehend those actions with which we—whilst swimming in the sea of life—might be able to build a raft or even a ship.'

Schwemmer[432] offers a summary of the programme so indicated—that is, for subjecting every word and every step in the justificatory process to methodological rules in the following requirement:

that at no stage in a train of thought which is to serve as an argument, on the one hand for assertions, on the other for demands or norms, may we use a word without satisfying ourselves of its common use. And that every assertion, demand, or norm which we put forward has to be justified step by step so that on each occasion on which—as we understand it—a new mental act (of understanding or cognition) is required to sustain a current line of thought, that act is expressly stipulated in a distinct step. These demands give a *programmatic formulation of the constructive method.*[433]

2. THE PRESUPPOSED PURPOSE OF CONSTRUCTIVIST ETHICS

A first attempt at applying the constructive method in order to advance ethics was published by Lorenzen in 1969.[434] Schwemmer gave a systematic elaboration of this attempt in his *Philosophie der Praxis* (1971). The sections relating to ethics in the

[431] Lorenzen, 'Methodisches Denken', in his *Methodisches Denken* (Frankfurt-on-Main, 1974), 29.

[432] The text sometimes speaks of either Schwemmer or Lorenzen although reference is to the book brought out by them jointly. This is possible because the Forward to *Konstruktive Logik, Ethik und Wissenschaftstheorie* indicates which author wrote which chapter.

[433] Lorenzen and Schwemmer, *Konstruktive Logik, Ethik und Wissenschaftstheorie*, p. 10 (my italics). An almost identical formulation is to be found in Schwemmer, 'Grundlagen einer normativen Ethik', in *Praktische Philosophie und konstruktive Wissenschaftstheorie*, ed. F. Kambartel (Frankfurt-on-Main, 1974), p. 75.

[434] Lorenzen, *Normative Logic and Ethics* (Mannheim and Zurich, 1969), pp. 73 ff.

book *Konstruktive Logik, Ethik und Wissenschaftstheorie* (*Constructive Logic, Ethics, and Theory of Science*) published in 1973 are also by him and will be the main source of what follows here.

The constructive method does not provide a sufficient programme in itself for setting the foundations of ethics. It only stipulates that one give word usage a secure common basis and proceed step by step and methodically. But it does not say which words are to be employed nor which steps are permitted or required.

The question now arises of how constructivist ethics is to start off free of any presuppositions. According to Schwemmer this problem can be solved for the time being by starting off with a presupposition—that is, with a methodically unsupported preconception, after all. Only after constructing ethics on the basis of this preconception will it become possible and necessary to test and if need be to correct the preconception itself.[435] This immediately arouses a suspicion of a circularity in argument. This circularity, however, is said to be avoided in that the construction of ethics signifies practising new ways of behaving which can be used to criticize the preconception from which it was itself developed.[436] The preconception to be taken for granted by ethics concerns the purpose of ethics.[437] The purpose of ethics consists of the elimination of conflict by non-coercive means.[438]Ethics has the task of 'drawing up principles for the elimination of conflict through speech'.[439] Thus the idea of 'purpose-rationality' (*Zweckrationalität*) forms the foundation of constructivist ethics.[440] This means that in the field of ethics the rules for rational argumentation which are to be justified have authority only over those who accept the purpose of ethics. This

[435] Lorenzen and Schwemmer, *Konstruktive Logik, Ethik und Wissenschaftstheorie*, pp. 16 ff.

[436] Ibid., 19–20.

[437] Schwemmer, *Philosophie der Praxis*, p. 20; and his 'Grundlagen einer normativen Ethik', p. 76.

[438] Schwemmer, *Philosophie der Praxis*, p. 106 and 'Grundlagen einer normativen Ethik', p. 77.

[439] Lorenzen and Schwemmer, *Konstruktive Logik, Ethik und Wissenschaftstheorie*, p. 109.

[440] Cf. ibid., 107, 115, 116. The idea of purpose-rationality seems to underlie the whole constructive philosophy. The introduction of any part of language is to be made intelligible by citing purposes (ibid., 21).

aim cannot be justified within ethics itself. There is therefore an act of will underlying the acceptance of the rules of discourse.

> The decision in favour of talk and against force . . . may be shown to be a possibility . . . but the actual realization of this possibility is no longer a matter of 'purpose-rational' [*zweckrationaler*] requirements but rather of practising speaking and generalizing itself—and to this extent it is not 'enforceable'.[441]

Persuading someone to follow moral principles 'can only be attempted by trying to follow these principles on a reciprocal basis'.[442]

This constitutes a considerable difference between Habermas and Schwemmer.[443] This difference could be characterized by saying that according to Schwemmer the rules of discourse taken altogether constitute the apodosis of a hypothetical imperative while according to Habermas they are categorically demanded of all who speak and think—that is, who can act as rational beings. Subject to several modifications, Habermas's thesis was accepted above. Schwemmer's idea, however, need not be rejected because of this. Whoever takes up a practical discourse as defined by Habermas's rules, is pursuing the goal of non-coercive elimination of conflict. To this extent, Habermas's theory includes that of Schwemmer.

3. THE PRINCIPLES OF CONSTRUCTIVIST ETHICS

For deliberations to achieve their purpose of eliminating conflict they should be governed by two principles: the principle of rationality and the principle of morality.

3.1 The principle of rationality, which Schwemmer also calls 'the principle of deliberation',[444] is the stipulation that one ought to realize three levels of rational communality.[445]

[441] Schwemmer, 'Appell und Argumentation. Aufgaben und Grenzen einer praktischen Philosophie', in *Praktische Philosophie*, pp. 199 ff.

[442] Lorenzen and Schwemmer, *Konstruktive Logik, Ethik und Wissenschaftstheorie*, p. 121.

[443] Habermas, *Legitimation Crisis*, pp. 109–10.

[444] Schwemmer, 'Grundlagen einer normativen Ethik', p. 82.

[445] Lorenzen and Schwemmer, *Konstruktive Logik, Ethik und Wissenschaftstheorie*, pp. 115–16.

At the *first level* both the speaker and the addressee must establish a common lexicon of usage.[446] This requirement can be readily accepted. The only question is how it is to be satisfied. According to the constructivist programme this requires the creation of a constructively built up language, an 'ortho-language'. 'The first task of practical philosophy is the reconstruction of a minimum of vocabulary so that we can argue for or against the acceptance of norms.'[447] Construction of such a language is said to occur through the practice of reciprocal interaction.[448]

Colloquial speech can be employed here in a subsidiary capacity, to the extent that it is controlled by reciprocal interaction (empragmatic language).[449] This makes it possible to describe situations of linguistic innovation, thereby making it unnecessary actually to enter into such situations.[450] But in principle the construction of the 'ortho-language' should be feasible without referring back to ordinary language.[451]

It may be doubted whether this is either possible or intelligible. There is much to be said in favour of the view that communication problems can be completely resolved through the methods of analytic philosophy. Ordinary language is the immediate starting-point for this. When obscurities arise, the expressions employed are logically analysed. On the basis of such an analysis it is possible both to avoid misunderstandings and to make determinations regarding a common use of language. Artificial languages may be used as an instrument for the analysis of colloquial expressions. Thus it makes sense, for example, to reconstruct concepts such as 'ought' and 'permitted' by means of deontic logic.

It will not be possible in the course of this investigation to attempt to settle whether the constructivist approach is tenable

[446] Ibid., 115; Schwemmer, 'Grundlagen einer normativen Ethik', p. 83.

[447] Lorenzen, *Normative Logic and Ethics*, p. 75. On constructing an 'ortho-language' cf. ibid., 76 ff. and Schwemmer, *Philosophie der Praxis*, pp. 37 ff.

[448] Cf. Lorenzen and Schwemmer, *Konstruktive Logik, Ethik und Wissenschaftstheorie*, pp. 21 ff.

[449] Ibid., 18, 41.

[450] Ibid.

[451] Ibid., 18.

at all[452] and, if it is, whether it is to be preferred to the analytic one. Such clarification is in any event unnecessary for the purposes of this investigation. The results of analytic philosophy show that its methods are capable of solving communication problems.[453] The requirements of the first level of rational communality can be met by them. Should constructivist philosophy also prove capable of providing a range of instruments beyond these, which can do the same or even more, this would be entirely welcome.

Discussions which take place to elucidate communication problems are to be understood as discourse of its own kind. Such discourse will here be called 'linguistic-analytical'. It is concerned, for example, with the discovery of ambiguities, indeterminacies, emotive components of meaning, and absurdi-

[452] An objection is indicated here. According to Schwemmer the situations of interaction in which new terms are first introduced must already be characterized by common pursuit of purposes (Lorenzen and Schwemmer, p. 21). It is, however, questionable whether there can first be purposes and then langage. If by 'purposive acting' one understands 'consciously acting directed towards something', then language always seems to be given with the purposes, for quite a lot is to be said for the view that it is not possible consciously to direct oneself towards something without having recourse to language. If, however, it is rather the case that 'purposive acting' is to be understood as 'achieving something (objectively purposeful) unconsciously' (like bees searching for honey) then the situation would not be suited to learning language. This objection becomes even stronger if, like Schwemmer, one rests not merely upon purposes at large but rather on common purposes. A closely analogous objection can be raised against Schwemmer's idea, namely that there exists a 'pre-linguistic need-determined ordering of the world', and that this is capable of being 'fixed' by the use of 'signs' in a situation in which terminology is being introduced (Schwemmer, 'Appell und Argumentation', p. 171). It could also be said of ants that they have available to them a 'need-determined ordering of the world'. Yet this ordering could serve as a 'natural basis for understanding' only if the parties to a situation in which terminology is being introduced already understand it, at least rudimentarily, as intelligible—that is, if they grasp it linguistically. It is for this reason that the Erlangen approach—in relation to the thesis of the complete development of language by constructivist means—would seem to be very problematic. There is, therefore, quite a lot to be said for the view that ordinary language (which, as Schwemmer correctly observes, owes its trustworthiness to its rootedness in contexts of action) must remain the foundation of securing understanding.

[453] Two examples of this from the extensive literature are: Austin, *Philosophical Papers* (on ordinary language philosophy) and Carnap, *Meaning and Necessity*, 2nd edn. (Chicago and London, 1956) (on the philosophy of ideal language).

ties. The goal of this discourse is to secure clear and meaningful speech. In order to guarantee this it must be possible for any speaker at any time to go over to it. This leads to the discovery of a further rule of discourse:

Every speaker must be able to go over to a linguistic-analytical discourse at any time.

The *second level* of rational communality is set up by Schwemmer as follows: 'provided the speaker him or herself accepts the statements which he or she enjoins the addressee to accept'.[454] This demand relates to the sincerity and seriousness of the discussion. Whoever suggests that another should accept a given statement must accept it him or herself. This requirement, like those of intelligibility and freedom from contradiction, is basic to every communication.[455] It will be formulated explicitly as a basic rule of speech later in the discussion.

Finally, at the *third level*, the shared nature of words and sentences is no longer restricted to the speaker and the addressee. The requirement is rather that the words should be made teachable and the statements acceptable to anyone at all. Generalization should be two-sided:

on the one hand the statements are directed to anyone at all (in the situation in question) and on the other hand what is stated in them should be stated 'generally' without recourse to proper names or individual expressions. This twofold generalization is held to constitute the *third level* of rational communality. The *principle of rationality* is thus the requirement to bring about this third level of rational communality in talk culminating in resolutions. This principle should determine what is to count as *rational deliberation*.[456]

According to Schwemmer, rational practical deliberations disclose three levels of justification as well as the three levels of rational communality. The first level concerns the justification of an action by adducing a purpose for it, the second is the justification of the purpose by reference to a norm, and the third stage is that of justifying the norm.

It is held that the principle of rationality of practical

[454] Lorenzen and Schwemmer, *Konstruktive Logik, Ethik und Wissenschaftstheorie*, pp. 115–16.

[455] Cf. Austin, 'Other Minds', in his *Philosophical Papers*, pp. 82, 115.

[456] Lorenzen and Schwemmer, *Konstruktive Logik, Ethik und Wissenschaftstheorie*, p. 116.

deliberation can be refined a step further by invoking these distinctions. With regard to the second-level justification, the generalization rule of the principle of rationality leads to the following requirement: 'Every norm advanced as justifying the adoption of a purpose should be admissible as a reason for any further adoptions of purpose, in particular one's own.'[457]

It is obvious that this principle, which Schwemmer calls the *principle of practical rationality*, is the same as the combination of Hare's principle of universalizability and the principle of prescriptivity.[458] To be sure, Schwemmer also offers formulations which are reminiscent of Habermas's generalization principle which demands that everyone must be able to accept the norm under discussion.[459] Thus Schwemmer states that 'the generalization of sentences employed in reaching a decision . . . in practical deliberation consists of the *common acceptance* of the norms'.[460] Furthermore, one of the conditions of the third level of rational communality, cited above, is said to consist 'in making the sentences acceptable to anyone at all'.[461] It is not clear how this requirement relates to the principle of practical rationality which is explicitly formulated by Schwemmer.[462] In view of the fact that these two conceptions of the principle of generalizability are consistent with one another[463] it can, however, be assumed that Schwemmer advocates both.

As a result of this Schwemmer's requirement of generalizability shares the weaknesses of both Hare's and Habermas's versions of the principle of generalizability. It says nothing about the content of the norm which one must be prepared to apply to any case including one's own situation, and gives no information as to which norm may be accepted by everyone.

[457] Ibid., 117. A substantively identical formulation is to be found in Schwemmer, 'Grundlagen einer normativen Ethik', p. 85.

[458] Cf. above, pp. 69 ff.

[459] Cf. above. pp. 115–16, 133.

[460] Schwemmer, 'Grundlagen einer normativen Ethik', p. 84 (my italics); there is a similar formulation in Lorenzen and Schwemmer, *Konstruktive Logik, Ethik und Wissenschaffstheorie*, p. 116.

[461] Lorenzen and Schwemmer, *Konstruktive Logik, Ethik und Wissenschaftstheorie*, p. 116.

[462] For a criticism of this lack of clarity cf. F. Kambartel, *Praktische Philosophie*, 24–5.

[463] Cf. above, p. 116.

Schwemmer expressly notes this with respect to the principle of practical rationality which corresponds to Hare's principle of universalizability.

The requirement of consistency expressed through this principle is not sufficient for arriving at the aim of practical deliberations, the non-coercive settlement of conflict. Different people may consistently advocate incompatible norms.[464] Schwemmer argues that there is, therefore, a need for a principle which allows one to answer the question of which norms are to be adopted from a number of incompatible ones.

3.2 This is the task of the principle of morality. In order to formulate this principle Schwemmer first introduces several new terms. If someone (also) abides by a norm N (a purpose Z) in order to be able to abide by a norm N′ (a purpose Z′), N is to be called 'subnorm' in respect of N′, and N′ 'supernorm' in respect of N (Z 'under purpose' in respect of Z′ and Z′ 'over purpose' in respect of Z).[465]

In the same vein he now states what is required by the principle of morality through the following formulation:

> If there is a conflict situation, establish the mutually compatible supernorms in respect of the norms which are used as reasons for mutually incompatible purposes, and establish in respect of these supernorms subnorms which are mutually compatible.[466]

The usefulness of the principle seems to be limited. Assume that in order to abide by the supernorms N'_1 and N'_2, A pursues N_1, and B N_2. Let N_1 and N_2 be incompatible. N_2 would, however, be compatible with N_3, which might likewise be chosen as a subnorm in respect of N'_1 and N'_2. If A is indifferent as between N_1 and N_3, it makes sense for him or her to substitute N_3 for N_1. In such a case the morality principle would yield a conclusion. However, it would be inconclusive were A to be

[464] Lorenzen and Schwemmer, *Konstruktive Logik, Ethik und Wissenschaftstheorie*, p. 118.

[465] Ibid., 119.

[466] Ibid., 119–20. There is a newer version which diverges slightly from the one cited above in Schwemmer, 'Grundlagen einer normativen Ethik', p. 88. What is missing here is the requirement to set up subnorms which are compatible with one another. However, this ought to be quite obvious.

unwilling to make such a substitution. There might be good grounds for this. One might wish to abide by N_1 for its own sake and not only as a means of realizing N'_1 and N'_2. A might wish to abide by N_1 as a means of realizing other supernorms not accepted by B. N_3 might lead to indirect consequences which A is not prepared to take on board. A can deploy all these points in arguing that it is not A but B who should modify his or her norms. The morality principle contains no criteria for justifying such a demand. It leaves open the question of which and of how incompatible norms or purposes are to be modified. Schwemmer's principle of morality therefore provides a specific argument form applicable in certain situations, rather than a generally applicable procedure of moral justification.[467]

Even if the morality principle is thereby to be viewed as a decision-making criterion of very limited application, nevertheless its underlying idea is worth retaining. This idea is expressed in the formulation of the principle of morality put forward by Schwemmer in his *Philosophy of Praxis*: 'Let us join together . . . in shaping our knowledge and our understanding and also our will.'[468] According to this, the 'compatibility requirement'[469] taken from the morality principle is not[470] to be realized by bringing the actually existing wishes and demands into some optimal relationship (however that might be fixed); the justification of these wishes and demands themselves is the subject-matter of discourse. 'Moral philosophy has the task of formulating principles which allow us to work on merely subjectively "given" wantings and so to discipline them that our decisions about how to act are justifiable.'[471] The task of practical discourse thus consists (among other things) of overcoming the subjectivity of normative conceptions as these actually exist. In this sense Lorenzen aptly speaks of 'transsubjectivity' as the foundation of morals.[472]

[467] Cf. Kambartel, *Praktische Philosophie*, p. 15.

[468] Schwemmer, *Philosophie der Praxis*, p. 126.

[469] On this concept cf. Schwemmer, 'Begründen und Erklären', in *Methodologische Probleme einer normativ-kritischen Gesellschaftstheorie*, ed. J. Mittelstraß (Frankfurt-on-Main, 1970), p. 54.

[470] One must add: 'not only'.

[471] Lorenzen, *Normative Logic and Ethics*, p. 79.

[472] Ibid., 82.

4. THE CRITICAL GENESIS OF NORMS

Despite the import and fundamental basic idea expressed in the morality principle it has little to offer towards solving the problem of the justification of norms. By contrast, Lorenzen makes a considerable stride forward in taking up several fundamental ideas of Hegelian and Marxist dialectical theory in order to outline the doctrine of the 'factual' and the 'critical normative genesis' of norm systems,[473] which has been developed in detail by Schwemmer.[474]

This piece of theorizing matters not only because it contains an interesting procedure for the criticism and justification of norms but also because it offers methods for bringing into consideration the needs and normative views of persons affected by, but not parties to, a given discussion or deliberation. This is of great importance since, in most cases, those who take part in practical discourses that actually occur are by no means identical with those who are affected by them. One has only to think of the deliberations of a bench of judges.

The version of the theory of factual and of critical genesis put forward in *Konstruktive Logik, Ethik and Wissenschaftstheorie* is a very complicated one. Definitions are stipulated for no fewer than seventy-three terms.[475] There is discussion of no fewer than eighteen stages, steps, or transitions.[476] Moreover, it remains open to doubt whether the work carried out to date is yet a complete account of the theory.[477] For all these reasons, only some of its basic points will be presented here.

The achievement of a full account of factual and of critical genesis is a task for the 'cultural sciences', which the Erlangen School contrasts with the 'natural sciences'. The cultural

[473] Cf. Ibid., 84 ff. and id., 'Das Problem des Szientismus', *Philosophie und Wissenschaft*, ed. L. Landgrebe, Ninth German Philosophy Congress (Meisenheim am Glan, 1972), pp. 33–4.

[474] Cf. in particular Lorenzen and Schwemmer, *Konstruktive Logik, Ethik und Wissenschaftstheorie*, pp. 190–221; Schwemmer, 'Grundlagen einer normativen Ethik', pp. 89–95, and his 'Begründen und Erklären', pp. 72–9.

[475] Cf. the enumeration in the 'Ortholexicon', Lorenzen and Schwemmer, *Konstruktive Logik, Ethik und Wissenschaftstheorie*, pp. 233 ff.

[476] Ibid., 191, 192, 196, 197, 201, 212.

[477] Cf. Schwemmer, 'Begründen und Erklären', p. 43.

sciences have three tasks assigned to them: interpretation of culture, critique of culture, and reform of culture.[478]

The task of interpreting a culture consists in establishing what system of norms is operative in a society or group. This is said to require more than simple observation and asking questions. Such a direct approach would leave the observer under the influence of his or her own subjective interpretations,[479] nor could the poser of questions avoid presupposing that the self-conceptions of those questioned were true and not themselves open to reinterpretation.[480] It is therefore argued that in order to arrive at an objective determination of which norms are operative, it is necessary to understand the history of the normative system. This requires a firm foundation from which to start off. Schwemmer sees such a basis in natural or culturally invariant needs.[481] From this 'basis of interpretation',[482] it is possible to understand both the formation of further culturally determined needs arising with the division of labour and the development of norms occurring within this process. A description of currently operative norms is the end-point of such a process of comprehension. Such a description is to be empirically tested[483] as far as possible.[484]

This factual genesis is a necessary prelude to critical genesis or critique of a culture. In cultural critique the normative system established by interpreting a culture is assessed according to whether it promotes or hampers the observance of the principle of rationality. The observance of this principle is hampered

[478] Lorenzen and Schwemmer, *Konstruktive Logik, Ethik und Wissenschaftstheorie*, p. 191.

[479] Cf. ibid., 197.

[480] Schwemmer, 'Begründen und Erklären', p. 59.

[481] Lorenzen and Schwemmer, *Konstruktive Logik, Ethik und Wissenschaftstheorie*, p. 196.

[482] Ibid., 195.

[483] Ibid., 197–8. On the empirical testing of assertions of actions, purpose, and norms cf. Schwemmer, 'Begründen und Erklären', pp. 62 ff.

[484] It neither can nor need be discussed here whether such a process of comprehension of the origin of the normative system, starting out from culturally invariant needs, is possible. For purposes of this investigation it is enough that it is in general possible to describe the origin of norms. It may remain an open question which method should be adopted. It can hardly be doubted that the possibility exists.

where the normative system leads to a singling out of certain purposes in a purely *de facto* way, that is, without any rational deliberation as to whether or not they can be justified. Such *de facto* singling out involves a distortion of the deliberative setting, while avoiding or preventing it, rectifies the situation.[485]

In order to discover such distortions and rectifications it is necessary to construct a rational deliberation for every step in the factual genesis undertaken in the interpretation of culture. This involves determining with respect to each step 'whether or not, if it had been debated, it would have been justified according to the principles of deliberation and of morality'.[486]

Critical reconstruction of the factual genesis, or in short *critical genesis* of a normative system, is to be the name given to this process of applying critical assessment of norms and enactments at every stage of the factual genesis of a norm-system, or to the deliberation constructed for each stage of factual genesis, an assessment from whose acceptance follows a planning of genesis.[487]

Special difficulties are presented in trying to posit norms for carrying out the rectification of dialogues. The justification of such norms presupposes extensive knowledge of social scientific regularities. This is the task of the third stage following on from interpretation of culture and critique of culture, namely that of cultural reform.[488] The goal of cultural reform is 'to make possible action in accordance with the principles of rationality and of morality'.[489]

Even this rough sketch makes it evident that the theory of factual and critical genesis contains fertile ideas. It seems entirely plausible that a norm can (also) be criticized in terms of its genesis. Two cases are of particular interest here.

The first case occurs when a norm which was entirely reasonable at an earlier period has lost it's point in the light of changes in the prevailing conditions.[490] A person who wishes to

[485] Lorenzen and Schwemmer, *Konstruktive Logik, Ethik und Wissenschaftstheorie*, pp. 209–10.

[486] Schwemmer, 'Grundlagen einer normativen Ethik', p. 94.

[487] Lorenzen and Schwemmer, *Konstruktive Logik, Ethik und Wissenschaftstheorie*, p. 212.

[488] On this cf. ibid., pp. 213 ff.

[489] Ibid., 193.

[490] Cf. Stevenson, *Ethics and Language*, pp. 123–4.

adhere to such a norm even under the changed circumstances can be shown that if this norm had been discussed anew at every change in the prevailing conditions it would no longer be valid today. This would as a rule mean that the individual in question would not have learnt the particular norm in the course of his or her upbringing and would therefore not advocate it today. Where no new reasons can be found in favour of the norm this line of reasoning can be adduced as a strong argument against it.

The second case concerns a norm which did not come into being in reasonable conditions and which would not have been approved of in any initial deliberation. It is again conceivable that someone could have been so successfully brought up in the spirit of a particular norm that it never occurs to him or her that the norm may be wrong and that he or she is therefore prepared to apply the norm consistently, to take on board its consequences, and to bring his or her other convictions into harmony with it. It is, of course, possible for conditions to change to such a degree that good grounds or reasons can now be adduced even for a norm with such unreasonable beginnings; however, if this is not the case, then reference to its unreasonable genesis ought to be a strong argument against it.

Several more cases could be featured. This, however, will not be necessary, for the ideas which have been put forward here could only be applied to them in a more complicated way. More important is a quite different variant of the genetic argument not considered by Lorenzen and Schwemmer: the conviction that a norm is valid may arise not only as a result of unreasonable conditions of a society but also as a result of unreasonable conditions of individual socialization. Distinguishing such a case from the other one cited would make sense even if all distortions in individual socialization could be traced back to distortions in societal development. If such a reduction does not prove possible consideration of this case is absolutely mandatory. Just as there is a need to bring into play the historical and social sciences in analysing distortions in societal development, so, in the case of individual development, psychology and in particular, psychoanalysis must be brought to bear.

The rule of discourse tentatively put forward in the discussion of Habermas's theory can now be formulated as follows:

Every norm put forward in discourse must be able to stand up to testing of both its social and its individual genesis.

5. POINTS TO REMEMBER

It is not possible to discuss the constructivists' programme thoroughly within the framework of this investigation.[491] There is only a need to mention once again the doubts rehearsed above with respect to the constructivist claim that it is possible to dispense with everyday language in building up the sciences and ethics. In any case no such fundamental discussion is called for. Quite independently of the tenability of constructivism, constructivist ethics yields a number of interesting insights for a theory of rational discourse.

(1) First, note should be taken of the demand for the fixing of a common use of words. This demand converges with that of analytic philosophy (and, it must be said, with that of any philosophy which is to be taken seriously) for linguistic clarity and precision. It must therefore be possible to make a transition from practical over into linguistic-analytical discourse with respect to any linguistic obscurity which may occur. It must remain an open question whether and to what extent the constructive method is acceptable as a method of linguistic-analytical discourse. In any case the methods developed in analytic philosophy are applicable in linguistic-analytical discourse.

(2) In considering the principle of rationality, interesting parallels arose with different forms of the principle of generalizability as previously worked out. The principle of practical rationality corresponds to a combination of Hare's principles of universalizability and prescriptivity. In addition there were formulations which coincided with Habermas's conception of the principle of generalizability.

(3) The morality principle did indeed prove unable to

[491] For a critique of the programme of constructivism cf. W. Wieland, 'Praxis und Urteilskraft', *Zeitschrift für philosophische Forschung*, 28 (1974), 17 ff.; for a criticism from the point of view of critical rationalism cf. H. H. Keuth 'Dialectics versus Critical Rationalism', *Ratio*, 15 (1973), 28 ff.

sustain the role in which Schwemmer wished to cast it. Yet it expresses an idea well worth remembering, namely, that practical discourse is not (only) a procedure for optimally reconciling subjective desires and normative views, but is also above all an arrangement in which normative views and thereby ideas concerning the justification of subjective desires are modified.

(4) The most important contribution of constructivist ethics towards a theory of rational discourse is the idea of critical genesis. It must, of course, be observed that only the basic idea of the genetic argument is adopted in this work. The requirement of critical testing of historical development needs to be supplemented by the requirement of critical testing of the emergence of normative convictions in the experience of individuals.

IV. Chaim Perelman's Theory of Argumentation

The philosopher and jurist Chaim Perelman, born in Warsaw and for many years a professor in Brussels, started out studying the logician Gottlob Frege.[492] Later he turned to the logical analysis of value-judgments and evaluative concepts. He arrived at the view that value-judgments can be justified neither purely through empirical observation (naturalism) nor by any sort of self-evidence (intuitionism).[493] In his study of justice which appeared in 1945, he therefore arrived at the conclusion that at least the basic principles of every normative system are arbitrary.[494] Perelman was not, however, satisfied with this as a conclusion. From the Fifties on he set about trying to show through a theory of argumentation that there exists a veritable armoury of further possibilities of rational argument and justification beyond those of empirical testing and logical deduction. His particular conviction was that the possibility of the practical use of reason can be demonstrated in a general theory of argumentation.[495]

Such a theory, elaborated in great detail, was presented by Perelman together with L. Olbrechts-Tyteca in 1958 under the title *The New Rhetoric: A Treatise on Argumentation*.[496] Perelman and Olbrechts-Tyteca see their theory as a revival of the ancient

[492] C. Perelman, *Étude sur Frege*, thesis. (Brussels, 1938) and id., 'Éude sur Gottlob Frege', *Revue de l'université de Bruxelles*, 44 (1938/9), 224–7.

[493] On this cf. above, pp. 34 ff.

[494] Perelman, 'Concerning Justice', in his *The Idea of Justice and the Problem of Argument*, trans. J. Petrie (London and New York, 1963), 59 ff.

[495] id., *Justice* (New York, 1967), p. 59.

[496] id., and L. Olbrechts-Tyteca, *La Nouvelle Rhétorique: Traité de l'argumentation*, vols. i and ii (Paris, 1958) (trans.: J. Wilkinson and P. Weaver, *The New Rhetoric: A Treatise on Argumentation* (Notre Dame and London, 1969). Please note that in the following footnotes the pages of the English translation corresponding to the French edition will be added in brackets.

tradition of rhetoric.[497] They rely particularly on Aristotle, Cicero, and Quintilian. Their interest, however, is not historical in essence but rather logical and systematical. It is therefore possible to pass in silence over the question of how far they do justice to the ancient tradition.[498]

The following reflections concentrate entirely on the question of whether Perelman[499] has succeeded in laying the foundations for a tenable theory of practical argumentation. Answering this question will determine the soundness of his thesis that it is possible for reason to have practical application.

1. THE THEORY OF ARGUMENTATION AS A LOGICAL THEORY (IN THE WIDER SENSE)

A theory of argumentation may be pursued as a theory in psychology. In such a case it would, for example, examine the effects of certain arguments. Perelman expressly rejects this line of inquiry.[500] He presents his theory as belonging to the realm of logic in the wider sense.[501]

> I chose to follow Gottlob Frege, who studied the laws of formal logic by analysing the reasoning of mathematicians. I began to analyse reasonings concerning the good and the bad, the just and the preferable, as they are found in the writings of philosophers, politicians, lawyers, and preachers.[502]

Perelman is not trying to replace formal logic in his anaylsis. He rather wishes to augment it: 'The new rhetoric does not aim at displacing or replacing formal logic, but at adding to it a field of

[497] Ibid., 1 ff. (pp. 1 ff.). Cf. also Perelman and Olbrechts-Tyteca, 'Act and Person in Argument', *Ethics*, 61 (1950/1), 251; Perelman, 'Rhetoric and Philosophy', *Philosophy and Rhetoric*, 1 (1968), 15 ff.

[498] For Perelman's assessment of the history of rhetoric cf. his 'The Social Contexts of Argumentation', in *The Idea of Justice*, pp. 158–9.

[499] In what follows, for reasons of simplicity, the text speaks only of Perelman even when discussing the book brought out together by Perelman and Olbrechts-Tyteca.

[500] Perelman and Olbrechts-Tyteca, *La Nouvelle Rhétorique*, p. 12 (p. 9).

[501] Cf. ibid., 13 (p. 10). Such a wider use of the term 'logic' is not unusual. Cf. e.g. Popper, *The Logic of Scientific Discovery*, pp. 53–4.

[502] Perelman, 'The New Rhetoric', in *Pragmatics of Natural Language*, ed. Bar-Hillel (Dordrecht, 1971), 145.

reasoning that, up to now, has escaped all efforts at rationalization, namely, practical reasoning.'[503] Perelman gives two different reasons for his view of the theory of argumentation as a theory in logic rather than psychology. First, logical analysis of the different argumentational structures must precede any investigation of their psychological effectiveness. To investigate the effectiveness of different argument forms it is first necessary to acquaint oneself with them. Second, psychological investigations have nothing to say about the merits of different argumentations. They are themselves the subject-matter of a methodological evaluation.[504] In parallel with these two arguments Perelman's theory is divided into *analytic* and *normative* parts. The degree to which it contains psychological or sociological parts, despite its self-characterization as a theory of logic, will become clear in the course of the narrative.

2. ARGUMENTATION AS A FUNCTION OF AUDIENCE

The basic concept of Perelman's theory is that of the 'audience' ('auditoire'). The audience is the collectivity or ensemble of all those whom the speaker wishes to influence by his or her argumentation.[505] Identification of the audience addressed by a speaker requires knowledge of the speaker's intentions. The audience of a speaker in parliament may thus be his or her parliamentary party, the parliament, or the whole nation. The goal of every piece of argumentation is to gain or to strengthen the adherence ('adhésion') of the audience.[506] In order to achieve this the speaker has to adapt his or her speech to the audience.[507] The same assertion can serve as an argument in favour of a thesis of the speaker's before one audience and as an argument against the same thesis before another audience. Thus

[503] Ibid., 148. Similarly, Perelman and Olbrechts-Tyteca, *La Nouvelle Rhétorique*, p. 13 (p. 10).

[504] Perelman and Olbrechts-Tyteca, *La Nouvelle Rhétorique*, p. 12 (p. 9).

[505] Ibid., 25 (p. 19).

[506] Ibid., 18, 24, 59 (pp. 13, 19, 45).

[507] Ibid., 31 ff. (pp. 23 ff.). Cf. Perelman, *Justice*, p. 81, and his 'The New Rhetoric', p. 146.

the argument that a particular measure will ease social tensions is persuasive with those who want social peace but not with those who desire confrontation.[508] The following, therefore, is a sound rule of argumentation: 'l'adaptation du discours à l'auditoire, quel qu'il soit'.[509] The speaker must match his or her speech to the audience, whoever that might be. Argumentation is thus a function of the audience ('l'argumentation est fonction de l'auditoire').[510]

3. DEMONSTRATION AND ARGUMENTATION

The role of the audience distinguishes argumentation from demonstration. By 'demonstration' Perelman understands logical deduction. Within a logical calculus a proof consists of deriving a formula from given axioms in accordance with fixed rules of inference. Such a proof is either correct or incorrect quite independently of the assent of any audience.

Logicians are free in their choice of axioms. They are bound only by formal criteria such as the postulate of non-contradiction. The logician's proof is accordingly only valid within his or her own system. By contrast, according to Perelman, whoever engages in argument must secure assent both to the *premisses* and also to *every step in the proof*. 'The explicit adherence of the interlocutors is indispensable at every step, in order to allow the reasoning to proceed.'[511] It is self-evident that the premisses of an argument must win the assent of the listeners. More interesting is Perelman's second claim to the effect that, most of the time,[512] the statement to be substantiated does not follow logically from the statements put forward as justifying grounds for it and that for this reason even the transition from these statements to the

[508] Perelman and Olbrechts-Tyteca, *La Nouvelle Rhétorique*, p. 26 (p. 20).

[509] Ibid., 33 (p. 25). Cf. also p. 612 (p. 461).

[510] Ibid., 58 (p. 44). Similarly pp. 7, 24 (pp. 5, 19). Cf. also Perelman, 'Rhetoric and Philosophy', 15 ff.

[511] Perelman, 'The Dialectical Method and the Part Played by the Interlocutor in Dialogue', in *The Idea of Justice*, p. 167. Cf. also Perelman and Olbrechts-Tyteca, *La Nouvelle Rhétorique*, p. 87 (p. 65).

[512] Perelman, 'The Dialectical Method', p. 166.

statement to be substantiated requires the assent of the audience.[513]

It must be conceded in Perelman's favour that in the majority of justificatory arguments actually advanced, the conclusion does not follow logically from the premisses. In justifying the value-judgment that a certain form of government is good, for example, it may be urged that this form of government secures maximum individual freedom. The former does not follow from the latter. Nevertheless, in discussing Hare's theory it was shown that such cases presuppose a rule of the kind: 'Forms of government which secure a maximum of individual freedom are good'. The value-judgment mentioned is logically derivable from the observation advanced in favour of it, taken together with the general statement. As stated above,[514] it is for this reason that Hare arrives at the conclusion that: 'the notion of a reason, as always, brings with it the notion of a rule which lays down that something is a reason for something else.'[515] This means that every argument can be understood as enthymematic; it can always be supplemented by premisses of the kind cited so that the conclusion follows logically from the premisses.[516]

This would at least not seem to contradict the intent of Perelman's work. When he writes that the link between the premisses and the conclusion requires assent,[517] this can be rephrased by saying that the presupposed but not expressly stated premisses must be approved by the audience. If Perelman does not expressly refer to such premisses, this might be explained by the apt observation that the citing of such premisses is either superfluous or not very significant in the course of actual argumentation. It is superfluous in cases like the one given, in which there exists no doubt as to the content of the premisses; it is not very significant in cases in which the premisses are so narrowly focused that the transition occurring

513 It is here that Perelman's model of argumentative justification is distinguished from Aristotelian dialectical inference. Although in both the premisses are only probable or plausible (ἔνδοξα), in Aristotle, however, the conclusion follows logically from the premisses (*Topica*, 100a/100b).

514 Cf. above, p. 66.

515 Hare, *Freedom and Reason*, p. 21.

516 On the concept of enthymeme cf. the literature cited above, p. 88.

517 Perelman and Olbrechts-Tyteca, *La Nouvelle Rhétorique*, p. 87 (p. 65).

in the argument is simply reformulated. Nevertheless, it is useful, even in such cases, to insist on the enthymematic character of the arguments expressed. Formulation of the presupposed premisses makes it quite clear what needs to be justified should the transition be called into question.

4. THE CONCEPT OF THE UNIVERSAL AUDIENCE

The above points concern the logical structure of *reasons*. Many of Perelman's considerations centre round the question of what *effects* can be brought about by what means with respect to what audience. To give just a few examples, he occupies himself with the effects of the usage of different tenses,[518] the influence of the esteem a speaker expresses for his audience,[519] and with the effect of characterizing the arguments of one's opponent as trite.[520] In the course of these observations, argumentation is understood technically as a means of influencing its audience. In this sense Perelman speaks of the 'conditioning of the audience by the discourse' ('conditionnement de l'auditoire par le discours').[521] These observations concerning the effects of arguments belong to a descriptive, psychological, or socio-psychological theory of argumentation. Perelman's claim to be proceeding in a logical-analytical mode must to this extent at least be qualified.

However, the concept of the audience also contains the key to a normative theory of argumentation: the value of an argument, according to Perelman, is determined by the value of the audience it succeeds in convincing.[522] At the heart of Perelman's theory as a normative theory of argumentation, therefore, lies the designation of an audience which can only be convinced by means of rational arguments. Perelman calls this 'the universal audience' ('auditoire universel'). Assent on the part of the universal audience is the criterion of rationality and objectivity in argumentation.[523]

518 Ibid., 216 (p. 160).

519 Ibid., 431 (p. 320).

520 Ibid., 620 (p. 408).

521 Ibid., 11 (pp. 8–9).

522 Ibid., 432 (p. 321).

523 Ibid., 40 (p. 31). The agreement of the universal audience—that is, rationality and objectivity—is according to Perelman the goal above all of the philosopher. The judge and the legislator on the other hand should execute their decisions solely according to the wishes and convictions of the society

The concept of the universal audience raises several problems. Perelman, like Habermas, must acknowledge that the agreement of all can never be obtained. Whoever appeals to the universal audience does not usually even start out on the assumption that all beings who belong to it will take cognizance of his or her arguments; even less can he or she hope that everyone will actually agree with him or her. But he or she does start out assuming that *if* they were to take congnizance of the arguments and to understand them, they would also come to agree to the theses proposed. 'L'accord d'un auditoire universel n'est donc pas une question de fait, mais de droit.'[524]

The ideal character of this audience gives rise to comparatively unimportant difficulties. More problematic is Perelman's thesis that the composition of this ideal audience depends on the ideas of particular individuals and diverse cultures.[525] Perelman says even of the philosopher, whom he regards as a person particularly dedicated to rational argument, that he or she appeals 'to the universal audience as he imagines it . . . It is this audience, with its convictions and its aspirations, that the philosopher wants to convince'.[526] According to this the character of the universal audience depends on individual and social contingencies. An audience is only a universal audience for those who recognize it as such. For those who do not so recognize it, it is particular.[527] This severely limits the normative

which appointed and/or elected them (Perelman, *Justice*, pp. 68, 71). This remains unconvincing for two reasons. On the one hand the judge also strives, *within the area of discretion left to him or her*, for a reasonable solution. On the other hand the philosopher must also, in a way which remains to be worked out, make contact in his or her argumentation with certain ideas embedded in the traditions of his or her listeners. However, this problem need not be discussed in full here, for the immediate concern here is a general theory of practical argumentation. It will have to be taken up again in discussing the question of the extent to which legal discourse is also governed by the claim to correctness.

524 Perelman and Olbrechts-Tyteca, *La Nouvelle Rhétorique*, p. 41 (p. 31). Cf. also id., 'Act and Person in Argument', p. 252: 'Of course, the universal audience never actually exists; it is an ideal audience, a mental construction of him who refers to it.'

525 id., *La Nouvelle Rhétorique*, p. 43 (p. 33) and id., 'Act and Person in Argument', p. 252.

526 Perelman, *Justice*, p. 82. Cf. also his 'Rhetoric and Philosophy', pp. 21–2.

527 Perelman and Olbrechts-Tyteca, *La Nouvelle Rhétorique*, p. 44 (p. 34).

role of the universal audience. It is a norm only for those who accept it as a norm.

There is, however, a further variant of this concept to be found in Perelman. In his *Justice*, in reliance on Kant's categorical imperative, he posits the following requirement: 'You must conduct yourself as if you were a judge whose *ratio decidendi* was to furnish a principle valid *for all men*'.[528] Corresponding to this, the agreement of the universal audience is the agreement 'of all reasonable men'[529]—in short, 'of all'.[530]

Several of these formulations suggest that the universal audience consists of the totality of human beings as they are. However, this is not Perelman's view. The universal audience is 'enlightened humanity'[531]; it is made up of people as reasonable beings.[532] This raises the question of what is to be understood by 'enlightened' and 'reasonable', and how these qualifications relate to the definition of the universal audience as the totality of all human beings. It may be assumed that the following definition does justice to Perelman's theory: those who enter into the argumentation game are 'enlightened' and 'reasonable'. Presuppositions of this are that one is in possession of information and has the competence to process this information.[533] Basically every human being has the capacity to acquire both. It is, of course, possible that despite the same subjective effort, and the same objective help, different people may develop quite different argumentative capabilities. Furthermore, it must be admitted that those who acquire only limited capability may hinder rather than advance the progress of arguments. But this in no way alters the fact that in principle anyone above the limits of imbecility can participate in

528 Perelman, *Justice*, p. 77 (my italics). Similarly his 'Évidence et preuve', *Dialectica* 11 (1957), p. 33 (trans.: 'Self-Evidence and Proof', in *The Idea of Justice and the Problem of Argument*, p. 124).

529 Perelman, *Justice*, p. 75. Similarly, ibid., 79; id., 'La Règle de justice', *Dialectica*, 14 (1960), 238 (trans.: 'The Rule of Justice', in *The Idea of Justice and the Problem of Argument*, p. 87).

530 id., 'Betrachtungen über die praktische Vernunft', *Zeitschrift für philosophische Forschung*, 20 (1966), 220.

531 Ibid., 221.

532 id., *Justice*, pp. 75, 78.

533 In this sense Perelman speaks of the universal audience as of 'all men who are rational and competent with respect to the issues that are being debated' ('Rhetoric and Philosophy', p. 21).

argumentation. Where practical discourse is concerned, the participation of the less capable is mandatory if only because their interests too are affected.[534] The universal audience may thus be defined as the totality of human beings in the state in which they would find themselves if they were to develop their argumentational capabilities.

Such a state of affairs corresponds to Habermas's ideal speech situation. Perelman's agreement of the universal audience is Habermas's consensus arrived at under ideal conditions. In relation to the generalizability principle this means that, according to Perelman too, a judgment of value or obligation is only to be acknowledged as rationally justified if everyone can agree to it.

It has therefore been shown that the meaning of the expression 'universal audience' contains at least two components for Perelman: (1) the audience which individuals or a society represent to themselves as the designated one and (2) the totality of human beings as participants in arguments. It does not seem inconceivable that the two definitions are mutually consistent; whoever appeals to the universal audience is appealing to the totality of human beings as participants in argumentation, and in doing so his or her conception of these people is shaped by his or her preconceived ideas of those beings. This is particularly the case when a speaker appeals to an audience by way of monologue.[535] To the extent that an

[534] On this cf. Popper's apposite remarks in *The Open Society and its Enemies*, ii. 226: 'Admittedly, intellectual gifts may be different . . . and they may contribute to reasonableness. . . . According to our view, however, we not only owe our reason to others, but we can never excel others in our reasonableness in a way that would establish a claim to authority.'

[535] Many of Perelman's utterances suggest the view that argumentation before the universal audience is always 'monological'. Thus he distinguishes between the 'rhetorical perspective of a speaker who is seeking to convince an audience, and . . . the dialectical perspective of the person who criticizes the theses of his adversary and justifies his own' ('Rhetoric and Philosophy', p. 23). Argumentation before the universal audience would seem, according to this, to belong to the rhetorical perspective and thus to be one-sided. Perelman nevertheless expressly stresses that this is not the case: 'Nor does anyone have the right to assert that rhetorical discourse is unilateral' ('Reply to Mr. Zaner', *Philosophy and Rhetoric*, 1 (1968), 170). Argumentation before the universal audience thus embraces the dialectical perspective mentioned above.

interchange of arguments takes place, so far do preconceived ideas lose in weight; they in their turn become the subject-matter of discourse. The second component then becomes decisive. This element will be in the forefront of what follows. The main question of interest here is the extent to which such a broadly formulated concept can serve as a standard of evaluation for arguments.

5. PERSUADING AND CONVINCING

Two further important distinctions are bound up with the concept of the universal audience: that between persuading ('persuader') and convincing ('convaincre'), and that between an efficacious ('efficace') and a valid ('valable') argument. Whoever tries to get the assent of a particular audience alone is making an attempt at persuasion; whoever strives for the assent of the universal audience evinces a desire to convince.[536] Corresponding to this, arguments which gain the assent of the universal audience are valid, whilst those which are only accepted by a particular audience are only efficacious.[537] To be sure Perelman stresses that often no sharp dividing-line can be drawn between convincing and persuading[538] and that there is an interrelation between efficacy and validity.[539]

6. PERELMAN'S ANALYSIS OF THE STRUCTURE OF ARGUMENTATION

As already explained, Perelman has two reasons for classifying his investigations as belonging to logic: first, because they aim to

[536] Perelman and Olbrechts-Tyteca, *La Nouvelle Rhétorique*, p. 36 (p. 28); Perelman, 'Reply to Mr. Zaner', p. 169. A very similar definition is to be found in Kant, *Critique of Pure Reason*, p. 645: 'If the judgment is valid for everyone, provided only he is in possession of reason, its ground is objectively sufficient, and the holding of it to be true is entitled *conviction*. If it has its ground only in the special character of the subject, it is entitled *persuasion*.'

[537] Perelman and Olbrechts-Tyteca, *La Nouvelle Rhétorique*, pp. 613–14. (p. 463).

[538] Ibid., 38 (p. 29).

[539] Ibid., 615 (p. 464).

determine the value of arguments (the normative part); second, because they have the structure of arguments as their subject-matter (the analytic part).[540] Before asking how it is that reference to the universal audience can mark off an argument as rational, Perelman's analysis of the structure of argumentation will be examined. In so doing, it is not possible to do more than present the rudiments of Perelman's great variety[541] of observations, for which, moreover, he makes no claims to completeness or to being definitive.[542]

Perelman's basic distinction is that between *premisses* and *techniques of argumentation*.

6.1 By 'premisses of argumentation' he understands those matters of agreement which constitute the starting-point of arguments.[543] He divides these premisses into two classes: members of the one concern the real ('réel'), members of the other the preferable ('préférable').[544] Premisses concerning the real are subdivided into facts and truths on the one hand[545] and presumptions ('présomptions')[546] on the other. In the realm of the preferable, he distinguishes values,[547] hierarchies ('hiérarchies'),[548] and *loci* ('lieux').[549] By 'hierarchies' Perelman understands relations of preference; under '*loci*', following the ancient concept of *topos*, he understands premisses of a general kind which can serve as a foundation for the justification of values and hierarchies.[550]

540 Cf. ibid., 12 (p. 9).

541 Strawson has discussed the diversity of discursive means uncovered by Perelman (review of Perelman and Olbrechts-Tyteca, '*Traité de l'argumentation*, *Mind*, 68 (1959), 420). He observes: 'there is almost no feature of language, or of conceptual thought in general, which may not find a place as a factor in discursive persuasion.'

542 Perelman and Olbrechts-Tyteca, *La Nouvelle Rhétorique*, pp. 252–3, 610 (pp. 188–9, 460).

543 Ibid., 87–8 (pp. 65–6).

544 Ibid., 88 (p. 66).

545 Ibid., 89 ff. (pp. 67 ff.). The expression 'fact' is to designate particular individual objects, the expression 'truths' complex ones (e.g. theories).

546 Ibid., 93 ff. (pp. 70 ff.).

547 Ibid., 99 ff. (pp. 74 ff.).

548 Ibid., 107 ff. (pp. 80 ff.).

549 Ibid., 112 ff. (pp. 83 ff.).

550 Ibid., 113 (p. 84).

In *The New Rhetoric* Perelman is still of the view that only premisses concerning the real lay claim to validity before the universal audience, while values, hierarchies, and *topoi* can only gain the assent of particular audiences.[551] This only varies with respect to very abstract values such as the Good and the Beautiful, because of their high level of generality.[552] In later works he does, however, start from the view that practical questions—that is, those concerning the preferable—are also amenable to discussion before the universal audience.[553]

6.2 Under the heading of techniques of argumentation, Perelman treats of the various argument forms ('schèmes d'arguments')[554] on the one hand and, on the other, the interaction between arguments, the argument structure, and the structure of argumentation.[555]

6.2.1. He divides the different argument forms into two classes: those of association ('liaison') and those of dissociation. By the process of association he understands the joining together of separate elements into a unity, by that of dissociation the splitting up of a unity into separate elements.[556]

Three types of argument count as associative ones: (1) quasi-logical arguments, (2) those based on the structure of reality, and (3) those establishing the structure of the real. Quasi-logical arguments gain their power of conviction from their similarity with logically valid conclusions.[557] Arguments with reference to transitivity form one group of quasi-logical arguments. An example of such an argument is: 'Our friends' friends are our friends'.[558] An example of arguments based on the structure of reality are those based on causal links.[559] Finally, Perelman divides arguments establishing the structure of reality into those

551 Ibid., 88, 99 (pp. 66, 74).
552 Ibid., 102 (p. 76) and also id., 'Acts and Person in Argument', p. 252.
553 Perelman, *Justice*, pp. 75 ff.
554 Perelman and Olbrechts-Tyteca, *La Nouvelle Rhétorique*, p. 252 (p. 187).
555 On these concepts cf. above, pp. 92–3.
556 Perelman and Olbrechts-Tyteca, *La Nouvelle Rhétorique*, p. 255 (p. 190).
557 Ibid., 259 (p. 193).
558 Ibid., 306 (p. 227).
559 Ibid., 354 (p. 263).

relating to a particular case (for example for the purposes of generalization)[560] and those which draw analogies.[561]

Dissociation is not simply a matter of breaking up the links forged by association. By the process of dissociation, the concepts employed in argumentation are themselves altered by means of further subdivision. It thus makes possible quite novel solutions.[562] An example of dissociation is the distinction between appearance and reality.[563]

6.2.2. In the second part of his investigation of the techniques of argumentation, Perelman treats of the interaction of arguments. Of particular interest here is the concept of convergence. Perelman distinguishes two types of convergence. The first type occurs when different independent arguments lead to the same result.[564] This case may be spoken of as *additive strengthening*. In the second type the premisses of an argument are established by means of further arguments.[565] Here one can speak of *regressive strengthening*.[566] The pursuit of regressive strengthening leads to the ordering of the argument into an ever more complete system.[567] A further form of interaction worth mentioning is that between an argument, and an argument about this argument.[568] This relation corresponds to that between discourse and meta-discourse.

6.2.3. There is no more to be said here by way of a sketch of Perelman's analysis of the structure of argumentation. The main failing of this analysis lies in the omission to apply the instruments of analytic philosophy. This already applies to the first part, in the investigation of the premisses of argumentation. The logical structures of these premisses should have been

[560] Ibid., 471 ff. (pp. 350 ff.).
[561] Ibid., 499 ff. (pp. 371 ff.).
[562] Ibid., 550 ff. (pp. 411 ff.).
[563] Ibid., 556 ff. (pp. 415 ff.).
[564] Ibid., 624 (pp. 471).
[565] Ibid., 629 (p. 474).
[566] Additive strengthening uses arguments of the same level, regressive strengthening uses arguments of different levels. On this cf. above, pp. 87, 92–3.
[567] Ibid., 626 (p. 472).
[568] Ibid., 253–4, 610 (pp. 189–90, 460).

been worked out. A distinction should have been made, for example, between simple (atomic) and composite (molecular) judgments, between singular and general judgments, and between those of value and those of obligation.

The refusal to use modern analytic tools is particularly noticeable in the investigation of the techniques of argumentation. The distinction between arguments based on the structure of reality and those establishing it is not intelligible. Perelman's interesting exposition of analogies, to name but one example, could have been taken considerably further by recourse to modern logic.[569]

It might be thought that this demand for precision is inappropriate to the subject. Argumentation is not concerned with precise conclusions like mathematics, but with the use of various linguistic methods for convincing speech-partners. This can be readily admitted. However, it does not follow from this that a *theory* of argumentation may dispense with the application of the methods of modern logic. That it cannot be dispensed with is shown by the fact that every analysis of an argument must start by looking into its logical structure. Only in this way is it possible to uncover hidden premisses systematically and to make evident the interpolation of persuasive means to bridge gaps in the argument where the transition is logically inconclusive. It is still a widely held misconception that modern logic has to be restricted in its application so as to include only realms with long chains of reasoning in artificial languages. This view misconstrues the character of logic as an analytic tool. Frege compares it to a microscope which makes visible a great deal of what remains hidden to the naked eye. To be sure, he himself points out that whoever looks through a microscope may indeed observe with greater precision and in more detail than the naked eye, but that at the same time, for many purposes, the eye is superior to the microscope.[570] However, this would only be an argument against the application of modern logic to the theory

[569] On this cf., from among the juristic literature, the investigations of e.g. Heller, *Logik und Axiologie der analogen Rechtsanwendung* (Berlin, 1961) and U. Klug, *Juristische Logik*, 3rd edn. (Berlin, Heidelberg, and New York, 1966), 97 ff.

[570] G. Frege, *Begriffsschrift* (Halle, 1879), p. v (trans. T. W. Bynum, *Conceptual Notation and Related Articles* (Oxford, 1972), 104–5.

of argumentation if—to continue the metaphor—viewing through a microscope excluded all other forms of observation. This is surely not a sustainable view.

Despite the shortcomings indicated, Perelman's analysis contains many interesting insights. Following Perelman, a distinction will be made between the analysis of sentences occurring in arguments and the analysis of argument forms. Also of significance is his distinction between the combination of sentences (association) and the breaking up of concepts (dissociation). The latter is a highly important argumentational method. Furthermore, it is worth holding on to the concepts of additive and regressive strengthening as well as that of meta-discourse.

7. THE RATIONALITY OF ARGUMENTATION

The analysis hitherto discussed of the structure of argumentation deals with argumentation both before a particular and before a universal audience. It has not yet to say anything concerning the validity of arguments. It must now be asked to what extent reference to the universal audience yields criteria of validity.

7.1 Whoever appeals to the universal audience is also appealing to him or herself, for the speaker is also a member of this audience. For this reason, assertions which the speaker does not believe and suggestions which he or she does not accept are excluded from argumentation before the universal audience. The previously established conditions of sincerity and seriousness[571] therefore apply here also.

7.2 Whoever is partisan, provided he or she is sincere, convinces only those among whose number he counts him or herself. Whoever wishes to convince everyone must be non-partisan. This presupposes the presentation of any available

[571] Perelman and Olbrechts-Tyteca, *La Nouvelle Rhétorique*, p. 58 (p. 44). Cf. also Perelman, 'Reply to Mr. Zaner', p. 170.

counter-arguments. The rule *audiatur et altera pars* holds good.[572] This principle of impartiality on the part of a speaker corresponds to the requirement relative to discussions whereby every speaker has the right to introduce any argument into the discourse. Thus at this point too there is a marked parallelism between the theories of Perelman and Habermas.

7.3 It was already established above that the concept of the universal audience is bound up with a requirement of generalizability corresponding to Habermas's view. Whoever wishes to convince everyone may only propose norms which everyone can accept.[573]

The requirements mentioned up till now and the requirements corresponding to them were already discussed earlier. However, it was also noted there that they relate to necessary but not to sufficient conditions of rational moral argumentation. The question therefore arises of whether Perelman can offer further and, as it were, more substantive criteria.

7.4 Perelman begins by observing that with regard to the starting-point of arguments there is no distinction between argumentation before the universal and a particular audience; the speaker must rely on that to which the audience assents at the outset.[574] What this means is that every argumentation is tied to some footing in attitudes and convictions. This corresponds to the insight already established in the preceding discussions both of analytical ethics and of Habermas's, Lorenzen's, and Schwemmer's theories, namely that every argument occurs in a historical and social context.[575] However, argumentation before the universal audience is distinguished from that before a particular audience, in that in the former the speaker attempts to move from these starting-points to theses to which all can assent.

However, this rather pinpoints than resolves the problem. No

572 Perelman and Olbrechts-Tyteca, *La Nouvelle Rhétorique*, p. 160 (p. 119); Perelman, *Justice*, p. 80.

573 Perelman, *Justice*, p. 81 and id., 'Self-Evidence and Proof', p. 124.

574 id., *Justice*, p. 64 and also id., 'Les Cadres sociaux de l'argumentation', p. 125.

575 id., *Justice*, pp. 81–2.

way is indicated which will lead to a justified consensus with certainty. On the contrary, the embeddedness of argumentation in a specific historic and social context rather supports the view that on many occasions speakers will not reach an agreement. Add to this the impossibility of processing all relevant information,[576] and it becomes clear that in many cases it is impossible conclusively to designate a solution as the only correct one. However, for Perelman this is no reason for giving up. On the contrary, from this finding he derives several important further standards for argumentation addressed to the universal audience.

7.5 The postulate of openness to criticism and the requirement of tolerance[577] are the outcome of the provisional nature of every result. The first, to use Habermas's terminology, concerns the readiness to begin and carry on discourses; the second relates to actions. Apart from these rules governing behaviour towards others is the requirement that a speaker strive for universality even if it cannot be attained. 'The characteristic of rational argumentation is the aim to universality—an aim whose realization is never assured.'[578] It is aimed at the 'realization of the ideal of universal community' ('la réalisation de l'idéal de communion universelle').[579] The relationship of this 'communion universelle' to Habermas's ideal speech situation is unmistakable.

7.6 The criteria of rational argumentation discussed so far are, taken in themselves, still relatively weak. However, their weight increases when brought into association with Perelman's *principle of inertia* ('inertie'). The principle of inertia states that an opinion which has been accepted in the past may not be abandoned again without sufficient reason.[580] It thus has the character of a rule allocating the burden of argumentation or

[576] Perelman already goes into this problem, which was also greatly stressed by Luhmann, in Perelman and Olbrechts-Tyteca, *La Nouvelle Rhétorique*, p. 160 (p. 119).

[577] Perelman, *Justice*, pp. 83 ff.

[578] Ibid., 83.

[579] id., 'La Règle de justice', p. 238.

[580] Perelman and Olbrechts-Tyteca, *La Nouvelle Rhétorique*, p. 142 (p. 106), and Perelman, 'Betrachtungen über die praktische Vernunft', p. 219.

burden of proof: the appeal to an existing practice does not require justification, 'change only must be justified'.[581] According to Perelman this principle forms 'the foundation of the stability of our intellectual and social life'.[582] It underlies the appeal to precedent and to accepted norms in both legal science and ethics.[583]

This does not mean 'that what is must remain forever'.[584] It merely states that it is unreasonable to abandon a view, hitherto accepted, for no reason. Whoever doubts or criticizes something must present a reason for that doubt or that criticism. Furthermore, it gives justifying grounds for the inadmissibility of universal doubt.[585] With this the realm which is in need of justification is considerably narrowed. It is not necessary to justify everything, but only those things which are subjected to doubt for given reasons.[586] This does not only mean a considerable lessening of the burden for argumentation, it makes argument actually possible. Argumentation cannot begin without presuppositions.

The principle of inertia thus makes a certain substantive contribution to the problem of justifying norms.[587] Of course, the

581 Perelman, *Justice* p. 10. Similarly id., 'Justice and Reasoning', in *Law, Reason, and Justice: Essays in Legal Philosophy*, ed. G. Hughes (New York and London, 1969), 208 and 'La Régle de justice', p. 237.

582 id., 'Betrachtungen über die praktische Vernunft', p. 219.

583 Perelman and Olbrechts-Tyteca, *La Nouvelle Rhétorique*, p. 144 (p. 107).

584 Perelman, *Justice*, p. 10.

585 id., 'Betrachtungen über die praktische Vernunft', p. 219.

586 Perelman and Olbrechts-Tyteca, 'Act and Person in Argument', p. 252.

587 Within the framework of Perelman's theory this principle fulfils a further important function. It demands that like always be treated like. But this is the content of the rule of formal justice. Perelman is therefore of the opinion that this rule can be justified by the principle of inertia (id., *La Nouvelle Rhétorique*, p. 294 (pp. 218–19) and Perelman, 'Betrachtungen über die praktische Vernunft', p. 219). The rule of formal justice demands: 'persons who belong to one and the same essential category ought to be treated in the same way' (Perelman, 'Concerning Justice', p. 29). Here it corresponds to Hare's principle of universalizability (cf. above, pp. 65 ff). Nevertheless like Hare's principle it leaves it open to debate when several people are basically 'like' and how they are to be treated if they are so (cf. 'La Règle de justice', p. 236). To determine this is the task of concrete justice ('Concerning Justice', pp. 36, 48). Finding this concrete justice is the stuff of rational argumentation. Perelman's rule of formal justice does indeed not contain anything new, yet the attempt to justify it through the principle of inertia is interesting.

value of this contribution is limited, for only those norms which are not the subject of doubt can be readily admitted into the justificatory process. However, it says nothing about when something is to be doubted and about how the matter should be decided in cases of doubt. Perelman provides no further criteria here and has to leave this to the reasonableness of those participating in discussion.

8. POINTS TO REMEMBER

Despite these and several other weaknesses already discussed above, such as the imprecise nature of the concept of the universal audience and the rejection of modern analytic methods in the analysis of the structure of argumentation, many important findings are to be taken from Perelman's work. It is not without interest to note that a number of points of agreement emerged between this and the other theories discussed here.

(1) The close kinship between Habermas's concept of the ideal speech situation and Perelman's concept of the universal audience became apparent. According to both conceptions a norm (rule etc.) is capable of generalization where all can agree to it.

(2) Furthermore, it is of great moment that Perelman on the one hand gears rational argumentation to the idea of universality, yet on the other hand ties it to historically and socially given stances on matters of conviction and attitude. Argumentation can neither begin with nothing nor begin with some definitive origin. It attempts to arrive at generally acceptable results from what is actually given in convictions and attitudes, by means of a process of rational elaboration.

(3) In such a process it is often not possible to define a result as the only and lasting, correct one. This gives rise to the obligations of openness to criticism and of tolerance.

B. OUTLINE OF A THEORY OF GENERAL RATIONAL PRACTICAL DISCOURSE

Outline of A Theory of General Rational Practical Discourse

This section of the book will draw together the results of the discussion so far, into a general theory of rational practical discourse. It will only be possible to recapitulate in brief the most important findings to be retained of the investigation so far, along with the main outlines of the arguments which justify them. What follows will therefore only be fully comprehensible in the light of the previous discussions.

1. THE PROBLEM OF THE JUSTIFICATION OF NORMATIVE STATEMENTS

It was shown that normative expressions such as 'good' and 'ought' which occur in normative statements (judgments of value and obligation)[1] do not refer to any kind of non-empirical object, characteristic, or relation as is assumed by intuitionism,[2] nor are they reducible to empirical expressions as is claimed by naturalism.[3] Normative statements accordingly cannot be tested either by reference to any non-empirical entities or by the methods of the empirical sciences.

This does not, however, amount to a reason for conceptualizing normative terms in the emotivist or subjectivist way (or any variant thereon)[4] as giving expression to or descriptions of feelings or attitudes explicable in psychological or sociological terms yet which cannot be shown to be correct or true.[5]

[1] On these concepts cf. above, p. 60.

[2] On intuitionism cf. above, pp. 37 ff.

[3] On naturalism cf. above, pp. 34 ff.

[4] On emotivism and subjectivism cf. above, pp. 39 ff.

[5] The discussion so far has shown that there are a number of arguments in favour of the truth value of normative statements (cf. above, pp. 46, 56 ff., 83, 104 ff., and 129). However, it remains to be shown whether these arguments justify designating normative statements as 'true' in exactly the same way as

Emotivist or subjectivist theories do not allow properly for the fact that a claim to correctness is always implicated in any judgment of value or obligation.[6] If someone casts doubt on such a judgment, its justification is then open to discussion. In such discussion reasons (G) can be adduced for and against the disputed normative statements (N). To be sure, mere reference to the fact that normative statements are amenable to discussion is as yet no conclusive reason for speaking of their amenability to justification or their correctness. Such discussions might be no more than contrivances for persuading, for exerting psychological influence. The crucial question is whether there are criteria or rules for distinguishing good from bad reasons, valid from invalid arguments.

The discussion of Hare and Toulmin showed that whenever anyone puts forward a reason or ground G (for example, 'A lied') in support of a normative statement N (for example, 'A behaved badly') this presupposes a rule R (for example, 'Lying is bad') from which, together with G, N follows logically.[7] In this case N can be said to be 'justifiable through G and R'. Whoever wishes to question the justifying of N by resort to G and R can attack either G or R. If R is the subject of attack, there is a need to provide justifying arguments for the rule expressed by 'Lying is bad'. In this process of second-order justification a statement like 'Lying causes avoidable suffering' (G′) can be put forward as such an argument. This in its turn presupposes some rule (R′) such as: 'Whatever brings about avoidable suffering is bad'.[8] If one now wishes to provide justifying arguments for R′ on this model, there is a need for a further rule R″, and so on.

The only way of avoiding an infinite regress would seem to be by breaking off the process of justification at some point and substituting for it a decision not itself amenable to justification. The upshot of this, however, would be that one could ascribe 'correctness' only in a very limited sense to the purportedly

empirical ones. This must remain the subject-matter of a separate investigation. The following pages will therefore only speak of the correctness of normative statements.

[6] Cf. above, pp. 107–8, 127 ff.

[7] Cf. Hare, *Freedom and Reason*, p. 21; Toulmin, *The Uses of Arguments*, p. 97, as well as above, pp. 66, 84 ff.

[8] Cf. above, p. 87.

justified statement N. The arbitrary nature of this decision would be carried over into the whole justificatory process which is dependent on it. The attempt to set about justifying normative statements in this continuous manner thus leads either to an infinite regress or to a decision which can at best be explained psychologically and sociologically but which is not amenable to justification. The only way out of these two alternatives would be by recourse to a logical circle—hardly acceptable.

This 'Münchhausen-Trilemma'[9] (as H. Albert calls it) is, however, not without remedy. It can be avoided by dropping the demand for ever further justification of every statement by another statement, in favour of a set of requirements governing the procedure of justification. These requirements can be formulated as rules of rational discussion. The rules of rational discussion do not relate only to statements as do the rules of logic, but reach out beyond them to govern the conduct of the speaker. To this extent they can be called 'pragmatic rules'. Observance of these rules does certainly not guarantee the conclusive certainty of all[10] results, but it does nevertheless mark the results out as rational ones. Rationality is accordingly not to be equated with conclusive certainty. This characterizes the basic idea of the theory of rational practical discourse.

Discourses are sets of interconnected actions devoted to testing the truth or correctness of the things we say.[11] Discourses concerned with the correctness of normative statements are practical discourses. It remains to be shown that legal discourse

[9] Cf. Albert, *Traktat über kritische Vernunft*, p. 13; Popper, *The Logic of Scientific Discovery*, p. 94.

[10] Of course, as the theory of discursive necessities shows, several results are necessarily required; cf. above, pp. 17, 132.

[11] Discourses are thus primarily events in which several individuals participate. Nevertheless, this does not exclude the possibility of speaking of 'inner discourses'. Inner discourses are the reflections of one person in which the possible counter-arguments of imaginary opponents are evaluated. It is possible to speak of successful inner discourses in a weaker sense, to the extent that all known counter-arguments have been appraised in a non-partisan way. An inner discourse can be said to succeed in a stronger sense to the extent that this has occurred with respect to all conceivable counter-arguments of all conceivable opponents. It must remain an open question how far and in what way these conditions can be met. It will only be noted that although the theory drawn up here does indeed offer the basis for a theory of inner discourse too, such a theory would have to solve a number of additional problems as well.

can be understood as a special case of general practical discourse under limiting conditions such as statute, legal dogmatics, and precedent.

2. POSSIBLE THEORIES OF DISCOURSE

A theory of discourse can be empirical, analytical, and/or normative. It is *empirical* when, to give just a few examples, it describes and explains the correlation between certain groups of speakers and the use of certain arguments, the effects of arguments, or the prevailing views of certain groups concerning the validity of arguments. It is *analytical* when it deals with the logical structure of actually occurring and possible arguments. Finally, it is *normative* when it proposes and justifies criteria for the rationality of discourses.

There are a number of connections between these three characteristics. Both empirical and normative theories presuppose informed positions on the logical structure of arguments. The relationship between empirical and normative theories is more problematic. Among the tasks of empirical theory is that of giving a descriptive account of the rules which individuals or given social groups acknowledge as binding. But giving such an account is not tantamount to justifying these rules. They would only be justified within the framework of a normative theory, and then only by the addition of some such further premiss as that the rules observed by particular academics at certain times are reasonable ones.

3. THE JUSTIFICATION OF RULES OF DISCOURSE

The theory of rational discourse is a normative theory of discourse. It therefore addresses the problem of how the rules of rational discourse can be justified. At first glance, this problem would seem not to admit of any solution. The rules of rational practical discourse can be understood as norms for the justification of norms. Does their justification not require third-order norms and so on, so that the infinite regress described in relation to norms of the same level also applies in relation to norms of different levels? Before giving up, the possible ways of arriving at rules of discourse should first be investigated. There are four possible routes.

3.1 The first way consists in conceptualizing rules of discourse as technical rules. Technical rules are rules which prescribe means as appropriate to particular ends.[12] Lorenzen and Schwemmer take this path when they attempt to establish the good sense of their rules by postulating non-coercive conflict resolution as their end.[13] This mode of justification can be termed '*technical*'.

There are two objections to the technical mode of justification. The one is that the end it postulates needs to be justified in its turn. But what rules are to be applied in this process, if the aim is supposed to be that which justifies all rules? The other is that an aim which might justify the observance of *all* rules of discourse is either so general that it becomes possible to postulate incompatible norms as a means to its attainment—this is the case with such aims as happiness or the dignity of human beings—or the state of affairs designated as the aim is itself defined by the observance of these norms.

This is the case when, for example, the purpose of non-coercive conflict resolution is understood not as a state of social pacification, also rejected by Schwemmer,[14] but as a state in which conflicts are rationally resolved. Setting as an end, a state of affairs already defined by the rules which it is intended to justify, holds true particularly of 'ends' such as justice and truth. There are not two separate kinds of things:[15] on the one hand justice and truth, as ends, and on the other hand rules-as-means

[12] On this cf. Wright, *Norm and Action* (London, 1963), 9 ff.

[13] Cf. above, p. 141; and also Grice, who claims to have formulated his rules in such a way that they serve the aim of a 'maximally effective exchange of information' (*Logic and Conversation*, p. 35).

[14] Lorenzen and Schwemmer, *Konstruktive Logik, Ethik und Wissenschaftstheorie*, p. 109.

[15] Instructive on this point is J. Ladd, 'The Place of Practical Reason in Judicial Decision', in *Rational Decision, Nomos*, vol. vii, ed. C. J. Friedrich (New York, 1964), 140. According to Ladd, the aim of the judge should be the 'impartial administration of justice or of the law'. This aim is to be pursued by acting in accordance with a number of rules and principles. 'These rules and principles play the logical function of defining the end itself.'

according to which they can be established or discovered; on the contrary, what is just or true is that which is established or discovered by applying these rules.[16]

This does not mean that the technical mode of justification is of no value at all. It will not serve as a procedure for justifying all rules. But it is indispensable to the justification of more concrete rules in terms of limited aims.[17] Of course, these aims would themselves need to be justified.

3.2. A second possibility consists in showing that certain rules have *de facto* validity—that is, that they are actually observed to a considerable extent, or that the particular results realizable through the observance of certain rules correspond to the normative convictions we actually have. This mode of justification can be called '*empirical*'.[18]

[16] This observation does not run counter to the distinction between definitional and criteriological theories of truth. (On this cf. N. Rescher, *The Coherence Theory of Truth* (Oxford, 1973), 1 ff.; H. J. Wolff, 'Begriff und Kriterium der Wahrheit', in *Gegenwartsprobleme des Internationalen Rechts und der Rechtsphilosophie*, Festschrift for R. Laun, ed. D. S. Constantopoulos and H. Wehberg (Hamburg, 1953), 587 ff.) Should this distinction prove feasible and meaningful, and there are indications in favour of this, then, to the extent that the observation concerns the concept 'truth' it would fall to be understood in the sense of a criteriological theory of truth. Should the distinction between definitional and criteriological theories of justice also prove possible, the same would hold true of the concept of 'just'. Of course the acceptance of the distinction between definitional and criteriological theories does not exclude the assumption that there exist close relations between such theories.

[17] The six main norms put forward by Arne Naess for an unbiased exchange of views can be seen as examples of such more concrete rules. These norms include those (1) against tendentious 'beating about the bush', (2) against tendentious rendition, (3) against tendentious ambiguity, (4) against the setting up of bogeymen, (5) against tendentious opening statements, and (6) against the tendentious preparation of contributions to the discussion (*Kommunikation und Argumentation* (Kronberg, 1975), 160 ff.). Naess justifies his norms via the aim of 'effective exchange of ideas' (ibid., 161).

[18] The term 'empirical' is not intended to imply that within the framework of this mode of justification it is possible to cite quite general facts as reasons. Only those arguments are to be included which make reference to a certain class of facts, namely the factual validity of rules and the actual confirmation of normative convictions. Calling such arguments 'empirical' in the present context can be justified by pointing out that the sentences describing these facts are not themselves normative but rather norm-describing and to this extent empirical sentences.

As already indicated above in the discussion of the relationship between an empirical and a normative theory of discourse, the main problem for the empirical mode of justification lies in the transition from the observation that a norm is actually operational or corresponds to actually existing convictions, to the conclusion that it is rational. This is a special case of deriving an 'ought' from an 'is'. Such a move would only be admissible if one were to accept the premiss that the prevailing practice is rational.

This premiss is certainly not entirely misguided. The existence of a prevailing practice is after all proof of its possibility. This is by no means certain in the case of proposed but untried methods. A further advantage of the empirical mode of justification lies in the fact that it provides a framework in which it is possible to point out contradictions within an existing practice and inconsistencies between actually held normative convictions. In this way a partner in the justificatory process may be moved to give up certain rules or convictions in order to maintain others which contradict them but seem of greater importance to him or her. It therefore makes sense to analyse prevailing practice and to take it as a prima facie starting-point.[19]

On the other hand the history of science or procedural law, for example, shows that the practice of a specific historical period is not only not the only possible one but need not necessarily be the best. A statement such as Hegel's: 'What is rational is actual and what is actual is rational'[20] cannot be taken literally, to say the least. An empirical justification of the kind indicated is therefore always only provisional in view of possible corrections by reference to other modes of justification.

[19] This is the aim of Kriele's demand that theory must 'achieve its standards for the judgment of practice from the observation of practice, that is it must learn from the experience of practice itself what constitutes good and bad practice' (*Theorie der Rechtsgewinnung*, p. 22). Of course this does not mean that the theory can confine itself to pure description and analysis of practice. In order to discover whether a certain practice is a good practice, theory must ask whether there are good reasons in favour of this practice (ibid., 288). The nature of these good reasons, on the other hand, will hardly be derivable from practice.

[20] G. W. F. Hegel, *Philosophy of Right*, trans. T. M. Knox (Oxford, 1965), 10.

3.3 Another path which often cuts across other modes of justification is taken by those who analyse the system of rules defining a language game and propose the adoption of the system of rules worked out in this way. The language games can be actually existing ones or hypothetical ones. The crucial factor for this mode of justification is that the presentation of the system of rules as defining a practice is considered the real motive for adopting the practice. This of course does not exclude the option of using other modes of justification as well, such as pointing out that the rules are already ('ever-presently') actually observed and are only to be intentionally strengthened once more, or that the observance of the rules has particular consequences. The only matter of importance is that the presentation of a system of rules is seen to constitute a reason or motive for its acceptance, regardless of whether or not any further reasons are given. This mode of justification is to be called '*definitional*'.[21]

The definitional mode of justification suffers from one weakness which makes it a matter of some doubt whether it is to count as a mode of justification at all. No further reasons are adduced in favour of the system of rules to be justified; it is simply elucidated and presented. This is meant to suffice as a motive or a reason. The definitional mode of justification thereby rests to some degree upon mere fiat or arbitrary will. Nevertheless, it should not be abandoned as pointless. It does make a difference whether one decides in favour of an explicitly formulated and comprehensively presented system of rules or whether one chooses something wholly lacking in conceptual

[21] Popper's argument moves in this direction in attempting to define 'empirical science . . . by means of its methodological rules'. These methodological rules he calls 'conventions', which must conform to the supreme rule that there be no protection 'against falsification' (*The Logic of Scientific Discovery*, p. 54). The supreme rule gives expression to the 'rationalist attitude' whose adoption is a matter of simple choice. 'That is to say, a rationalist attitude must be first adopted if any argument or experience is to be effective, and it cannot therefore be based upon argument or experience' (*The Open Society and its Enemies*, ii. 230). One can indeed draw attention to the consequences of opting for or against such an attitude, but to do so would not determine the case for this attitude (ibid., ii. 232). Albert takes the point with particular sharpness, speaking of the 'rationalism of criticalism' as the 'sketch of a way of life' whose adoption involves a moral decision (Traktat über kritische Vernunft, pp. 40–1).

and analytic endeavour. The definitional mode of justification can be advantageous in another way too. It allows the construction of completely new systems of rules.

3.4 A fourth and last way consists in showing that the validity of certain rules is a condition of the possibility of linguistic communication. Apel calls such a mode of justification 'transcendental-pragmatic'.[22] Habermas, however, is hesitant about the use of the word 'transcendental' as given currency by Kant. He gives two reasons for this: (1) rules of discourse, unlike Kant's philosophy, are not concerned with the constituents of experience but rather with the generation of arguments,[23] and (2) in working out these rules it is not possible to make a clear distinction between logical and empirical analysis.[24] He therefore suggests the expression 'universal-pragmatic' for the 'reconstruction of general and unavoidable presuppositions of possible processes of understanding'.[25] This expression is preferable since it is better suited to avoiding misunderstanding. The fourth mode of justification will therefore be called '*universal-pragmatic*'.

A weaker version of this mode of justification consists in showing that: (1) the validity of certain rules is constitutive[26] of the possibility of certain speech acts, and that (2) we cannot do without these speech acts save by giving up those forms of behaviour which we regard as peculiarly human.[27] The speech act of asserting would seem to belong to this category.

The mode of justification just described gives rise to many problems. Not only are these concerned with the questions of which rules can be rightfully characterized as 'general and unavoidable presuppositions of possible processes of understanding', which are constitutive of which speech acts, and

[22] Apel, *Towards a Transformation of Philosophy*, pp. 256 ff. and his 'Sprechakttheorie und transzendentale Sprachpragmatik zur Frage ethischer Normen', in id. (ed.), *Sprachpragmatik und Philosophie* (Frankfurt-on-Main, 1976), 116 ff.

[23] Habermas, 'What is Universal Pragmatics?' pp. 23–4.

[24] Ibid., 24–5.

[25] Ibid., 21. On the procedure for such a rational reconstruction cf. pp. 8 ff.

[26] On this concept cf. Searle, *Speech Acts*, pp. 33 ff.

[27] On this cf. ibid., 186 n. 1.

which speech acts are necessary for peculiarly human forms of behaviour; over and above that it is a question of importance from the standpoint of theory of science namely whether or not such justification is in the end possible at all. This dispute can be seen as a new variant of the old controversy between logical-empirical and transcendental-philosophical attitudes. It will not be entered into here.[28] It will only be observed that the boundaries in this dispute are no longer in the least clear cut. It can nevertheless be stated that where certain rules can be shown to be generally and necessarily presupposed in linguistic communication, or are constitutive of peculiarly human ways of behaviour, it is quite possible to speak of a justification of these rules. Of course, such justification will only be possible for relatively few fundamental rules.

3.5 The exposition of these four modes of justification lays no claim to completeness. It is quite conceivable that there are yet other methods; certainly other classifications are possible, and in any event further differentiation is possible within the individual modes of justification. However, the above observations show clearly that no mode of justification is without its weaknesses. Technical justification involves presupposing ends which are themselves not justified. In addition to this there is always the danger of excessively abstract aims or of aims which already contain the rules to be justified. The empirical method makes existing practice the standard of rationality. The definitional method is, in the last analysis, arbitrary, and the universal-pragmatic mode at best serves as a justification procedure for a few fundamental rules.

Nevertheless, each of these methods seems to contain an important element. Rules which can be justified in the universal-pragmatic mode are to be retained as valuable primary material. *De facto* binding rules are significant in two respects. Those engaged in theory of discourse must themselves be guided by them at least in the first instance, in the process of giving any justifications. How else can they begin? Furthermore, it can be said in favour of these rules, that they have

[28] On this cf. the essays by Apel, Habermas, Kanngießer, Schnelle, and Wunderlich, in *Sprachpragmatik und Philosophie*.

succeeded. This is indeed no proof of their rationality. But it does at least show that to date no criticism has been brought to bear against them which has proved sufficiently trenchant to lead to their abandonment. Take into account that the possibility of criticizing them did not always exist, but nevertheless often arose, and it is not possible to deny them limited reasonableness. In addition, empirically discovered rules can be scrutinized as to their appropriateness and set against other systems of rules constructed according to different criteria of appropriateness. Finally, the definitional method enhances the possibility of criticizing systems of rules by explicitly formulating them and by constructing new rules, opens up the way to new modes of procedure.

This review makes it clear that a discourse about rules of discourse is itself meaningful. Such a discourse can be called '*discourse-theoretical discourse*'. The four possible modes of justification applicable in discourse-theoretical discourse have just been outlined. How they are to be applied in detail must be left to the participants in discourse. Rules are already observed in the course of discussion within the framework of these four modes of justification. These rules consist partly of those actually valid for the group of speakers and partly of rules already provisionally justified. It is not unreasonable not to proceed exclusively by means of justified rules. Since this is not possible, and since it is reasonable to get discussion started, it is also reasonable to begin in the first instance on the basis of rules which are not themselves justified.

4. THE RULES AND FORMS OF GENERAL PRACTICAL DISCOURSE

The rules defining rational practical discourse are of quite diverse kinds. There are rules which are only valid for practical discourses and rules which are also valid in other language games. There are commands, prohibitions, and permissions. Some rules demand strict observance; others contain demands which can only be approximately met. In addition, there are rules governing behaviour within practical discourse and rules which deal with moving over into other forms of discourse. Finally, argument forms must be distinguished from the rules of discourse.[29]

In the following, the rules and forms worked out in the preceding investigation will be explicitly formulated. It is not least the aim of such an explicit formulation to highlight shortcomings more clearly. Such shortcomings may relate to the content of the rules, to the incomplete nature of their enumeration, to the superfluity of some rules and forms, and to the inadequacy of their formal expression. Should it prove possible to eliminate these shortcomings, it ought to be possible one day to construct something like a code of practical reason. Such a code would be a synopsis and an explicit formulation of all the rules and forms of rational practical argumentation partly mentioned and partly only sporadically subjected to analysis in so many different writings.

4.1. The Basic Rules

The validity of the first group of rules is a precondition for the possibility of every linguistic communication which gives rise to any question of truth or correctness:

(1.1) No speaker may contradict him or herself.

(1.2) Every speaker may only assert what he or she actually believes.

(1.3) Every speaker who applies a predicate F to an object *a* must be prepared to apply F to every other object which is like *a* in all relevant respects.

(1.4) Different speakers may not use the same expression with different meanings.

(1.1) makes reference to the rules of logic. These rules are presupposed here. There are two further remarks to be made. First, it should be pointed out that the rules of logic are also applicable to normative statements. This is not without its

[29] The difference between rules and forms will become clearer when they are set out below. Here it will only be noted that the forms can be reformulated into rules—that is, into rules which require that in certain argument situations one must employ certain forms and only certain forms of argument. It is for this reason that one often only speaks of rules.

problems. If logic is regarded as 'the science of the most general laws of truth'[30] and if, furthermore, one is of the opinion that normative statements do not have truth-value, one might arrive at the belief that the rules of logic do not hold for normative statements. This problem is discussed under the heading 'Jørgensen's Dilemma'.[31] However, this 'dilemma' can easily be avoided. One way out consists in choosing values like 'valid' and 'invalid',[32] or 'lawful' and 'not lawful'[33] instead of the values 'true' and 'false'; a second way out lies in showing that the very occurrence of expressions such as 'and', 'if . . . then . . .', 'all', and 'some' in normative sentences is itself a ground for supposing that logical relations obtain between such sentences.[34] The third and probably the best way is to construct semantics (model theories) which allow of the ascription of truth and falsity to normative sentences.[35]

The second point is closely related to the first. The reference to the rules of logic expressed in (1.1) does not relate only to classical logic but above all also to deontic logic,[36] which has been developing for some years amid stormy and unresolved controversy. The prohibition against self-contradiction therefore relates also to deontic inconsistencies.

(1.2) secures the sincerity of the discussion. (1.2) is constitu-

[30] Frege, 'Logik' in *Schriften zur Logik und Sprachphilosophie. Aus dem Nachlaß*, ed. G. Gabriel (Hamburg, 1971), 39 and his 'The Thought: A Logical Inquiry' in P. F. Strawson (ed.), *Philosophical Logic* (Oxford, 1967), p. 18.

[31] J. Jørgensen, 'Imperatives and Logic', *Erkenntnis*, 7 (1937/8), 288 ff.; Ross, 'Imperatives and Logic', *Theoria*, 7 (1941), 55–6; and id., *Directives and Norms* (London, 1968), 139.

[32] Ross, *Directives and Norms*, pp. 177 ff.

[33] R. Schreiber, *Logik des Rechts* (Berlin, Göttingen, and Heidelberg, 1962), 65–6.

[34] Hare, *The Language of Morals*, pp. 20 ff.

[35] On such semantics cf. S. Kanger, 'New Foundations for Ethical Theory', *Deontic Logic: Introductory and Systematic Readings*, ed. R. Hilpinen (Dordrecht, 1971), pp. 44 ff.; J. Hintikka, 'Some Main Problems of Deontic Logic', *Deontic Logic*, pp. 67 ff. On model theory in general cf. S. A. Kripke, 'Semantical Considerations on Modal Logic', *Reference and Modality*, ed. L. Linsky (Oxford, 1971), 63 ff.

[36] On deontic logic cf. the writings of Wright, in particular, 'Deontic Logic', *Logical Studies* (London, 1957), 58–74; *Norm and Action* (London, 1963); *An Essay in Deontic Logic and the General Theory of Action* (Amsterdam, 1968); 'Deontic Logic Revisited', *Rechtstheorie*, 4 (1973), 37–46.

tive of every linguistic communication.[37] Without (1.2) it would not even be possible to lie, for in the absence of the presupposition of a rule requiring sincerity, deception is inconceivable. (1.2) does not thereby exclude the utterance of conjectures; it only demands that they be marked out as such.

(1.3) relates to the use of expressions by one speaker, (1.4) to the use of expressions by different speakers. (1.3) is formulated in stronger terms inasmuch as it demands a readiness for self-consistency in the application of terms. This would, however, not amount to an essential difference if (1.4) were to be strengthened so as to say that only those who are prepared to apply an expression in every case to which it is applicable use that expression at all. Under this condition (1.3) and (1.4) could be united into a single rule requiring all speakers to use all expressions with the same meaning. The reason for not doing this here lies above all in the fact that (1.3) and (1.4) contain quite different aspects of this general rule, aspects which it is worth distinguishing.

(1.3) relates to the self-consistency of the speaker. Applied to evaluative expressions (1.3) assumes the following form:

(1.3′) Every speaker may assert only those value judgments or judgments of obligation in a given case which he or she is willing to assert in the same terms for every case which resembles the given case in all relevant respects.

(1.3′) is a formulation of Hare's principle of universalizability.[38]

(1.4) requires communality in the use of language.[39] It is a matter of controversy how this communality is to be established and secured. Representatives of the Erlangen School stipulate that every expression should be subjected to the rules of an 'ortho-language' to achieve communality. For this, ordinary language can only be used in a subordinate role. The

[37] On the requirement of sincerity cf. Austin, 'Other Minds', pp. 82, 115; *How to Do Things with Words*, p. 15; Searle, *Speech Acts*, p. 65; Grice, *Logic and Conversation*, p. 34; O. Weinberger, 'Wahrheit, Recht und Moral', *Rechtstheorie*, 1 (1970), 131 ff. Cf. also above, pp. 145, 169.

[38] On this cf. above, pp. 65 ff.

[39] On this cf. above pp. 142 ff. On the communality of the use of language as an indispensable presupposition of every argumentation cf. also Perelman and Olbrechts-Tyteca, *La Nouvelle Rhétorique*, pp. 19 ff. (pp. 15 ff.).

practicability of this programme was questioned above.[40] There is quite a lot to be said in favour of starting out from ordinary language and only making stipulations concerning word usage where obscurities and misunderstandings arise. Analysis of the expressions used is a presupposition of any such stipulation. Artificial languages such as that of deontic logic may be employed as an instrument for this analysis.

Discussions carried out to elucidate communication problems can be understood as discourse *sui generis*. This type of discourse was called 'linguistic-analytical discourse' above.[41] Apart from the establishment of a common use of language, linguistic-analytic discourse is concerned with securing clear and meaningful speech. To this extent (1.4) might be further refined.

(1.1)–(1.4) are to be called '*basic rules*' because of their elementary character.

4.2 The Rationality Rules

Practical discourse is concerned with the justification of assertions of normative sentences.[42] In discussing such assertions, further assertions are drawn up, and so on. Assertions are also needed to refute something, to answer questions, and to justify suggestions. It is not possible to have practical discourse without assertions.

Whoever makes an assertion not only wishes to express a belief that something is the case but also implicitly claims that what is being said can be justified—that is, is true or correct. This applies equally to normative and non-normative statements.[43]

The claim to justifiability does not include a claim to the effect that the speaker him or herself is capable of giving a justification. It is quite sufficient for the speaker to refer to some other determinate or determinable person as capable of justifying

[40] Cf. above, pp. 143–4.

[41] Cf. above, p. 144.

[42] On the possibility of speaking of the speech act of asserting in regard to normative statements too cf. above, pp. 64 ff.

[43] Cf. Habermas, 'Wahrheitstheorien' p. 200; Patzig, 'Relativismus und Objektivität moralischer Normen', p. 75; Frankena, *Ethics*, pp. 79 ff. as well as above, pp. 127 ff.

what has been said. Reference to the competence of others to justify is, like every other argument, itself open to discussion. Thus it can be asked whether the authority invoked by the speaker really guarantees the correctness of the statements made. It is possible and, as a rule, necessary in this process to go into the question of whether or not what is said is in substance correct. In this way even the reference to the competence of determinate or determinable other people can be regarded as a justification argument. Nevertheless, it is not enough for the speaker simply to be of the opinion that someone at some time will be in a position to justify his or her statement, unless reasons can be given for this opinion.

Furthermore, the claim to justifiability does not mean that a speaker has to justify every assertion at any time to anyone at all. However, when a speaker refuses to provide a justifying argument, he or she has to be able to give reasons which justify this refusal.[44]

The following rule thus holds good for the speech act of asserting:

(2) Every speaker must give reasons for what he or she asserts when asked to do so, unless he or she can cite reasons which justify a refusal to provide a justification.[45]

This rule may be called the '*general justification rule*'.

Whoever gives justifying reasons for something at least pretends to accept the other party as a partner of equal standing, at least with regard to what concerns the justificatory process, and neither to practise coercion him or herself nor rely on coercion exercised by others. Furthermore, he or she claims to be able to defend the assertion not only to the speech-partner in question but to anyone at all. Language games which do not at least purport to fulfil these conditions cannot be regarded as justifications. The requirements of equal standing, universality,

[44] On these limitations with respect to the claim of justifiability cf. above, p. 128.

[45] On such a rule cf. Wunderlich, 'Zur Konventionalität von Sprechhandlungen', p. 20; Grice, *Logic and Conversation*, pp. 32 ff.; Schnelle, *Sprachphilosophie und Linguistik*, pp. 42 ff. On the question of whether such a rule is to be regarded as a rule constitutive of the speech act of asserting or simply as a general postulate of conversation cf. above, p. 129.

and freedom from coercion can be formulated as three rules. These rules correspond to the conditions laid down by Habermas for the ideal speech situation[46] in the weakened version accepted above.[47] The first rule concerns entry into discourse. It goes as follows:

(2.1) Everyone who can speak may take part in discourse.

The second rule governs the freedom of discussion. It can be subdivided into three provisions:

(2.2) (a) Everyone may problematize any assertion.
(b) Everyone may introduce any assertion into the discourse.
(c) Everyone may express his or her attitudes, wishes, and needs.

(c) is of significance particularly in practical discourse. Finally, the third rule has the task of shielding discourse from coercion. It stipulates that:

(2.3) No speaker may be prevented from exercising the rights laid down in (2.1) and (2.2) by any kind of coercion internal or external to the discourse.

It may be doubted whether (2.3) is a rule of discourse at all. It could also be regarded as a condition of realizing (2.1) and (2.2). However, it will suffice here to point out its special status.

It might be thought that little has been gained by setting out these rules. In reality, it is quite out of the question that all speakers should avail themselves of the rights provided for in rules (2.1) and (2.2). Furthermore, it may be doubted whether the freedom from coercion required by (2.3) could ever be achieved.[48]

Nevertheless, these rules are not meaningless. Justificatory arguments which would not be accepted when (2.1)–(2.3) (including the additional rules of discourse) were satisfied, are to be regarded as invalid. So together with the remaining rules of discourse they form a *negative hypothetical criterion* for the

[46] Cf. Habermas, 'Wahrheitstheorien', pp. 255–6.
[47] Cf. above, pp. 120–1, 127 ff.
[48] On this cf. above, pp. 121 ff.

correctness of normative statements. Their role as a *positive criterion* is more problematic. A distinction must be made between their function as a criterion for discussions which have actually occurred or are occurring, and their function as a criterion for hypothetical discussions. With regard to actual discussions, rules (2.1)–(2.3) can only be approximately satisfied. In addition, there always exists some possibility of error about the degree to which they have been satisfied. However, it can be said that where (2.1)–(2.3) are satisfied to the highest degree possible in the situation to be assessed, they do yield something akin to a provisional criterion. With regard to their role as a positive hypothetical criterion, the difficulty arises that there is a need for prognoses concerning the behaviour of *all* those affected in relation to the discussion. This calls for extensive empirical inquiry. The criterion will be as uncertain in application as these prognoses are. This uncertainty, however, does not make the criterion meaningless. But it does furnish grounds for treating as reversible, conclusions reached by reference to it.

Linked to the role of (2.1)–(2.3) as criteria for the correctness of normative statements is their role as an *instrument of criticism* of unjustifiable limitations of the rights and opportunities of discourse-partners. For they show that some limitations can be justified, namely those which in comparison with other limitations or with no limitations at all offer a better chance of arriving at a result which would also be generated under ideal conditions. Furthermore, they define an *ideal* which can be approached through practice[49] and organizational arrangements. Empirical knowledge must be brought into play both in testing limitations and in answering the question of the degree to which an approximation to this ideal is possible under certain circumstances. Finally, these rules yield an '*explication*' of the claim to truthfulness or correctness. The claim to justice is a special case of the claim to correctness. An explication of this concept is therefore made possible by reference to these rules.

(2) along with (2.1)–(2.3) defines the most important

[49] On the question of how such practice is possible cf. O. Ludwig and W. Menzel, 'Diskutieren als Gegenstand und Methode des Deutschunterrichts', *Praxis Deutsch*, 14 (1976), 13–22, as well as the eight didactic models put forward in this issue.

conditions for the rationality of discourses. They are therefore to be called '*rationality rules*'.

4.3 Rules for Allocating the Burden of Argument

(2.2.a) allows everyone to problematize any assertion. If this were unqualified it would let any speaker be driven into a corner by childish and mechanical repetition of the question 'why?'. It would also be possible to present everything said by the other parties to the deliberation as completely dubious. Each of these moves is quite simple for a speaker who can ask questions or express doubts without ever having to give reasons for so doing. The rules worked out so far do indeed regulate the burden of putting forward justifications in the case of assertions, but not with respect to posing questions or registering doubts.

This gives rise to a question of great importance for discourses, namely that of the extent and distribution of burdens of argument or of burdens of justification.[50] This problem has cropped up in various connections in the discussion so far. According to Singer, the generalization principle demands that anyone wishing to treat one person differently from another must provide a reason for so doing.[51] In Lorenzen's dialogical logic, for example, whoever asserts that all *x*'s have the characteristic F ((*x*)F*x*) is obliged to show with regard to any *a* that it is an F (F*a*).[52] Finally, Perelman's principle of inertia stipulates that a view or practice which has once been accepted should not be abandoned without some reason.[53]

The distribution of the burden of argument stipulated by Singer results from the principle of universalizability (1.3′) together with the justification rule (2). Whoever proposes to treat A differently from B asserts, inasmuch as he or she presupposes (1.3′), that there exists a relevant difference

[50] These expressions are used synonymously in this investigation. A. Podlech differentiates between them in a way not needed here in his *Gehalt und Funktionen des allgemeinen verfassungsrechtlichen Gleichheitssatzes* (Berlin, 1971), 87–8.

[51] Singer, *Generalization in Ethics*, p. 31. Cf. above, pp. 65 ff.

[52] Lorenzen and Schwemmer, *Konstruktive Logik, Ethik und Wissenschaftstheorie*, p. 46. Cf. above, p. 138.

[53] Perelman and Olbrechts-Tyteca, *La Nouvelle Rhétorique*, p. 142 (p. 106). Cf. above, pp. 171 ff.

between them. This assertion has to be justified. The following rule therefore applies:

(3.1) Whoever proposes to treat a person A differently from a person B is obliged to provide justification for so doing.[54]

A further justification of (3.1) is to be found in the rationality rules according to which all are equal and reasons must therefore be put forward in order to justify any deviation from this condition. The rationality rules provide justifying grounds for a presumption of equality.[55]

It is not possible to discuss the justification of a dialogical construction of logic in this investigation. For this reason it will only be pointed out here that it is to be taken for granted that the rules of logic impose the strictest commitments in argument. Whoever asserts '$p \rightarrow q$' must, if his or her speech partner advances '$\neg q$', either accept '$\neg p$' or refute '$\neg q$' or give up '$p \rightarrow q$'.

In addition, Perelman's principle of inertia is of considerable significance. According to (2), when a speaker asserts something, his or her discussion-partner or collocutor has the right to call for a justifying reason. By contrast, a statement or norm which is presupposed as true or valid within the speaker's community, yet is not expressly asserted or discussed, may, according to this principle, only be doubted or questioned by giving some reason for so doing:

(3.2) Whoever attacks a statement or norm which is not the subject of the discussion must state a reason for so doing.

Finally, it is not admissible for a speaker to persist in demanding ever more reasons from his or her partner.[56] The partner or collocutor would soon run out of reasons. Once the

[54] For a very similar interpretation of the 'pragmatic content' of the constitutional principle of equality cf. Podlech, *Gehalt und Funktionen*, p. 89.

[55] On this cf. Rawls, 'Justice as Fairness', *The Philosophical Review*, 67 (1958), 166: 'There is a presumption against the distinctions and classifications made by legal systems and other practices to the extent that they infringe on the original and equal liberty of the persons participating in them.'

[56] Cf. Austin, 'Other Minds', p. 84: 'If you say, "that's not enough", then you must have in mind some more or less definite lack. . . . If there is no definite lack, which you are at least prepared to specify on being pressed, then it's silly (outrageous) just to go on saying "That's not enough".'

collocutor has cited a reason as is required by the justification rule, he or she is only obliged to make any further response in the event of counter-arguments:

(3.3) Whoever has put forward an argument is only obliged to produce further arguments in the event of counter-arguments.

(2.2.b) and (2.2.c) allow any speaker to introduce, whenever he or she pleases, any number whatever of assertions and utterances about his or her attitudes, wishes, and needs. In this way anyone can at any time advance assertions about the weather, for example, as well as utterances about his or her perceptions of it, without the existence of any connection at all with the problem under discussion. It is not necessary to exclude such utterances completely. If they only crop up once in a while, they do not necessarily harm the discussion. It must be left to the participants in a discourse to decide when they should be excluded. Moreover, it is not appropriate to exclude them by setting up a requirement that only relevant points be made,[57] as if it were a matter for discourse theory to determine issues of relevancy. That is entirely a matter for the parties to an argument. This suggests the following rule:

(3.4) Whoever introduces an assertion or an utterance about his or her attitudes, wishes, or needs into a discourse, which does not stand as an argument in relation to a prior utterance, must justify this interjection when required to do so.

4.4 The Argument Forms

Before embarking upon further rules of discourse, it will make sense to take a look first at the argument forms characteristic[58] of practical discourse.

Singular normative statements (N) are the immediate subject-matter of practical discourse. There are two basic ways

[57] On such a requirement cf. Grice, *Logic and Conversation*, p. 34.

[58] It should be stressed that only those argument forms specific to general practical discourses are dealt with here. Besides these there exist many argument forms which occur both in general practical as well as in other discourses. On this cf. the discussion of Perelman's analyses above, pp. 164 ff.

of justifying them. In the first, reference is made to a *rule* (R) presupposed as valid; in the second the *consequences* (F) of observing the imperatives implied[59] in N, are pointed out.[60]

There is an important structural relationship between these two ways. Whoever appeals to a rule in the course of providing a justificatory argument is at least presupposing that the conditions for applying this rule have been met. These conditions of application might be the characteristics of some person, action, or object, or the existence of a certain state of affairs, or the occurrence of a specific event. This means that whoever cites a rule as a reason presupposes that a statement (T) describing such characteristics, states of affairs, or events is true.

On the other hand whoever asserts something about consequences as a reason for N presupposes a rule to the effect that the achievement of these consequences is obligatory or good. This is so by reason of the generalization: 'the notion of a reason, as always, brings with it the notion of a rule which lays down that something is a reason for something else'.[61]

One can therefore distinguish argument forms as shown:

(4.1) T
R
—
N

(4.2) F
R
—
N

(4.1) and (4.2) are sub-forms of the more general form:

(4) G
$R^{\cdot}$
—
$N^{\cdot}$[62]

There can be theoretical discourse both about the truth of T and about whether or not F really is a consequence of the action

[59] On the possibility of imperatives being implied by normative propositions (value-judgments and judgments of obligation) cf. above, p. 59.

[60] On these two kinds of justification cf. Toulmin, *The Place of Reason in Ethics*, p. 132, and also above, pp. 81 ff.

[61] Hare, *Freedom and Reason*, p. 21. Cf. also above, p. 66.

[62] '$R^{\cdot}$' in contrast to 'R', and as well as to 'R″', denotes a rule of any level whatever, '$N^{\cdot}$' in contrast to 'N' any normative proposition (not just a singular one). The introduction of '$R^{\cdot}$' and '$N^{\cdot}$' is necessary in order to be able to express the generality of (4).

in question.[63] The requirement that one must always be able to open up such a discourse at any time is supported by a rule of its own to be introduced below.

The main focus of interest here is disputes about R. There are different ways of defending R. R may be justified by giving an account of the state of affairs which prevails when R holds (S_R) or by pointing out some future state which will come to pass if R holds (S_F). S_R and S_F are to be distinguished in that in order to describe S_R it is necessary to include some reference to R in addition to indicating consequences which can be described independently of R. Provided one bears in mind these differences, it is nevertheless justifiable, for reasons of simplicity, to speak of the *consequences of the rule R* (F_R) both in the case of S_R and in that of S_F.

The thesis that giving a reason for an assertion presupposes a rule to the effect that the reason given counts as a reason for such an assertion, also holds good when R is justified through F_R. A second order rule (R′) is therefore necessary.[64]

Besides drawing attention to F_R, it is also possible to adduce a further rule R′ which requires R under some condition T′ which is not classifiable as a consequence of R. T′ could, for example, involve pointing out what is by no means morally irrelevant, namely that a certain rule was decided upon in a certain way.

This yields two second-level argument forms:[65]

(4.3) $\dfrac{F_R \quad R'}{R}$ (4.4) $\dfrac{T' \quad R'}{R}$

(4.3) and (4.4) are also sub-forms of the basic form (4).[66]

[63] It should be stressed that it is the answer to this question which is the decisive problem in many discourses. Many disputes about practical questions could be settled immediately were there sufficient certain empirical knowledge on which to draw. It would nevertheless be wrong to conclude from this that all practical problems are soluble merely by procuring empirical information.

[64] On such rules of the second level cf. above, p. 87.

[65] On the different levels of justification cf. above, p. 82.

[66] In (4.1)–(4.4) the conclusion in each case follows from the general normative statement together with an empirical statement. Starting out from the position of a true empirical statement and a false conclusion the general normative premiss must be false. The four forms therefore not only represent

In each case of (4.1)–(4.4) the application of a specific rule leads to a specific result. However, different rules can yield different and mutually inconsistent results both when the justifying arguments involved are of the same form and when they are of different forms. In such cases it must be decided which justifying argument is to take precedence. The rules invoked to justify such decisions are called '*priority rules*'.[67]

There are priority rules which prescribe that certain rules are

the *justification* of normative statements—corresponding to them over and above this are four forms of *testing* general normative statements. In the process of such testing it may be asked whether logical consequences which cannot be accepted as correct may be yielded by a general normative statement, perhaps the premiss R of a justification of form (4.2) (the hypothesis) together with an empirical statement to be accepted as true. Should this be the case the general normative statement must be rejected or modified. In the case of (4.2) the following pattern of inference would underlie such testing:

$([(F \wedge R) \rightarrow N] \wedge \neg N \wedge F) \rightarrow \neg R$

In practical discourses arguments corresponding to (4.1)–(4.4) can thus be used both in justifications and for testing. Since the various forms of testing can be arrived at through the forms of justification according to the rules of logic (1.1) there is no need to go into them here. The relationship of justification and testing is yielded by the rules of discourse. Whoever makes an assertion must give a reason for so doing (2). He or she does not, however, have to continue justifying any assertion ever further. Further arguments need only be adduced in response to counter-arguments (3.3). These counter-arguments may contain a test of the aforementioned kind, and themselves become the object of such testing. There thus occurs an interplay between justification and testing.

In this, justification takes priority. Testing occurs in practical discourses only where something is being asserted. When something is asserted, however, then according to (2) at least one reason for it must always be cited. Moreover, the object of such testing always consists of general statements. In practical discourse, general normative statements only become relevant in the course of justification of singular normative statements. Even more importantly, the testing of normative statements always requires further normative statements. Whoever asserts such a statement in the course of such testing must by reason of the general justification rule (2) always give at least one reason in favour of it—that is, must cite a justification of the form (4.1)–(4.4). A mere reference to evidence or intuition is not admissible. This results from the untenability of intuitionism (cf. above, pp. 38 f.). It is for these reasons, as well as for reasons of simplicity of exposition, that reference is made throughout to justifications in particular. It would always be possible to extend the arguments to testing.

[67] On the concept of a priority rule cf. Baier, *The Moral Point of View*, pp. 99 ff. and also above, p. 94.

to take precedence over others under all circumstances; but there are also priority rules which lay down that certain rules are to take precedence over others only under specified conditions (C). Let P be a relation of precedence between two rules. The priority rules can then be of two forms:

(4.5) R_iPR_k and $R_i'PR_k'$
(4.6) $(R_iPR_k)C$ and $(R_i'PR_k')C$

The priority rules in their turn can be justified by arguments of the forms (4.3) and (4.4).[68] Where conflict arises between priority rules, recourse must be had to second-order priority rules.

A great deal of further differentiation is possible within the various forms. Drawing attention to negative consequences, for example, presents a particularly important variant of (4.2) and (4.3). There may perhaps be further forms. However, the analysis presented here is sufficient for the theory of rational discourse which is the concern of the present investigation.

It highlights one factor in particular: the different argument forms can (except in so far as the two-stage character of justification imposes a limitation) be combined and iterated entirely *ad lib*. The various combinations of argument forms constitute an argument structure.[69] A distinction must be made here between a regressive and an additive argument structure.[70] Justificatory arguments can be combined with testing procedures and testing procedures lead on into justification. Argument structures which occur in this way are always finite.

[68] (4.5) and (4.6) themselves are not argument forms, but rather forms of rules. The insertion of (4.5) or (4.6) for R in (4.3) or (4.4), however, yields four further argument forms as follows: two sub-forms each of (4.3) and (4.4). Since (4.3) and (4.4) are sub-forms of (4), it is possible to speak of the existence of two groups of sub-forms of (4), characterized by (4.5) and (4.6) as conclusions. This is what was meant when in the Introduction there was a remark to the effect that six forms are distinguished here. What must be stressed is that all six are sub-forms of (4).

[69] On the concept of argument structure cf. above, pp. 92–3.

[70] An additive argument structure exists when an assertion or rule is justified by means of various arguments which are independent of one another. It would also be possible to speak of several justifications in such a case. In a regressive structure, the one argument would act as the support of the other. On this cf. above, p. 169.

It is never possible to justify all rules, for there are always some which simply have to be accepted if the process of justification is to be possible at all.[71] The demand for rationality does not mean that all rules are to be simultaneously justified, but only that any rule can be subjected to the process of justification.

4.5 The Justification Rules

The formulas (4.1)–(4.6) only specified *forms* of argument employable in practical discourses. It is already a gain for rationality if arguments are conducted in these forms and not countered by means such as flattery, accusations, and threats. On the other hand, any normative statements and rules whatever may be justified in these forms. A search should therefore be carried out for rules which govern the justificatory arguments to be conducted in these forms.

4.5.1 The various versions of the principle of generalizability form a first important group of rules.[72] According to the preceding discussion, three versions of the requirement of generalizability should be distinguished here: those of Hare, Habermas, and Baier.[73]

[71] Toulmin, *The Uses of Argument*, pp. 100, 106, as well as above, p. 87.

[72] These rules can in the main be justified by means of the rules already cited. This might be put forward as a reason for not receiving them into the list of rules. However, there are at least considerations of expediency in favour of such a move.

[73] Singer's generalization argument, which has already been mentioned several times (above, pp. 97–8), will not be taken up here. The following justification will be given for this: It is fairly certain that this argument will lead back to other principles. Singer derives it from the principle of universalizability (1.3′), together with a principle of consequences which might be viewed as a negative variant of (4.2) (*Generalization in Ethics*, pp. 63 ff.). Hoerster justifies it through a 'principle of fairness' (*Utilitaristische Ethik und Verallgemeinerung*, pp. 108 ff.). Should Singer's derivation be tenable, it could be traced back to rules and forms which have already been taken up here, which would involve further definition of (4.2). Hoerster's principle of fairness declares it to be 'immoral, to enjoy the fruits of an enterprise undertaken by many and yet to leave the burdens or sacrifices necessarily involved in the enterprise only to the others' (ibid., p. 112). Everything is in favour of the view that such a way of behaving would not be accepted in a practical discourse. Singer's argument can thus, insofar as regards the

Hare's principle of universalizability has already been formulated as rule (1.3′). From this principle, together with that of prescriptivity,[74] Hare arrives at a requirement of the following kind:[75]

(5.1.1) Everyone who makes a normative statement that presupposes a rule with certain consequences for the satisfaction of the interests of other persons must be able to accept these consequences,[76] even in the hypothetical situation where he or she is in the position of those persons.[77]

In short, everyone must be able to agree to the consequences for everyone else of the rules he or she presupposes or asserts.

Habermas's version of the generalizability principle is the direct result of the structure of discourse as determined by the rationality rules ((2.1)–(2.3)). If everyone deliberates about practical questions on an equal footing, then only those normative statements and rules which everyone can accept will be generally agreed upon.

(5.1.1) takes the normative views of individual speakers as its starting-point. Habermas's principle of generalizability relates to the common views to be worked on in discourse. It can be formulated as follows:

(5.1.2) The consequences of every rule for the satisfaction of the interests of each and every individual must be acceptable to everyone.[78]

justification put forward by him and by Hoerster, be viewed as implied by the rules and forms as well as the conditions of general practical discourse. This makes it appear unnecessary to receive Singer's argument into the list of rules summarized here. To be sure, it would certainly be quite useful to include this argument in a more elaborate theory of discourse.

[74] On this cf. above, pp. 69 ff.

[75] On the question of whether this requirement follows solely from the principle of universalizability, together with the principle of prescriptivity, cf. above, pp. 70–1.

[76] 'Consequences' are here to be understood as both the factual consequences of the observance of a rule, and the constraints which directly result from observance of the imperatives implied by the rules.

[77] On the problems related to (5.1.1), particularly its limited efficiency, cf. above, pp. 72 ff.

[78] On this and on the question of the compatibility of (5.1.1) and (5.1.2) cf. above, p. 116.

In short, everyone must be able to agree to every rule.[79] (5.1.2) shares the ideal character of the rationality rules.

Baier's principle can be justified by two requirements governing discourse: openness and sincerity. It can be understood as a concretization of (1.2). It immediately excludes a whole number of rules as unjustifiable:[80]

(5.1.3) Every rule must be openly and universally teachable.

4.5.2 Even (5.1.1)–(5.1.3) do not yet offer anything like a guarantee of rational *agreement*. (5.1.1) makes it possible to proceed from the various, actually extant normative convictions of any speaker whoever; (5.1.2) shares the ideal character of the rationality rules, and (5.1.3) excludes only relatively few moral rules.

It is not possible to present a procedure which secures a rational agreement in each case. However, much would already have been gained if a procedure could be found which at least increased the probability of adjusting mutually inconsistent but actually held views in the direction of rational agreement. Such a procedure has been proposed by Habermas and also—in an elaborated and detailed form—by Lorenzen and Schwemmer in the programme of critical genesis.[81] In such a genesis, the development of the system of moral rules is retrospectively reconstructed by the participants in the discourse. It can then be established for the various developmental stages, to what extent the conditions of rational discourse were realized. Corresponding to this, the rules evolved in this developmental process and which now govern our practical reasoning can be criticized. This gives rise to the formulation of the following additional rule of discourse:

(5.2.1) The moral rules underlying the moral views of a speaker must be able to withstand critical testing in terms of their historical genesis. A moral rule cannot stand up to such testing if:

> (a) even though originally amenable to rational justification, it has in the meantime lost its justification, or

[79] For Perelman's very similar requirements cf. above, p. 163.
[80] Cf. above, pp. 95–6. [81] Cf. above, pp. 133–4, 149 ff.

(b) it was not originally amenable to rational justification and no adequate new grounds have been discovered for it in the meantime.[82]

The testing of the socio-historical origin of norms proposed by Lorenzen and Schwemmer must be supplemented by testing normative views in their individual development:[83]

(5.2.2) The moral rules underlying the moral views of a speaker must be able to withstand critical testing in terms of their individual genesis. A moral rule does not stand up to such testing if it has only been adopted on grounds of some unjustifiable conditions of socialization.

It must remain an open question during this investigation what are to count as 'unjustifiable conditions of socialization'. Here it can only be remarked that conditions of socialization can certainly not be justified if they result in the individual concerned being unable or unwilling to participate in discourses.

4.5.3 A final rule of this group results from the fact that practical discourses are conducted for the purposes of resolving practical questions as they actually occur. It is of course possible to conduct practical discourse just for the fun of it, but this possibility is parasitic on the aforementioned one. This gives rise to the conclusion that practical discourses must yield results which are practically realizable:

(5.3) The actually given limits of realizability are to be taken into account.[84]

The application of (5.3) presupposes considerable empirical knowledge.

(5.1)–(5.3) have direct and decisive impact on the content of statements and rules to be justified. They are therefore to be called '*justification rules*'.

[82] Cf. above, pp. 151–2.

[83] Cf. above, pp. 152–3.

[84] (5.3) requires both that the realizability of a norm be logically possible at all and that it lies in the realm of the actually possible. On the first requirement cf. Kutschera, *Einführung in die Logik der Normen, Werte und Entscheidungen*, pp. 69–70.

4.6 The Transition Rules

It has already been observed that many problems arise in practical discourses which cannot be resolved through practical argumentation. These problems include questions of fact, particularly the prediction of consequences; linguistic problems, especially problems of understanding; and questions relating to practical discussion itself. In such cases it must be possible to make a transition into other forms of discourse. This possibility is guaranteed through the following rules:

(6.1) It is possible for any speaker at any time to make a transition into a theoretical (empirical) discourse.

(6.2) It is possible for any speaker at any time to make a transition into a linguistic-analytical discourse.[85]

(6.3) It is possible for any speaker at any time to make a transition into a discourse-theoretical discourse.[86]

(6.1)–(6.3) are to be called '*transition rules*'. (6.1) is of particular significance. Speakers often agree about normative premisses but are in dispute about the facts. It is frequently the case that the necessary empirical knowledge cannot be attained with desirable certainty. In this situation there is a need for rules of reasonable presumption.

5. THE LIMITS OF GENERAL PRACTICAL DISCOURSE

Observance of the stated rules and utilization of the described forms of argument do indeed increase the probability of reaching agreement on practical issues, but they do not guarantee that agreement can be reached on every subject nor that any agreement obtained will be final and irreversible. The reason for this lies in the facts that the rationality rules (2.1)–(2.3), in particular, can only be partially fulfilled; that not all steps in argumentation are fixed ones; and that every discourse must latch on to historically given, and hence changeable, normative preconceptions.

[85] Cf. above, pp. 144–5.
[86] Cf. above, p. 187.

To the extent that the outcomes of discourse cannot lay claim to any final certainty, it is necessary that they should always be open to revision. This requirement is borne out by the rules set out above, in particular the rationality rules which lay down that anyone can at any time dispute any rule and any normative statement, including even the rules and statements which have hitherto been regarded as indisputably sound.

To be sure, several judgments of value and of obligation as well as several rules are stringently required and flatly excluded by the rules of discourse. This holds true, for example, of rules which completely exclude some human beings from participation in discourses by imposing the legal status of a slave on them. In this sense it is possible to speak respectively of '*discursive impossibility*' and '*discursive necessity*'.[87] Rules of discourse can be used as premisses in the justification of such discursively necessary or discursively impossible rules.

In those instances in which two incompatible normative statements or rules can be justified without violating any of the rules of discourse,[88] one can speak of '*discursive possibility*'. This situation in its turn can be the subject of practical discourse. In such discourses, rules are justified which make it possible to decide between two incompatible and discursively possible solutions. Examples of such rules are the rules of parliamentary legislation based on the principle of representation and the majority principle. Rules such as these, as well as those legal rules established by procedures governed by them, are necessary and to this extent reasonable, because there are limits to the possibility of arriving at compelling solutions in practical

[87] Cf. above, pp. 17, 132.

[88] The concept of a violation of a rule of discourse must be defined differently according to the distinct character of the different rules. In the case of non-ideal rules, as for example (1.1) (freedom from contradiction), (1.3′) (universalizability), and (5.3) (realizability), it is in principle always ascertainable whether or not there has been a violation. The ideal rules like (2.1) (universality of participation) and (5.1.2) (universality of agreement) on the other hand are only approximately realizable. Accordingly, one would speak of their being fulfilled in any given situation if there were conformity to them to an optimal degree in the given context.

discourse.[89] The limits of general practical discourse provide justifying grounds for the necessity of legal rules.[90] This brings about the transition into legal discourse.

[89] A similar idea is to be found in Kant, whose principle of the 'freedom of every member of society as a human being' (*Kant's Political Writings*, ed. H. Reiss, trans. H. B. Nisbet (Cambridge, 1970), 74—a translation of 'On the Common Saying: "This May be True in Theory, but it does not Apply in Practice" ') requires that 'only the united and consenting Will of all—that is, a general united Will of the people by which each decides the same for all and all decide the same for each—can legislate' (*The Metaphysical Elements of Justice*, p. 78). Kant establishes that such a consent of an entire people is problematic. 'An entire people cannot, however, be expected to reach unanimity, but only to show a majority of votes (and not even of direct votes, but simply of the votes of those delegated in a large nation to represent the people). Thus the actual principle of being content with majority decisions must be accepted unanimously and embodied in a contract; and this itself must be the ultimate basis on which a civil constitution is established' ('On the Common Saying', p. 79).

[90] Such legal rules usually have not only the function of facilitating solutions where no discursive agreement can be reached, but also that of securing the presuppositions under which it is in fact possible for discourses to be conducted. On this requirement cf. Wieland, 'Praxis und Urteilskraft', pp. 40 ff. However, the fact that legal rules can make it possible for discourses to be conducted does not mean that they are not themselves amenable to discursive justification.

C. A THEORY OF LEGAL ARGUMENTATION

I. Legal Discourse as a Special Case of General Practical Discourse

1. TYPES OF LEGAL DISCUSSION

There are quite different types of legal discussions. A distinction can be made between discussions in legal science (legal dogmatics),[1] judicial deliberation, debates in courts of law, legislative treatment of legal questions (whether in legislatures themselves or before commissions or committees), discussions of legal questions among students or among jurists or lawyers or among legally qualified personnel in administration or industry, as well as debates on legal problems in the media, at any rate where these take the form of juristic arguments.

The differences between these forms of discussion, which can in turn be divided into further sub-groups, are manifold. Several of them, such as court-room negotiation and judicial deliberation, are institutionalized. This is not the case with others, like the discussion of legal questions among lawyers. With some of the forms it is a question of arriving at a conclusion within a limited time period; with others such as discussions in legal science (dogmatic discussions), there is no time limit. Some result in binding decisions, whilst others only suggest, or lay the groundwork for, or criticize decisions. Some forms, such as the public discussion of judgments, allow of a transition at any time from legal to general practical arguments, whilst in others, such

[1] Under the concept of legal scientific (dogmatic) discussion in the present context, are to be understood discussions of an institutionally organized profession of academic lawyers where these discussions are either concerned directly with the resolution of actual or imaginary legal cases, or with justifying or criticizing dogmatic propositions, constructions, and theories with at least some reference to the resolution of legal cases. The concept of legal dogmatics will be discussed in more detail below, pp. 250 ff. For a different use of terminology cf. O. Ballweg, *Rechtswissenschaft und Jurisprudenz* (Basle, 1970), 7 ff., 90ff., 123. He calls what is here termed 'dogmatic legal science', 'jurisprudence', and limits the expression 'legal science' to the analysis and theory of 'jurisprudence'.

as legal scientific (dogmatic) discussions, this is certainly not possible without constraints.

Just as diverse as the differences are the similarities and connections. The most important common feature consists in the fact that within all the forms argumentation is (at least in part) *legal*.

The question of what distinguishes legal reasoning from general practical reasoning is one of the central questions of the theory of legal discourse. One point can be established even at this stage: legal reasoning is characterized by its relationship with valid law, however this is to be determined.

This highlights one of the most important differences between legal reasoning and general practical reasoning. In the context of legal discussion not all questions are open to debate. Such discussion takes place under certain constraints.

The extent and kinds of constraint are very different within the different forms. The freest or least constrained is discussion of a legal scientific kind. Constraints are greatest in the context of a trial. Here roles are unequally distributed, the participation of the defendant is not voluntary,[2] and the obligation to tell the truth is limited. The reasoning process in limited in time[3] and regulated by the rules of procedural law. The parties are entitled to be guided by their own interests. Frequently, perhaps even commonly, they are not concerned with arriving at a correct or just outcome but rather at one that is advantageous to themselves. The other forms can be ranged between these extremes with respect to the extent of the various constraints.

2. THE SPECIAL CASE THESIS

The thesis has been stated above that legal discourse is a special case of general practical discourse.[4] This was supported on the ground that: (1) legal discussions are concerned with practical

[2] On this cf. H. Rottleuthner, 'Zur Soziologie richterlichen Handelns II', *Kritische Justiz*, 4 (1971), 81 ff.

[3] On this cf. Wieacker, 'Zur praktischen Leistung der Rechtsdogmatik', 329, and K. Makkonen, *Zur Problematik der juridischen Entscheidung*, trans. B. Assmuth (Turku, 1965), 26.

[4] Above, pp. 15, 19.

questions—that is, what should or may be done or not done—and (2) these questions are discussed under the claim to correctness. It is a matter of a 'special case' because legal discussions (3) do take place under constraints of the kind described.

The special case thesis is accordingly open to attack on all three points. It is possible to assert that legal discussions: (1) are not concerned with practical questions, (2) do not carry with them any claims to correctness, or (3) do indeed make such claims but the constraints governing legal discussions make it unjustifiable to designate them 'discourses'.

2.1 The first objection is the easiest to counter. It is certainly the case that there are many discussions relating to legal questions which are concerned not with substantiating normative statements but rather with the establishment of facts. This does not only include investigations in legal history, sociology of law, and legal theory but also descriptions of valid law and predictions of future judicial behaviour.[5] This is not the place to discuss whether and to what extent these activities are possible without entering into practical questions. The only important point is that quite apart from these activities, there exists legal reasoning orientated to solving practical questions. It plays a central role both in legal practice and in the realm of legal science.[6] This is what we are concerned with here.

[5] On this cf. the investigation into the concept of legal dogmatics below, pp. 250 ff.

[6] It should be noted that the broad concept of legal science used here, which includes argumentation related to the resolution of practical questions, does indeed conform to what is regarded as self-evident by probably most jurists working in the field of dogmatics, but it is by no means self-evident. According to Kelsen, for example, legal science should limit itself to the knowledge and description of positive legal norms (*Pure Theory of Law*, pp. 70 ff.). The task of legal science is the 'value-free description' of valid law (ibid., 79). Kelsen does indeed see that a legal norm cannot give rise to a definite, clear-cut decision in every case if only because of the vagueness of the expressions used to formulate it. Nevertheless, the task of legal science should be limited to elaborating the various possible meanings with respect to any doubtful cases which occur (ibid., 355 ff.). The option in favour of one of several possible decisions should be reserved for the 'authentic interpretation' of the courts (ibid., pp. 236 ff., 353 ff.), for this involves a value-judgment and not a question of scientific truth (ibid., 356). Underlying Kelsen's view in the conviction that value-judgments

2.2 The claim to correctness involved in legal discourses is clearly distinguishable from that involved in general practical discourses. There is no claim that the normative statement asserted, proposed, or pronounced in judgments is absolutely rational, but only a claim that it can be rationally justified within the framework of the prevailing legal order. Precisely what this means has to be elucidated in the framework of the theory of legal discourse.

A whole series of quite distinct arguments can be adduced for the 'claim-to-correctness thesis'. First it may be observed that justifying arguments are put forward in all forms of legal discourse. Anyone who justifies something is thereby implicitly claiming that the justification is sound and the assertion therefore correct.[7] It is not permissible in legal discourses any more than in general practical discourses to assert something and then to refuse to justify it without giving reasons. It is therefore true of legal statements, just as of general normative statements, that they make a claim to correctness[8]—a claim to be upheld in quite different ways, of course. This claim to correctness is not rendered invalid by the fact that the person justifying some position is only following his or her subjective interests. What holds true here is similar to the case of promising. The fact that in making a promise I may secretly intend not to keep it, in no way affects the obligation which has objectively come into existence as a result of the promise.

The demand for justification and the claim to correctness bound up with it, can, at least as far as concerns judicial decisions, be justified beyond this through positive law.

and judgments of obligation have no truth-value and are not rationally justifiable, and therefore cannot be the subject of scientific inquiry. It is the thesis of this work that the latter is not the case. If and presumably only if this thesis is tenable, then the above use of the broad concept of legal science has been justified.

[7] Cf. above, pp. 130 ff., 191–2.

[8] On this cf. above, pp. 127 ff. and also Larenz, *Methodenlehre der Rechtswissenschaft*, p. 276, where in reference to Hare and Frankena he observes: 'If moral value-judgments already raise a claim, through their meaning, of being capable of being approved by every reasonable person and in this sense of being "valid", then this must be true to an even greater degree of legal value-judgments'.

According to the law as it is currently in force in the Federal Republic of Germany and doubtless most other states, judges are under a duty to justify their decisions.[9] This places judicial decisions within the scope of the claim to correctness by virtue of positive law. A further grounding for this is in the legal system of the Federal Republic of Germany derivable from Article 20, paragraph 3 of the Constitution (*Grundesetz*) which subjects every exercise of jurisdiction to 'legislation and the rule of law' ('Gesetzund Recht').

It is a quite different question whether it is necessarily the case that this claim is implicit in the issuance of judicial decisions as such. This would be the case if the concept of a judicial decision included the concept of the claim to correctness. The answer to this question depends on how one defines the concept of a judicial decision. There are good reasons for defining this concept within the framework of an analytic legal theory, in such a way that it does not embrace this claim.[10] On the other hand it will be said that a judgment such as: 'Mr N. is hereby sentenced to ten years' imprisonment in the name of the people, although there are no good reasons in favour of this' is not defective solely on moral grounds. Its defectiveness rather resembles that of an utterance such as: 'The cat is on the mat but I do not believe it.'[11] It is, of course, quite possible for such a

[9] Cf. para. 30, sect. 1, *BVerfGG*; para. 313, sect. 1, No. 6, *ZPO* (Code of Civil Procedure); paras. 267, 275, sect. 1, *StPO* (Code of Criminal Procedure); para. 117, sect. 2, No. 5, *VwGO* (Code of Procedure of the Administrative Court); paras. 60, sect. 2; 75, sect. 2; 96, sect. 2, *ArbGG* (Code of Procedure of the Labour Court); also J. Brüggemann, *Die richterliche Begründungspflicht* (Berlin, 1971), 91 ff. On the limitation of the judicial duty of justification cf. para. 313a, *ZPO*, valid since 1 July 1977. Its narrow presuppositions, in particular the requirement of a renunciation by the parties to a justification, show, however, that para. 313a, *ZPO*, also takes a fundamental duty of justification as its starting-point. For a criticism of para. 313a, *ZPO* cf. H. Putzo, 'Die Vereinfachungsnovelle', *NJW*, 30 (1977), 5–6.

[10] Reasons can be cited in favour of this which quite generally support using the expression 'legal norm' in such a way that it includes no reference to moral norms. Cf. Hart, 'Positivism and the Separation of Law and Morals', pp. 615 ff. On the thesis that there exists no necessary connection between legality and justifiability cf. also Kriele, *Theorie der Rechtsgewinnung*, p. 168.

[11] On the mistaken nature of this utterance cf. Austin, *How to Do Things with Words*, pp. 48 ff., and his 'The Meaning of a Word', *Philosophical Papers*, pp. 63 ff.

judgment to be executed in fact and to be accepted by the members of a legal community, particularly if it remains an isolated case. However, this in no way alters its defects. It is for this reason that there is something to be said for the view that although the lack of a claim to correctness with respect to a given decision does not necessarily deprive the decision of its character as a valid judicial one, yet such a decision always remains defective in more than a morally relevant sense.

It is a quite separate question to what extent the claim to correctness implicit in the issuance of legal judgments and legal justifications is in fact taken seriously and satisfied, and whether and to what extent it matters at all in the light of the acceptance of judicial decisions. Extensive social scientific investigations would be needed to answer this question.[12] Such research would, among other things, lead to an empirical testing of Luhmann's views to the effect that legal decision-making and justification, as well as the acceptance of such decisions and justifications, can only be adequately understood by abandoning the traditional concepts of rationality, truth, correctness, and justice in favour of a structuralist-functional theory of systems.[13]

Here it is not possible to do more than give a few reasons for the supposition that empirical investigation would show that the claim to correctness is constitutive of the practice of legal justification and decision-making, and hence that Luhmann's thesis does not apply.

It is possible to point first to the fact that there are legal deliberations which involve long and intensive discussion on the correctness of a decision and which are, moreover, understood by the participants as a search for a correct decision.[14] There is also much to be said for the view that discussions of a judgment

[12] Esser, *Vorverständnis und Methodenwahl*, p. 121: 'Moreover, there is need for a well-aimed research programme into the question which I regard as central, namely that of the necessity to secure consensus on a decision's legitimacy and legality.'

[13] Cf. Luhmann, *Legitimation durch Verfahren*, pp. 57 ff.; id., *Rechtssystem und Rechtsdogmatik* (Stuttgart, Berlin, Cologne, and Mainz, 1974), 15 ff.; id., *Rechtssoziologie*, vol. ii (Reinbek, 1972), 259 ff.

[14] On this cf. Wieacker, 'Zur praktischen Leistung der Rechtsdogmatik', p. 330: 'In the substantive deliberations of a bench of judges or in the scientific discussions of professional jurists, exchange of arguments wholly becomes the means of a common advance to a practical truth.'

in learned journals or the press, for example, can be seen as disputes about the correctness of the judgment. Furthermore, it may be acceptable for judicial proceedings *also* to have the function of 'isolating [the defendant] as a source of trouble and establishing social order independently of his agreement or objection'.[15] Judicial justification *can*, however, also fulfil other functions: 'It is, rather, to treat a rational being rationally, that is, as a rational being, by *explaining* to him through reasons why a decision that adversely affects his interests has been reached.'[16] Luhmann himself considers it necessary 'for non-participants to come to a conviction that there is nothing strange going on, that truth and right are established with serious, sincere, and arduous endeavour and that they too, if need be, would have secured their rights by recourse to this institution.'[17] This can be interpreted as a paraphrasing of the claim to correctness.

None of this amounts to proofs. However, it does serve to strengthen the suggestion that one reference to rationality expressed by the claim to correctness has as yet not been 'overtaken by evolution', and that 'a mode of socialisation' cut off from norms in need of justification has as yet not been established.[18]

2.3 What has been said up till now is still not sufficient to justify the special case thesis. It would be possible to concede that the legal discussions examined here are indeed concerned with practical questions and that they do make claims to correctness which are in fact significant, yet, in light of the constraints which govern legal discussions, to deny that these

[15] Luhmann, *Legitimation durch Verfahren*, p. 121.

[16] J. Ladd, 'The Place of Practical Reason in Judicial Decision', 144. Cf. Müller, *Juristische Methodik*, p. 106, where he writes that the justification should 'convince those affected', and Larenz, *Methodenlehre der Rechtswissenschaft*, p. 347 n. 83.

[17] Ibid., 123. Cf. Zippelius, who puts forward the empirical claim that a judicature which cannot rely on reasons which are accepted must 'soon also lose the general agreement, the overall consensus on which Luhmann wishes to found the legitimacy of the system.' ('Legitimation durch Verfahren?', in Festschrift for K. Larenz, ed. G. Paulus *et al.* (Munich, 1973), p. 302).

[18] On this problem cf. Habermas, *Legitimation Crisis*, pp. 94, 120. Cf. also above, p. 126.

can count at all as forms of discourse. It must be asked whether this objection is significant.

It is easiest to answer this question with respect to the freest form of legal discussion, namely debates in legal science. No claim is made here to the effect that the normative statement to be justified would receive universal assent in a free-ranging discussion, but it is claimed that everyone governed by the validly prevailing legal order must agree to the statement in question.[19] It is to this kind of argumentation, occurring under certain constraints, yet nevertheless rational, that reference will be made. Such reference to rational argumentation not only justifies talking of legal discourses, but makes such talk seem necessary at least as long as the constraints are not disguised.[20]

Sound reasons can thus be adduced for the special case thesis with respect to legal scientific discussion. It is much more problematic to decide whether this holds true for the reasoning occurring in the context of various legal proceedings. Several features of such proceedings indicate the contrary: the limitations imposed by the procedural rules, time constraints, and the actual motivations of the participants who often if not usually are concerned to achieve a judgment which is to their advantage rather than a correct or just outcome. In addition, in regard to criminal proceedings there is the asymmetrical distribution of roles already mentioned above. It is for these reasons that Habermas conceptualizes a trial as a strategic undertaking rather than as discourse.[21]

At a first glance these reasons would seem incontrovertible. Nevertheless, it should be observed that, although the parties in

[19] This, incidentally, is entirely consistent with holding that a legal statement can only be said to be possible rather than conclusive. In the present instance it is being claimed that agreement is to the effect that it is possible.

[20] Add to this, that it is precisely in legal scientific discussions that one enters into counter-arguments to a high degree. The extent of the consideration and weighing of counter-arguments is regarded as a criterion of the quality of legal scientific inquiries and opinions. To this extent legal scientific treatises—like many other scientific inquiries—are a written form of inner discourse. On this concept cf. above, p. 179.

[21] Habermas, 'Theorie der Gesellschaft oder Sozialtechnologie?', pp. 200–1.

civil proceedings, for example, may be concerned with their own advantage, unless they are striving for a settlement this is not the subject of their negotiation. The argumentation before a court is fundamentally differentiated from that which goes on in negotiations aimed at a settlement. In the arguments they put forward both the parties and their lawyers raise claims to correctness even if they are subjectively only following their own interests. The reasons they put forward in favour of a certain decision could, at least in principle, be included in legal scientific treatises. It is not unusual, particularly in proceedings in the higher courts, to take justifying arguments from learned discussions. Beyond this, the arguments brought forward in court often find their way into judicial justifications and it can hardly be disputed that these are made under a claim to correctness.

It would therefore appear that the various kinds of judicial proceeding cannot be easily categorized as either discourse or strategic undertaking. This gives credence to the suggestion that the distinction is too simplistic. It does not do justice to many phenomena which cannot be unambiguously classified as one or the other.

This difficulty in achieving a clear categorization of proceedings before judges does indeed exclude the possibility of designating them simply as discourses, but on the other hand it does mean that they cannot be theoretically understood without reference to the concept of discourse. This last point connects particularly to the fact that the participants claim to be arguing rationally. Thus, in civil proceedings, the parties do not as a rule wish to convince each other—this has previously already been shown to be impossible—nevertheless, they claim to speak in such a way that every rational person would have to agree with their viewpoint. They at least purport to be making arguments such that they would gain assent under ideal conditions. Discourse theory is thus not only suited to the theoretical understanding of the reasoning involved, it is necessary to understanding it.

This makes it clear that the theory of rational discourse as theory of legal reasoning does not presuppose that all legal disputes are to be viewed as discourse in the sense of non-coercive unfettered communication, but only that, in legal disputes, discussion proceeds under a claim to correctness and accordingly by reference to ideal conditions.[22]

3. TRANSITION TO A THEORY OF LEGAL ARGUMENTATION

This, then, is the core of the special case thesis: the claim to correctness is indeed also raised in legal discourse, but this claim, unlike that in general practical discourse, is not concerned with the absolute rationality of the normative statement in question, but only with showing that it can be rationally justified within the framework of the validly prevailing legal order. But what is to count as a rational justification within the validly prevailing legal order?

In order to answer this question, the following pages will outline the basic features of a theory of legal reasoning. In the course of this it will be possible to fall back to a considerable extent on the conclusions worked out so far.

[22] A quite separate question is whether today's structure of the different forms of process is to be regarded as rational. This must not be answered in the negative simply by alluding to the fact that the freedom of the participants in the discussion is limited. Rather more decisive is whether, in view of the need for a decision, the limitations set down by the rules of legal process offer a sufficient chance of arriving at outcomes which would also have resulted under ideal conditions (cf. above, p. 194). In favour of the current structure it can be argued that given that the participants argue against one another, the judge is subjected in a particularly forceful way to the reasons for and against any specific decision. (On this cf. Kriele, *Theorie der Rechtsgewinning*, p. 147.) Reasons against the rationality of current criminal process have been put forward by H. Rottleuthner, 'Zur Soziologie richterlichen Handelns II', pp. 83 ff., where he points out the prevailing distortion of communication. It would only be possible to discover which structure of the various forms of process could best satisfy the criterion cited above through extensive empirical investigation.

II. The Outline of a Theory of Legal Argumentation

Legal discourses are concerned with the justification[23] of a special case of normative statements, namely those which express legal judgments. Two aspects of justification can be distinguished: *internal justification* and *external justification*.[24] Internal justification is concerned with the question of whether an opinion follows logically from the premisses adduced as justifying it.[25] The correctness of these premisses is the subject-matter of external justification.[26]

1. INTERNAL JUSTIFICATION

Problems associated with internal justification have been widely discussed under the heading 'legal syllogism'. Meanwhile, there is a considerable range of publications in which this problem area is dealt with by applying methods of modern logic.[27]

The simplest form of internal justification has the following structure:

[23] [*Translator's note*: This footnote refers to the distinction between 'Rechtfertigung' and 'Begründung' discussed in n. 3 on p. 34. It once again points out that the two terms are more or less interchangeable.]

[24] On these concepts cf. J. Wróblewski, 'Legal Syllogism and Rationality of Judicial Decision', *Rechtstheorie*, 5 (1974), 39 ff., and his 'Legal Decision and its Justification', in *Le Raisonnement juridique, Akten des Weltkongresses für Rechts-und Sozialphilosophie*, ed. H. Hubien (Brussels, 1971), 412 ff.

[25] id., *Le Raisonnement juridique*, p. 412: 'Internal justification deals with the validity of inferences from given premisses to legal decision taken as their conclusion.'

[26] Ibid.: 'External justification of legal decision tests not only the validity of inference, but also the soundness of premisses.'

[27] Cf. Klug, *Juristische Logic*, 3rd. edn. (Berlin, Heidelberg, and New York, 1966), 47 ff.; G. Rödig, *Die Theorie des gerichtlichen Erkenntnisverfahrens* (Berlin, Heidelberg, and New York, 1973), 163 ff.; Wróblewski, 'Legal Syllogism and Rationality of Judicial Decision', pp. 33 ff.; Schreiber, *Logik des Rechts* (Berlin,

(J.1.1) .(1) $(x)\ (Tx \rightarrow ORx)$
.(2) Ta
(3) ORa (1), (2)[28]

'x' is an individual variable ranging over the domain of natural and juristic persons; 'a' is an individual constant, a proper name for example; 'T' a predicate at any chosen level of complexity appropriate to comprehending the operative facts of the norm (1) as a characteristic of persons; and 'R' is a similarly appropriately complex predicate which expresses that which the norm-subject has to do.

There are legal questions in respect of which a justification of the form (J.1.1) is sufficient. The following is an example:

.(1) Soldiers on official business must tell the truth (paragraph 13, section 1, German Military Regulations).
.(2) Mr M. is a soldier.
(3) Mr M. must tell the truth when on official business. (1), (2)

(J.1.1) satisfies the requirement of justification through universal rules laid down by the principle of universalizability (1.3′).[29] The principle of universalizability underlies the principle of formal justice. The principle of formal justice demands the observance of 'a rule which lays down the obligation to treat in a certain way all persons who belong to a given category.'[30] It is a requirement of the observance of a rule in a legal justification that, as in the case (J.1.1), the legal judgment follows logically from this rule. Otherwise, it would be possible to adduce a rule in the course of the justification and yet to assert any conclusion whatever. The following rules for internal justification can thus be formulated as a concretization of the principle of universalizability:

Göttingen, and Heidelberg, 1962), 24 ff. For an analysis of the legal syllogism by means of traditional logic cf. in particular K. Engisch, *Logische Studien zur Gesetzesanwendung*, 2nd edn. (Heidelberg, 1960).

[28] On problems relating to this scheme of inference and an explanation of the symbols cf. above, pp. 67 ff. For a scheme of inference of this kind as 'basic form for legal inference' cf. Klug, *Juristische Logik*, pp. 52 ff.
[29] On this cf. above, pp. 65 ff.
[30] Perelman, *The Idea of Justice and the Problem of Argument*, p. 40.

(J.2.1) At least one universal norm must be adduced in the justification of a legal judgment.

(J.2.2) A legal judgment must follow logically from at least one universal norm together with further statements.

(J.2.1) and (J.2.2), just like the principle of universalizability, should not be overestimated. They do not lay down anything about the content of the universal norm, nor do they exclude the possibility of changing the universal norm by, for example, introducing exceptions. But such exceptions must in their turn be of universal application.

Of great significance is that (J.2.1) and (J.2.2) apply both in those cases in which a positive legal norm can be used in justification, and in those where no such positive legal norm is available. If no rule can be derived from statute law then a rule must be formulated.[31]

The justification formula (J.1.1) is insufficient for some more complex cases. Such more complex cases arise when, for example, (1) a norm such as paragraph 823, section 1 of the German Civil Code contains several alternative statements of operative facts, or (2) application of the norm involves supplementing it with other clarificatory, limiting, or referential legal norms,[32] or (3) there are several possible legal

[31] (J.2.1) and (J.2.2) thereby serve to secure what Luhmann has called a 'universalistic decision-making practice' (Luhmann, *Rechtssystem und Rechtsdogmatik*, p. 29). Wieacker views universalizability as a necessary feature of legal decision-making. Cf. his 'Über strengere und unstrenge Verfahren der Rechtsfindung', pp. 440 ff., and 'Zur Topikdiskussion', pp. 411 ff. Wieacker not only provides conceptual (analytic) arguments in favour of this view, but also a legal-positivist justification: since the justifications required by rules of procedure, for example by para. 313, sect. 1, no. 6, *ZPO*, 'can be tested by courts of next higher instance, they must be intellectually objectified (in this sense: rational); and since they are tested by appellate courts for "infraction of the *law*" (para. 549, *ZPO*) and "non-application or incorrect application of the *law*" (para. 550, *ZPO*) they must acknowledge a *general* rule (statute or legal principle: art. 2, *EGBGB* (Introductory Law to the Civil Code); art. 20, GG) as a ground for determination' ('Über strengere und unstrenge Verfahren der Rechtsfindung' p. 442). Cf. also Kelsen, *Pure Theory of Law*, p. 244: 'The court-created individual norm is justifiable only as application of such a not positive, general norm.'

[32] On these concepts cf. Larenz, *Methodenlehre der Rechtswissenschaft*, pp. 239 ff. Such clarificatory, limiting, or referential rules can in their turn either be taken from statutes or formulated by those applying the law.

consequences,[33] or (4) the expressions used in formulating the norm allow of several interpretations.

A simple example will serve to clarify this. Suppose it has been established that *a* killed his wife in her sleep, and that there were neither special circumstances nor reasons to justify this deed or to exclude or mitigate guilt. The judge in such a case—no less than the legal scientist discussing it—must test whether the norm stated[34] in paragraph 211, section 1 of the German Criminal Code ('Whoever commits murder is punished by life imprisonment') is applicable. This norm can be stated in the following logical form:[35]

(1) $(x)\ (Tx \rightarrow ORx)$.

'T' is defined in terms of nine characteristics (M^1_1–M^1_9)[36] in paragraph 211, section 2. Paragraph 211, section 2 can be reduced to the following formula:

(2) $(x)\ (M^1_1x \vee M^1_2x \vee \ldots M^1_9x \leftrightarrow Tx)$.

From (1) and (2) follows:

(3) $(x)\ (M^1_1x \vee M^1_2x \vee \ldots M^1_9x \rightarrow ORx)$.

(3) states that in those instances, when at least one of the characteristics is present, the legal consequence OR*x* obtains. 'M^1_5' has the meaning '. . . treacherously killed a human being'. From (3) thus follows:

(4) $(x)\ (M^1_5x \rightarrow ORx)$.

According to the definition used by the courts, treacherous

[33] On this cf. Wróblewski, 'Legal Syllogism and Rationality of Judicial Decision', pp. 43 ff.

[34] On the possibility of expressing norms by means of indicative sentences, as occurs in the criminal code, cf. Wright, *Norm and Action*, pp. 101–2.

[35] It should be stressed that there could be a number of further formalizations of para. 211, sect. 1, *StGB*. One might perhaps understand it as a reaction-guiding norm addressed to the courts and stipulate that it is the court as addressee of the norm which comes within the range of the deontic operator. (On this cf. Makkonen, *Zur Problematik der juridischen Entscheidung*, pp. 27 ff.; H. H. Keuth, *Zur Logik der Normen* (Berlin, 1972), 25 ff.) There is no need to decide here which formalization is the best. The one adopted in the text is not impossible—'. . . is punished by life imprisonment' can be understood as a predicate—and is sufficient for the purposes of this investigation.

[36] The index '1' in 'M^1_9' means that one is dealing here with a characteristic of the first decompositional step, the index '9' that 'M' is the ninth of several characteristics.

killing consists of 'knowingly taking advantage of the victim's unsuspecting and defenceless condition, to kill him or her' (M^2_5).[37]

Hence, likewise valid is:

(5) $(x)\ (M^2_5x \leftrightarrow M^1_5x)$.

'M^2_5', in its turn, is to be deemed satisfied when the wrongdoer kills someone who is not expecting an attack and who only has a limited opportunity of warding off the attack (M^3_5).[38]

Hence, likewise valid is:

(6) $(x)\ (M^3_5x \leftrightarrow M^2_5x)$.

It now becomes apparent that someone who kills a sleeping person in the absence of any special defensive precautions taken by the victim (S) is to be designated as an individual to whom 'M^3_5' applies, so that the following has to be accepted:[39]

(7) $(x)\ (Sx \rightarrow M^3_5x)$.

But *ex hypothesi*

(8) Sa

holds good. Accordingly it follows from (1)–(8) that

(9) ORa.

The concern here is not with the soundness of the premisses used in justifying (9). This is the subject-matter of external justification. In the present context the only matters of importance are the insight which this example affords into the structure of internal justification.

The most important insight is that with the help of each of the premisses (2), (5), (6), and (7) in the development of the applicable norm (1), an ever more concrete norm is obtained. The chain of ever more concrete norms can be specified in the following way:

(3)	$(x)\ (M^1_1x \vee M^1_2x \vee \ldots M^1_9x \rightarrow ORx)$	(from [1] and [2])
(4)	$(x)\ (M^1_5x \rightarrow ORx)$	(from [3])
(5′)	$(x)\ (M^2_5x \rightarrow ORx)$	(from [4] and [5])
(6′)	$(x)\ (M^3_5x \rightarrow ORx)$	(from [5′] and [6])
(7′)	$(x)\ (Sx \rightarrow ORx)$	(from [6′] and [7])

[37] *BGHSt* 23, 119 (120); similarly *BGHSt* 9, 385 (390); 11, 139 (143).

[38] *BGHSt* 23, 119 (120). Cf also A. Schönke and H. Schröder, *Strafgesetzbuch. Kommentar*, 18th edn., rev. T. Lenckner, P. Cramer, A. Eser, and W. Stree (Munich, 1976), para. 211, subsect. 13a.

[39] *BGHSt* 23, 119 (120).

Each of these norms, together with the conditions set out in the antecedent proposition, is sufficient to justify the legal judgment under scrutiny. This is indicative of the normative relevance of the premisses (2), (5), (6), and (7). These premisses can be understood as rules for the usage of the expressions used in the preceding stages of the justification. Without embarking on any further differentiation, they will here be called 'word usage rules'. Such rules, as the example illustrates, exhibit the stronger form (x) $(Fx \leftrightarrow Gx)$ and the weaker form (x) $(Fx \rightarrow Gx)$. In any justification, premisses of the stronger form can be replaced by those of the weaker. The weaker form should therefore be viewed as the standard form.

If it is not certain whether *a* is an instance of T—that is, if the simplest form of internal justification set out above (J.1.1) is therefore not immediately applicable—then there have to be added rules at least of the standard form concerning the usage of T. In the absence of such rules it would be possible to treat two individuals *a* and *b*, who are alike in all the relevant aspects, as T in the one case and not in the other. This would contradict the principle of universalizability. The demand for additional word usage rules can thus be justified by appeal to the principle of universalizability. This demand not only applies to the cases in which it is doubtful whether '*a*' is a T, but also to the cases in which doubts develop at further stages of the justification. The following third rule of internal justification therefore holds good:

(J.2.3) Whenever it is open to doubt whether *a* is a T or an M^i, a rule must be put forward which settles this question.[40]

(J.2.3) together with (J2.2) yields the following both rudimentary and general form of internal justification:

[40] On a requirement corresponding to (J.2.3) cf. Larenz, *Methodenlehre der Rechtswissenschaft*, p. 300: 'Even if the judge has to interpret a particular expression or a particular legal provision on account of the particular case to be decided, he or she may nevertheless not interpret just for this case but only in such a way that the interpretation also stands for any and all other like cases. It would be a contradiction of the requirement of justice to treat like cases alike, as of the legal security sought by the law, if the courts were to interpret the same determination in like cases now one way, now another.'

(J.1.2) .(1) $(x)\ (Tx \rightarrow ORx)$
.(2) $(x)\ (M^1x \rightarrow Tx)$
.(3) $(x)\ (M^2x \rightarrow M^1x)$

.
.
.

.(4) $(x)\ (Sx \rightarrow M^nx)$
.(5) Sa
(6) ORa (1)–(5)[41]

(J.1.2) is rudimentary in that it does not allow for the possibility of a more complex structure of operative facts and legal consequences. (J.1.2) is general in that it reveals the logical structure of any case in which the specific description (S*a*) of the facts of the case is subsumed within a general concept by means of decompositional steps.[42]

The question arises of how many decompositional steps are needed. Two rules can be formulated for this:

(J.2.4) The number of decompositional steps required, is that number which makes possible the use of expressions whose application to a given case admits of no further dispute.

In such a case, whatever is M^n becomes S.[43]

[41] The schema (J.1.2) makes it clear that the problem of whether interpretation depends on establishing the major or the minor premiss can be treated as one of terminology. From (2)–(5) in (J.1.2), follows 'Ta' (5′). From (1) and (5′) follows (6). One might thus view (1) as the major premiss (5′) as the minor premiss, and (2)–(5) as justification of the minor premiss. An alternative to this would be to regard the norm '$(x)\ (Sx \rightarrow ORx)$' (4′) which follows from (1)–(4) as the major premiss (5) as the minor premiss, and (1)–(4) as justification of the major premiss. (4′) would be something like Ehrlich's 'norm of decision' (*Fundamental Principles of the Sociology of Law*, trans. W. Möll (Cambridge, Mass., 1936), chap. 6). Between these possibilities, an increasing number of decompositional steps gives rise to an increasing number of further solutions.

[42] (J.1.2) concerns the justification of a command. (J.1.2) might easily be more generally understood by replacing the deontic operator 'O' with a variable for deontic operators. In this way (J.1.2) would also represent the logical form of justification of prohibitions and permissions. It is only for reasons of simplicity that such a variable is not used here.

[43] On this cf. Rödig, *Die Theorie des gerichtlichen Erkenntnisverfahrens*, p. 183.

When there are very few and very broad decompositional steps, their normative content fails to emerge with great clarity. On the one hand they are easily open to attack, on the other hand such attacks often become non-specific. A multiplicity of steps may be laborious but it does lead to clarity. It therefore makes sense to stipulate as follows:

(J.2.5) As many decompositional steps as possible should be articulated.

The rules and forms discovered so far concern the formal structure of legal justification. Their main emphasis lies in securing universalizability. They can therefore be called '*rules and forms of formal justice*'.

The foregoing observations might give rise to several misunderstandings. The most serious misunderstanding would be to interpret the requirement of logical deducibility expressed by (J.2.2) as claiming that legal justification consists solely in deduction from given norms. The example cited shows that no such assertion is here being made. It makes it clear that in more complex cases a whole range of premisses such as (5), (6), and (7) is needed in the justification of legal judgments, premisses which cannot be inferred from any statute. In many cases even the norm from which one starts is not a norm of positive law. The requirement of deducibility leads to precisely the opposite of a concealment of the creative element in the determination of law: those premisses which do not derive from positive law are brought right out into the open. This is perhaps the most important aspect of the demand for internal justification. It is the task of external justification to justify those premisses which cannot be derived directly from positive law.

It would be a further misunderstanding to think that the model given above fails to take sufficient account of the interplay between fact and norm—to say that it starts out too one-sidedly from the norm to be decomposed and therefore does not do justice to the requirement of 'casting one's glance back and forth'.[44] This is also not the case. In order to justify the rules

[44] This concept was introduced into the discussion of legal method by Engisch with an almost casual remark (*Logische Studien zur Gesetzesanwendung*, p. 15, and also the clarification in his *Einführung in das juristische Denken*, p. 203 n. 36, p. 206 n. 54). It won particular acceptance in legal hermeneutics

necessary for the individual steps in the process of decomposition it is necessary to consider most closely both the peculiarities of the fact and the characteristics of the norm. This occurs in the context of external justification, within which all the arguments admissible in legal discourse are allowed. The rules to be put forward in internal justification, which bridge the gap between a norm and a description of the facts, can, if one so wishes, be viewed as the result of the process characterized by the metaphor of wandering back and forth.

This makes it clear at the same time that the forms of internal justification do not claim to reproduce the course of deliberations as these actually occur in the mind of the decision-maker. A clear distinction must be made between the process of discovery and the process of justification.[45] The model of finding and confirmation of 'norm hypotheses' worked out by Kriele can count as a description of the process of discovery.[46] The only matter of interest here is that the reflections of the decision-maker must lead to a justification which corresponds to the forms described. Of course, this is not to say that the requirements of the justification process do not exercise a reciprocal influence on the discovery process.

Furthermore, it is very easy either to over or underestimate the significance of the forms and rules of internal justification.

Engisch correctly observes that 'reaching a conclusion as such gives rise to a minimum of effort; the main difficulty lies in finding premisses for it'.[47] Nevertheless, the demand for internal justification is not pointless. In the course of internal justification

(Larenz, *Methodenlehre der Rechtswissenschaft*, pp. 183 ff., 263 ff.). It also plays a significant part in Kriele's model of legal decision-making (*Theorie der Rechtsgewinnung*, pp. 197 ff.). Esser critically observed that little has yet been achieved with this formula. If casting 'back and forth' is not to become 'wandering without end', there is a need for criteria 'which permit cutting off discussion in favour of a particular subsumption' (*Vorverständnis und Methodenwahl*, p. 79). It is the task of the theory of external justification to specify such criteria.

[45] On this cf. R. A. Wasserstrom, *The Judicial Decision* (Stanford and London, 1961), 27.

[46] Cf. Kriele, *Theorie der Rechtsgewinnung*, pp. 197 ff.

[47] Engisch, *Logische Studien zur Gesetzesanwendung*, p. 13; similarly Kriele, *Theorie der Rechtsgewinnung*, p. 51; Wróblewski, 'Legal Syllogism', p. 43.

it becomes clear which premisses need to be externally justified. Presuppositions which might otherwise have remained hidden must be explicitly formulated.[48] This increases the possibility of recognizing mistakes and criticizing them.[49] Finally, articulating universal rules facilitates consistency in decision-making and thereby contributes towards justice and legal certainty.

(J.1.1) and (J.1.2) as well as (J.2.1)–(J.2.5) thus undoubtedly secure a certain measure of rationality. The rationality guaranteed by them is, of course, relative to the rationality of the premisses. A decision as to the rationality of a judgment thus falls in the realm of external justification. To this the argument now turns.

2. EXTERNAL JUSTIFICATION

The justification of premisses used in the process of internal justification is the subject-matter of external justification. These premisses can be of quite different kinds. The following can be distinguished: (1) rules of positive law, (2) empirical statements, and (3) premisses which are neither empirical statements nor rules of positive law.

Corresponding to these different kinds of premisses are different methods of justification. Justification of a rule as a rule of positive law takes place by showing that it meets the criteria of validity of the legal order. A whole range of procedures can be brought into play in the justification of empirical premisses. These range from the methods of the empirical sciences to the maxims of rational presumption to the rules on the burden of proof in a trial. Finally, what can be called 'legal argumentation' or 'legal reasoning' serves to justify those premisses which are neither empirical statements nor rules of positive law.

[48] On this cf. Rödig, 'Über die Notwendigkeit einer besonderen Logik der Normen', p. 178, and his *Die Theorie des gerichtlichen Erkenntnisverfahrens*, p. 151. Cf. also U. Diederichsen, 'Die "reductio ad absurdum" in der Jurisprudenz', in Festschrift for K. Larenz, ed. G. Paulus, U. Diederichsen, and C.-W. Canaris (Munich, 1973), p. 156: 'Since the jurist is also tied to the basic principles of thinking . . . the evaluative part of a decision on a legal problem, for which he or she must take responsibility on the process of justification, only becomes quite clear if one has previously pictured the generally valid . . . structures of the justification of judgments.'

[49] Wasserstrom, *The Judicial Decision*, p. 173.

There are in fact many diverse relations between these three procedures of justification. Thus rules of positive law and empirical statements play a considerable role in the justification of premisses which are neither a matter of positive law nor empirical. In justifying a norm according to the criteria of validity of a legal order it may be necessary to interpret the rules defining the criteria of validity. This is of particular significance where there are constitutional limitations among the criteria of validity, for example a list of fundamental rights.[50] Legal reasoning may therefore be of decisive significance not only in the interpretation of a valid norm but also in establishing its validity. Indeed this also holds true for establishing empirical facts. Thus what is admitted into the justification as a fact may depend on the interpretation of a rule on the burden of proof. It is just because of these multiple 'cross-overs' that, unless one wishes to throw everything in together, there is a need to distinguish carefully between the three aforementioned methods of justification. It is only in this way that it becomes possible to analyse the interplay between them.

The justification of those premisses which are neither rules of positive law nor empirical statements will be at the forefront of the following discussion. In speaking of 'external justification' in what follows it is the justification of such premisses that is at issue.

2.1 The Six Groups of Rules and Forms of External Justification

In a rough classification it is possible to classify the argument forms[51] and rules of external justification into six groups: rules and forms of (1) interpretation, (2) dogmatic argumentation, (3) use of precedents, (4) general practical reasoning, (5) empirical reasoning,[52] and (6) the so-called special legal

[50] On this cf. Hart, *The Concept of Law*, pp. 102–3.

[51] On the concept of an argument form cf. above, p. 92.

[52] Empirical argumentation serves directly both the justification of empirical statements used in internal justification and also justification of empirical statements used in the external justification of non-empirical statements. It is the last-named mode of application that is under discussion here.

argument forms.[53] Should one wish to characterize these groups by means of only one word one would choose the following: (1) statute, (2) dogmatics, (3) precedent, (4) reason, (5) facts, and (6) special legal argument forms.

The first task of a theory of external justification is logical analysis of the argument forms brought together in these groups. The most important result of this analysis is an understanding of the necessity for and possibilities of linking them together. The examination of the interplay of different kinds of argument forms will make clear above all the role of empirical and of general practical reasoning in legal discourse.

2.2 Empirical Reasoning

Empirical reasoning itself cannot be examined in detail here. Only its relevance can be indicated. Its relevance consists in the fact that almost all legal—just as almost all general practical—argument forms include empirical statements. Statements of quite different kinds are under consideration here. Argument forms variously presuppose statements about particular facts, about individual actions, motives of agents, events, or states of affairs. Yet others require statements concerning laws of the natural or social sciences. Furthermore, a distinction can be made between statements about past, present, and future actions, events, or states of affairs. These statements in their turn can be ordered into different fields of knowledge such as economics, sociology, psychology, medicine, linguistics, etc.[54]

[53] On the classification of the rules and forms of external justification cf. Müller, who distinguishes the following six groups of 'elements of concretization': (1) methodological elements, (2) elements of normativity, (3) dogmatic elements, (4) theory-elements, (5) elements based on techniques of problem-solving, and (6) legal and constitutional-political elements respectively (*Juristische Methodik*, pp. 266, 146 ff).

[54] For an analysis of the empirical statements used in the Federal Constitutional Court cf. K. J. Philippi, *Tatsachenfeststellungen des Bundesverfassungsgerichts* (Cologne, Berlin, Bonn, and Munich, 1971). On the different kinds of knowledge necessary for legal argumentation cf. also C. Starck, 'Empirie in der Rechtsdogmatik', *JZ* (1972), 614. On the import of social-scientific knowledge only the following will be cited from the extensive literature: K.-D. Opp, *Soziologie im Recht* (Reinbek, 1973), 79 ff., and W. Naucke, *Über die juristische Relevanz der Sozialwissenschaften* (Frankfurt-on-Main, 1972), 34 ff.

This makes it clear that a thoroughgoing theory of empirical reasoning relevant to legal justification would have to deal with almost all the problems of empirical knowledge.[55] Added to this are the problems of the incorporation of empirical knowledge into legal reasoning. This problem is only to be resolved by way of interdisciplinary co-operation.[56]

In the theory of general practical discourse the significance of empirical knowledge was taken into account by means of the transition rule (6.1): It is possible for any speaker at any time to make a transition into a theoretical (empirical) discourse.

This rule also applies to legal discourse. Just as in the field of general practical discourse, here too, how to proceed in empirical discourse must remain an open question. Both in general practical and in legal discourse the problem arises that the necessary empirical knowledge is often not available with the desirable degree of certainty. Such a situation requires rules of rational presumption. At the same time the relevance of empirical knowledge for legal reasoning can hardly be overestimated.[57] In numerous legal disputes it is the appreciation of facts which plays the decisive role. There is no disagreement about the normative statements to be accepted; the decision turns only on the facts on which it is to be based.

It would of course be quite wrong to think that legal discourse is reducible to empirical discourse. This is no more possible with respect to legal discourse than with respect to general practical discourse. The reasons for this rehearsed in the theory of general practical discourse are also valid for legal discourse.

Although in the following discussion there is always some emphasis on the relevance of empirical arguments, yet the main focus is the relationship of general practical to legal argument forms. An attempt will be made to analyse the interplay of the different argument forms from this perspective.

[55] At this point one should refer to the entire literature in the field of epistemology as well as psychological and sociological literature on the cognitive process.

[56] Of course one's capability for interdisciplinary co-operation presupposes an appropriate training. On this cf. in particular Opp, *Soziologie im Recht*, pp. 219 ff.

[57] Cf. perhaps Rottleuthner, *Rechtswissenschaft als Sozialwissenschaft*, pp. 205 ff.

2.3 The Canons of Interpretation

The canons of interpretation have been the subject of wide-ranging discussion ever since the time of Savigny.[58] Even today there is as yet no agreement as to their number, their precise formulation, their rank order, and their value. There is little point in taking up a position in the debate without knowing what kind of thing these canons are. The discussion will start with an inquiry into their logical structure.

It will be helpful to discuss the logical structure of the canons in terms of a very simple model of internal justification. In what follows, the shortened version of (J.1.2) will be used:

(J.1.2′) .(1) $(x)\ (Tx \rightarrow ORx)$ (R)
.(2) $(x)\ (Mx \rightarrow Tx)$ (W)
.(3) Ma
(4) ORa (1)–(3)

From (1), the norm R, and (2), the word usage rule W, follows the concrete norm R′:

(2′) $(x)\ (Mx \rightarrow ORx)$.

Let R′ be designated as 'an interpretation of R in terms of W' (I^{R}_{W}).

One of the most important tasks for the canons is the justification of such interpretations. However, this does not exhaust their function. They can also be brought to bear directly in the justification of non-positive norms as well as of many other legal statements.

The following discussion of the canons will serve to give neither a complete nor a very detailed analysis of the argument forms traditionally brought together as arguments on interpretation. Its purpose is solely to elucidate the role of these argument forms in legal discourse. To this end it will be sufficient to emphasize several typical characteristics of some of the forms. Accordingly the canons will be classified into six groups; those of semantic, genetic, historical, comparative,

[58] F. C. von Savigny, *System des heutigen Römischen Rechts*, vol. i (Berlin, 1840), 212 ff.

systematic, and teleological interpretation.[59] It will become clear that these groups represent classes of quite different argument forms.

2.3.1 *The Individual Argument Forms*

(1) *Semantic argument* takes place when an interpretation R′ of R is justified, criticized, or said to be possible by reference to linguistic usage. In this case the rule N is to be understood as a *finding* about natural language or some technical language, in particular that of jurisprudence. Where N amounts to a *determination*[60] by the decision-maker in favour of one of these languages, there exists no semantic argument, since such a determination is not capable of being justified by reference to some existing usage. Such justification calls for further argument.

Semantic arguments can be used to justify or to criticize an interpretation or to show that it is at least semantically admissible. Accordingly, it is possible to distinguish three argument forms:

(J.3.1) By reason of W_i, R′ *must* be accepted as an interpretation of R.

(J.3.2) By reason of W_k, R′ *cannot* be accepted as an interpretation of R.

(J.3.3) It is *possible* both to accept and not to accept R′ as an interpretation of R, since neither W_i nor W_k holds.

Using arguments of this form implies an assertion of the validity or invalidity of W_i and/or W_k. The question of how to justify an assertion to the effect that a semantic rule does or does not hold will not be discussed here. It is possible to conceive of such widely divergent ways as an appeal on the part of the speaker to his or her own linguistic competence, empirical inquiry, and recourse to the authority of a dictionary.

Arguments of the form (J.3.1) and (J.3.2) are definitive whenever it is established by reference to a semantic rule that *a* comes under the norm R or that this is not the case. The

[59] For other classifications cf. above, p. 3.

[60] On the concepts of 'finding about' and 'determination for' a language cf. E. von Savigny, *Grundkurs im wissenschaftlichen Definieren* (Munich, 1970), pp. 22–3.

semantic argument is then sufficient to justify a decision through R.[61] The situation is quite different where (J.3.3) is applicable. In such a case semantic interpretation leads to the conclusion that a decision cannot be attained by semantic means alone.[62] It can only be observed that T is vague and that *a* comes within the range of vagueness of T.[63] The question of whether *a* falls under T cannot be answered by means of a finding about language but only by a determination. The argument forms to be discussed next serve, among other things, to justify such determinations.

(2) *Genetic argument* is at issue when an interpretation R′ of R is justified by saying that this interpretation corresponds to the intention of the legislator. Two basic forms of the genetic argument can be distinguished. The first basic form occurs when it is said that $I_W^R = R'$ was what the legislator directly intended; the second arises when it is claimed that the legislator adopted R as a means for advancing the goals $Z_1, Z_2 \ldots Z_n$ in the combination K ($[Z_1, Z_2 \ldots Z_n]$ K), and that the validity of R in the interpretation I_W^R is necessary in order to bring about ($Z_1, Z_2 \ldots Z_n$) K. This second basic form is a form of teleological argument. If ($Z_1, Z_2 \ldots Z_n$) K is abbreviated to Z, the two forms have the following structure:

(J.4.1) .(1) R′ ($= I_W^R$) is intended by the legislator.
(2) R′

[61] Of course arguments of the form (J.3.1) and (J.3.2) carry the justification of a decision only relative to a norm R (here: R_1). Should one not wish to accept the outcome justified by semantic arguments of the form cited, it is possible to modify R_1. In case of any undesired applicability this may occur by limiting R_1 ($(x)\ [T_1 x \rightarrow ORx]$) with the help of a characteristic F, appropriate to *a*, to R_2 ($(x)\ [T_1 x \wedge \neg Fx \rightarrow ORx]$) (teleological reduction). In case of any undesired inapplicability of R_1 it is possible to justify a norm R_3 ($(x)\ [T_2 x \rightarrow ORx]$) possibly through the argument form of analogy, under which T_2 *a* falls differently than under T_1. It can therefore be generally observed that anyone who wishes to argue against a decision justified through (J.3.1) or (J.3.2) must be in a position to justify a non-positive legal norm such as R_2 or R_3.

[62] Cf. here Savigny's pertinent observation on the cognition of vaguenesses: 'But it is just because of this that it concludes with clear insight into the nature of the existing doubt and does not at the same time involve its dissolution' (*System des heutigen Römischen Rechts*, p. 228).

[63] On the concept of vagueness cf. W. P. Alston, 'Vagueness', in *Encyclopedia of Philosophy*, viii. 218 ff. together with further bibliographies.

(J.4.2) .(1) R is, for the legislator, a means to end Z.
.(2) $\neg R' (= I^{R}_{W}) \rightarrow \neg Z$
(3) R′

R′ does not follow logically from the premiss(es) cited in either (J.4.1) or (J.4.2). (J.4.1) requires a further premiss or rule of inference[64] with something like the following content:

(a) The fact that the legislator enacted R with the intention that it should be interpreted according to W ($I^{R}_{W} = R'$) is a ground for the validity of R′.

Of greater interest are the presupposed premisses or rules of inference of (J.4.2):

(b) The fact that the legislator enacted R as a means to the end Z is a ground for holding that it is mandatory to apply R in such a way as to realize Z.

(c) If it is mandatory to realize Z then whatever means are necessary for the realization of Z are also mandatory.

(a) and (b) have been given a relatively weak formulation. The intention of the legislator is only *one* reason for an interpretation. This opens up the possibility of counter-reasons. The rule of inference (c) is of greater interest. Underlying it is the following schema:

(S) .(1) OZ
.(2) $\neg M \rightarrow \neg Z$
(3) OM[65]

[64] On the question of whether rules such as (a)–(c) are to be classified as premisses or rules of inference cf. above, pp. 88–9.

[65] An argument of the form (S) can be reduced without difficulty to a form such as (4.2) or (4.3). In a case of (4.2) say, the consequence F of an action *a* which is said to be mandatory through N were cited as a reason for N. Z in (S) corresponds to the description of the consequence F in (4.2). R in (4.2) signifies that an action is required then when it has F as a consequence. This is expressed in (S) not by citing a rule, but through OZ. The premiss $\neg M \rightarrow \neg Z$ is presupposed in (4.2) in the assertion that F is a consequence of *a*. N in (4.2) signifies that *a* is obligatory. In (S) the corresponding *a* is obligatory as the means M for Z (OM). It should be stressed again at this point that both (4.2) and (S) are the simplest basic forms. Not only can many more forms be distinguished, these forms themselves can be analysed in considerably more detail. All that is significant here is that arguments of the argument forms (S) cited above, as well as (J.4.2), can be reformulated into the forms corresponding to (4.2) or (4.3) in the manner put forward. This holds also for the further legal argument forms based on (S) which remain to be elaborated.

In everyday language, (S) can be formulated in some such way as follows:

.(1) It is mandatory that the state of affairs Z obtains.
.(2) Unless M obtains, Z does not obtain (that is, M is a condition of Z).
(3) It is mandatory that M obtains.

(S) can be viewed as a variant of a practical syllogism.[66] To demonstrate the validity of (S) would require fundamental reflections on both deontic logic and the theory of the means-end relationship. Such reflections cannot be pursued here. Nevertheless, the intuitive plausibility of (S) makes it reasonable to assume that although such inquiries would lead to many refinements, modifications, and limitations, the validity of (S) would remain fundamentally unaffected.[67] Subject to this reservation, (S) and thereby (c) and (J.4.2) can be accepted.

The forms of semantic interpretation include statements about the validity of semantic rules, while those of genetic interpretation include statements about the intention of the legislator. These statements are frequently not made explicit. It is simply stated that a certain interpretation corresponds to the wording of the norm, the will of the legislator or the purpose of the norm. In such cases the argument is incomplete. In order to complete it, statements of the kind indicated above are required. This will be called '*the requirement of saturation*'. The soundness of the arguments in the various forms depends on the soundness of the statements which have to be inserted to fulfil this requirement. Arguments of further forms are needed to justify the soundness of such statements.

To justify the statements needed to bring to saturation genetic argument forms is frequently very difficult and often impossible. This is bound up with the fact that on the one hand it remains unclear who is to be regarded as the subject of 'the intention of the legislator' and on the other hand it is often not possible to establish unequivocally in what the content of this intention consists. Is the totality of elected representatives the subject of

[66] On the various meanings of this concept cf. above, p. 88.

[67] For a scheme like (S) cf. O. Weinberger, *Rechtslogik* (Vienna and New York, 1970), 219–20, where he considers such a scheme as 'fairly convincing even if not immune to every doubt'.

the intention in question? If so, what happens when a majority of the representatives has no view at all about some particular prescription contained in one of the many bills to be enacted? Do they adopt the views of those in a ministry perhaps who drew up the statute and debated it in various committees and commissions? What if different opinions were expressed in this process, or if these expressions of opinion in their turn require interpretation?[68]

These questions highlight the difficulties of genetic argumentation.[69] It will only be pointed out here that both establishing the intent of participants in the legislative process and establishing a particular use of language consist in establishing facts.[70] Semantic and genetic reasoning are thus shown to be special cases of empirical reasoning.

(3) *Historical argument* is a term used for cases where facts concerning the history of the legal problems under discussion are advanced as reasons for or against some interpretive decision. A particularly interesting form of historical argument will be outlined. It consists in explaining that (1) a particular solution of the problem under discussion has already been implemented in the past, (2) this led to the consequence F, (3) F is undesirable, (4) the situations are not sufficiently dissimilar to exclude the occurrence possibility of F in the current situation, and (5) the solution in question is therefore not to be recommended in the present either. This is a case of learning from history. What is important is that an argument of this form not only presupposes historical, sociological, and economic knowledge, but by way of (3) also includes a normative premiss. This requires justification.

(4) In *comparative arguments* reference is made not to some legal state of affairs of the past but rather to that of another society. The above argument form can be changed into a

[68] On these problems cf. Larenz, *Methodenlehre der Rechtswissenschaft*, pp. 315 ff. as well as A. Mennicken, *Das Ziel der Gesetzesauslegung. Eine Untersuchung zur subjektiven und objektiven Auslegungstheorie* (Bad Homburg, Berlin, and Zurich, 1970), 30 ff., with numerous references.

[69] For a model of critical genetic argumentation cf. Esser, 'Bemerkungen zur Unentbehrlichkeit des juristischen Handwerkzeugs', *JZ* (1975), 555 ff.

[70] Cf. perhaps Wieacker, 'Über strengere und unstrenge Verfahren der Rechtsfindung', p. 432, where he speaks of the 'empirical intention of the historical legislator'.

comparative one through minor modification. Just as in the case of the historical argument, such a comparative argument form includes at least one normative premiss as well as many empirical ones.

(5) *Systematic argument* is an expression used as a reference both to the position of a norm in a legal text,[71] and to the logical or teleological relation of a norm to other norms, goals, and principles. Only the latter will be discussed here. When teleological relations come into play it is a case of a systematic-teleological argument.[72] Such arguments are better dealt with in the framework of teleological reasoning. Only those arguments solely concerned with logical relations between norms shall be viewed as strictly speaking 'systematic'.

The most important form of systematic argument, in this strict sense, is a reference to a contradiction between norms.[73] If the interpretation of R_1 through W, R'_1, contradicts the norm R_2, which is to be recognized as valid, then R'_1 must be abandoned. Of course a reference to contradictions only leads to a result when all interpretations of R_1 except one are excluded by other norms. This is often not the case.

(6) A comprehensive elucidation of the concept of *teleological argument* presupposes a detailed analysis of the concepts of ends and means as well as of the related concepts of willing, intention, practical necessity, and goal.[74]

Such a detailed analysis cannot be undertaken here. Nevertheless, it is possible even without a detailed investigation to gain some insights into the structure of teleological reasoning which are of significance for this work.

[71] On this argumentation from the 'outer system' cf. Larenz, *Methodenlehre der Rechtswissenschaft*, p. 313.

[72] On the connection between systematic and teleological arguments cf. Larenz, *Methodenlehre der Rechtswissenschaft*, p. 315; Engisch, *Einführung in das juristische Denken*, p. 79.

[73] Those arguments relating to the avoidance of contradictions between norms are instances of the application of the general rule of discourse (1.1); cf. above, pp. 188–9.

[74] For such an analysis cf. Stegmüller, 'Probleme und Resultate der Wissenschaftstheorie und Analytischen Philosophie', vol. i, Wissenschaftliche Erklärung und Begründung (Berlin, Heidelberg, and New York, 1974), pp. 518 ff.; Wright, 'On So-called Practical Inference', pp. 39 ff. In the legal literature, a critical position is taken up by Dreier, *Zum Begriff der 'Natur der Sache'* (Berlin, 1965), 103 ff.

It was shown whilst discussing genetic interpretation, that there are teleological arguments in which the person arguing can rely directly on the aims of the historical legislator. The focus here is on teleological arguments in which this is not the case. Following Larenz, they will be called 'objective-teleological'.[75]

Objective-teleological arguments are characterized by the fact that the individual arguing does not rely on the aims of any past or present actually existing person but rather on 'rational' aims, or on those 'objectively prescribed in the framework of the valid legal order'. This raises the question of what is to be regarded as a rational aim or as one objectively prescribed in the framework of the valid legal order. The answer of discourse theory goes as follows: those aims which decision-makers deciding within the framework of the valid legal order would posit on the basis of rational argumentation, are rational aims or aims objectively prescribed in the framework of the valid legal order. The community of those deciding in the framework of the valid legal order on the basis of rational argumentation is the hypothetical subject of the aims presupposed in objective-teleological arguments. The aims stated by the interpreter are hypotheses about the aims set by this hypothetical subject. Their correctness has to be justified by rational argumentation.

The aims involved in teleological interpretation are thus a matter not of empirical findings but rather of normative distinctions. Such a normatively determined aim is to be understood here as a prescribed state of affairs or event.[76]

The fact that a state of affairs or event is prescribed can be symbolized by 'OZ'. The fact that the interpretation $I^R_W = R'$ is necessary to bring about Z—that is, is a means to Z[77]—can be expressed by a sentence of the form: $\neg R'\ (= I^R_W) \rightarrow \neg Z$. The simplest form of objective-teleological argument thus has the

[75] Larenz, *Methodenlehre der Rechtswissenschaft*, p. 322.

[76] On the concepts of 'state of affairs' and 'event' cf. Wright, *Norm and Action*, pp. 25 ff.

[77] To say that $I^R_W = R'$ is a means to Z, can mean several things: (1) The application of R' in a concrete case, is a means to Z (2) general compliance with R' is a means to Z, (3) the validity of R' is a means to Z. The starting-point here will be that the validity of R' is a means to Z.

following form:

(J.5) .(1) OZ

.(2) $\neg R'\ (= I^{R}_{W}) \rightarrow \neg Z$

(3) R'

(J.5) corresponds to the genetic argument form (J.4.2), apart from the fact that Z is not asserted as something intended by the legislature but as something which ought objectively to be realized.[78] The general schema underlying it, as in the case of (J.4.2) is:

(S) .(1) OZ

.(2) $\neg M \rightarrow \neg Z$

(3) OM

(J.5) presupposes the soundness of two quite diverse premisses. 'OZ' (1) is a normative statement, while '$\neg M \rightarrow \neg Z$' (2) is an empirical one. To give grounds upholding the truth of (2) calls for knowledge based on empirical generalizations. Teleological arguments thus rely in part on empirical argumentation. When, as is not uncommon, there is no dispute about (1), the decision depends only on empirical arguments. This illustrates the considerable importance of empirical reasoning in legal discourse.

Here only the justification of (1) is of interest. For the most part, (1) is justified with reference to the applicable norm. It is claimed that it is necessary to bring about condition Z because of the binding character of R. Z is frequently justified by reference to a group of norms rather than to a single norm. Nevertheless in none of these cases does Z follow logically from the norms to which reference is made in the justification. Further arguments are therefore needed. Only where a norm immediately prescribes the pursuit of Z is this not the case.

In most cases not only one aim but several aims can be put

[78] (J.5) corresponds to the combination of the argument forms analysed by Dreier under the description 'technical practical' and 'objective practical argumentation from the nature of the thing'. (J.5) is objective practical to the extent that Z is described as something which objectively ought to be realized. (J.5) is technical practical because it includes the statement that R, when it is to serve the aim Z, must have the characteristic 'interpreted through W' confirmed in it (*Zum Begriff der 'Natur der Sache'*, pp. 106 ff., 108 ff., 120 ff., 124).

forward in favour of a norm or a group of norms. These aims usually either exclude one another or can only be realized by limiting each in the light of the other.[79] What is necessary in these cases is to justify the mandatory quality of a combination of aims ($[Z_1, Z_2 \ldots Z_n]K$). This presupposes the application of priority rules.

The most difficult problems of teleological reasoning arise when Z or $(Z_1, Z_2 \ldots Z_n)$ K—the following will once again only talk of Z—cannot be described solely by means of empirical expressions. This is the case when Z is defined as being a state of affairs in which certain norms hold good.[80]

A borderline case of such a state of affairs exists when Z can be determined as being the very state of affairs in which R′, the norm to be justified, holds. In such a case, reference to Z has no point other than to clarify what it means for R′ to be valid.

As a rule the description of such a state of affairs requires norms general in scope or principles.[81] Z is then the state of affairs in which the principles $P_1, P_2 \ldots P_n$ hold. Teleological argument accordingly turns into a kind of argument from principles.[82] The problem of reasoning from principles consists not so much in the justification of the principles but much more

[79] On the realization that a norm need not always have only one aim assigned to it cf. Esser, *Vorverständnis und Methodenwahl*, p. 102; Engisch, *Einführung in das juristische Denken*, p. 80.

[80] Cf. above, p. 199.

[81] By 'principles' in this context are meant normative statements of a high level of generality like: 'The dignity of man should be respected', 'Like cases should be treated alike' and 'Everyone should take responsibility for shortcomings in their sphere of business'. Because of their high level of generality, such statements cannot be used directly in the justification of a decision. Further normative premisses are needed. On the concept of principles cf. Esser, *Grundsatz und Norm in der richterlichen Fortbildung des Privatrechts* (Tübingen, 1956; repr. 1964), pp. 87 ff. and his *Vorverständnis und Methodenwahl*, p. 42; Canaris, *Systemdenken und Systembegriff*, pp. 48 ff.; Larenz, *Methodenlehre der Rechtswissenschaft*, p. 458. On the concept of generality cf. Hare, 'Principles', pp. 2–3 and above, pp. 66–7.

[82] Cf. Larenz, *Methodenlehre der Rechtswissenschaft*, pp. 323 ff., who—without distinguishing between states of affairs and principles—included principles such as the principle of equal treatment and ethico-legal principles among the 'objective-teleological criteria of interpretation'. Cf. also Engisch, *Einführung in das juristische Denken*, p. 81, who for reasons like those cited above, holds the view that the term 'interpretation on the basis of reasons' would be more fitting than that of 'interpretation on the basis of purpose'.

in the fact that the norm to be justified does not usually follow logically from the principles. There is a need for a concretization of the principles with the help of further normative statements.

2.3.2 *The Role of the Canons in Legal Discourse*

Six points will be raised with a view to clarifying the role of the canons of interpretation in legal discourse: (1) the range of their applicability, (2) their logical status, (3) the saturation requirement, (4) the different functions of the various forms, (5) the problem of their rank order, and (6) the resolution of the problem of their rank order within the theory of legal discourse.

(1) The different forms of argument have until now been represented as forms of argument for or against a particular interpretation I of a presupposed norm R, through a 'word usage rule' W ($I^R_W = R'$). Beyond that, apart from the argument forms of semantic interpretation, all the forms can be deployed in a large number of further contexts. In particular we should note the contexts of a conflict of norms, of a limitation of norms, and of the justification of norms which cannot be inferred from any statute. Thus in a situation of a conflict of norms, for example, reference may be made to the fact that the legislature accorded particular significance to one of the norms. When justifying a restrictive reading of a norm it is possible to refer to comparable and well-tried regulations in other states, and in justifying a norm which cannot be inferred from positive law one can advance as an argument an aim which ought to be pursued. To this extent, the traditional characterization of the argument forms discussed above under the heading of canons of interpretation, is too narrow.

(2) The logical status of the canons is subject to dispute. Rottleuthner denies that they have the character of rules. They are said to serve only 'to indicate viewpoints for questions of relevancy and to propose lines of inquiry'.[83] Hart calls them 'general rules for the use of language.'[84] Müller speaks of 'elements in the process of concretization' and 'moments in a

[83] Rottleuthner, *Richterliches Handeln*, p. 30, and his *Rechtswissenschaft als Sozialwissenschaft*, p. 197.

[84] Hart, *The Concept of Law*, p. 123.

unitary interpretative procedure',[85] Larenz of 'guiding perspectives to which variable weight is assigned'.[86]

The foregoing reflections have shown that the various argument forms do not in actual fact amount to rules. They do not lay down what must conditionally or unconditionally be done or striven after. On the other hand they are more than mere points of view or guidelines for raising questions. They can, to use a concept of Perelman's, best be described as 'schemata for arguments' ('*schèmes d'arguments*').[87] They amount to schemata for statements of a particular form such that a further statement of a particular form follows logically or may be justified by reference to a presupposed rule. It is for this reason that they are to be called 'argument forms'.[88]

As argument forms the canons give a special character to the structure of legal reasoning. A comprehensive analysis of all argument forms possible in legal discourse would yield something like a grammar of legal argumentation. To take the analogy further, however, this would tell us nothing about the issue of what one ought to say if speaking the language which follows this grammar. Still, it would have shown how one can proceed in order to arrive at a rational outcome.

(3) An argument of a particular form is only complete if it contains all the premisses belonging to this form. This may be called the requirement of saturation.[89] The premisses needed for completeness are of different kinds. Corresponding to these are quite different methods of justification.

Empirical justifications play a significant part. Observations about linguistic usage, claims about the will of the legislator or of individuals participating in the legislative process or about the state of the law at times past or those in other jurisdictions, as well as hypotheses which underlie assertions about consequences, are all subjects for empirical justification.

In addition to the empirical statements of the kind mentioned here, the argument forms contain normative premisses which

[85] Müller, *Juristische Methodik*, p. 145.
[86] Larenz, *Methodenlehre der Rechtswissenschaft*, p. 332.
[87] Perelman and Olbrechts-Tyteca, *La Nouvelle Rhétorique*, p. 252 (p. 187).
[88] On the concept of argument form cf. above, p. 92.
[89] Cf. above, p. 238.

cannot be inferred from the enacted law. Examples occur in cases of historical, comparative, and teleological interpretation, all of which presuppose the evaluation of states of affairs. The justification of these normative presuppositions certainly does not always depend directly on the methods of general practical discourse. The justification of some interpretation may perhaps initially deploy a comparative argument. In order to justify the evaluation presupposed in this argument, it might be possible to refer to the commitments to certain aims involved in other norms. It is only at this point that it may be necessary to resort to general practical arguments.

The requirement of saturation secures the rationality of the application of the canons. It excludes the possiblity of argument by recourse to bald assertion to the effect that a particular interpretation results from the wording or the historical origin or the purpose of the norm. It is always necessary to put forward either empirical or normative premisses whose truth or correctness can at any time be made the subject-matter of further discussion. The following rule accordingly precludes resort to empty assertions:

(J.6) Saturation—that is a full statement of reasons—is required in every argument which belongs among the canons of interpretation.

(4) The different forms fulfil different functions. The forms of semantic and genetic reasoning are concerned with the commitment of the decision-maker to the very words of the statute and to the intention of the legislator respectively. The historical and comparative forms allow for learning from the experiences of the past and of other societies. Systematic interpretation contributes among other things to freeing the legal order from contradiction. Finally, the teleological forms open up the field to general practical reasoning. All this only characterizes one particularly important function of the various forms in each case.

(5) It is already obvious from the different functions of the different forms that in the context of a discussion about a particular problem arguments using one form may lead to a quite different solution from arguments using another. This gives rise to a double uncertainty in the application of the

canons. A single form may achieve saturation in diverse ways and different forms may be used to justify different conclusions.

The question of the mutual relationships of the arguments of different forms is generally treated as the problem of constructing a catalogue of priorities or stages, or a rank ordering of the canons. To date no proposal for such a catalogue has met with general acceptance.[90] Different reactions have been voiced both as to the possibility of and the necessity for such a rank ordering. According to Esser, the 'hope that one might be able to draw up a catalogue of stages "among the sequence of steps in interpretation", is doomed to failure.'[91] Kriele has presented a number of significant arguments on this point.[92] Larenz tries to establish a certain determination of the relationship between the canons, but he too arrives at the conclusion that there is 'no definite rank order' of the different forms. 'They stand in a relation of reciprocity and their respective weight is not in the last analysis determined by the results they yield in individual cases.'[93] Müller advances a view of the rule of law as supporting priority for the semantic and systematic arguments.[94] Engisch is of the opinion that if it should turn out to be 'quite impossible to resolve' the issue of the relationship of interpretational methods then there is 'absolutely no prospect of overcoming the problems of legal decision-making in any way which gives rise to even vague confidence'.[95] He sets up a catalogue of stages for discussion, in which, in accordance with the subjective theory, the will of the legislator is initially to be the decisive factor and objective-teleological arguments are only to be brought in if the legislative will cannot be determined with certainty.[96] However, he reduces the value of this catalogue by observing that the dispute between objective and subjective theories of interpretation 'has not been conclusively resolved and like all true foundational problems will never admit of final resolution.'[97]

[90] Müller, *Juristische Methodik*, p. 198.

[91] Esser, *Vorverständnis und Methodenwahl*, p. 124–5.

[92] Kriele, *Theorie der Rechtsgewinnung*, pp. 85 ff.

[93] Larenz, *Methodenlehre der Rechtswissenschaft*, pp. 334–5.

[94] Müller, *Juristische Methodik*, pp. 202 ff.

[95] Engisch, *Einführung in das juristische Denken*, p. 225 n. 82d.

[96] Ibid., 230 ff.

[97] Ibid., 96. On the dispute between the subjective and the objective theory of interpretation cf. Mennicken, *Das Ziel der Gesetzesauslegung*, pp. 30 ff., 75 ff.

(6) Discourse theory in its turn can offer a solution neither by constructing a catalogue of stages, nor by deciding in favour of an objective or subjective theory of interpretation, nor by constructing a formula which puts them both in relation to one another. However, it can make a contribution to resolving the problem in that it indicates how the different argument forms can usefully be employed.

Here two characteristics of discourse theory show themselves in a favourable light. The first of these is the fact that discourse theory includes an account of the pragmatic dimensions of justification; the second is the fact that it does not attempt to provide criteria which are so strong as to enable one to determine a result with certainty simply on the basis of familiarity with discourse theory.[98] Rules and forms are set out whose observation and implementation increases the probability of achieving a correct, that is a rational or reasonable result in any discussion. It cannot be said on the basis of these rules and forms alone—except in the case of discursive necessity—what these results shall be. This requires an actually occurring or imaginary discussion.

In order to link this discussion to valid law it must be stipulated that those arguments which give expression to a link prima facie have the greater weight. If a proponent (P) appeals to the very words or the will of the historical legislator in support of a proposed solution, while by contrast his or her opponent (O) cites a rational aim in support of a divergent proposal, then P's arguments should take precedence unless O is not only able to give good reasons for his or her assertions but can also give good reasons for saying that his or her arguments are stronger than P's. In cases of doubt, P's reasons take precedence. The following rule on the burden of proof in argumentation thus holds as a pragmatic rule:

(J.7) Arguments which give expression to a link with the actual words of the law, or the will of the historical legislator, take precedence over other arguments, unless rational grounds can be cited for granting precedence to the other arguments.

This rule leaves open the question of when there exist rational

[98] Cf. above, p. 17 ff., 206.

grounds for assigning a lesser weight to arguments which express a link. This is left to the participants in legal discourse to decide. This, however, does not mean that this decision is arbitrary. Those grounds alone are rational which can be justified in a rational juristic discussion. All possible arguments of legal discourse are admissible in a discussion of this sort on the use of legal arguments. Of course general practical arguments will, in this situation, play the decisive part, since these very legal arguments which are under discussion cannot themselves be used to determine its outcome. The problem of rank ordering is thus shown as a problem to be resolved primarily through the methods of general practical reasoning.

Assigning the decision to the rationality of the participants in the argument does not mean that the determination of the relationship between the canons is always open and has to be actually investigated anew in each case. The participants in the discourse have to determine weights to be attached to various forms of argument in various contexts of interpretation. The weights they assign, since these have to be well-founded, are valid not only for the case under discussion but also for any other case which is similar in the relevant respects.[99] As a fundamental principle of discourse theory, the principle of universalizability in this way requires that the use of argument forms takes place according to rationally justifiable rules governing their interrelationships. This yields the following rule as a variant of the principle of universalizability:

(J.8) Determinations of the relative weight of arguments different in form must conform to weighting rules.

Such rules can only be developed with reference to particular contexts of interpretation and particular branches of law. Moreover, since the contexts of interpretation and the branches of law are subject to change, they never achieve final and conclusive certainty.

(J.8) is a rule of general practical discourse governing the use of the canons. Yet another general rule of discourse can be specified in an analogous way.

(2.2.a) and (2.2.b), which express the requirement of freedom of discussion, secure the admissibility of all arguments. In

[99] Cf. above, pp. 65 ff.

relation to legal argumentation this means that all arguments which might possibly be produced must be given due consideration. The following rule therefore holds:

(J.9) Every possibly proposable argument of such a form that it can be counted as one of the canons of interpretation must be given due consideration.[100]

To sum up, it can be said that although the canons do not offer a guarantee of 'finding one right answer . . . with a relatively high degree of certainty',[101] they are nevertheless more than mere instruments for secondary legitimation of a decision which can be reached and justified in alternative ways. They are forms in which legal reasoning has to be cast if it is to fulfil its claim to correctness, which, unlike that of general practical discourse, contains acknowledgement of the mandatory quality of legislation.

2.4 Dogmatic Reasoning

2.4.1 *Towards a Concept of Legal Dogmatics*

In order to discover the nature of dogmatic arguments and the role they play in legal discourse it is necessary to know what is meant by 'juristic dogmatics' or 'legal dogmatics'. This is far from clear. To be sure there is a growing number of publications on this subject, but a generally accepted theory of legal dogmatics is not yet in sight.

If one follows the terminology probably most prevalent among jurists, then 'juristic dogmatics' or 'legal dogmatics' is taken to mean legal science in the narrower and proper sense, [102] as it is actually pursued by them.[103] This legal science, in the

[100] For a parallel requirement cf. Larenz, *Methodenlehre der Rechtswissenschaft*, p. 335.

[101] Kriele, *Theorie der Rechtsgewinnung*, p. 85.

[102] On this cf. G. Radbruch, *Rechtsphilosophie*, 7th edn. (Stuttgart, 1970), 209.

[103] Instead of starting from prevailing terminology and those matters designated by the expressions 'juristic dogmatics' or 'legal dogmatics', one might begin with an analysis of the term 'dogmatics', an inquiry into its history and its application in other disciplines, particularly theology. This path is taken by a number of writers (e.g. U. Meyer-Cording, *Kann der Jurist heute noch*

narrower and proper sense, is a mixture of at least three activities: (1) that of describing the law in force, (2) that of subjecting it to conceptual and systematic analysis, and (3) that of working out proposals about the proper solutions to legal problems. As is clear from this, legal dogmatics is a 'multi-dimensional discipline'.[104]

Corresponding to the three activities above it is possible to distinguish three dimensions: descriptive-empirical, logical-analytical, and normative-practical.[105] There are different ways of proceeding within each of these dimensions. In the context of the descriptive-empirical dimension it is possible to distinguish, in particular, the description and prognosis of the practice of the courts and the determination of the actual will of the

Dogmatiker sein? Zum Selbstverständnis der Rechtswissenschaft (Tübingen, 1973), 7 ff.; Albert, 'Erkenntnis und Recht: Die Jurisprudenz im Lichte des Kritizismus', *Jahrbuch für Rechtssoziologie und Rechtstheorie*, 2 (1972), 82 ff.; E. J. Thul, 'Die Denkform der Rechtsdogmatik', *ARSP* 46 (1960), 241 ff. Cf. also D. de Lazzer, 'Rechtsdogmatik als Kompromißformular' in *Dogmatik und Methode*, Festschrift for J. Esser, ed R. Dubischar *et al.* (Kronberg, 1975), 87). This kind of shift towards conceptual-analytical, conceptual-historical, and comparative inquiries can certainly yield significant insights, so long as we postpone a decision on what juristic dogmatics is until the thing itself has come into view. Such inquiries only have meaning when they are pursued in sufficient depth. This cannot be done here. Apart from one observation to be made below, they will therefore be dispensed with here.

[104] Dreier, *Was ist und wozu Allgemeine Rechtstheorie?*, p. 15. Cf. also Meyer-Cording, *Kann der Jurist heute noch Dogmatiker sein?*, p. 41, who speaks of a 'mixture of very different activities', and K. Adomeit, 'Zivilrechtstheorie und Zivilrechtsdogmatik, mit einem Beitrag zur Theorie der subjektiven Rechte', *Jahrbuch für Rechtssoziologie und Rechtstheorie*, 2 (1972), 504, especially n. 8, where he tries to grasp the 'mixed character' of juristic dogmatics in an '8-operation model'.

[105] Several authors present a bipartite division rather than a tripartite one, that is into a descriptive-theoretical and a normative-practical dimension (cf. Dreier, *Was ist und wozu Allgemeine Rechtstheorie?*, p. 15), or into 'reporting' and 'proposing' statements (Adomeit, 'Zivilrechtstheorie und Zivilrechtsdogmatik', pp. 503 ff.). This could be justified by reference to the logical-analytical work already required in the description and elaboration respectively of proposals for regulation. On the other hand it must be admitted that it is precisely in the framework of juristic dogmatics that the logical-analytical dimension plays a role which, though linked with the other dimensions, remains clearly distinctive.

legislator.[106] The logical-analytical dimension includes both the analysis of legal concepts and the investigation of the logical relations between various norms and principles. Finally, the normative-practical dimension is pursued by those who make proposals for the interpretation of a norm or for a new norm or a new institution and justify them or those who criticize a decision at law on grounds of the practical shortcomings, and work out a counter-proposal. Numerous relations obtain between these three dimensions. Thus the description of the law in force presupposes a particular conceptual apparatus. Logical analysis of law in force is not possible in the absence of a description of it, and in order to work out proposals about norms and decisions it is necessary to have sound knowledge of the legal order, since these must fit into the legal order as it exists.

The gravamen of legal dogmatic pursuit may be variously distributed between and within these dimensions. Distribution of attention between them depends on the practical interests of the dogmatist, his or her background, assumptions about legal theory and the peculiarities of the area of law under scrutiny. Thus someone writing a legal commentary for practitioners will, above all, concentrate on describing the current practice of the courts, while someone who undertakes a fresh investigation of the concept of 'declaration of intention' will most likely place particular emphasis on analytical considerations. For someone for whom only the will of the legislator constitutes law in the strict sense, general practical arguments will play quite a different role than for the person whose conception of law is first and foremost as a rational ordering of human coexistence.

Besides this very wide conception of legal dogmatics as embracing the whole field of legal science in its narrower and proper sense, a number of more restricted conceptions can also be found. Of particular interest here are the narrower conceptions which may be characterized by such expressions as 'conceptual', 'logical', and 'systematic'.[107] In the way of perhaps

[106] Cf. R. Dreier, 'Zum Selbstverständnis der Jurisprudenz als Wissenschaft', *Rechtstheorie*, 2 (1971), 41 ff., where he distinguishes in this vein between the function of legal science as describing judge-made law and its function as describing legislation.

[107] In particular, stress is laid on the relation of the concept of dogmatics to the concept of the system. Thus Wieacker speaks of the 'concept of a system,

more colourful characterizations of these narrower conceptions of dogmatics, one comes across expressions such as 'the "social mathematics" of legal dogmatics' or 'the apparatus of argumentation endowed with absolute logicality'.[108]

Dogmatics as social mathematics was pursued in its purest form in the conceptual jurisprudence of the nineteenth century. The following remarks by Windscheid are typical of their kind:

When interpretation has completed its task there remains the question of the development of those concepts which are contained in the legal propositions generated by interpretation. The actual thought of the legal statement also presents itself in concepts, that is, in combinations of 'thought-elements'; it is a question of breaking the concepts down into their constituent parts and of bringing to light the 'thought-elements' contained in them. It is possible to go a longer or shorter way in this operation, for the elements discovered may themselves be shown to be compounds of simpler elements, and so on. Modern legal science has a decided tendency to go as far as possible in the breaking down of concepts. And this is its merit. For in fact not only a complete understanding of the law but also certainty in its application both depend on an exhaustive understanding of the content of the concepts contained in legal propositions. . . . the decision is the result of a calculation in which legal concepts are the factors; the more determinate the value of the factors, the more certain the outcome of the calculation will be. It is immediately obvious that the true system of rights, the inner interconnectedness of its propositions, can only be revealed by a complete understanding of legal concepts.[109]

There are, accordingly, three tasks for dogmatics: (1) logical analysis of legal concepts, (2) unification of this analysis into a

which [is] the formal constituent of dogmatics' (*Zur praktischen Leistung der Rechtsdogmatik*, p. 319 n. 22). Esser observes that the 'dogmatization of a legal subject . . . [compels] a move towards system-formation' (*Vorverständnis und Methodenwahl*, p. 97), and L. Raiser considers substituting for the expression 'legal dogmatics' the term 'systematic legal science' ('Wozu Rechtsdogmatik?', *DRiZ* (1968), 98).

[108] Simitis, 'Die Bedeutung von System und Dogmatik—dargestellt an rechtsgeschäftlichen Problemen des Massenverkehrs', *AcP* 172 (1972), 132.

[109] B. Windscheid, *Lehrbuch des Pandektenrechts*, 9th edn., rev. T. Kipp, vol. i (Frankfurt-on-Main, 1906), 110–11; similarly P. Laband, 'Das Staatsrecht des Deutschen Reiches', 2nd edn., in *Handbuch des Öffentlichen Rechts*, vol. ii, ed. M. von Seydel (Freiburg and Leipzig, 1894), 1–276, Forward.

system, and (3) application of the results of this analysis to justify legal decisions.

Since Jhering's day such a programme for legal dogmatics has been the subject of many criticisms.[110] The most important objection is founded on the impossibility of obtaining any new normative conclusion using only the methods of logical analysis and logical inference. Using conceptual analysis as a seemingly logical way of going about justifying decisions and norms which cannot be directly extracted from the law therefore means glossing over the normative premisses necessary for a justification which is conclusive in a truly logical way. This is what Jhering has in mind when he rails against the 'cult of logic which aims at transforming jurisprudence into a mathematics of law'.[111]

The fact that subjecting valid law to logical analysis is not sufficient *in and of itself* for justifying norms and decisions by no means entails, however, that the application of conceptual-systematic arguments is therefore unnecessary for or even detrimental to legal reasoning. It is much more likely that the application of conceptual-systematic arguments is necessary and rational *in conjunction with* other arguments, in particular those of general practical reasoning. It is one of the most important but also one of the most complicated tasks of a theory of legal discourse to discern both the limits and the justifiable uses of conceptual-systematic argumentation.

In light of the ideas put forward in this book neither the application of the wider concept of legal dogmatics indicated above nor the narrow conception mentioned later would seem appropriate. If one were to use the wide conception which includes the activities of describing norms, as well as those of analysing and proposing them, then every argument occurring in legal discourse would be a dogmatic one. On the other hand it would be too narrow to conceive of dogmatics as confined to the logical analysis of legal norms. So confined, dogmatic argu-

[110] Cf. the literature brought together in W. Krawietz's article, 'Begriffsjurisprudenz', in *Historisches Wörterbuch der Philosophie*, vol. i, ed. J. Ritter (Basle, 1971), cols. 809 ff.

[111] R. von Jhering, *Der Geist des Römischen Rechts*, vol. iii, 3rd edn. (Leipzig, 1877), 311–12. Cf. also Ehrlich, *Die juristische Logik*, pp. 299 ff., and P. Heck, *Begriffsbildung und Interessenjurisprudenz* (Tübingen, 1932), 94 ff.

ments would have little to contribute to the justification of normative statements.

In order to determine at what point between these two extremes it would be right to settle for a conception of legal dogmatics adequate for the definition of the concept of dogmatic argument, it will be helpful to ask what conditions such a conception must satisfy. Five conditions can be stated:

(1) Since legal dogmatics is supposed to provide a basis for arguments, it is desirable in the present context to take the term 'legal dogmatics' as comprising congeries not of activities but of *propositions*.[112]

(2) These propositions *relate to the enacted norms and to case law*,[113] but are not identical with the description of enacted norms or the rulings or *rationes decidendi* stated in judicial decisions. In the former case dogmatics would be nothing more than a record of codifications; in the latter it would be exhausted by compilations of precedents. This does not of course mean that propositions in legal dogmatics have nothing to do with judicial rulings or *rationes decidendi*. The courts can take over dogmatic propositions and themselves participate in the development of dogmatics.

(3) The propositions of legal dogmatics make up a *coherently interrelated whole*. How this coherent interrelatedness is made up cannot of course be easily determined. Three points can be stressed: (a) the propositions may not contradict one another, (b) the same legal concepts occur in the formulations of different propositions, and (c) to the extent that they contain the same legal concepts there is a scope for relations of inference between

[112] On this distinction cf. W. Krawietz, 'Was leistet Rechtsdogmatik in der richterlichen Entscheidungspraxis?', *ÖZöR* 23 (1972), 55; Rottleuthner, *Rechtswissenschaft als Sozialwissenschaft*, p. 176. Many writers seem to understand by the term 'legal dogmatics' both a system of propositions and also one or several specific activities. Cf. Wieacker, 'Zur praktischen Leistung der Rechtsdogmatik', pp. 319, 322. Savigny speaks of 'a dogmatic' as of a class of propositions (*Juristische Dogmatik und Wissenschaftstheorie*, p. 121) and of 'dogmatics' as of an activity (ibid., 106, and id., 'Die Jurisprudenz im Schatten des Empirismus. Polemische Anmerkungen zu Hans Albert: *Erkenntnis und Recht*', *Jahrbuch für Rechtssoziologie und Rechtstheorie*, 2 (1972), 98).

[113] On the elaboration of case law as the task of juristic dogmatics cf. Larenz, *Methodenlehre der Rechtswissenschaft*, pp. 201, 216.

them, resting on these concepts.[114] Of course this list only draws attention to some particularly elementary formal relations.

(4) In any piece of legal dogmatics the propositions are composed, justified, and tested in the framework of an *institutionally organized legal science.* This feature, grounded in the pragmatics of the propositions of legal dogmatics, highlights what is probably the most important difference between dogmatic and general practical propositions. The fact that dogmatics is institutionally organized gives rise to a very considerable widening of the discussion in respect of its time-scale and its subject-matter. With regard to the time-scale, conclusions of past discussions can be taken up again, tested against experiences, and thereby rejected or maintained. So far as concerns subject-matter, the effects of one solution can be checked by reference to the solutions of other questions. Furthermore, institutionalization means that for given periods of time a basic core of statements stands as more or less undisputed. This makes the discussion of disputed points easier. The advantages of institutionalization will be discussed further in the discussion of the function of dogmatics.

(5) Legal dogmatics has *normative content.* Its propositions can be advanced as arguments for deciding questions which cannot be answered by reference to empirical arguments alone.

Drawing together the demands listed in these five conditions yields the following definition: Legal dogmatics is (1) a class of propositions which (2) relate to enacted norms and case law but are not identical with a description of them, and (3) stand in some coherent mutual interrelationship, (4) are composed and discussed in the framework of an institutionally organized legal science, and (5) have normative content. This definition leaves a number of questions open. Probably the most important unanswered question is that of the kinds of propositions which are to be considered as belonging to legal dogmatics.

[114] An example of an inquiry into the relations of inference between dogmatic propositions is to be found in Savigny, 'Zur Rolle der deduktiv-axiomatischen Methode in der Rechtswissenschaft', *Rechtstheorie*, ed. G. Jahr and W. Maihofer, (Frankfurt-on-Main, 1971), 316 ff.

2.4.2 *The Propositions of Legal Dogmatics*

Only a very rough classification can be outlined here. A detailed and methodologically up-to-date analysis of the propositions occurring in the various dogmatics has, as far as can be seen, not yet been presented. The classification offered here is thus very tentative in character. However, it will be sufficient in the context of the limited inquiry pursued here into the role of dogmatic arguments in legal discourse.

(1) *The definitions of 'genuine legal concepts'*,[115] to use Radbruch's words, traditionally lie at the centre of dogmatics. Classic examples of genuine legal concepts are those of contract, administrative acts, and self-defence. The content of these concepts depends on the norms governing the way contracts come into being, the operation of administrative acts, and the legal soundness of a plea of self-defence. If there were no such norms, these concepts would not signify anything.[116] These concepts thus do not refer to brute facts, to use an expression of Searle's,[117] but rather to institutional facts, to facts which like a victory in a game of chess, for example, only exist given the existence of corresponding rules.[118] This relationship of genuine legal concepts to legal norms also makes it clear that a proposal to change one of these concepts entails a proposal to change the norms to which they refer, and that anyone designating a specific state of affairs by means of one of these concepts thereby subsumes this state of affairs under the norms constituting the

[115] Radbruch, *Rechtsphilosophie*, p. 219.

[116] On the question of whether this means that those concepts can in principle be eliminated from the language of jurisprudence cf. Keuth, *Zur Logik der Normen*, pp. 41 ff.

[117] Searle, *Speech Acts*, pp. 50 ff., and his 'How to derive "Ought" from "Is"', in *Theories of Ethics*, ed. P. Foot (Oxford, 1967), 111–12.

[118] On this cf. Engisch, *Einführung in das juristische Denken*, p. 110, who calls those concepts 'normative legal concepts' 'which, in contrast to descriptive concepts, aim at entities which are not simply perceptible or discoverable but only become imaginable and comprehensible in connection with the world of norms.' From these, Engisch distinguishes those concepts which need to be filled out by values such as 'dishonourable' and 'obscene' which he also calls 'normative concepts' (ibid., 111, 123). Here only the former and from among these, only those relating to institutional facts constituted by legal norms, are to be understood as genuine legal concepts.

concept. It is in this sense that definitions of genuine legal concepts have normative content.

(2) While there is no doubt that the definitions of genuine legal concepts belong among the propositions of legal dogmatics, this remains less certain with respect to the *definitions of other concepts* occurring in legal norms. These concepts include those such as: 'in undertaking a performance' in paragraph 831, section 1, sentence 1 of the German Civil Code, 'treacherous' in paragraph 211 of the German Criminal Code and 'coherently built-up area' in paragraph 34 of the German Federal Building Code.[119] One might take the view that definitions of such concepts should be included in interpretation and not in legal dogmatics geared to the conceptual-systematic treatment of valid law. However, such a separation between interpretation and dogmatics would not be consistent with what is understood by dogmatics today. Definitions of concepts such as those cited play a considerable part in it, often under the euphemistic title of 'theory'. The four traditional theories on the concept of a 'taking away' in paragraph 242, section 1 of the German Criminal Code will be cited by way of an example: the theories of *apprehensio* (seizing), *contrectatio* (handling), *ablatio* (carrying off), and *illatio* (carrying in).[120] On the other hand, one would not wish to say that every proposed or applied rule of word usage in the interpretation of a norm is a proposition which properly belongs to legal dogmatics. Should one wish to do this then the formulations of countless rules of word usage applied or presupposed in the justification of legal judgments would have to be viewed as dogmatic propositions. This highlights the problem arising even more sharply in the discussion of further dogmatic propositions, namely that in many cases the semantic characteristics of a proposition fail to make it clear whether or not it is a proposition belonging to dogmatics. In the light of this the pragmatic criterion cited above is significant, that is that a proposition is a proposition of dogmatics if it is put forward, accepted, or at least discussed in the context of an institutionally organized legal science. The four definitions of the concept of taking away are, according to this, without doubt propositions

[119] This makes it clear that quite different kinds of concepts are brought together here under 'other concepts'.

[120] Cf. Welzel, *Das Deutsche Strafrecht*, 11th edn. (Berlin, 1969), 349.

of dogmatics; a rule employed for the first time in a court interpreting a new norm is not. This does not, of course, mean that a proposition loses the character of a dogmatic proposition whenever it is used by a court in the process of justification. In such a case the court is using a dogmatic proposition. It is precisely in order to be able to analyse such applications that there is a need for as accurate a conception as possible of the concept of the dogmatic proposition.

(3) The demarcation of dogmatic and non-dogmatic propositions becomes even more difficult with respect to propositions which express a *norm which lacks any statutory pedigree*. There is no doubt that such norms which cannot be extracted from statute law are also discussed as propositions of dogmatics. Let it suffice to mention Staub's proposal for the institution of positive breach of contract.[121] Once again the criterion of demarcation here is above all pragmatic in kind. It depends on whether the proposition in question is accepted or at least being discussed in the framework of a legal science. To this extent Rottleuthner is moving in the right direction with the following critical remark: 'Dogmatic propositions are those which the majority of lawyers holds to be correct.'[122] He merely goes too far in that he equates the concept of dogmatics with that of the prevailing opinion.[123] In order for a proposition to be designated dogmatic it is not necessary that the majority of lawyers should consider it to be correct but only that they should consider it to belong to dogmatics.

Empirical scrutiny of the opinion of lawyers is of course only one way of finding out whether a proposition is a dogmatic one. Much can be said for the possibility of proposing criteria which legal scientists may be assumed to presuppose. An important negative criterion (certainly not valid without exception) seems to be that the proposition in question must not contradict any

[121] Staub, *Die positiven Vertragsverletzungen*, 2nd edn., ed. E. Müller (Berlin, 1913).

[122] Rottleuthner, *Rechtswissenschaft als Sozialwissenschaft*, p. 178.

[123] On this cf. R. Schnur, 'Der Begriff der "herrschenden Meinung" in der Rechtsdogmatik', in Festschrift for E. Forsthoff, ed. K. Doehring (Munich, 1967), 43 ff. Esser, 'Herrschende Lehre und ständige Rechtsprechung', *Dogma und Kritik in den Wissenschaften*, Mainzer Universitätsgespräche, Summer Term 1961, (Mainz, 1962), pp. 26 ff.

valid norm. One of the most important positive criteria is that arguments are available in favour of the proposition which can be supported by reference to other norms or to propositions already acknowledged as dogmatic. A further positive criterion would seem to be that the proposition in question can be articulated in technical legal language. It would be very desirable, though it is not possible in the present context to investigate these kinds of criteria in more detail. They are, of course, relatively ill-defined. Thus the negative criterion cited does not hold without exceptions. In a wide range of cases it therefore depends on the actually existing convictions of legal scientists whether or not a proposition is accepted as dogmatic.[124] This also holds for the two remaining classes of dogmatic propositions to be introduced below.

(4) A further category of dogmatic propositions consists of *descriptions* and *designations* of *states of affairs* whose establishment, termination, or preservation is supposed to be the purpose of individual norms or groups of norms as well as determinations of priority relations between such states of affairs.[125]

(5) *Formulations* of *principles* form a final class. Principles are normative propositions of such a high level of generality that they can as a rule not be applied without the addition of further normative premisses and are usually subject to limitation on account of other principles.[126] Instead of being introduced into the discussion as normative propositions, principles can also be introduced as descriptions of states of affairs in which they hold good.[127]

A classification of the propositions of dogmatics is as yet not a theory of dogmatics. On the other hand such a theory presupposes analysis of the language of dogmatics if it does not wish to misrepresent the character of dogmatics as linguistic

[124] Cf. Dreier's related thesis 'that the limits of the legitimacy of dogmatic argumentation are defined less by a consistent methodology and much more by the social substratum on which dogmatics rests; that is, by the horizons of expectation and toleration of a professionalized estate of lawyers who have undergone specific training' ('Zur Problematik und Situation der Verfassungsinterpretation', in R. Dreier and F. Schwegmann, *Probleme der Verfassungsinterpretation* (Baden-Baden, 1976), 21.

[125] Dreier, 'Zur Problematik und Situation', p. 35.

[126] On the concept of principle cf. above, pp. 243–4.

[127] On this cf. above, p. 243.

activity. A first step towards such an analysis is a classification of the kind undertaken above.

Further constituents of a theory of dogmatics are an analysis of the application of dogmatic propositions in justifications and an investigation of the justification and testing of dogmatic propositions as well as a theory of the function of dogmatics. Four parts can accordingly be distinguished within an adequate theory of dogmatics: a theory (1) of the language of dogmatics, (2) of the application of the propositions of dogmatics, (3) of the justification of those propositions, and (4) the function of dogmatics.

2.4.3 *The Application of Dogmatic Propositions*

There are instances of the application of dogmatic propositions in which the proposition to be justified follows from these dogmatic propositions together with only empirical propositions, or by the addition of formulations of positive legal norms. There are also instances in which further normative premisses are needed. In the first case it is possible to speak of a *pure dogmatic justification*, in the second of an *impure dogmatic justification*. In the case of impure dogmatic justifications, there is a need for general practical arguments in addition to dogmatic arguments.

Furthermore, dogmatic propositions can be used without themselves being justified further. But it is also possible to use them in a justification and to put forward further arguments in their favour at the same time. The first case may be called a *non-justificatory* and the second a *justificatory application* of dogmatic propositions.

Non-justificatory application occurs above all when a dogmatic proposition is not generally disputed, that is, it is in accordance with prevailing opinion. This is not necessarily a sign of an uncritical attitude. As will be shown below, there are rational grounds for regarding non-justificatory application as mandatory to a certain degree. It is even necessary in works of critical dogmatics. No dogmatist can justify all the dogmatic propositions on which he or she relies in the discussion of a particular problem. There would be no end to the process. This is a corollary of the general proposition that nobody can simultaneously justify everything.

2.4.4 *The Justification and Testing of Dogmatic Propositions*

Dogmatic propositions cannot be logically inferred from either the formulations of the legal norms whose validity is to be presupposed on their own, or from empirical statements on their own. Were the former possible, they would have no normative content over and above that of the valid norm; nothing could be justified by means of them which could not also be justified through the valid norms. Were they derivable solely from empirical statements they would have no normative content whatsoever. This does not mean that valid norms and facts have no part to play in the justification of dogmatic propositions, quite the contrary. But it does show that neither is sufficient on its own.

It is possible on the other hand, to use dogmatic propositions in the justification of further dogmatic propositions. However, these in their turn would also need to be justified, and so on. At some point the dogmatic propositions will run out and other arguments become necessary. Since dogmatic propositions have normative content these other arguments can only be general practical arguments.

A distinction must be made between the justification and testing of dogmatic propositions.[128] Justification takes place when a proposition is derived from other propositions; testing takes place when it is asked whether the propositions derivable from a proposition on its own, or together with other propositions, are acceptable. Both the testing and justification of dogmatic propositions lead to general practical propositions, for the propositions which are applied to the refutation of dogmatic propositions cannot, as is the case with propositions used in justification, in their turn, always be dogmatic propositions. General practical propositions are thus the basis of both the justification and the testing of dogmatic propositions.

Every proposition which has normative content is a candidate

[128] On the testing of dogmatic propositions cf. Savigny, 'Übereinstimmende Merkmale in der Struktur strafrechtsdogmatischer und empirischer Argumentation', in Savigny, Rahlf, and Neumann, *Juristische Dogmatik und Wissenschaftstheorie*, pp. 120 ff. On the distinction between justification and testing, and on the relation of both in practical discourse, cf. above, pp. 199–200.

for justification or testing by means of general practical propositions. The special feature of dogmatic propositions consists in the fact that they can be *systematically* tested. Two modes of systematic testing can be distinguished. The first refers to the logical relations between the proposition to be tested and the remaining dogmatic propositions, as well as the formulations of legal norms presupposed valid (*systematic testing in the narrower sense*). The second refers to the relationship to be adjudged from a general practical point of view of those singular normative propositions which are justifiable with the help of the dogmatic proposition which is being tested, to the singular normative propositions justifiable with the help of the remaining dogmatic propositions and formulations of legal norms respectively (*systematic testing in the wider sense*).

The most important criterion of systematic testing in the narrower sense is whether the proposition under scrutiny fits without contradiction into the class of already accepted dogmatic propositions and valid legal norms.[129] It is of course possible that when the dogmatic proposition in question contradicts other dogmatic propositions, these latter propositions rather than the one being tested will be abandoned.

In the case of systematic testing in the wider sense it is a question of whether those decisions or singular normative propositions which are justifiable with the help of the dogmatic proposition under scrutiny can be justified according to the rules of general practical discourse *relative* to those singular normative propositions which are justifiable with the help of all other dogmatic propositions together with the formulations of legal norms. Such a testing may have the following form: there is a choice to be made between the dogmatic propositions S_1 and S_2. It is possible to justify the singular normative proposition N_1 with the help of S_1, together with a class of already recognized further premisses of various kinds which are not to be abandoned; the same holds of N_2 with the help of S_2. Taken on their own, both N_1 and N_2 are discursively possible.[130] The

[129] A dogmatic proposition (S) fits without contradiction into the class of already accepted dogmatic propositions and valid legal norms (K), when neither S nor a proposition derivable from S, together with already accepted propositions and the formulations of valid legal norms, contradicts a proposition of K.

[130] On this concept cf. above, p. 207.

participants in the discussion are inclined to favour N_1. It now transpires, however, that a previously accepted dogmatic proposition S_3 leads to N_3 and that N_3 is consistent with N_2 but not with N_1. 'Not consistent' here means that in the opinion of the discussants it would for general practical reasons not be justifiable to pronounce N_1 as a decision in one case and yet to pronounce N_3 as a decision in another case. In this situation the participants in the discourse must, if they wish to continue to adhere to S_3, abandon N_1 and thereby the dogmatic proposition S_1, although taken on its own, N_1 rather than N_2 would be favoured by them. This example illustrates the way in which the general practical basis of decision-making is widened by dogmatics. The outcome of one case can be compared with those of many others.

Legal dogmatics thus makes possible something like 'consistency control' in two ways. With respect to systematic testing in the narrower sense it is possible to ask whether the dogmatic propositions and the formulations of legal norms are logically consistent with one another and with respect to the wider sense, whether the decisions justifiable with the help of dogmatic propositions and legal norms are consistent with one another form a general practical perspective.[131]

Meeting the requirements of systematic testing in the narrower sense is only a necessary and not a sufficient condition for the acceptability of a dogmatic proposition. For this it is necessary that it can stand up to a systematic testing in the wider sense. It can do so when one is able to give a general practical justification for the decisions which can be supported with its help relatively to the decisions supportable with the help of all the other dogmatic propositions and the formulations of legal norms. Of course dogmatic reasoning cannot thereby be reduced to general practical reasoning, but general practical

[131] Esser seems to have these two kinds of consistency control in mind when he writes: 'Because of the pressure of trying to fit the attempts at resolution into a particular perspective, a test of rationalizing is carried out which, if taken seriously, exhibits the effects of an outcome on the more distant fate of the affected system and forces either a construction of alternatives or a coming to terms with all the consequences which now occur in the system' ('Möglichkeiten und Grenzen des dogmatischen Denkens im modernen Zivilrecht', *AcP* 172 (1972), 104; cf. also his *Vorverständnis und Methodenwahl*, pp. 92, 99).

reasoning does form the cornerstone of the process of proof and therewith the basis of dogmatic reasoning.

It is precisely this point that is stressed by a number of contemporary writers. Esser, for example, observes that dogmatic reasoning is 'an abbreviation of the argument from the consensually accepted "justice-content" of a proposal for conflict resolution'.[132] 'A dogmatic argument can only function by virtue of the "rationality" of the original content of the dogma.'[133] 'It can no longer remain a forbidden subject that every "dogmatic" decision rests on those pre-dogmatic judgments which ultimately justify it.'[134] Wieacker stresses that the arguments of dogmatics 'at least in modern societies . . . [are] justified through the persuasiveness of the "raisonnements" and the results offered.'[135] According to Simitis, it is necessary 'to risk the argumentative justification' of the results of dogmatic constructions.[136]

The dependency of dogmatics on general practical reasoning means that the propositions of dogmatics are in no way irrefutable. They are not dogmas in the conventional sense.[137] Following Popper, Esser aptly calls them hypotheses[138] and

[132] Esser, 'Dogmatik zwischen Theorie und Praxis', *Funktionswandel der Privatrechtsinstitutionen*, Festschrift for L. Raiser, ed. F. Baur, J. Esser, F. Kübler, and E. Steinhoff (Tübingen, 1974), 536.

[133] id., *Vorverständnis und Methodenwahl*, p. 93.

[134] id., 'Möglichkeiten und Grenzen des dogmatischen Denkens im modernen Zivilrecht', p. 108.

[135] Wieacker, 'Zur praktischen Leistung der Rechtsdogmatik', p. 321.

[136] Simitis, 'Die Bedeutung von System und Dogmatik', pp. 144–5.

[137] Cf. in particular Meyer-Cording, *Kann der Jurist heute noch Dogmatiker sein?*, pp. 7 ff. He demands the abandonment of the expression 'dogmatics' for this reason. (ibid., pp. 21, 32). Larenz and Raiser also have reservations about the use of this expression. Instead Raiser considers the expression 'systematic legal science' ('Wozu Rechtsdogmatik?', p. 98). In the absence of a better expression it seems sensible to follow Larenz and stick to the adopted terminology for the time being (*Methodenlehre der Rechtswissenschaft*, p. 210). On the origin and history of the expression 'dogmatics', as well as the related concepts of 'dogma' and 'dogmatism', cf. Meyer-Cording and Lazzer, 'Rechtsdogmatik als Kompromißformular', p. 87; M. Elze, 'Dogma', *Historisches Wörterbuch der Philosophie*, vol. ii, ed. J. Ritter (Basle, 1972), cols. 275–6; Nieke, 'Dogmatism', *Historisches Wörterbuch der Philosophie*, cols. 278–9.

[138] Esser 'Dogmatik zwischen Theorie und Praxis', p. 521 n. 8.

'tentative formulae'.[139] Bachof speaks of the 'provisional nature of the truth of legal dogmas',[140] Meyer-Cording of 'pragmatic proposals for solution'.[141] Even after accepting such a proposal 'dogmatic talk . . . can start up anew'.[142]

What has been said regarding the justification and testing of dogmatic propositions can be summarized in the following rules:

(J.10) Every dogmatic proposition must be justified by recourse to at least one general practical argument whenever it is subjected to doubt.

(J.11) Every dogmatic proposition must be able to stand up to systematic testing in both the narrower and the wider sense.

2.4.5 *The Functions of Dogmatics*

If it is indeed the case that to the extent that dogmatic propositions do not follow logically from the formulations of valid norms together with empirical statements they can in the last analysis only be justified by general practical arguments, the question arises whether and to what extent dogmatic reasoning even makes sense or is needed over and above general practical argumentation. Is there not something to be said for the view that in legal justifications, apart from legal norms, empirical statements, and some argument forms serving the application of these norms, only general practical arguments are of significance? In order to answer this question the functions of legal dogmatics, already mentioned in passing, will be examined a little more systematically. At least six functions of positive value can be distinguished: (1) the stabilization function, (2) the developmental function, (3) the burden-reducing function, (4) the technical function, (5) the control function, and (6) the heuristic function.

(1) The *stabilization function* is fulfilled in that particular solutions to practical questions can be retained and thereby

[139] id., 'Möglichkeiten und Grenzen des dogmatischen Denkens im modernen Zivilrecht', p. 101.

[140] O. Bachof, 'Die Dogmatik des Verwaltungsrechts vor den Gegenwartsaufgaben der Verwaltung', *VVDStRL* 30 (1972), 198.

[141] Meyer-Cording, *Kann der Jurist heute noch Dogmatiker sein?*, p. 40.

[142] Esser, 'Dogmatik zwischen Theorie und Praxis', p. 535.

reproduced as required[143] with the help of dogmatic propositions.[144] This is possible because legal dogmatics is part of an institutional setting. Because of this, certain ways of deciding can be fixed over long time periods. This point is of considerable significance in light of the wide range of discursive possibilities. If one were to reopen the discussion at any time the possibility would arise that—without violating rules of legal and of general practical discourse—one might always arrive at different outcomes. This would be in contradiction of the principle of universalizability and thereby an elementary aspect of the principle of justice.[145] The dogmatization of law or something equivalent from the point of view of the stabilization function is thus required by general practical principles.

This does not, however, mean that once accepted a dogmatic proposition must be strictly retained over an unlimited period of time. But it does exclude simply abandoning it for no reason. It is not enough that there should be equally good grounds in favour of a new solution as for the one to be overridden. The

[143] Esser, 'Möglichkeiten und Grenzen des dogmatischen Denkens im modernen Zivilrecht', p. 103.

[144] It is not to be supposed here that stability can only be achieved through dogmatics, that is, through systems of dogmatic propositions. So far as concerns the stabilizing function, casuistry seems to be equally effective. All that is of importance here is that dogmatics can also serve stability. On the relation between casuistry and dogmatics cf. Luhmann, *Rechtssystem und Rechtsdogmatik*, p. 18.

[145] On the connection between the stabilizing function and the principle of equal treatment cf. Luhmann, *Rechtssystem und Rechtsdogmatik*, p. 37. When there is talk of a situation in which in two or more discourses, it is the case that the rules of discourse which include the principle of universalizability (1.3′) have been followed and yet that there has been a violation of the principle of universalizability in relation to the totality of the discourses, what is happening is that the discourses are being considered from different points of view. In the first case, the participants in the discourse are disconnected in the sense that their personal non-identity makes the outcomes of prior discourses irrelevant to them for the purposes of (1.3′). In the second case, there occurs a loosening of the individuality of the discourse participants insofar as it is decisions of early participants which are ascribed to them. Such ascription is justified in every case of representative discourse, in which there is no identity of those who take part and those who are affected. For those who are affected, but do not take part, it is irrelevant if a change takes place in those who do take part. As against representatives (1.3′) accordingly imports stronger normative requirements than it does as against those who are both participants and persons affected.

reasons for the new solution must be sufficiently strong as to justify not only the new solution but also the break with tradition. Perelman's principle of inertia therefore holds.[146] Whoever puts forward a new solution carries the burden of proof.[147]

This shows that the stabilization effect of legal dogmatics must not be overestimated. It is not only limited by the fact that previously accepted dogmatic propositions can be rejected or revised. Many justifications require general practical propositions in addition to dogmatic ones. (In these cases we have impure dogmatic justifications.) Since it is often the case that several general practical propositions are discursively possible, quite different outcomes can frequently be justified by recourse to exactly the same dogmatic propositions. Luhmann is alluding to all this when he states that 'the function of dogmatics [lies] . . . not in putting fetters on one's mind but, quite to the contrary, in enhancing freedom in dealing with experiences and texts'.[148] This is certainly a sound point. It would, however, be a mistake to underestimate the stabilizing effect engendered by the principle of inertia with respect to previously accepted dogmatic propositions because of the freedoms undoubtedly present also in dogmatic argumentation.

(2) The *developmental function* is closely related to the stabilization function. The institutionalization of dogmatics, involving the expansion of legal discussion as to times, topics, and persons, makes it possible to differentiate dogmatic propositions to a considerably greater degree and to develop ways of testing them such as would never be possible in *ad hoc* discussions. This makes possible something like a developmental progress in dogmatics. Of course, progress in dogmatics is a considerably more complex matter than in the empirical sciences.[149] It is not only dependent on the activity of legal scientists but beyond this to a considerable degree on the activity of the legislature and on

[146] On this cf. above, pp. 171 ff.

[147] Cf. W. Brohm, 'Die Dogmatik des Verwaltungsrechts vor den Gegenwartsaufgaben der Verwaltung', *VVDStRL* 30 (1972), 248.

[148] Luhmann, *Rechtssystem and Rechtsdogmatik*, p. 16.

[149] On this cf. T. S. Kuhn, *The Structure of Scientific Revolutions* (Chicago, 1962), and also the contributions in I. Lakatos and A. Musgrave (eds.), *Criticism and the Growth of Knowledge* (Cambridge, 1970).

changes in the evaluative ideas prevalent in society. This, however, does not detract from the fact that progress is also possible in legal dogmatics[150]. The possibility of such progress is a strong argument in favour of the scientific character of legal dogmatics.

(3) It is possible for dogmatic justifications to adopt, at least provisionally, items which have previously been tested and accepted. This reduces the burden on the justificatory process to the extent that in the absence of some special ground fresh testing is unnecessary. One can be excused from discussing afresh every value question in every case. This *burden-reducing function*[151] is not only indispensable for the work of the courts which takes place under time constraints, but also of significance for legal scientific discussion. In this sphere too—as in all spheres—it is impossible to discuss everything all over again in every case.

To be sure, the value of the burden-reducing function depends on the degree of advancement achieved in a range of variables such as the simplicity, precision, richness, and confirmation of the tenets of dogmatics on the one hand, and on the other hand the extent to which sufficient consensus has emerged about the dogmatic tenets in question. Experience so far suggests that the central problem of legal dogmatics consists in the fact that these values cannot be satisfactorily brought into conjoint realization. If they were, it would be possible for there to be systems of legal dogmatics from which valuationally convincing solutions could be deduced in every possible case in a given field of law.

Since this is not possible, the burden-reducing function is of limited import. It is often necessary to make a choice between alternative dogmatic tenets before coming to a decision on an individual case, and this choice in its turn has to be justified.

[150] On advance in legal science cf. H. Dölle, 'Juristische Entdeckungen', *Verhandlungen des 42. Deutschen Juristentages, Düsseldorf 1957*, vol. ii (Tübingen, 1959) pp. B1–B22, and the contributions in *Fortschritte des Verwaltungsrechts*, Festschrift for H. J. Wolff, ed. C.-F. Menger (Munich, 1973).

[151] On this cf. Esser, 'Dogmatik zwischen Theorie und Praxis', pp. 522, 524; Bachof, 'Die Dogmatik des Verwaltungsrechts vor den Gegenwartsaufgaben der Verwaltung', p. 198; Luhmann, *Rechtssystem und Rechtsdogmatik*, p. 22; Lazzer, 'Rechtsdogmatik als Kompromißformular', p. 103.

Furthermore, it is frequently necessary to reject hitherto accepted tenets and often the case that general practical tenets as well as dogmatic tenets are needed for justification of a decision.

It must, therefore, indeed be admitted that dogmatics may not only have the effect of reducing the burden but also that of aggravating it.[152] Luhmann stresses the following: 'The difficulties of decision-making are thus compounded—not diminished!—by conceptual elaboration of the law—or, rather, the possibilities of rendering decision-making more difficult are increased.'[153] However, this is only one aspect. On the other side, it is hardly to be doubted that there are dogmatic propositions like, for example, definitions of legally relevant concepts which are sufficiently precise and generally recognized so that decision-making is rendered easier to the extent that it seems unproblematic beyond the point that facts have to be established. In such ordinary cases the burden-reducing function consists precisely in the fact that dogmatic tenets present no problems.[154]

The burden-reducing effect achieved in average cases must of course be paid for by giving rise to difficulties in borderline cases which would not arise in the absence of dogmatics. The question of whether this price is worth paying cannot be answered solely by reference to the advantages of burden-reduction in easy cases, but requires, in addition, reference to the other effects also yielded by dogmatics. Yet the fact that dogmatics can lead to questions which would not arise in its absence is, as will be shown, in no way to be viewed only as a disadvantage.

(4) Furthermore, the *technical function* is of considerable significance.

In order to have an overview of the totality or at least of as wide a realm as possible of the . . . meaning of concrete legal norms, it is necessary to

[152] On this cf. K. Zweigert, 'Rechtsvergleichung, System und Dogmatik', in Festschrift for E. Bötticher, ed. K. A. Bettermann and A. Zeuner (Berlin, 1969), 445–6, and Struck, 'Dogmatische Diskussionen über Dogmatik', *JZ* (1975), 86.

[153] Luhmann, *Rechtssystem und Rechtsdogmatik*, p. 23.

[154] To this extent it is not possible to agree with Struck, who is evidently of the opinion that dogmatic propositions play no part in average cases ('Dogmatische Diskussion über Dogmatik', p. 86).

construct general basic concepts, forms of statements, legal institutions, and so on because the only thing that can provide a quick overview is a presentation of the norms of the law which has been simplified in this way, which has a unitary and systematic character, and which matches with the reciprocally conditional relations subsisting among the norms.[155]

In this way dogmatics performs an informational function,[156] enhancing the law's 'teachability' and 'learnability'[157] and thus by the same token its amenability to being handed down.[158] In this connection Podlech draws attention to the law on the aftermath of war—for example legal rules on equalization of resultant burden and war-reparations, and the provisions of the (German) Act 131, of which no dogmatic elaboration has ever really taken place and which therefore 'can only be mastered casuistically by specialist practitioners'.[159]

Doubt can, of course, be cast on this very didactic function of dogmatics. Struck quite fairly entertains the thought that the didactic value of legal dogmatics has yet to be clearly proven—and that such proof would have to be in terms of modern educational science.[160] On the other hand one must admit that at least one means of mastering a subject area is that of subjecting it to a thoroughgoing conceptual analysis.

(5) The *control function*[161] already mentioned is an extremely important one. As explained above[162] two kinds of checking for

[155] W. Krawietz, 'Funktion und Grenze einer dogmatischen Rechtswissenschaft', p. 151 and similarly his 'Was leistet Rechtsdogmatik in der richterlichen Entscheidungspraxis?', p. 52. Cf. also Engisch, 'Begriffseinteilung und Klassifikation in der Jurisprudenz', in Festschrift for K. Larenz, ed. G. Paulus, U. Diederichsen, and C.-W. Canaris (Munich, 1973), 125 ff.

[156] Esser, 'Möglichkeiten und Grenzen des dogmatischen Denkens im modernen Zivilrecht', p. 101.

[157] Podlech, 'Rechtstheoretische Bedingungen einer Methodenlehre juristischer Dogmatik', *Jahrbuch für Rechtssoziologie und Rechtstheorie*, 2 (1972), 492.

[158] Luhmann, 'Sinn als Grundbegriff der Soziologie', in Habermas and Luhmann (edd.), *Theorie der Gesellschaft oder Sozialtechnologie*, p. 98.

[159] Podlech, 'Rechtstheoretische Bedingungen', p. 493. For the beginning of a dogmatic elaboration of these areas of the law cf. H. J. Wolff and O. Bachof, *Verwaltungsrecht*, vol. iii, 3rd edn. (Munich, 1973), para. 144.

[160] Struck, 'Dogmatische Diskussion über Dogmatik', pp. 85–6.

[161] On this cf. Luhmann, *Rechtssystem und Rechtsdogmatik*, pp. 19, 40 ff.; Krawietz, 'Was leistet Rechtsdogmatik in der richterlichen Entscheidungspraxis?', p. 77.

[162] Cf. above, pp. 262 ff.

consistency can be distinguished. Systematic testing in the narrower sense makes it possible to control for the logical compatibility of the propositions of dogmatics and in the wider sense makes it possible to check the general practical compatibility of judgments justifiable by recourse to a diversity of dogmatic propositions. In this way, studies in legal dogmatics facilitate the decision of cases not as isolated instances but as considered in the light of a whole line of cases already decided and yet to be decided. In like measure they give an enhanced reality to the principle of universalizability and accordingly serve the ends of justice.[163]

(6) The last remaining positive function of dogmatics to be mentioned here is the *heuristic function*. Dogmatics contains a great range of problem-solving models, distinctions, and viewpoints which would not readily occur to someone always beginning afresh. Even if this is not sufficient to determine a decision, it still remains a real help to make use of this apparatus. Questions are put and answers suggested which would otherwise be impossible or would remain hidden from view. A system of legal dogmatics can thus be 'a fruitful starting-point for making new findings and connections, since, to the same extent as it pulls together and enhances the fertility of our stage of understanding acquired with respect to particular problems, it becomes a trigger for new discoveries which would not have come to mind at all, much less gained ground if reflection were confined to individual points rather than having a systematic character.'[164]

2.4.6 *Dogmatic and General Practical Argumentations*

The achievements which have been set out together with the limitations which have come into the picture suggest taking an *instrumental* view of legal dogmatics.[165] Legal dogmatics is a tool

[163] On this cf. Wieacker, 'Zur praktischen Leistung der Rechtsdogmatik', p. 335.

[164] Esser, *Vorverständnis und Methodenwahl*, p. 101. Cf. also Luhmann, *Rechtssystem und Rechtsdogmatik*, pp. 22–3.

[165] Such an instrumental conception of juristic dogmatics is to be found in Esser, 'Dogmatik zwischen Theorie und Praxis', p. 518; Wieacker, 'Zur praktischen Leistung der Rechtsdogmatik', p. 333; H. Dölle, 'Rechtsdogmatik und Rechtsvergleichung', *Rabels Zeitschrift für ausländisches und internationales Privatrecht*, 34 (1970), 408.

which can bring about results unattainable solely through the medium of general practical discourse. Several of these achievements, such as the contribution to satisfying the principle of universalizability[166] in the framework of the stabilization and control functions, are requirements of general practical reason; others, such as the heuristic function, are desirable for like reasons. Thus far legal dogmatics is a rational activity.

The rational character of the application of legal dogmatics is, of course, turned upside down the moment it is no longer used as an 'instrument for determining the right in matters of practical reason or morality'.[167] This is particularly the case when legal dogmatics are used to conceal the true grounds of a decision or to provide purportedly autonomous programmes for decision-making. It is beyond dispute that such a misapplication of argument from legal dogmatics is possible. The extent to which it occurs is a question for empirical investigation. That it does occur is nothing remarkable. Specious justification and question-begging (*petitio principii*) occur in general practical reasoning too. The point of present interest is that it is just as possible for dogmatic reasoning to be rational as to be fallacious.

Dogmatic argumentation is rational as long as its linkage back into general practical reasoning is not lost from view. This linkage is not broken as long as justifications are given in doubtful cases for the dogmatic propositions in dogmatic arguments. Dogmatic propositions can in turn be applied in such justifications; but, as shown above, general practical arguments are required in the last resort.

Dogmatic argumentation is bound up with general practical reasoning in yet another respect. A distinction was made above between pure and impure dogmatic justifications. In pure dogmatic justifications the conclusion to be justified follows solely from dogmatic propositions together with valid norm formulations and empirical statements. In impure dogmatic justifications general practical propositions are required over and above this. In such cases, which are far from uncommon, there exists a direct relationship between dogmatic and general practical reasoning.

[166] Cf. the general rule of discourse (1.3′).

[167] Wieacker, 'Zur praktischen Leistung der Rechtsdogmatik', p. 333.

In conclusion, the application of dogmatic arguments can be acknowledged as not only not contradicting a single one of the principles of discourse theory but as being a kind of reasoning which is required by it in the special context of legal discourse. The following rule thus holds:

(J.12) Whenever dogmatic arguments are possible they should be used.

2.5 The Use of Precedent

A theory of legal reasoning which failed to go into an account of the role of precedent would miss one of the most characteristic aspects of legal argumentation. Nowadays, even in continental European law, the importance—at least the de facto importance—of precedent is acknowledged on all sides.[168] What is disputed is its theoretical standing. The dispute focuses above all on the question of whether precedent is to be accorded the character of a source of law.[169] This question cannot be discussed here. The following discussion will rather be limited to two areas: (1) the role to be ascribed to the observance of precedent as this is seen from the standpoint of the theory of legal discourse outlined here, and (2) the relationship of arguments based on

[168] Cf. perhaps Larenz, 'Über die Bindungswirkung von Präjudizien', in Festschrift for H. Schima, ed. H. W. Fasching and W. Kralik (Vienna, 1969), 249; O. A. German, *Präjudizien als Rechtsquelle* (Stockholm, Göteborg, and Uppsala, 1960), 11; Kriele, *Theorie der Rechtsgewinnung*, pp. 243 ff.

[169] G. Less expressly answers this question in the affirmative (*Von Wesen und Wert des Richterrechts* (Erlangen, 1951), 59 ff.). Cf. also H. W. Kruse, *Das Richterrecht als Rechtsquelle des innerstaatlichen Rechts* (Tübingen, 1971), 7 ff. For arguments in favour of a correction of traditional theory on legal sources cf. also Kriele, *Theorie der Rechtsgewinnung*, p. 289; Wieacker, *Gesetz und Richterkunst*, pp. 16–17.; German, *Präjudizien als Rechtsquelle*, pp. 45 ff. Against the character of precedents as a legal source are, among others, Larenz, 'Über die Bindungswirkung von Präjudizien', pp. 247 ff.; Esser, 'Richterrecht, Gerichtsgebrauch und Gewohnheitsrecht', in Festschrift for F. von Hippel, ed. J. Esser and H. Thieme (Tübingen, 1967), 95 ff. On the need for a differentiated approach, particularly in respect of the distinction between the question of reasons concerning the origin, the binding nature, and the cognition of law, and also in respect of the need to solve 'the problem of the sources of the cognition of law, not abstractly but in their relations with situations and also specifically with roles', cf. Dreier, 'Probleme der Rechtsquellenlehre', in Festschrift for H. J. Wolff, ed. C.-F. Menger (Munich, 1973), 4 ff.

precedent to other possible arguments of legal discourse. Whatever is said in relation to the former point has, of course, some bearing on the problem of the status of precedent as a source of law.

2.5.1 *The Rule on the Burden of Argument*

The basic reason for following precedents is the principle of universalizability,[170] the requirement that we treat like cases alike, which lies behind justice as a formal quality.[171] This immediately reveals one of the decisive difficulties of following precedent: no two cases are ever completely identical. It is always possible to find a difference. The actual problem thus shifts to one of determining which differences are relevant.[172] Before going into this, another point is of importance. It is possible for a case to be exactly like a previously decided case in all relevant circumstances and yet a different decision is sought because one's assessment of the circumstances has altered in the mean time. If one were to adhere solely to the principle of universalizability, such a decision would be impossible. Thus, wholly to exclude any change of mind is, however, inconsistent with the claim to correctness implicated in every act of deciding. On the other hand satisfying the claim to correctness precisely involves satisfying the principle of universalizability. To be sure, it is only one condition. A general condition is justifiability by argument. In this situation the possibility arises of demanding respect for precedent as a matter of principle while nevertheless allowing exceptions subject to imposing the *burden of argument* on anyone who proposes to make an exception.[173] Here Perelman's principle of inertia holds good, with its demand that a decision may only be altered if sufficiently good reasons can be adduced for so doing.[174] Whether this burden of argument is discharged

[170] On this cf. above, pp. 65 ff., and p. 190 (Rule 1.3')).

[171] On this cf. Perelman, *The Idea of Justice and the Problem of Argument*, pp. 11 ff.

[172] Kriele, Theorie der Rechtsgewinnung, p. 269.

[173] On this cf. in particular ibid., 243, 247, 253, 276.

[174] Perelman and Olbrechts-Tyteca, *La Nouvelle Rhétorique*, pp. 42–3 (32–3) and pp. 294 ff. (218 ff). Perelman expressly emphasizes that the principle of inertia underlies the appeal to precedents. On this principle of inertia cf. above, pp. 171 ff.

in a given case can, of course, only be determined by reference to real or imaginary discourse partners.

The hypothesis considered up till now was one in which the noteworthy facts were adjudged identical. This must be distinguished from those cases in which attention is drawn to special facts or where the absence of certain facts is indicated in favour of making a distinction as to what should be the rule. In such cases it will also be necessary to accept the burden of argument.[175] The borderline between cases which are still so alike that there exists such a burden of argument and those which reach the point of being so different that it need no longer be discharged is of course ill-defined.

A doctrine of precedent based on the aforementioned rule on the burden of argument has several valuable functions. These functions in part correspond to those for the use of dogmatic arguments. Before discussing them it will be appropriate to comment in brief on the relationship between dogmatic arguments and arguments from precedent.

The most important point is this: while on the one hand countless statements from legal dogmatics are directly incorporated into precedents, on the other hand results handed down judicially are taken over into dogmatics, which purports to state the law as it is currently in force.[176] What is distinctive about legal disputes pursued as a science is that such a legal science involves a greater degree of thoroughness in the conceptual-analytical elaboration of its theses, that it proposes principles for the solution of cases even in advance of any such case's arriving before a court for decision, and that it can hold out alternative decisions as possibilities. The distinctiveness of legal decision-making when it is creating precedents is to be seen above all by contrast in the fact that judicial opinions contain statements whose point is not the communication of suggestions but the performance of actions. To adopt a previously mentioned distinction of Austin's, such statements have quite a different illocutionary force from those of legal science.[177] This should, of

[175] Cf. above, p. 196 (Rule (3.1)).

[176] In this connection Esser aptly speaks of precedents steering the '"course" between theory and practice' (*Vorverständnis und Methodenwahl*, p. 189).

[177] Cf. above, p. 55.

course, not detract from the fact that there exists a considerable degree of parallelism, at least as to content, between the propositions of dogmatics and the propositions of case law. It is indeed for this reason that much of what was said about the function of dogmatics also applies to the function of the utilization of precedent.

This holds in particular for the stabilization, developmental,[178] and burden-reducing[179] functions. Reference should here be made to what was said above. By securing stability, the practice of following precedent contributes at the same time to legal certainty and the protection of confidence in judicial decision-making.

Legal certainty and protection of confidence are, of course, not its only goals. If they were, it would not be permissible to depart from precedent in the limits set by the principle of inertia. From the standpoint of discourse theory the most important reason for the rationality of a doctrine of precedent which conforms to the principles of universalizability and inertia is yielded by the limits to which general practical argument is subject. As explained above, the rules of discourse do not always enable us to find just one right answer. There often remains a considerable area of discursive possiblity.[180] Filling this gap with changing inconsistent solutions would be in contradiction of the requirement of consistency set by the principle of universalizability. The introduction of a burden of argument in favour of precedent cannot be viewed as an error in the rules of discourse, as long as the possibility of rejecting any maxim of decision-making recognized as wrong, remains open. This limitation of the range of what is discursively possible achieved by precedent should therefore be recognized as rational.[181] The following

[178] On this cf. Kriele, *Theorie der Rechtsgewinnung*, pp. 264 ff.

[179] Ibid., 262 ff. [180] Cf. above, p. 207.

[181] Cf. Kriele, p. 258. It is not possible to agree with Larenz, who is of the view that it is 'not precedent as such which "binds" but solely the correctly interpreted or concretized norm within it' (*Methodenlehre der Rechtswissenschaft*, p. 422). Precedents are of significance precisely because it is often not possible to distinguish which of several proposals for a solution is the correct one. In this situation, the pure fact that a proposed solution has already been previously applied, is a good reason to choose it once more. On the other hand one must agree with Larenz that a precedent 'must not be, so to speak, taken over "blind"'. The "presumption" of correctness is already insufficient where there

rules can therefore be formulated as the most general rules for the utilization of precedent:

(J.13) If a precedent can be cited in favour of or against a decision it should be so cited.

(J.14) Whoever wishes to depart from a precedent carries the burden of argument.

Until now the rule on the burden of argument has been justified as a rule of legal discourse. A further question is whether it can be regarded as a 'principle of our positive law'.[182] This question touches on the other one mentioned above about the status of precedent as a source of law. An attempt to answer it would lead to the general problem of the legal standing of the rules of discourse. It will suffice here simply to acknowledge the problem.

2.5.2 *The Application of Precedent and Legal Argumentation*

The extent of the bond governed by the burden of argument rule depends on the range of possibilities for deviating from case law. It is necessary to distinguish between the techniques of divergence and the reasons for divergence.

The techniques of divergence are the constituent parts of the techniques for the application of case law. It is not possible here even to make a start at presenting the many theories which have been elaborated, particularly in Anglo-American legal science.[183] Only some points will be emphasized which are of significance for the question of the relationship of arguments based on case law to other possible arguments of legal discourse.

Application of a precedent implies the application of the norm underlying the decision in case law. 'Case law is also a law of norms.'[184] The question is, what is to count as a norm to be observed from the point of view of case law. Many theories have

exist serious doubts in regard to it' (ibid., 422, 423 n. 144). For several reasons justifying departure from precedents cf. German, *Präjudizien als Rechtsquelle*, pp. 35 ff.

[182] Kriele, *Theorie der Rechtsgewinnung*, p. 248.

[183] On this cf. Kriele, *Theorie der Rechtsgewinnung*, pp. 282 ff.; German, *Präjudizien als Rechtsquelle*, pp. 21 ff.

[184] Kriele, *Theorie der Rechtsgewinnung*, p. 270.

been put forward in answer to this revolving around the distinction between *ratio decidendi* and *obiter dictum*.[185] The more limited question posed here will make it possible to point out two factors rather than embark on a full discussion of these theories, namely the possibility of *distinguishing* and *overruling*. The technique of distinguishing is used where the norm to be observed from the point of view of case law is understood so narrowly—for example, through the introduction of a feature not present in the facts of the case—that it no longer applies. In this process the precedent as such remains worth considering. By contrast the technique of overruling consists in rejection of precedent. Only one point is of interest here: both distinguishing and overruling require justification. According to Kriele, this requires considerations of right reasons.[186] It is certainly correct that general practical arguments play a special role in such situations. But apart from this, all further additional arguments possible in legal discourse are admissible.

The application of precedent is thus shown to be a method of argumentation which is itself required on general practical grounds (the principle of universalizability/the rule on the burden of argument) and is to this extent rational. Furthermore, its use presupposes further arguments, particularly general practical ones.

2.6 The Application of Special Legal Argument Forms

Special legal argument forms[187] are here understood to be those particular argument forms dealt with in legal methodology such as analogy, *argumentum e contrario*, *argumentum a fortiori*, and *argumentum ad absurdum*. The following reflections have the sole aim of making clear the role of these forms in legal discourse. So

[185] For a presentation of the state of the dispute cf. ibid., 282 ff., and W. Schlüter, *Das Obiter dictum* (Munich, 1973), 77 ff.

[186] Kriele, *Theorie der Rechtsgewinnung*, pp. 246, 286.

[187] On this terminology cf. Klug, *Juristische Logik*, p. 97; Klug speaks of 'special arguments of legal logic'. Of course this is not quite correct, since the forms characterized here as 'legal' are also applicable to other domains. Of course, it has been in the jurisprudential context that many of them have been exposed to particular development. This justifies the terminology used above.

far as concerns their logical analysis, they rely above all on investigations carried out in more recent times using the methods of modern logic.[188]

All special legal argument forms can be expressed in the forms of valid logical inference. This is not too surprising since the same is possible with respect to every argument form. Anyway, nearly all cases require a special recasting of the premisses and frequently the introduction of special premisses which usually remain unarticulated in argumentation as it actually occurs. The formulation of special legal argument forms as valid logical inference forms has two advantages: it makes it possible to understand their logical structure, and it makes their non-logical content apparent.

Traditional notations include quite different forms. Klug discusses the following case of *argumentum e contrario* as an example of an inference form which is logically valid without addition of any special premisses:

(J.15) .(1) $(x)\ (OGx \rightarrow Fx)$
(2) $(x)\ (\neg Fx \rightarrow \neg OGx)$ (1)[189]

(J.15) is a logically valid inference. However, the possibility of such an argument presupposes that the norm which forms the starting-point has the logical form exhibited in (1). It must ordain that *only* where *x* is a case of an F is the legal consequence in question to follow. Whether this is the case depends on its interpretation. This in its turn can, of course, often rely on appropriate formulations in the text of the norms, but frequently requires further arguments. All arguments possible for legal discourse are admissible as such further arguments.[190] Even a form as simple as (J.15) refers to the entire profusion of

[188] On this cf. ibid., 97 ff.; Heller, *Logik und Axiologie der analogen Rechtsanwendung*; Diederichsen, 'Die "reductio ad absurdum" in der Jurisprudenz', pp. 155 ff.; Schreiber, *Logik des Rechts*, 57 ff.

[189] On this schema cf. Klug, *Juristische Logik*, p. 128. The symbols match the ones used here.

[190] It is too narrow when Klug considers only a teleological analysis to be necessary in such cases (ibid., 129). Teleological arguments are only one class of the arguments possible here. In order to justify holding that the facts of the cases fulfil a necessary condition for a particular legal consequence, it is possible for example to refer to legislative interest.

conceivable legal arguments. This holds for all cases of the application of logical inference forms in legal argumentation.[191]

Special legal argument forms would hardly have become the subject of so much discussion if they had no concern other than application of generally valid logical inference forms in legal argumentation. But there is more to it than this and that is exactly why they are of interest. Analogy is the most widely discussed case.[192]

Analogy can also be presented as a valid logical inference. This is possible in quite different ways. A particularly easy way has been chosen here. 'F sim *x*' means '*x* resembles an F'. The analogical inference can then be formalized as follows:

(J.16) .(1) $(x)\ (Fx \vee F\ \text{sim}\ x \rightarrow OGx)$
.(2) $(x)\ (Hx \rightarrow F\ \text{sim}\ x)$
(3) $(x)\ (Hx \rightarrow OGx)$ (1), (2)

(J.16) corresponds to Klug's formula (9.6).[193] Klug's example can thus be fitted into (J.16). In this, *x* is to be understood as a variable about transactions.

.(1) For all *x*: If *x* is a contract of sale (F) or a contract for a transaction similar to sale (F sim) then paragraphs 433 ff. BGB shall be applicable (G) to *x*.

.(2) For all *x*: If *x* is a contract concerned with the transfer for value of a commercial enterprise (H) then *x* is a contract for a transaction similar to sale (F sim).

(3) For all *x*: If *x* is a contract concerned with the transfer for value of a commercial enterprise (H) then paragraphs 433 ff. BGB shall be applicable (G) to *x*. (1), (2).

This example makes it clear that the real problem of analogical

[191] For an interpretation of the variables in the schemata of sentential logic by reference to juristic sentences cf., in addition, Diederichsen's example dealing with the possible subjective filing of an action ('Die "reductio ad absurdum" in der Jurisprudenz', pp. 170–1).

[192] Only the form of analogy called 'statutory analogy' or 'single analogy' by Larenz, will be dealt with here. On these concepts Engisch, *Einführung in das juristische Denken*, p. 147; Larenz, *Methodenlehre der Rechtswissenschaft*, pp. 368–9.

[193] Klug, *Juristische Logik*, p. 120. This has been formulated in the language of the calculus of classes and has the following form: $((\alpha \subset \beta)\ \&\ ((\beta \cup \gamma) \subset \delta)) \rightarrow (\alpha \subset \delta)$. α corresponds to H*x*, β to F sim *x*, γ to F*x* and δ to OG*x*.

reasoning does not lie in the inference from (1) and (2) to (3), but rather in the justification of (1) and (2). Klug therefore suggests that an inference such as (J.16) should not be called 'analogical inference' but rather 'the inference which brings to a conclusion the process of legal analogical reasoning'.[194] This raises the question of how premisses (1) and (2) can be justified.

(1) is not usually a norm which can be expressly found in enacted law. The norm which can be found in enacted law is usually of the form:

(1.a) $(x)\ (Fx \rightarrow OGx)$.

In order to arrive at (1) from this a rule of the following kind is needed:

(1.b) States of affairs which are alike from a legal point of view should have like legal consequences.[195]

(1.b) is a special case of the principle of universalizability (1.3')[196] and thereby of the principle of equality. Underlying analogy, therefore, are the principles of universalizability and equality respectively.[197] This means that in justifying the second premiss of (J.16)—that is, in the determination of likeness—all the difficulties of applying the principle of equality arise. Of course it is possible to provide an analysis of the logical structures of relations of likeness.[198] But such an analysis on its own cannot yield a conclusion as to the existence of a legally relevant likeness. Many authors have therefore remarked that

[194] Klug, *Juristische Logik*, p. 121. Cf. also Heller, *Logik und Axiologie der analogen Rechtsanwendung*, p. 46.

[195] On such a proposition cf. Heller, *Logik und Axiologie der analogen Rechtsanwendung*, p. 118; Engisch, *Einführung in das juristische Denken*, p. 256 n. 166*c*.

[196] Cf. above, p. 190.

[197] Engisch, *Einführung in das juristische Denken*, p. 256 n. 166*c*; Larenz, *Methodenlehre der Rechtswissenschaft*, p. 366; Zippelius, *Einführung in die juristische Methodenlehre*, pp. 69–70; id., 'Rechtsphilosophische Aspekte der Rechtsfindung', *JZ* (1976), 153.

[198] On this cf. Klug's explication of the concept of likeness by recourse to the concept of 'spheres-of-likeness' and Heller's view of analogy as structural likeness (*Juristische Logik*, pp. 79–80, 120; Heller, *Logik und Axiologie der analogen Rechtsanwendung*, pp. 24 ff.).

analogy is based on an evaluation.[199] In order to justify this evaluation all the arguments possible in legal discourse are admissible. This does not mean that analogy is superfluous as an argument form. It is a formal structure of what might be called substantive arguments whose point can be exhibited only in a structure like this. As such it is bound up with the concept of discourse in two ways. On the one hand it relies on the principle of universalizability which is constitutive of both general practical and legal discourse; on the other hand it can only be brought into play where it is backed up with arguments.

The same holds for the argument from unacceptability as analysed by Diederichsen.[200] A case of such an argument from unacceptability occurs, for example, when in order to support the thesis that a particular interpretation I of a norm R through a word usage rule W ($I^R_W = R'$) is inadmissible, it is stated that this would result in unacceptable, meaningless, incomprehensible, or suchlike results.[201] Let Z stand for such an unacceptable result which—at least from the point of view of the arguing parties—is regarded as prohibited ($O\neg Z$). Using the schema (S) presented above, the argument then has the following structure:[202]

(J.17) .(1) $O\neg Z$
.(2) $R' \rightarrow Z$
(3) $\neg R'$

Premisses (1) and (2) must be justified. In particular, it must be shown that Z is to be regarded as prohibited and that R′ really does result in Z. The former can be established *inter alia* by general practical arguments, the latter only by empirical

[199] Cf. Larenz, *Methodenlehre der Rechtswissenschaft*, p. 367; Diederichsen, 'Traditionelle Logik für Juristen', *Juristische Analysen*, 2 (1970), 780; Esser, *Vorverständnis und Methodenwahl*, p. 183; Weinberger, 'Über die Offenheit des rechtlichen Normensystems' in Festschrift for W. Wilburg (Graz, 1975), 447; Heller, *Logik und Axiologik der analogen Rechtsanwendung*, p. 110; Klug, *Juristische Logik*, p. 123.

[200] Diederichsen, 'Die "reductio ad absurdum" in der Jurisprudenz', pp. 175 ff.

[201] For examples from adjudication cf. ibid., 157, 175 ff.

[202] What was cited above concerning the validity of (S) holds for this schema. Cf. above, pp. 237–8.

arguments. Of course, (J.17) is a particularly strong example of an argument from unacceptability. Weaker forms would involve showing that Z is not absolutely prohibited but only as supposing it to be the worst of available alternatives. What is of importance here is that the demand for the justification of (1) connects up this form of argument with legal discourse.

Let this outline suffice for present purposes. It makes it clear that at least the three argument forms discussed above are special cases of the application of the rules and forms of general practical discourse. (J.15) is a valid logical form of inference, (J.16) is required by the principle of universalizability, and (J.17) is a case of taking consequences into consideration. To the extent that these forms refer back to the rules and forms of general practical discourse, their application can be called rational. But it has also become clear that, as with the canons of interpretation, the application of such forms is only rational to the extent that saturation is achieved, and the statements inserted for this purpose can be justified in legal discourse. The following rule therefore holds for the use of these forms:

(J.18) Special legal argument forms must have the reasons for them stated in full—that is, must achieve saturation.

2.7 The Role of General Practical Arguments in Legal Discourse

The role of general practical arguments in legal discourse has already been alluded to in the preceding discussion. The only concern here will be to draw together what has already been stated.

General practical reasoning may be required (1) in the justification of the normative premisses necessary to satisfy the different argument forms,[203] (2) in justifying a choice between different argument forms leading to different results,[204] (3) in the justification and testing of propositions of legal dogmatics,[205]

[203] Cf. above, pp. 238, 245–6, 284.
[204] Cf. above, pp. 248–9.
[205] Cf. above, pp. 262 ff.

(4) in justifying any cases of distinguishing or overruling,[206] and (5) directly in justifying statements used in internal justification.

The application of general practical arguments is, of course, by no means the only method applied in these five situations. It is always at least conceivable that propositions of legal dogmatics or of case law might be used instead of general practical arguments. The application of dogmatic propositions or those of case law is not only possible in achieving saturation of the various different argument forms, but also in justifying a choice between different argument forms yielding diverse outcomes. The principle of universalizability requires that one proceed in accordance with weighting rules in the various situations of requiring choice (J.8).[207] These rules on weighting may assume the character of propositions of legal dogmatics or those of case law. Dogmatic propositions can also be adduced to justify an instance of distinguishing or overruling. Finally, it is possible to justify propositions of legal dogmatics in their turn by further dogmatic propositions.

Of course the possibility of inserting dogmatic propositions and statements of case law into the five situations described above can only partially supplant general practical reasoning. It often does so incompletely and always only provisionally.

It supplants it only *partially* because there are by no means always appropriate propositions of legal dogmatics or of case law available. Where there are no such statements available, general practical reasoning intervenes directly.

Supplanting is often only *incomplete* because although it is not unusual to be able to draw on a proposition of legal dogmatics or of case law, nevertheless this statement is not the necessary one (for example for achieving saturation of an argument form), and the statement which is necessary does not follow logically from the statement cited (even together with empirical statements and the formulations of valid legal norms). In such a situation there is a need for additional premisses with a normative content which have to be justified by recourse to general practical reason. What takes place is what was above called an 'impure

[206] Cf. above, p. 279.
[207] Cf. above, p. 249.

dogmatic justification'[208] together with what can be correspondingly called 'impure justification through case law'.

The most important point is that the supplanting of general practical arguments is always only *provisional*. Statements of legal dogmatics cannot continue to be justified by even more statements of legal dogmatics. In the last analysis, in order both to test them and to justify the applicability of case law, general practical arguments are necessary.[209] It is in this sense that general practical reasoning forms the basis of legal reasoning.

[208] Cf. above, p. 261.
[209] Cf. above, pp. 265–6, 278–9.

III. Legal and General Practical Discourse

The preceding chapters have made plain the inextricable link of legal to general practical discourse. Summarizing what has been said so far, it is possible to distinguish four aspects of this link: (1) the need for legal discourse in view of the nature of general practical discourse, (2) the partial correspondence in the claim to correctness, (3) the structural correspondence between rules and forms of legal discourse and those of general practical discourse, and (4) the need for general practical reasoning in the framework of legal reasoning.

1. THE NEED FOR LEGAL DISCOURSE IN VIEW OF THE NATURE OF GENERAL PRACTICAL DISCOURSE

The need for legal discourse arises out of the weakness of the rules and forms of general practical discourse. This weakness consists in the fact that these rules and forms define a decision-making procedure which in many cases leads to no result at all and which, when it does lead to a result, in no way guarantees conclusive certainty. There are three reasons for this weakness: (1) the rules of discourse do not stipulate which normative premisses are to form the starting-point for parties to any discourse. The actual normative convictions, which are often mutually inconsistent, form the starting-point of discourse. Since (2) not all the steps in argumentation are fixed, and (3) there are several rules of discourse which can only be approximately satisfied, there always remains the possibility of not reaching agreement. In fact, some normative statements are required by the rules of discourse as being discursively necessary. Their negation is inconsistent with them (that is discursively impossible).[210] However, there remains a wide range of

[210] Cf. above, p. 17.

discursive possibilities in which both a particular normative statement and its negation may be justified without infringing the rules of discourse.[211]

In light of this situation and of the actually given need for a decision it is reasonable, that is justifiable, in a practical discourse, to agree on procedures to limit the range of the discursively possible in as rational a way as one can. Examples of such procedures are the rules of parliamentary legislation which are grounded in the principles of majority voting in and of representation, and the various rules of procedure.

The legal norms which emerge from legislative procedures do not solve all problems. It is repeatedly made clear that they in no way fully determine legal decision-making. Four reasons have been cited for this: (1) the vagueness of legal language, (2) the possibility of conflicts between norms, (3) the fact that there can be cases which call for legal resolution, but whose resolution is not provided for by any existing valid norm, and also (4) the possibility in special cases of making a decision which goes against the strict letter of the law.[212] If one were always inclined to fill in this area of uncertainty by no other means than recourse to general practical reasoning, the weaknesses of general practical discourse would continue to be transmitted to a considerable degree into legal decision-making. So it is only rational to introduce special forms and rules of legal argumentation and to institutionalize it as legal science, while also embedding it in the context of precedents. In this way it is possible further to reduce the range of discursive possibilities in the area of uncertainty left by legal norms.

General practical reasoning is not superseded by legal reasoning in this process. As has been shown again and again, legal reasoning remains throughout dependent on general practical arguments. The uncertainty due to the nature of general practical discourse can therefore never be fully eliminated. Nevertheless, as an element of legal reasoning, general practical reasoning takes place under conditions which considerably increase its determinative capability, not least in virtue of the institutionalization of legal discourse as legal science.

[211] Cf. above, pp. 135–6, 207.

[212] On this point cf. above, pp. 1–2.

2. THE PARTIAL CORRESPONDENCE IN THE CLAIM TO CORRECTNESS

A further aspect of the inextricable link lies in the claim to correctness which is also constitutive of legal reasoning.[213] Unlike the case of general practical discourse, this claim does not relate to whether or not the normative statement in question is absolutely rational, but rather only to whether it can be rationally justified within the framework of the valid legal order.[214] The rationality of legal argumentation is thus, to the extent that it is determined by statute, relative to the rationality of legislation. Absolute rationality in legal decision-making would presuppose the rationality of legislation. A condition of this is that practical questions be rationally resolved in the society in question. In order to arrive at a theory of legal discourse which would also embrace these conditions of rationality, the theory of general rational practical discourse would have to be expanded to include a theory of legislation and then a normative theory of society of which the theory of legal discourse would form a part. The aims pursued here are more limited in scope. The only question to be asked is what it means to decide rationally in the framework of a valid legal order. This point must be explained in the theory of legal argumentation. Of course such a theory brings in a whole range of important questions which also have to be addressed by a theory of legislation and a normative theory of society. These theories can thus be distinguished but not strictly separated.

3. THE STRUCTURAL CORRESPONDENCE BETWEEN THE RULES AND FORMS OF LEGAL DISCOURSE AND THOSE OF GENERAL PRACTICAL DISCOURSE

The inextricable link between legal and general practical discourse becomes especially obvious in the structural correspondence between the rules and forms of legal discourse and those of general practical discourse.

[213] On this point cf. above, pp. 127 ff., 214 ff.
[214] Cf. above, p. 220.

(1) The rules and forms of internal justification are instances of the application of the *principle of universalizability* (1.3′)[215] which corresponds to the principle of formal justice to treat like cases alike.[216] The rules and forms of internal justification are the basic structure of legal argumentation. The same principle thus forms the foundation of both general practical and legal discourse.

(2) *Empirical argumentation* always plays an important part and often a decisive role in both general practical and legal discourse. There is frequently agreement about the normative premisses, but disagreement centres on the facts. Rule (6.1)[217] therefore holds for both forms of discourse, that is the rule which allows the transition into a theoretical (empirical) discourse at any time. The same problem thus arises in both forms of discourse, namely that the necessary empirical knowledge is often not available with sufficient certainty. Rules about rational presumptions are therefore required by both forms of discourse.[218]

(3) Several of the argument forms grouped under the heading of *canons* of interpretation help to build up the authority-bound character of legal argumentation which, as already stated, is by no means irrational. Others are rather variants of general practical argument forms. The teleological argument form (J.5)[219] discussed above, for example, can be seen as a variant of the general argument from consequence (4.3).[220]

(4) *Dogmatic legal science* can be understood as an institutionalization of practical discourse conditioned upon the existence of a legal order. This institutionalization makes it possible to achieve outcomes which would not be possible using only the methods of general practical discourse.[221] The discussion broadens out considerably in respect of times, persons, and topics. In this way both the consistency and the differentiation

[215] Cf. above, pp. 65 ff., 190.
[216] Cf. above, p. 222.
[217] Cf. above, pp. 206, 233.
[218] Cf. above, p. 206.
[219] Cf. above, p. 242.
[220] Cf. above, pp. 199, 237–8.
[221] Cf. above, pp. 266 ff.

of decision-making can be increased. The former is required directly by the principles of non-contradiction,[222] universalizability,[223] and inertia,[224] the latter indirectly by the rationality rules' (2.2)[225] requirement of openness and consideration of all arguments. Satisfying these requirements corresponds to the stabilizing,[226] developmental,[227] control,[228] and heuristic[229] functions performed by legal dogmatics.

(5) The principles of universalizability and inertia[230] form the foundation of the *doctrine of precedent*. This means that this too rests on general practical principles.

(6) Finally, this holds for the application of *special legal argument forms* too. The variant of the *argumentum e contrario* was an instance of applying a logical rule and thus of (1.1),[231] analogy was shown to be a special case of the application of the principle of universalizability (1.3′), and the argument from unacceptability a variant of the basic form of the argument from consequence (S)[232] and (4.3)[233] respectively.

4. THE NEED FOR GENERAL PRACTICAL ARGUMENTS IN THE FRAMEWORK OF LEGAL REASONING

The aspect of the inextricable link between the two forms of discourse which is most often stressed is not that outlined above of their structural correspondence but rather that of the requirement for general practical arguments in the framework of legal discourse. The reasons for this have been repeatedly stressed above, and have already been comprehensively

[222] Cf. above, pp. 188–9, rule (1.1).
[223] Cf. above, p. 190, rule (1.3′).
[224] On this point cf. above, p. 196, rules (3.1) and (3.2).
[225] Cf. above, p. 240.
[226] Cf. above, pp. 266 ff.
[227] Cf. above, pp. 268–9.
[228] Cf. above, pp. 271–2.
[229] Cf. above, p. 272.
[230] Cf. above, pp. 275–6.
[231] Cf. above, pp. 188, 280.
[232] Cf. above, pp. 237, 283.
[233] Cf. above, p. 199.

described.[234] It was established that legal argumentation is throughout dependent on general practical argumentation and that it therefore makes sense to say that general practical reasoning forms the foundation of legal reasoning.

This conclusion would appear to be somewhat contradictory of the thesis presented above to the effect that legal discourse is necessary precisely because of the weaknesses of general practical discourse, and that legal discourse particularly, by virtue of its institutionalization as legal science and its ties to case law, can yield results which are unattainable in general practical reasoning. Why should there be a need for legal reasoning, and how can it achieve these outcomes if in the last analysis it is after all dependent on general practical reasoning?

The answer is obvious from what has already been said. The fact that legal reasoning depends on general practical reasoning does not mean that it is identical with it or reducible to it. The general practical reasoning required for legal discourse takes place in special forms and according to special rules and under special conditions. These special forms and rules lead to both a consolidation and a differentiation of the mode of reasoning. Each is required on general practical grounds. Legal reasoning can thus be viewed as a special form of general practical reasoning which is required on general practical grounds, structurally dependent on general practical principles, and demanding general practical argumentation, and which occurs in special forms, according to special rules, and under special conditions, and is therefore particularly powerful and not reducible to general practical reasoning.

5. THE LIMITS AND NECESSITY OF THE THEORY OF RATIONAL LEGAL DISCOURSE

The fact that legal reasoning does indeed take place in special forms, according to special rules, and under special conditions but always remains dependent on general practical reasoning means that although the weaknesses of general practical

[234] Cf. above, pp. 284 ff.

discourse are mitigated to a considerable degree in legal discourse, they can never be eliminated.

For anyone only prepared to accept as a theory of rational legal argumentation a procedure guaranteeing certainty of outcome, the theory proposed here will be unacceptable on this ground alone. However, no procedure guaranteeing certainty is yet in sight. Anyone who equates rationality with certainty must renounce the idea of a theory of rational legal argumentation.

There is, however, no reason for insisting on this identification. Even in the natural sciences, which are often held up in contrast with jurisprudence as the paradigm of genuine science, there can be no question of reaching conclusive certainty. The fact that certainty is unattainable cannot therefore in and of itself be regarded as a sufficient reason for denying the scientific character of jurisprudence or its nature as a rational activity.

It is not the generation of certainty which constitutes the rational character of jurisprudence but rather its conformity to a number of conditions, criteria, or rules. An attempt has been made in this book to work out such conditions, criteria, and rules. A systematic presentation of them can be regarded as an explanation of the concept of rational legal argumentation.

It would be hard to raise serious objections to the view that it is not the certainty of outcomes but rather conformity to such conditions, criteria, or rules which constitutes the rational character of legal reasoning. More problematic is the question of what is to be counted as belonging among them. It is easy to agree on a minimal content. Constituents of this are the requirements of consistency (non-contradiction), of instrumental rationality, and of the truth of the empirical statements used. These requirements are not trivial, nor has their significance for legal reasoning yet been sufficiently clarified. Nevertheless, they alone are insufficient as a foundation for the analysis of a concept of rational legal argumentation. A legal argument may be internally consistent, faithful to the principles of instrumental rationality, only resting on true empirical statements, and yet—possibly because of the aims it espouses—be properly called 'irrational'. An explanation of the concept of rational legal argumentation must therefore start out from stronger criteria than those mentioned above.

The theory proposed here is an attempt to give such stronger criteria. This not only serves as the analysis of an interesting concept. If it is a sound thesis that the claim to be arguing rationally is implicit in legal discourse, then the analysis of what is to be understood by rational legal argumentation is a prerequisite of the theoretical comprehension of such discourse.

The explanation of the concept of rational legal argumentation in this investigation consisted in the presentation of a number of rules which reasoning must follow and a number of forms which reasoning must take, if it is to make good the claim implicit in it. Where a discussion is in accordance with these rules and forms, then the result yielded by it can be called 'correct'. The rules and forms of legal discourse thus constitute a criterion for the correctness of legal decisions.

As a special case of general practical discourse, legal discourse includes the rules and forms of general practical discourse. Their application as criteria for correct decisions necessitates reference to hypothetical discourses and hypothetical consensus. To the extent that general practical arguments are required by legal reasoning, the theory of rational legal discourse suffers from the uncertainties of the theory of general practical discourse as a hypothetical criterion for the correctness of normative statements. These uncertainties do not, of course, render discourse theory inoperable as a criterion of correctness—it may particularly be of service as a negative criterion—but they do mean that a judgment as to the correctness of a decision (except in the realm of the discursively necessary) is always provisional in nature—that is, it can always be contested.

The value of the rules and forms of legal discourse is not limited to the explanation of the concept of rational legal argumentation (and thus the claim to correctness) and to their function as a hypothetical criterion of correctness. They also contain requirements for actually occurring arguments. As such they form a standard against which to measure the limitations necessary in legal determinations and litigation. In so doing, it is necessary to start out from the formula cited above—that is, that in a particular situation those limitations are justified which in comparison with others, or with no limitations at all, offer the greatest chance of arriving at a decision which would also have been the outcome under ideal conditions. In this way discourse theory offers something like a context-specific criterion for the rationality of decision-making procedures as well as for the decisions generated by them.

Finally, the function of the theory of rational legal discourse as the definition of an ideal is not to be underestimated. As such it reaches out beyond the realm of legal science. Lawyers can, of course, contribute to the realization of rationality and justice, yet this cannot be achieved in isolation within their own sphere of professional competence. This presupposes a rational and just social order.

To make a contribution to this subject was not the task undertaken in this book. Its goals were more limited. They will have been achieved if the book succeeds in making it a little clearer that, and how, jurisprudence is possible as a special branch of practical reason.

Appendix

Table of the Rules and Forms Obtained

It should be stressed that this table does not summarize the progress of thought in the investigation, but a particular class of results from it. The page numbers refer to the places in the text where the formulas are to be found.

I. THE RULES AND FORMS OF GENERAL PRACTICAL DISCOURSE

1. *The Basic Rules*

(1.1)	No speaker may contradict him or herself.	188
(1.2)	Every speaker may only assert what he or she actually believes.	188
(1.3)	Every speaker who applies a predicate F to an object *a* must be prepared to apply F to every other object which is like *a* in all relevant respects.	188
(1.3′)	Every speaker may assert only those value judgments or judgments of obligation in a given case which he or she is willing to assert in the same terms for every case which resembles the given case in all relevant respects.	190
(1.4)	Different speakers may not use the same expression with different meanings.	188

2. *The Rationality Rules*

(2)	Every speaker must give reasons for what he or she asserts when asked to do so, unless he or she can cite reasons which justify a refusal to provide a justification.	192
(2.1)	Everyone who can speak may take part in discourse.	193

(2.2) (a) Everyone may problematize any assertion. 193
(b) Everyone may introduce any assertion into the discourse. 193
(c) Everyone may express his or her attitudes, wishes, and needs. 193

(2.3) No speaker may be prevented from exercising the rights laid down in (2.1) and (2.2) by any kind of coercion internal or external to the discourse. 193

3. *Rules for Allocating the Burden of Argument*

(3.1) Whoever proposes to treat a person A differently from a person B is obliged to provide justification for so doing. 196

(3.2) Whoever attacks a statement or norm which is not the subject of the discussion must state a reason for so doing. 196

(3.3) Whoever has put forward an argument is only obliged to produce further arguments in the event of counter-arguments. 197

(3.4) Whoever introduces an assertion or an utterance about his or her attitudes, wishes, or needs into a discourse, which does not stand as an argument in relation to a prior utterance, must justify this interjection when required to do so. 197

4. *The Argument Forms*

(4) $\dfrac{\begin{array}{c} G \\ R^{\cdot} \end{array}}{N^{\cdot}}$ 198

(4.1) $\dfrac{\begin{array}{c} T \\ R \end{array}}{N}$ (4.2) $\dfrac{\begin{array}{c} F \\ R \end{array}}{N}$ 198

(4.3) $\dfrac{\begin{array}{c} F_R \\ R' \end{array}}{R}$ (4.4) $\dfrac{\begin{array}{c} T' \\ R' \end{array}}{R}$ 199

(4.5) R_iPR_k and $R_i'PR'_k$

(4.6) $(R_iPR_k)C$ and $(R_i'PR_k')C$ 201

5. *The Justification Rules*

(5.1.1) Everyone who makes a normative statement that presupposes a rule with certain consequences for the satisfaction of the interests of other persons must be able to accept these consequences even in the hypothetical situation where he or she is in the position of those persons. 203

(5.1.2) The consequences of every rule for the satisfaction of the interests of each and every individual must be acceptable to everyone. 203

(5.1.3) Every rule must be openly and universally teachable. 204

(5.2.1.) The moral rules underlying the moral views of a speaker must be able to withstand critical testing in terms of their historical genesis. A moral rule cannot stand up to such testing if:

(a) even though originally amenable to rational justification, it has in the mean time lost its justification, or

(b) it was not originally amenable to rational justification and no adequate new grounds have been discovered for it in the mean time. 204

(5.2.2) The moral rules underlying the moral views of a speaker must be able to withstand critical testing in terms of their individual genesis. A moral rule does not stand up to such testing if it has only been adopted on grounds of some unjustifiable conditions of socialization. 205

(5.3) The actually given limits of realizability are to be taken into account. 205

6. *The Transition Rules*

(6.1) It is possible for any speaker at any time to make a transition into a theoretical (empirical) discourse. 206

(6.2) It is possible for any speaker at any time to make a transition into a linguistic-analytical discourse. 206

(6.3) It is possible for any speaker at any time to make a transition into a discourse-theoretical discourse. 206

II. THE RULES AND FORMS OF LEGAL DISCOURSE

1. *The Rules and Forms of Internal Justification*

1.1 Forms

1.1.1 The Simplest Form

(J.1.1) .(1) $(x)\ (Tx \rightarrow ORx)$
.(2) Ta
(3) ORa (1), (2) 222

1.1.2 The Most General Form

(J.1.2) .(1) $(x)\ (Tx \rightarrow ORx)$
.(2) $(x)\ (M^1x \rightarrow Tx)$
.(3) $(x)\ (M^2x \rightarrow M^1x)$
.
.
.
.(4) $(x)\ (Sx \rightarrow M^nx)$
.(5) Sa
(6) ORa (1)–(5) 227

1.2 Rules

(J.2.1) At least one universal norm must be adduced in the justification of a legal judgment. 223

(J.2.2) A legal judgment must follow logically from at least one universal norm together with further statements. 223

(J.2.3) Whenever it is open to doubt whether *a* is a T or an M^i, a rule must be put forward which settles this question. 226

(J.2.4) The number of decompositional steps required, is that number which makes possible the use of expressions whose application to a given case admits of no further dispute. 277

(J.2.5) As many decompositional steps as possible should be articulated. 228

2. *The Rules and Forms of External Justification*

2.1 Rules and Forms of Empirical Reasoning
(6.1) holds good. Special rules and forms were not elaborated. 223

2.2	Rules and Forms of Interpretation	
2.2.1	Forms of Semantic Interpretation	
(J.3.1)	By reason of W_i, R′ *must* be accepted as an interpretation of R.	235
(J.3.2)	By reason of W_k, R′ *cannot* be accepted as an interpretation of R.	235
(J.3.3)	It is *possible* both to accept and not to accept R′ as an interpretation of R, since neither W_i nor W_k holds.	235
2.2.2	Forms of Genetic Interpretation	
(J.4.1)	.(1) R′ $(= I^R_W)$ is intended by the legislator. (2) R′	236
(J.4.2)	.(1) R is, for the legislator, a means to end Z. .(2) $\neg R' (= I^R_W) \rightarrow \neg Z$ (3) R′	237
2.2.3	Basic Form of Teleological Interpretation	
(J.5)	.(1) OZ .(2) $\neg R' (= I^R_W) \rightarrow \neg Z$ (3) R′	242
2.2.4	Forms of historical, comparative, and systematic interpretation were not elaborated.	
2.2.5	Rules	
(J.6)	Saturation—that is a full statement of reasons—is required in every argument which belongs among the canons of interpretation.	246
(J.7)	Arguments which give expression to a link with the actual words of the law, or the will of the historical legislator, take precedence over other arguments, unless rational grounds can be cited for granting precedence to the other arguments.	248
(J.8)	Determinations of the relative weight of arguments different in form must conform to weighting rules.	249
(J.9)	Every possibly proposable argument of such a form that it can be counted as one of the canons of interpretation must be given due consideration.	250
(J.10)	Every dogmatic proposition must be justified by recourse to at least one general practical argument whenever it is subjected to doubt.	266
(J.11)	Every dogmatic proposition must be able to stand up to systematic testing in both the narrower and the wider sense.	266
(J.12)	Whenever dogmatic arguments are possible they should be used.	274

2.4	The Most General Rules for the Application of Precedent	
(J.13)	If a precedent can be cited in favour of or against a decision it should be so cited.	278
(J.14)	Whoever wishes to depart from a precedent carries the burden of argument.	278
2.5	Special Legal Argument Forms	
2.5.1	Forms	
(J.15)	.(1) $(x)\ (OGx \rightarrow Fx)$ (2) $(x)\ (\neg Fx \rightarrow \neg OGx)$ (1)	280
(J.16)	.(1) $(x)\ (Fx \vee F\ \text{sim}\ x \rightarrow OGx)$.(2) $(x)\ (Hx \rightarrow F\ \text{sim}\ x)$ (3) $(x)\ (Hx \rightarrow OGx)$ (1), (2)	281
(J.17)	.(1) $O\neg Z$.(2) $R' \rightarrow Z$ (3) $\neg R'$	283
2.5.2	Rule	
(J.18)	Special legal argument forms must have the reasons for them stated in full—that is, must achieve saturation.	284

Bibliography

Adomeit, K., 'Zivilrechtstheorie und Zivilrechtsdogmatik, mit einem Beitrag zur Theorie der subjektiven Rechte', *Jahrbuch für Rechtssoziologie und Rechtstheorie*, 2 (1972), 503–22.

Albert, H., *Traktat über kritische Vernunft*, 2nd edn. (Tübingen, 1969).

—— Erkenntnis und Recht: Die Jurisprudenz im Lichte des Kritizismus', *Jahrbuch für Rechtssoziologie und Rechtstheorie*, 2 (1972), 80–96.

Alston, W. P., 'Vagueness', in *Encyclopedia of Philosophy*, ed. P. Edwards (New York and London, 1967), viii. 218–21.

Ambrose, A. and M. Lazerowitz (eds.), *Ludwig Wittgenstein: Philosophy and Language* (London and New York, 1972).

Anderson, A. R. and N. D. Belnap, 'Enthymemes', *Journal of Philosophy*, 58 (1961), 712–22.

Apel, K.-O., Towards a Transformation of Philosophy, trans. G. Adey and D. Frisby (London, Boston, and Henley, 1980).

—— 'Sprechakttheorie und transzendentale Sprachpragmatik zur Frage ethischer Normen', in id. (ed.), *Sprachpragmatik und Philosophie* (Frankfurt-on-Main, 1976) 10–173.

Aristotle, *The Works of Aristotle*, viii. *Metaphysics*, trans. W. D. Ross, 2nd edn. (Oxford, 1928).

—— *The Nicomachean Ethics*, trans. D. Ross (London, 1954).

—— *Topica*, trans. W. A. Pickard-Cambridge, in *The Works of Aristotle*, i. *Logic* (Oxford, 1928).

—— *Topica*, Germ. trans. E. Rolfes, 2nd edn. (Leipzig, 1922; repr. Hamburg, 1968).

Austin, J. L., *How to Do Things with Words* (London, Oxford, and New York, 1962).

—— 'Performative und konstatierende Äußerung', in *Sprache und Analysis*, ed. and trans. R. Bubner (Göttingen, 1968), 140–53.

—— *Philosophical Papers*, ed. J. O. Urmson and G. J. Warnock, 2nd edn. (London, Oxford, and New York, 1970).

Ayer, A. J., *Language, Truth and Logic*, (Harmondsworth, 1971).

Bachof, O., 'Die Dogmatik des Verwaltungsrechts vor den Gegenwartsaufgaben der Verwaltung', *VVDStRL* 30 (1972), 193–244.

Baier, K., *The Moral Point of View* (Ithaca and London, 1958).

Ballweg, O., *Rechtswissenschaft und Jurisprudenz* (Basle, 1970).

Bar-Hillel, Y., 'On Habermas' Hermeneutic Philosophy of Language', *Synthèse*, 26 (1973), 1–12.

Beardsmore, R. W., *Moral Reasoning* (London, 1969).

Berki, R. N., 'Interests and Moral Ideals,' *Philosophy*, 49 (1974), 265–80.

Berlin, I. *et al.* (eds.) *Essays on J. L. Austin* (Oxford, 1973).

Bird, O., 'The Re-Discovery of the Topics', *Mind*, 70 (1961), 534–9.

BOKELOH, A., 'Der Beitrag der Topik zur Rechtsgewinnung', thesis (Göttingen, 1972).

BRANDT, R. B., *Ethical Theory* (Englewood Cliffs, NJ, 1959).

BROAD, C. D., *Five Types of Ethical Theory* (London, 1930).

BROCK, D. W., 'Recent Work in Utilitarianism', *American Philosophical Quarterly*, 10 (1973), 241–76.

BROHM, W., 'Die Dogmatik des Verwaltungsrechts vor den Gegenwartsaufgaben der Verwaltung', *VVDStRL* 30 (1972), 245–312.

BROUWER, L. E. J., *Over de Grondslagen der Wiskunde* (Amsterdam and Leipzig, 1907) (trans.: A. Heyting (ed.), *Collected Works*, vol. i (Amsterdam and New York, 1975).).

BRÜGGEMANN, J., *Die richterliche Begründungspflicht* (Berlin, 1971).

CANARIS, C.-W., *Systemdenken und Systembegriff in der Jurisprudenz* (Berlin, 1969).

CARNAP, R., *Philosophy and Logical Syntax* (London, 1935).

—— *Meaning and Necessity*, 2nd edn. (Chicago and London, 1956).

CHISHOLM, R. M., 'Contrary-to-Duty Imperatives and Deontic Logic', *Analysis*, 24 (1963), 33–6.

DIEDERICHSEN, U., 'Topisches und systematisches Denken in der Jurisprudenz', *NJW* 19 (1966), 697–705.

—— 'Traditionelle Logik für Juristen', *Juristische Analysen*, 2 (1970), 765–83.

—— 'Die "reductio ad absurdum" in der Jurisprudenz', in Festschrift for K. Larenz, ed. G. Paulus, U. Diederichsen, and C.-W. Canaris (Munich, 1973), 155–79.

DIEẞLHORST, M., *Die Natur der Sache als außergesetzliche Rechtsquelle verfolgt an der Rechtsprechung zur Saldotheorie*, (Tübingen, 1968).

DÖLLE, H., 'Rechtsdogmatik und Rechtsvergleichung', *Rabels Zeitschrift für ausländisches und internationales Privatrecht*, 34 (1970), 403–10.

—— 'Juristische Entdeckungen', *Verhandlungen des 42. Deutschen Juristentages, Düsseldorf 1957*, vol. ii (Tübingen, 1959), B1–B22.

DREIER, R., *Zum Begriff der 'Natur der Sache'* (Berlin, 1965).

—— 'Zum Selbstverständnis der Jurisprudenz als Wissenschaft', *Rechtstheorie*, 2 (1971), 37–54.

—— 'Probleme der Rechtsquellenlehre', in Festschrift for H. J. Wolff, ed. C.-F. Menger (Munich, 1973), 3–36.

—— 'Zu Luhmanns systemtheoretischer Neuformulierung des Gerechtigkeitsproblems', *Rechtstheorie*, 5 (1974), 189–200.

—— *Was ist und wozu Allgemeine Rechtstheorie?* (Tübingen, 1975).

—— 'Zur Problematik und Situation der Verfassungsinterpretation', in R. Dreier and F. Schwegmann, *Probleme der Verfassungsinterpretation* (Baden-Baden, 1976), 13–47.

EDWARDS, P., *The Logic of Moral Discourse* (New York and London, 1955).

EHRLICH, E., *Die juristische Logik* (Tübingen, 1918).

—— *Fundamental Principles of the Sociology of Law*, trans. W. Möll (Cambridge, Mass., 1936).

EICHENHOFER, E., 'Frequenzanalytische Untersuchungen juristischer Argumentation', *Rechtstheorie*, 5 (1974), 216–22.

ELZE, M., 'Dogma', *Historisches Wörterbuch der Philosophie*, vol.ii, ed. J. Ritter (Basle, 1972), cols. 275–7.

ENGISCH, K., *Logische Studien zur Gesetzesanwendung*, 2nd edn. (Heidelberg, 1960).

—— *Einführung in das juristische Denken*, 5th edn. (Stuttgart, Berlin, Cologne, and Mainz, 1971).

—— 'Begriffseinteilung und Klassifikation in der Jurisprudenz', in Festschrift for K. Larenz, ed. G. Paulus, U. Diederichsen, and C.-W. Canaris (Munich, 1973), 125–53.

ESSER, J., *Grundsatz und Norm in der richterlichen Fortbildung des Privatrechts* (Tübingen, 1956; repr. 1964).

—— 'Herrschende Lehre und ständige Rechtsprechung', *Dogma und Kritik in den Wissenschaften*, Mainzer Universitätsgespräche, Summer Term 1961 (Mainz, 1962), 26–35.

—— 'Richterrecht, Gerichtsgebrauch und Gewohnheitsrecht', in Festschrift for F. von Hippel, ed. J. Esser and H. Thieme (Tübingen, 1967), 95–130.

—— *Vorverständnis und Methodenwahl in der Rechtsfindung*, 2nd edn. (Frankfurt-on-Main, 1972).

—— 'Möglichkeiten und Grenzen des dogmatischen Denkens im modernen Zivilrecht', *AcP* 172 (1972), 97–130.

—— 'Dogmatik zwischen Theorie und Praxis', in *Funktionswandel der Privatrechtsinstitutionen*, Festschrift for L. Raiser, ed. F. Baur, J. Esser, F. Kübler, and E. Steinhoff (Tübingen, 1974), 517–39.

—— 'Bemerkungen zur Unentbehrlichkeit des juristischen Handwerkzeugs', *JZ* (1975), 555–8.

FANN, K. T. (ed.), *Symposium on J. L. Austin* (London and New York, 1969).

FØLLESDAL, D. and R. HILPINEN, 'Deontic Logic: An Introduction', in *Deontic Logic: Introductory and Systematic Readings*, ed. R. Hilpinen (Dordrecht, 1971), 1–35.

FOOT, P., 'Moral Arguments', *Mind*, 67 (1958), 502–13.

—— 'Moral Beliefs', in *Theories of Ethics*, ed. ead. (Oxford, 1967), 83–100.

FRANKENA, W. K., *Ethics* (Englewood Cliffs, NJ, 1963).

—— 'The Naturalistic Fallacy', in *Theories of Ethics*, ed. P. Foot (Oxford, 1967), 50–63.

—— 'Decisionism and Separatism in Social Philosophy', in *Rational Decision*, ed. C. J. Friedrich, *Nomos*, 7 (1964), 18–25.

FREGE, G., *Begriffsschrift* (Halle, 1879) (trans.: T. W. Bynum, *Conceptual Notation and Related Articles* (Oxford, 1972)).

—— 'Der Gedanke. Eine logische Untersuchung', in ead., *Logische Untersuchungen*, ed. G. Patzig (Göttingen, 1966), 30–73 ('The Thought: A Logical Inquiry', trans. A. M. and M. Quinton, in *Philosophical Logik*, ed. P. F. Strawson (Oxford, 1967), 17–38).

—— 'Logik', in *Schriften zur Logik und Sprachphilosophie. Aus dem Nachlaß*, ed. G. Gabriel (Hamburg, 1971), 35–73.

FURBERG, M., *Saying and Meaning: A Main Theme in J. L. Austin's Philosophy* (Oxford, 1971).

GAUTHIER, D. P., 'Hare's Debtors', *Mind*, 77 (1968), 400–5.

GEORGE, R., 'Enthymematic Consequence', *American Philosophical Quarterly*, 9 (1972), 113–16.

GERMAN, O. A., *Präjudizien als Rechtsquelle* (Stockholm, Göteborg, and Uppsala, 1960).

GREWENDORF, G. and G. MEGGLE, 'Zur Struktur des metaethischen Diskurses', *Seminar: Sprache und Ethik. Zur Entwicklung der Metaethik* (Frankfurt-on-Main, 1974), 7–31.

GRICE, H. P., *Logic and Conversation* (typescript, 1968).

HABERMAS, J., 'Der Universalitätsanspruch der Hermeneutik', in *Hermeneutik und Dialektik*, Festschrift for H.-G. Gadamer, ed. R. Bubner, K. Cramer, and R. Wiehl (Tübingen, 1970), 73–103.

—— 'Towards a Theory of Communicative Competence', in *Recent Sociology*, ed. H. P. Dreitzel, vol. ii (London, 1970), 115–48.

—— 'Vorbereitende Bemerkungen zu einer Theorie der kommunikativen Kompetenz', in id. and N. Luhmann (eds.), *Theorie der Gesellschaft oder Sozialtechnologie—Was leistet die Systemforschung?* (Frankfurt-on-Main, 1971), 101–41.

—— 'Theorie der Gesellschaft oder Sozialtechnologie? Eine Auseinandersetzung mit Niklas Luhmann', in id. and N. Luhmann (eds.), *Theorie der Gesellschaft oder Sozialtechnologie—Was leistet die Systemforschung?* (Frankfurt-on-Main, 1971), 142–290.

—— *Theory and Practice*, trans. J. Viertel (London, 1974).

—— 'Einige Bemerkungen zum Problem der Begründung von Werturteilen', in *Philosophie und Wissenschaft*, ed. L. Landgrebe, Ninth German Philosophy Congress (Meisenheim am Glan, 1972), 89–99.

—— *Erkenntnis und Interesse*, 2nd edn. (Frankfurt-on-Main, 1973).

—— 'A Postscript to Knowledge and Human Interests', *Philosophy of the Social Sciences*, 3 (1973), 157–89.

—— 'Wahrheitstheorien', in *Wirklichkeit und Reflexion*, Festschrift for W. Schulz, ed. H. Fahrenbach (Pfullingen, 1973), 211–65.

—— *Legitimation Crisis*, trans. T. A. MacCarthy (London, 1976).

—— 'Sprachspiel, Intention und Bedeutung. Zu Motiven bei Sellars und Wittgenstein', in *Sprachanalyse und Soziologie*, ed. R. Wiggershaus (Frankfurt-on-Main, 1975), 319–38.

—— 'Historischer Materialismus und die Entwicklung normativer Strukturen', in id., *Zur Rekonstruktion des Historischen Materialismus* (Frankfurt-on-Main, 1976) 9–48 (trans: *Communication and the Evolution of Society*, trans. T. A. MacCarthy (Boston, 1979, 95–129)).

—— 'What is Universal Pragmatics?' *Communication and the Evolution of Society*, trans. T. A. MacCarthy (Boston, 1979), 1–68.

—— 'Zwei Bemerkungen zum praktischen Diskurs', in id., *Zur Rekonstruktion des Historischen Materialismus* (Frankfurt-on-Main, 1976), 338–46.

—— and N. LUHMANN (edd.), *Theorie der Gesellschaft oder Sozialtechnologie—Was leistet die Systemforschung?* (Frankfurt-on-Main, 1971).

HANSSON, B., 'An Analysis of Some Deontic Logics', in *Deontic Logic: Introductory and Systematic Readings*, ed. R. Hilpinen (Dordrecht, 1971), 121–47.

HARE, R. M., review of S. E. Toulmin, *The Place of Reason in Ethics*, *Philosophical Quarterly*, 1 (1950/1), 371–4.

—— *The Language of Morals* (London, Oxford, and New York, 1952).

—— 'Universalisability', *PAS* 55 (1954/5), 295–312.
—— 'Geach: Good and Evil', *Analysis*, 17 (1956–7), 103–11.
—— *Freedom and Reason* (Oxford, 1963).
—— 'Austin's Distinction between Locutionary and Illocutionary Acts', in id., *Practical Inferences* (London and Basingstoke, 1971), 59–73.
—— 'Meaning and Speech Acts', in id., *Practical Inferences* (London and Basingstoke, 1971) 74–93.
—— 'Wissenschaft und praktische Philosophie', in *Philosophie und Wissenschaft*, ed. L. Landgrebe, Ninth German Philosophy Congress (Meisenheim am Glan, 1972) 79–88.
—— 'Wrongness and Harm', in id., *Essays on the Moral Concepts* (London and Basingstoke, 1972) 92–109.
—— 'Principles', *PAS* 73 (1972/3), 1–18.
—— 'Rawls' Theory of Justice', *Philosophical Quarterly*, 23 (1973), 144–55, 241–52.
HART, H. L. A., *The Concept of Law* (Oxford, 1961).
—— 'Positivism and the Separation of Law and Morals', *Harvard Law Review*, 71 (1958), 593–629.
HASSEMER, W., 'Juristische Argumentationstheorie und juristische Didaktik', *Jahrbuch für Rechtssoziologie und Rechtstheorie*, 2 (1972), 467–80.
HECK, P., *Begriffsbildung und Interessenjurisprudenz* (Tübingen, 1932).
HEGEL, G. W. F., *Philosophy of Right*, trans. T. M. Knox (Oxford, 1965).
HELLER, T., *Logik und Axiologie der analogen Rechtsanwendung* (Berlin, 1961).
HINTIKKA, J., 'Some Main Problems of Deontic Logic', in *Deontic Logic: Introductory and Systematic Readings*, ed. R. Hilpinen (Dordrecht, 1971) 59–104.
HÖFFE, O., 'Rationalität, Dezision oder praktische Vernunft. Zur Diskussion des Entscheidungsbegriffs in der Bundesrepublik', *Philosophisches Jahrbuch*, 80 (1973), 340–68.
HOERSTER, N., 'Zum Problem der Ableitung eines Sollens aus einem Sein in der analytischen Moralphilosophie', *ARSP* 55 (1969), 11–39.
—— *Utilitaristische Ethik und Verallgemeinerung*, 2nd edn. (Freiburg and Munich, 1977).
—— 'Grundthesen analytischer Rechtstheorie', *Jahrbuch für Rechtssoziologie und Rechtstheorie*, 2 (1972), 115–30.
—— 'R. M. Hares Fassung der Goldenen Regel', *Philosophisches Jahrbuch*, 81 (1974), 186–96.
HOHFELD, W. N., 'Some Fundamental Legal Conceptions as Applied in Judicial Reasoning', in *Fundamental Legal Conceptions as Applied in Judicial Reasoning and Other Legal Essays*, ed. W. W. Cook (New Haven, Conn., 1923), 23–114.
HUNTER, J. F. M. '"Forms of Life" in Wittgenstein's *Philosophical Investigations*', *American Philosophical Quarterly*, 5 (1968), 233–43.
JHERING, R. VON, *Der Geist des Römischen Rechts*, vol. iii, 3rd edn. (Leipzig, 1877).
JØRGENSEN, J., 'Imperatives and Logic', *Erkenntnis*, 7 (1937/8), 288–96.
KALINOWSKI, G., *Einführung in die Normenlogik*, trans. W. Klein (Frankfurt-on-Main, 1973).

KAMBARTEL, F. (ed.), *Praktische Philosophie und konstruktive Wissenschaftstheorie* (Frankfurt-on-Main, 1974), 9–33.
KAMLAH, W., *Philosophische Anthropologie* (Mannheim, Vienna, and Zurich, 1973).
KAMLAH, W. and P. LORENZEN, *Logische Propädeutik oder Vorschule des vernünftigen Redens*, rev. edn. (Mannheim, Vienna, and Zurich, 1967).
KANGER, S., 'New Foundations for Ethical Theory', in *Deontic Logic: Introductory and Systematic Readings*, ed. R. Hilpinen (Dordrecht, 1971), 36–58.
KANT, I., *Critique of Pure Reason*, trans. N. K. Smith (London, 1933).
—— *Groundwork of the Metaphysic of Morals*, trans. H. Paton, in *The Moral Law*, 3rd edn. (London, 1964).
—— *Kant's Political Writings*, ed. H. Reiss, trans. H. B. Nisbet (Cambridge, 1970).
—— *The Metaphysical Elements of Justice*, trans. J. Ladd (Indianapolis, 1965).
—— *On History*, trans. L. W. Beck (Indianapolis, 1963).
KELSEN, H., *Pure Theory of Law*, trans. M. Knight (Berkeley, Calif., 1967).
—— *Reine Rechtslehre*, 2nd edn. (Vienna, 1960).
—— *What is Justice?* (Berkeley, Calif., 1959).
—— 'Zur Theorie der Interpretation', in *Die Wiener rechtstheoretische Schule. Ausgewählte Schriften von Hans Kelsen, Adolf Julius Merkl* und *Alfred Verdross*, ed. H. Klecatsky, R. Marcic, and H. Schambeck (Vienna, Frankfurt, Zurich, Salzburg, and Munich, 1968) ii., 1363–73.
KEMMERLING, A., 'Regel und Geltung im Lichte der Analyse Wittgensteins', *Rechtstheorie*, 6 (1975), 104–31.
KENNY, A., *Wittgenstein* (London, 1973).
KERNER, G. C., *The Revolution in Ethical Theory* (Oxford, 1966).
KEUTH, H. H., *Zur Logik der Normen* (Berlin, 1972).
—— 'Dialectics versus Critical Rationalism', *Ratio*, 15 (1973), 28–43.
KILIAN, W., *Juristische Entscheidung und elektronische Datenverarbeitung* (Frankfurt-on-Main, 1974).
KLUG, U., *Juristische Logik*, 3rd edn. (Berlin, Heidelberg, and New York, 1966).
KRAWIETZ, W., 'Funktion und Grenzen einer dogmatischen Rechtswissenschaft', *Recht und Politik*, 6 (1970), 150–8.
—— 'Begriffsjurisprudenz', in *Historisches Wörterbuch der Philosophie*, vol. i, ed. J. Ritter (Basle, 1971), cols. 809–13.
—— 'Was leistet Rechtsdogmatik in der richterlichen Entscheidungspraxis?', *ÖZöR* 23 (1972), 47–80.
KRIELE, M., 'Offene und verdeckte Urteilsgründe. Zum Verhältnis von Philosophie und Jurisprudenz heute', in *Collegium Philosophicum*, Festschrift for J. Ritter, ed. E.-W. Böckenförde *et al.* (Basle and Stuttgart, 1965), 99–117.
—— *Theorie der Rechtsgewinnung*, 2nd edn. (Berlin, 1976).
KRIPKE, S. A., 'Semantical Considerations on Modal Logic', in *Reference and Modality*, ed. L. Linsky (Oxford, 1971).
KUHN, T. S., *The Structure of Scientific Revolutions* (Chicago, 1962).
KRUSE, H. W., *Das Richterrecht als Rechtsquelle des innerstaatlichen Rechts* (Tübingen, 1971).

KUTSCHERA, F. VON, *Einführung in die Logik der Normen, Werte und Entscheidungen* (Freiburg and Munich, 1973).

—— *Sprachphilosophie* (Munich, 1971).

LABAND, P., 'Das Staatsrecht des Deutschen Reiches', 2nd edn., in *Handbuch des Öffentlichen Rechts*, vol. ii, ed. M. von Seydel (Freiburg and Leipzig, 1894), 1–276.

LADD, J., 'The Place of Practical Reason in Judicial Decision', in *Rational Decision, Nomos*, vol. vii, ed. C. J. Friedrich (New York, 1964), 126–44.

LAKATOS, I. and A. MUSGRAVE (edd.), *Criticism and the Growth of Knowledge* (Cambridge, 1970).

LARENZ, K., 'Über die Bindungswirkung von Präjudizien', in Festschrift for H. Schima, ed. H. W. Fasching and W. Kralik (Vienna, 1969), 247–64.

—— *Methodenlehre der Rechtswissenschaft*, 3rd edn. (Berlin, Heidelberg, and New York, 1975).

LAZZER, D. de, 'Rechtsdogmatik als Kompromißformular', in *Dogmatik und Methode*, Festschrift for J. Esser, ed. R. Dubischar *et al.* (Kronberg, 1975), 85–112.

LENK, H., 'Zu Wittgensteins Theorie der Sprachspiele', *Kant-Studien*, 58 (1967), 458–80.

LESS, G., *Von Wesen und Wert des Richterrechts* (Erlangen, 1951).

LORENZEN, P., *Normative Logic and Ethics* (Mannheim and Zurich, 1969).

—— 'Das Problem des Szientismus', *Philosophie und Wissenschaft*, ed. L. Landgrebe, Ninth German Philosophy Congress (Meisenheim am Glan, 1972), 19–34.

—— 'Methodisches Denken', in id., *Methodisches Denken* (Frankfurt-on-Main, 1974), 24–59.

LORENZEN, P. and W. KAMLAH, *Logische Propädeutik oder Vorschule des vernünftigen Redens*, rev. edn. (Mannheim, Vienna, and Zurich, 1967).

LORENZEN, P. and O. SCHWEMMER, *Konstruktive Logik, Ethik und Wissenschaftstheorie* (Mannheim, Vienna, and Zurich, 1973).

LÜDERSSEN, K., *Erfahrung als Rechtsquelle. Abduktion und Falsifikation von Hypothesen im juristischen Entscheidungsprozeß. Eine Fallstudie aus dem Kartellstrafrecht* (Frankfurt-on-Main, 1972).

LUDWIG, O. and W. MENZEL, 'Diskutieren als Gegenstand und Methode des Deutschunterrichts', *Praxis Deutsch*, 14 (1976), 13–22.

LUHMANN, N., 'Systemtheoretische Argumentationen. Eine Entgegnung auf Jürgen Habermas', in J. Habermas and id. (eds.), *Theorie der Gesellschaft oder Sozialtechnologie—Was leistet die Systemforschung?* (Frankfurt-on-Main, 1972), 291–405.

—— *Rechtssoziologie*, vol. ii (Reinbek, 1972).

—— 'Gerechtigkeit in den Rechtssystemen der modernen Gesellschaft', *Rechtstheorie*, 4 (1973), 131–67.

—— *Rechtssystem und Rechtsdogmatik* (Stuttgart, Berlin, Cologne, and Mainz, 1974).

—— 'Die Systemreferenz von Gerechtigkeit. In Erwiderung auf die Ausführungen von Ralf Dreier', *Rechtstheorie*, 5 (1974), 201–3.

—— *Legitimation durch Verfahren*, 2nd edn. (Darmstadt and Neuwied, 1975).

LYCAN, W. G. and A. OLDENQUIST, 'Can the Generalization Argument be Reinstated?', *Analysis*, 32 (1971/2), 76–81.

LYONS, D., *Forms and Limits of Utilitarianism* (Oxford, 1965).
MAKKONEN, K., *Zur Problematik der juridischen Entscheidung*, trans. B. Assmuth (Turku, 1965).
MCGUINESS, B. F., 'Comments on Professor von Wright's "Wittgenstein on Certainty"', in *Problems in the Theory of Knowledge*, ed. G. H. von Wright (The Hague, 1972), 61–5.
MENGER, C.-F. (ed.), *Fortschritte des Verwaltungsrechts*, Festschrift for H. J. Wolff (Munich, 1973).
MENNICKEN, A., *Das Ziel der Gesetzesauslegung. Eine Untersuchung zur subjektiven und objektiven Auslegungstheorie* (Bad Homburg, Berlin, and Zurich, 1970).
MEYER-CORDING, U., *Kann der Jurist heute noch Dogmatiker sein? Zum Selbstverständnis der Rechtswissenschaft* (Tübingen, 1973).
MITTELSTRAß, J. (ed.), *Methodologische Probleme einer normativ-kritischen Gesellschaftstheorie* (Frankfurt-on-Main, 1975).
MOORE, G. E., *Principia Ethica* (Cambridge, 1903).
—— 'Facts and Propositions, *Proceedings of the Aristotelian Society*, suppl. vol. 7 (1927), 171–206.
MORRIS, C. W., 'Foundations of the Theory of Signs', International Encyclopedia of Unified Science (Chicago, 1938), vol. i.
MORSCHER, E., 'Das Sein-Sollen-Problem logisch betrachtet. Eine Übersicht über den gegenwärtigen Stand der Diskussion', *conceptus*, 8 (1974), 5–29.
MORSCHER, E. and G. ZECHA, 'Wozu deontische Logik?' *ARSP* 58 (1972), 363–78.
MÜLLER, F., *Juristische Methodik*, 2nd edn. (Berlin, 1976).
NAESS, A., *Kommunikation und Argumentation*, trans. A. von Stechow (Kronberg, 1975). [Norwegian edn.: *En del elementaere logiske emner*, 11th edn. (Oslo, Bergen, and Tromsø, 1975).]
NAUCKE, W., *Über die juristische Relevanz der Sozialwissenschaften* (Frankfurt-on-Main, 1972).
NIEKE, W., 'Dogmatismus', in *Historisches Wörterbuch der Philososphie*, vol. ii, ed. J. Ritter (Basle, 1972), cols. 277–9.
NIELSEN, K., 'Good Reasons in Ethics: An Examination of the Toulmin-Hare Controversy', *Theoria*, 24 (1958), 9–28.
—— 'Problems of Ethics', in *Encyclopedia of Philosophy*, ed. P. Edwards (New York and London, 1967), iii. 117–34.
—— 'On Moral Truth', *Studies in Moral Philosophy*, American Philosophical Quarterly, Monograph Series, i. (Oxford, 1968), 9–25.
—— 'Covert and Overt Synonymity: Brandt and Moore and the "Naturalistic Fallacy"', *Philosophical Studies*, 25 (1974), 51–6.
NOWELL-SMITH, P. H., *Ethics* (Harmondsworth, 1954).
OGDEN, C. K. and J. A. RICHARDS, *The Meaning of Meaning* (London, 1923).
OPP, K.-D., *Soziologie im Recht* (Reinbek, 1973).
OTTE, G., 'Zwanzig Jahre Topik-Diskussion: Ertrag und Aufgaben', *Rechtstheorie*, 1 (1970), 183–97.
PATZIG, G., 'Sprache und Logik', in id., *Sprache und Logik* (Göttingen, 1970), 5–38.
—— 'Satz und Tatsache', in id., *Sprache und Logik* (Göttingen, 1970) 39–76 (trans.: 'Facts and Sentences', *Contemporary German Philosophy*, vol. ii, ed. D. E. Christensen *et al.* (Pennsylvania, 1983), 176–99).

—— 'Relativismus und Objektivität moralischer Normen', in id., *Ethik ohne Metaphysik* (Göttingen, 1971), 62–100.

Perelman, C., *Étude sur Frege*, thesis (Brussels, 1938).

—— 'Étude sur Gottlob Frege', *Revue de l'université de Bruxelles*, 44 (1938/9), 224–7.

—— 'Évidence et preuve', *Dialectica*, 11 (1957), 21–35.

—— *The Idea of Justice and the Problem of Argument*, trans. J. Petrie (London and New York, 1963).

—— *Justice* (New York, 1967).

—— 'Les Cadres sociaux de l'argumentation', *Cahiers Internationaux de Sociologie*, 26 (1959), 123–9.

—— 'La Règle de justice', *Dialectica*, 14 (1960), 230–8.

—— 'Betrachtungen über die praktische Vernunft', *Zeitschrift für philosophische Forschung*, 20 (1966), 210–21.

—— 'Rhetoric and Philosophy', *Philosophy and Rhetoric*, 1 (1968), 15–24.

—— 'Reply to Mr. Zaner', *Philosophy and Rhetoric*, 1 (1968), 168–70.

—— 'Justice and Reasoning', in *Law, Reason, and Justice: Essays in Legal Philosophy*, ed. G. Hughes (New York and London, 1969), 207–15.

—— 'The New Rhetoric', in *Pragmatics of Natural Language*, ed. Y. Bar-Hillel (Dordrecht, 1971), 145–9.

Perelman, C. and L. Olbrechts-Tyteca, 'Act and Person in Argument', *Ethics*, 61 (1950/1), 251–69.

—— *La Nouvelle Rhétorique: Traité de l'argumentation*, vol. i, vol. ii (Paris, 1958) (trans.: J. Wilkinson and P. Weaver, *The New Rhetoric: A Treatise on Argumentation* (Notre Dame and London, 1969)).

Philippi, K. J., *Tatsachenfeststellungen des Bundesverfassungsgerichts* (Cologne, Berlin, Bonn, and Munich, 1971).

Piaget, J., 'Piaget's Theory', in *Carmichal's Manual of Child Psychology*, ed. P. H. Mussen, 3rd edn. (New York, London, Sydney, and Toronto, 1970), i. 703–32.

Pike, N., 'Rules of Inference in Moral Reasoning', *Mind*, 70 (1961), 391–9.

Pitcher, G., *The Philosophy of Wittgenstein* (Englewood Cliffs, NJ, 1964).

Podlech, A., 'Wertungen und Werte im Recht', *AöR* 95 (1970), 185–223.

—— *Gehalt und Funktionen des allgemeinen verfassungsrechtlichen Gleichheitssatzes* (Berlin, 1971).

—— 'Rechtstheoretische Bedingungen einer Methodenlehre juristischer Dogmatik', *Jahrbuch für Rechtssoziologie und Rechtstheorie*, 2 (1972), 491–502.

—— 'Recht und Moral', *Rechtstheorie*, 3 (1972), 129–48.

Popper, K. R., *The Logic of Scientific Discovery* (New York, Hagerstown, San Francisco, and London, 1968).

—— 'Normal Science and its Dangers', in *Criticism and the Growth of Knowledge*, ed. I. Lakatos and A. Musgrave (Cambridge, 1970), 51–8.

—— *The Open Society and its Enemies*, vol. i vol. ii, *The Spell of Plato*, 5th edn. (London, 1966).

Posner, R., 'Diskurs als Mittel der Aufklärung. Zur Theorie der rationalen Kommunikation bei Habermas und Albert', in *Linguistik und Sprachphilosophie*, ed. M. Gerhard (Munich, 1974), 280–303.

Putzo, H., 'Die Vereinfachungsnovelle', *NJW* 30 (1977), 1–10.

Quine, W. V. O., *Methods of Logic* (London, 1952).
Radbruch, G., *Rechtsphilosophie*, 7th edn. (Stuttgart, 1970).
Raiser, L., 'Wozu Rechtsdogmatik?', *DRiZ* (1968), 98.
Rawls, J., 'Two Concepts of Rules', *Philosophical Review*, 64 (1955), 3–32.
—— 'Justice as Fairness', *Philosophical Review*, 67 (1958), 164–94.
—— *A Theory of Justice* (Cambridge, Mass., 1971).
Reiner, H., 'Die "Goldene Regel"', *Zeitschrift für philosophische Forschung*, 3 (1948), 74–105.
Rescher, N., *The Coherence Theory of Truth* (Oxford, 1973).
Rhees, R. (ed.), *Discussions of Wittgenstein* (London, 1970).
Rödig, G., 'Über die Notwendigkeit einer besonderen Logik der Normen', *Jahrbuch für Rechtssoziologie und Rechtstheorie*, 2 (1972), 163–85.
—— *Die Theorie des gerichtlichen Erkenntnisverfahrens* (Berlin, Heidelberg, and New York, 1973).
Roellecke, G., 'Grundfragen der juristischen Methodenlehre und die Spätphilosophie Ludwig Wittgensteins', in Festschrift for G. Müller, ed. T. Ritterspach and W. Geiger (Tübingen, 1970), 323–39.
Ross, A., 'Imperatives and Logic', *Theoria*, 7 (1941), 53–71.
—— 'On Moral Reasoning', *Philosophical Yearbook*, 1 (1964), 120–32.
—— *Directives and Norms* (London, 1968).
Ross, W. D., *The Right and the Good* (Oxford, 1930).
—— *The Foundations of Ethics* (Oxford, 1939).
Rottleuthner, H., 'Zur Soziologie richterlichen Handelns II', *Kritische Justiz*, 4 (1971), 60–88.
—— *Richterliches Handeln. Zur Kritik der juristischen Dogmatik* (Frankfurt-on-Main, 1973).
—— *Rechtswissenschaft als Sozialwissenschaft* (Frankfurt-on-Main, 1973).
Rüssmann, H., 'Die Begründung von Werturteilen', *Juristische Schulung*, 15 (1975), 352–8.
Ryle, G., *The Concept of Mind* (New York, Melbourne, Sydney, and Cape Town, 1949).
Savigny, E. von, *Die Philosophie der normalen Sprache*, 1st edn. (Frankfurt-on-Main, 1969).
—— *Grundkurs im wissenschaftlichen Definieren* (Munich, 1970).
—— 'Zur Rolle der deduktiv-axiomatischen Methode in der Rechtswissenschaft', in *Rechtstheorie*, ed. G. Jahr and W. Maihofer (Frankfurt-on-Main 1971), 315–51.
—— 'Die Jurisprudenz im Schatten des Empirismus. Polemische Anmerkungen zu Hans Albert: *Erkenntnis und Recht*', *Jahrbuch für Rechtssoziologie und Rechtstheorie*, 2 (1972), 97–108.
Savigny, E. von, J. Rahlf, and U. Neumann, *Juristische Dogmatik und Wissenschaftstheorie* (Munich, 1976).
Savigny, F. C. von, *System des heutigen Römischen Rechts*, vol. i, (Berlin, 1840).
Scheler, M., *Der Formalismus in der Ethik und die materiale Wertethik*, 5th edn. (Berlin and Munich, 1966).
Schlink, B., 'Inwieweit sind juristische Entscheidungen mit entscheidungstheoretischen Modellen theoretisch zu erfassen und praktisch zu bewältigen?', *Jahrbuch für Rechtssoziologie und Rechtstheorie*, 2 (1972), 332–46.

SCHLÜTER, W., *Das Obiter dictum* (Munich, 1973).
SCHNELLE, H., *Sprachphilosophie und Linguistik* (Reinbek, 1973).
SCHNUR, R., 'Der Begriff der "herrschenden Meinung" in der Rechtsdogmatik', in Festschrift for E. Forsthoff, ed. K. Doehring (Munich, 1967), 43–64.
SCHÖNKE, A. and H. SCHRÖDER, *Strafgesetzbuch. Kommentar*, 18th edn., rev. T. Lenckner, P. Cramer, A. Eser, and W. Stree (Munich, 1976).
SCHREIBER, R., *Logik des Rechts* (Berlin, Göttingen, and Heidelberg, 1962).
SCHWEMMER, O., *Philosophie der Praxis*, (Frankfurt-on-Main, 1971).
—— 'Grundlagen einer normativen Ethik', in *Praktische Philosophie und konstruktive Wissenschaftstheorie*, ed. F. Kambartel (Frankfurt-on-Main, 1974), 73–95.
—— 'Appell und Argumentation. Aufgaben und Grenzen einer praktischen Philosophie', in *Praktische Philosophie und konstruktive Wissenschaftstheorie*, ed. F. Kambartel (Frankfurt-on-Main, 1974), 148–211.
—— 'Begründen und Erklären', in *Methodologische Probleme einer normativ-kritischen Gesellschaftstheorie*, ed. J. Mittelstraß (Frankfurt-on-Main, 1975), 43–87.
SCHWEMMER, O. and P. LORENZEN, *Konstruktive Logik, Ethik und Wissenschaftstheorie* (Mannheim, Vienna, and Zurich, 1973).
SEARLE, J. R., 'How to Derive "Ought" from "Is" ', in *Theories of Ethics*, ed. P. Foot (Oxford, 1967), 101–14.
—— *Speech Acts* (Cambridge, 1969).
SILVERSTEIN, H. S., 'A Note on Hare on Imagining Oneself in the Place of Others', *Mind*, 81 (1972), 448–50.
SIMITIS, S., 'Die Bedeutung von System und Dogmatik—dargestellt an rechtsgeschäftlichen Problemen des Massenverkehrs', *AcP* 172 (1972), 131–54.
SINGER, M. G., *Generalization in Ethics* (New York, 1961).
SMART, J. J. C., 'Extreme and Restricted Utilitarianism', *Philosophical Quarterly*, 6 (1956), 344–54.
SMART, J. J. C. and B. WILLIAMS, *Utilitarianism For and Against* (Cambridge, 1973).
SMART, R. N., 'Negative Utilitarianism', *Mind*, 67 (1958), 542–3.
SOBEL, J. H., 'Generalization Arguments', *Theoria*, 31 (1965), 32–60.
SPECHT, E. K., 'Die sprachphilosophischen und ontologischen Grundlagen im Spätwerk Ludwig Wittgensteins', *Kant-Studien*, 84 (1963).
SPENDEL, G., 'Die Goldene Regel als Rechtsprinzip', in Festschrift for F. von Hippel, ed. J. Esser and H. Thieme (Tübingen, 1967), 491–516.
SPRUTE, J., 'Topos und Enthymem in der aristotelischen Rhetorik', *Hermes*, 103 (1975), 68–90.
STALLBERG, F. W., 'Legitimation und Diskurs—Zur Habermas-Analyse Wolfgang Fachs', *Zeitschrift für Soziologie*, 4 (1975), 96–8.
STARCK, C., 'Empirie in der Rechtsdogmatik', *JZ* (1972), 609–14.
STAUB, H., *Die positiven Vertragsverletzungen*, 2nd edn., ed. E. Müller (Berlin, 1913).
STEGMÜLLER, W., *Hauptströmungen der Gegenwartsphilosophie*, 4th edn. (Stuttgart, 1969).
—— *Probleme und Resultate der Wissenschaftstheorie und Analytischen Philosophie*,

vol. i, *Wissenschaftliche Erklärung und Begründung* (Berlin, Heidelberg, and New York, 1974).

STEVENSON, C. L., 'Persuasive Definitions', *Mind*, 47 (1938), 331–50.

—— *Ethics and Language* (New Haven, Conn. and London, 1944).

—— 'The Emotive Meaning of Ethical Terms', in id., *Facts and Values* (New Haven, Conn. and London, 1963), 10–31.

—— 'Retrospective Comments', in id., *Facts and Values* (New Haven, Conn. and London, 1963), 186–232.

STRAWSON, P. F., 'Ethical Intuitionism', *Philosophy*, 24 (1949), 23–33.

—— review of L. Wittgenstein, *Philosophical Investigations*, *Mind*, 63 (1954), 70–99.

—— review of C. Perelman and L. Olbrechts-Tyteca, *Traité de l'argumentation*, *Mind*, 68 (1959), 420–1.

—— 'Truth', in *Truth*, ed. G. Pitcher (Englewood Cliffs, NJ 1964), 32–53.

—— 'Austin and "Locutionary Meaning"', in *Essays on J. L. Austin*, ed. I. Berlin *et al.* (Oxford, 1973), 46–68.

STRUCK, G., *Topische Jurisprudenz* (Frankfurt-on-Main, 1971).

—— 'Dogmatische Diskussion über Dogmatik', *JZ* (1975), 84–8.

TARSKI, A., 'The Semantic Conception of Truth and the Foundations of Semantics', *Philosophy and Phenomenological Research*, 4 (1943/4), 341–75.

—— 'On the Concept of Logical Consequence', in id., *Logic, Semantics, Metamathematics* (Oxford, 1956), 409–20.

—— *Introduction to Logic and to the Methodology of Deductive Sciences*, 3rd edn. (Oxford and New York, 1965).

TAYLOR, C. C. W., review of R. M. Hare, *Freedom and Reason*, *Mind*, 74 (1965), 280–98.

THORNTON, M. T., 'Hare's View of Morality', *Mind*, 80 (1971), 617–19.

THUL, E. J., 'Die Denkform der Rechtsdogmatik', *ARSP* 46 (1960), 241–60.

TOULMIN, S. E., *The Place of Reason in Ethics* (Cambridge, 1950).

—— *The Uses of Argument* (Cambridge, 1958).

URMSON, J. O., *The Emotive Theory of Ethics* (London, 1968).

VIEHWEG, T., *Topik und Jurisprudenz*, 5th edn. (Munich, 1974).

—— 'Systemprobleme in Rechtsdogmatik und Rechtsforschung', in *System und Klassifikation in Wissenschaft und Dokumentation*, ed. A. Diemer (Meisenheim am Glan, 1968), 96–104.

—— 'Some Considerations Concerning Legal Reasoning', in *Law, Reason, and Justice: Essays in Legal Philosophy*, ed. G. Hughes (New York and London, 1969), 257–69.

WARNOCK, G. J., *Contemporary Moral Philosophy* (London and Basingstoke, 1967).

WASSERSTROM, R. A., *The Judicial Decision* (Stanford and London, 1961).

WEINBERGER, O., *Rechtslogik* (Vienna and New York, 1970).

—— 'Wahrheit, Recht und Moral', *Rechtstheorie*, 1 (1970), 129–46.

—— 'Über die Offenheit des rechtlichen Normensystems', in Festschrift for W. Wilburg (Graz, 1975) 439–51.

WEISCHEDEL, W., *Recht und Ethik* (Karlsruhe, 1956).

WELZEL, H., *Naturrecht und materiale Gerechtigkeit*, 4th edn. (Göttingen, 1962).

—— *Das Deutsche Strafrecht*, 11th edn. (Berlin, 1969).

WHITE, A. R., *Truth* (London and Basingstoke, 1970).

WIEACKER, F., *Gesetz und Richterkunst* (Karlsruhe, 1958).

—— 'Zur praktischen Leistung der Rechtsdogmatik', *Hermeneutik und Dialektik*, Festschrift for H.-G. Gadamer, vol. ii, ed. R. Bubner, K. Cramer, and R. Wiehl (Tübingen, 1970), 311–36.

—— review of C.-W. Canaris, *Systemdenken und Systembegriff in der Jurisprudenz*, *Rechtstheorie*, 1 (1970), 107–19.

—— 'Zur Topikdiskussion in der zeitgenössischen deutschen Rechtswissenschaft', in *Xenion*, Festschrift for P. J. Zepos, ed. E. von Caemmerer, J. H. Kaiser, G. Kegel, W. Müller-Freienfels, and H. J. Wolff (Athens, 1973), 391–415.

—— 'Über strengere und unstrenge Verfahren der Rechtsfindung', in *Im Dienst an Recht und Staat*, Festschrift for W. Weber, ed. H. Schneider and V. Götz (Berlin, 1974), 421–43

WIELAND, W., 'Praxis und Urteilskraft', *Zeitschrift für philosophische Forschung*, 28 (1974), 17–42.

WINCH, P., *The Idea of a Social Science*, 4th edn. (London, 1965).

—— (ed.), *Studies in the Philosophy of Wittgenstein* (London and New York, 1969).

WINDSCHEID, B., *Lehrbuch des Pandektenrechts*, 9th edn., rev. T. Kipp, vol. i (Frankfurt-on-Main, 1906).

WITTGENSTEIN, L. *Blue and Brown Books* (Oxford, 1975).

—— *On Certainty*, ed. G. E. M. Anscombe and G. H. von Wright (Oxford, 1969).

—— *Philosophical Investigations*, trans. G. E. M. Anscombe (Oxford, 1953).

—— *Tractatus Logico-philosophicus*, *Schriften*, vol. i (Frankfurt-on-Main, 1969), 7–83 (trans.: D. F. Pears and B. F. McGuinness (London, 1961)).

WOLFF, H. J., 'Begriff und Kriterium der Wahrheit', in *Gegenwartsprobleme des Internationalen Rechts und der Rechtsphilosophie*, Festschrift for R. Laun, ed. D. S. Constantopoulos and H. Wehberg (Hamburg, 1953), 587–605.

WOLFF, H. J. and O. BACHOF, *Verwaltungsrecht*, vol. i, 9th edn. (Munich, 1974); vol. iii, 3rd edn. (Munich, 1973).

WRIGHT, G. H. VON, 'Deontic Logic', in id., *Logical Studies* (London, 1957), 58–74.

—— *Norm and Action* (London, 1963).

—— *The Logic of Preference* (Edinburgh, 1963).

—— *The Varieties of Goodness* (London and New York, 1963).

—— *An Essay in Deontic Logic and the General Theory of Action* (Amsterdam, 1968).

—— 'A New System in Deontic Logic', in *Deontic Logic: Introductory and Systematic Readings*, ed. R. Hilpinen (Dordrecht, 1971) 105–20.

—— 'Wittgenstein on Certainty', in id. (ed.), *Problems in the Theory of Knowledge* (The Hague, 1972) 47–60.

—— 'On So-called Practical Inference', *Acta Sociologica*, 15 (1972/3), 39–53.

—— 'Deontic Logic Revisited', *Rechtstheorie*, 4 (1973), 37–46.

—— *Explanation and Understanding* (Ithaca and London, 1971).

WRÓBLEWSKI, J., 'Legal Decision and its Justification', in *Le Raisonnement*

juridique, Akten des Weltkongresses für Rechts- und Sozialphilosophie, ed. H. Hubien (Brussels, 1971), 409–19.
—— 'Legal Syllogism and Rationality of Judicial Decision', *Rechtstheorie*, 5 (1974), 33–46.
WUNDERLICH, D., 'Zur Konventionalität von Sprechhandlungen', in id. (ed.), *Linguistische Pragmatik* (Frankfurt-on-Main, 1972), 11–58.
—— *Grundlagen der Linguistik* (Reinbek, 1974).
ZIPPELIUS, R., 'Legitimation durch Verfahren?', Festschrift for K. Larenz, ed. G. Paulus, U. Diederichsen, and C.-W. Canaris (Munich, 1973), 293–304.
—— *Einführung in die juristische Methodenlehre*, 2nd edn. (Munich, 1974).
—— 'Rechtsphilosophische Aspekte der Rechtsfindung', *JZ* (1976), 150–3.
ZWEIGERT, K., 'Rechtsvergleichung, System und Dogmatik', in Festschrift for E. Bötticher, ed. K. A. Bettermann and A. Zeuner (Berlin, 1969), 443–9.

Index of Names

Index of Subjects

The manufacturer's authorised representative in the EU for product safety is Oxford University Press España S.A. of El Parque Empresarial San Fernando de Henares, Avenida de Castilla, 2 - 28830 Madrid (www.oup.es/en or product.safety@oup.com). OUP España S.A. also acts as importer into Spain of products made by the manufacturer.
Printed and bound by CPI Group (UK) Ltd, Croydon, CR0 4YY
14/09/2026
02216287-0008